Call
of
the
Night

〈 3 〉

KOTOYAMA

N I G H T S

19TH NIGHT If I Can Be of Help ——————— 5

20TH NIGHT Reproduce ——————————— 25

21ST NIGHT Dropout from the School of Love ——— 41

22ND NIGHT Cheers! ——————————————— 59

23RD NIGHT All of Us ———————————— 79

24TH NIGHT Vampire Love Guru ——————— 95

25TH NIGHT She's Been Busy ————————— 113

26TH NIGHT You Know Those Harem Manga? ——— 135

27TH NIGHT What Are You to Her? ——————— 153

28TH NIGHT They Say Love Is Blind ——————— 169

29TH NIGHT No Fair ——————————————— 185

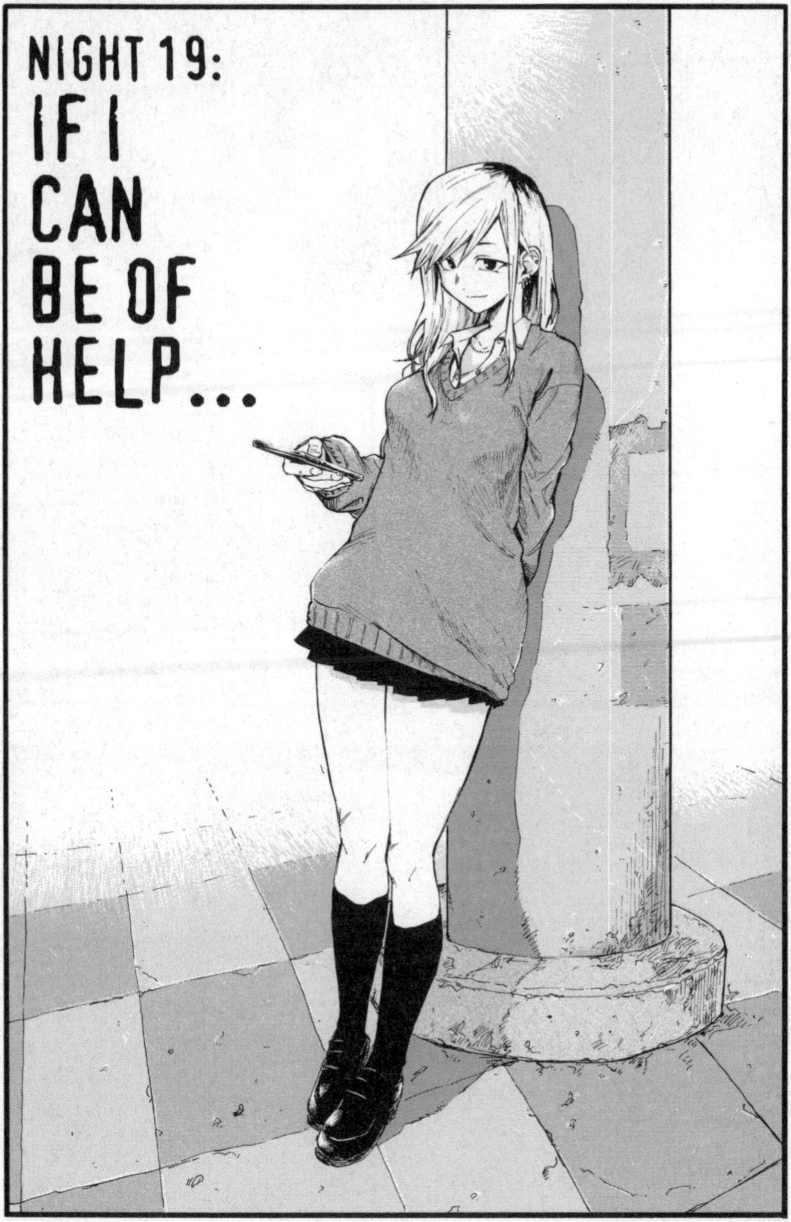
NIGHT 19:
IF I CAN BE OF HELP...

DING DONG
...
SHE ISN'T HERE EITHER.
WHERE COULD NAZUNA BE?
SHE ISN'T ANSWERING HER WALKIE-TALKIE.
WELL, I'LL RUN INTO HER SOONER OR LATER.
AND SO BEGINS ANOTHER NIGHT OF RANDOM WANDERING.
I'M OUT EARLIER THAN USUAL. THERE ARE STILL NORMAL PEOPLE AROUND.
I HOPE I DON'T BUMP INTO ANYONE I KNOW.
FDGT
FDGT
OH!

YAMORI!
YIPE
!!
BDMP
BDMP
BDMP
BDMP
I KNEW IT WOULD HAPPEN SOONER OR LATER...
...BUT THIS IS SOONER!
SOMEONE I KNOW HAS SEEN ME AND SAID HI.
WHO IS IT? WHAT SHOULD I DO? RUN?
THERE'S NO WAY OUT. BRACE YOURSELF, KO...
UH...
HEY THERE.
Are you okay?

...YEAH, I GET IT.
I HAVE THE SAME WORRY.
IF I'M OUT SHOPPING ON THE WEEKEND AND I SEE MY BOSS, I HIDE.
BIP
YOU TOO, HUH?
ARE YOU ON YOUR WAY HOME FROM WORK?
YES. I GOT OUT EARLY TODAY.
TNK
EARLY FOR *YOU*, YOU MEAN...
OH.
I OWE YOU A THANK-YOU.
HERE, HAVE ONE.
YOU OWE ME?
YOU DON'T HAVE TO. I DIDN'T REALLY DO ANYTHING.
I JUST NAGGED YOU.
ACTUALLY, I WAS KIND OF A PAIN IN THE ASS.
YOU MADE A PROMISE TO ME.

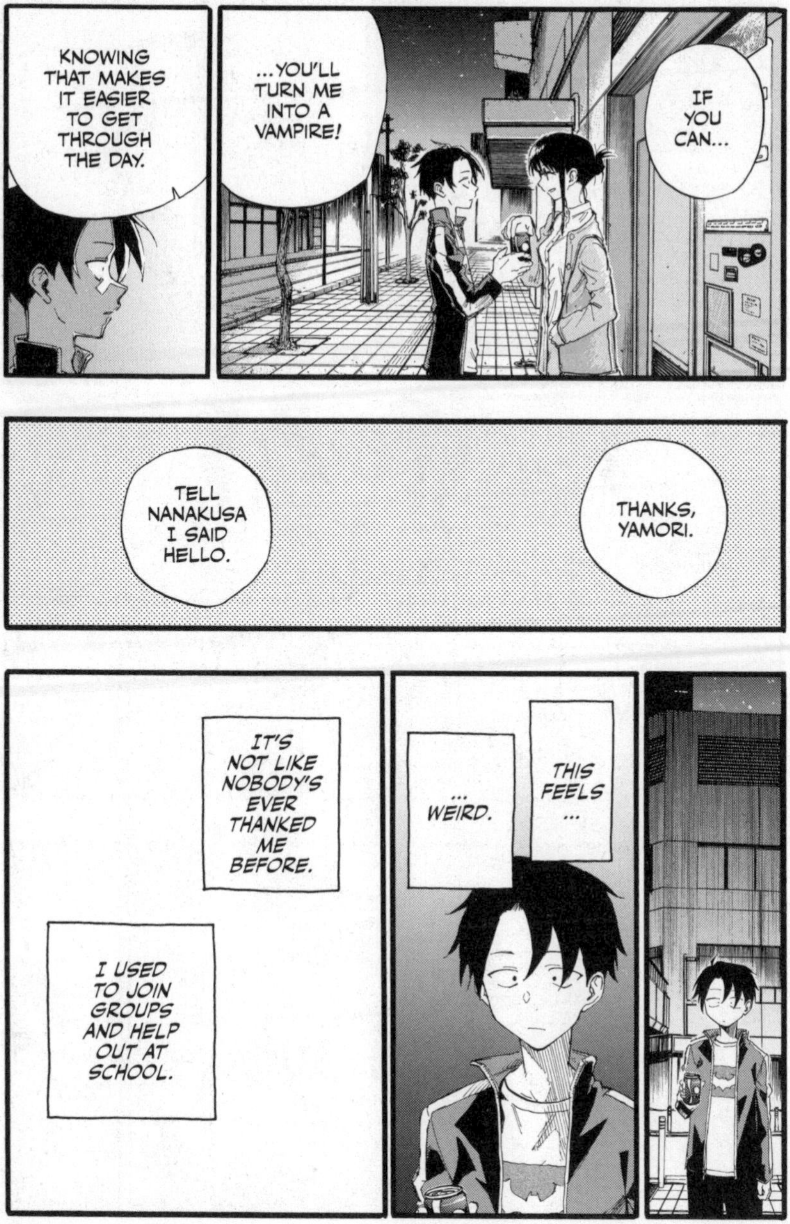
IF YOU CAN...
...YOU'LL TURN ME INTO A VAMPIRE!
KNOWING THAT MAKES IT EASIER TO GET THROUGH THE DAY.
THANKS, YAMORI.
TELL NANAKUSA I SAID HELLO.
THIS FEELS ...
... WEIRD.
IT'S NOT LIKE NOBODY'S EVER THANKED ME BEFORE.
I USED TO JOIN GROUPS AND HELP OUT AT SCHOOL.

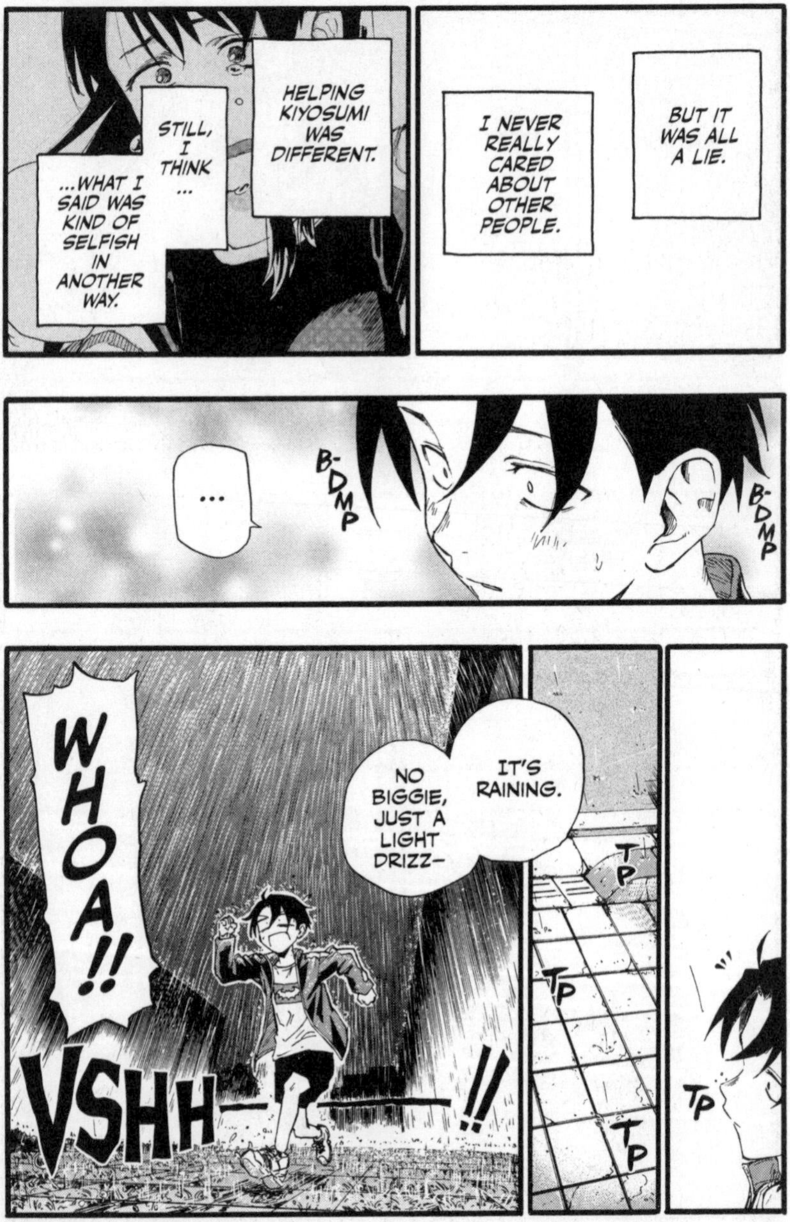
BUT IT WAS ALL A LIE.
I NEVER REALLY CARED ABOUT OTHER PEOPLE.
HELPING KIYOSUMI WAS DIFFERENT.
STILL, I THINK ...
...WHAT I SAID WAS KIND OF SELFISH IN ANOTHER WAY.
B-DMP
B-DMP
...
TP
TP
TP
TP
IT'S RAINING.
NO BIGGIE, JUST A LIGHT DRIZZ—
WHOA!!
VSHH——!!

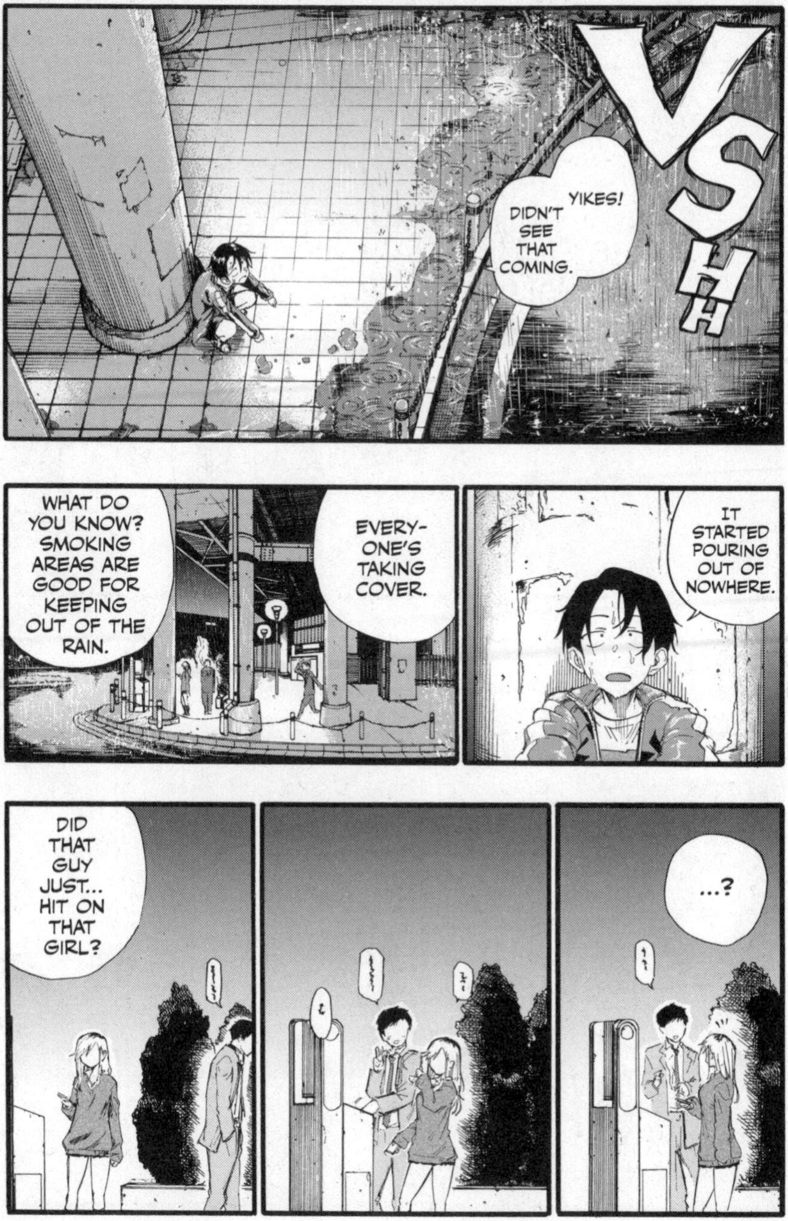
VSHH
YIKES! DIDN'T SEE THAT COMING.
IT STARTED POURING OUT OF NOWHERE.
EVERY-ONE'S TAKING COVER.
WHAT DO YOU KNOW? SMOKING AREAS ARE GOOD FOR KEEPING OUT OF THE RAIN.
...?
DID THAT GUY JUST... HIT ON THAT GIRL?

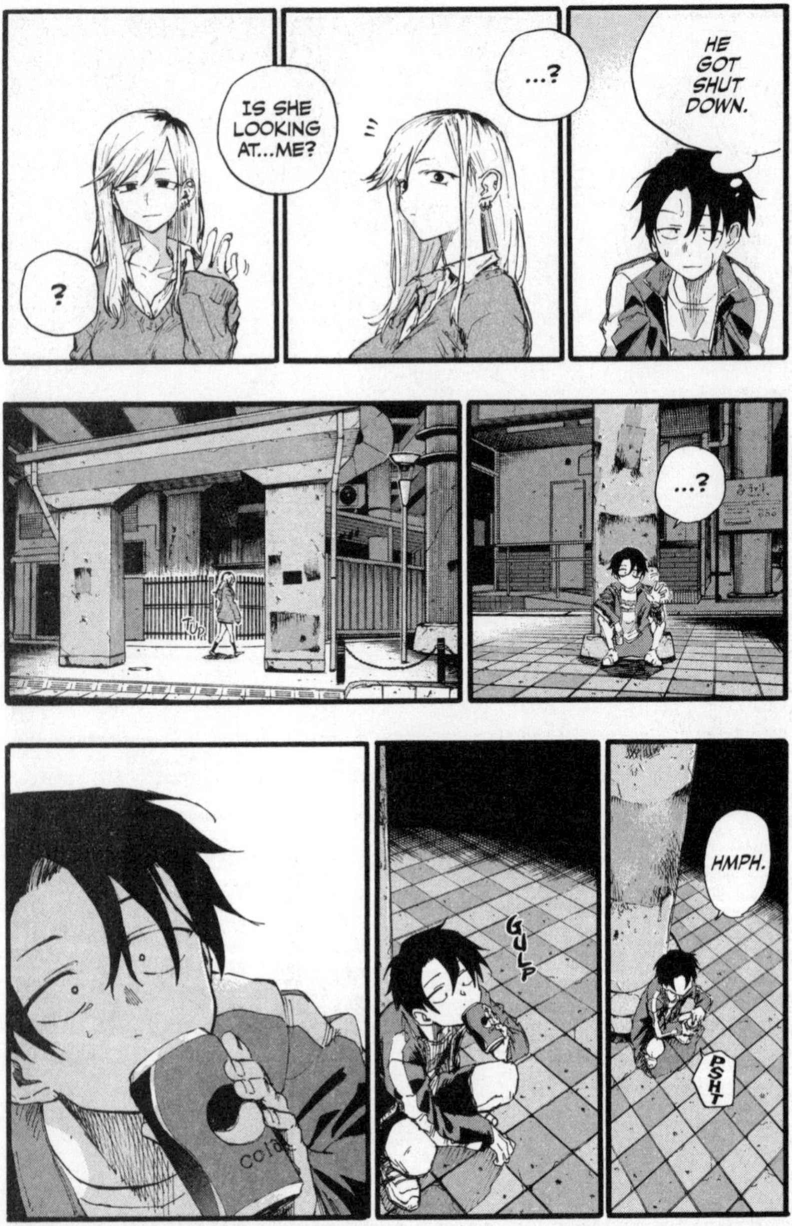
HE GOT SHUT DOWN.
...?
IS SHE LOOKING AT...ME?
?
...?
TUP
HMPH.
PSHT
GULP
cold

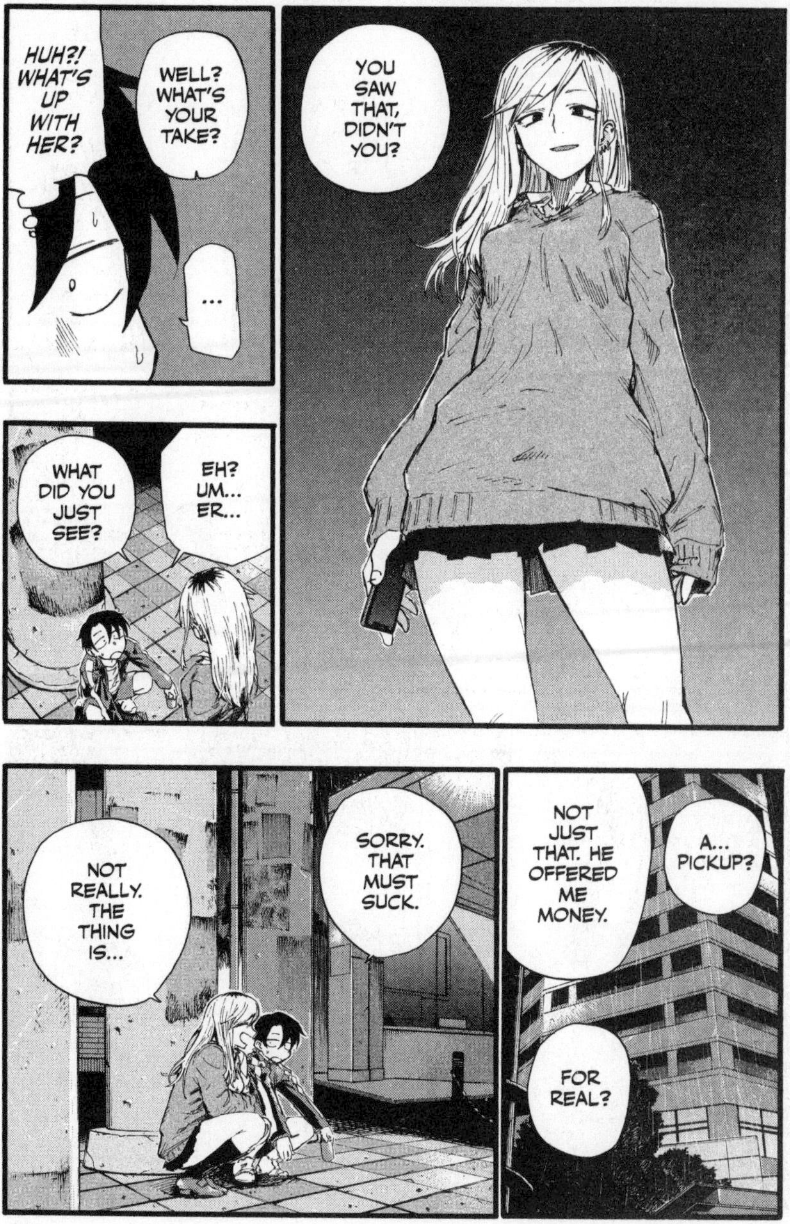
YOU SAW THAT, DIDN'T YOU?
WELL? WHAT'S YOUR TAKE?
HUH?! WHAT'S UP WITH HER?
...
EH? UM... ER...
WHAT DID YOU JUST SEE?
A... PICKUP?
NOT JUST THAT. HE OFFERED ME MONEY.
FOR REAL?
SORRY. THAT MUST SUCK.
NOT REALLY. THE THING IS...

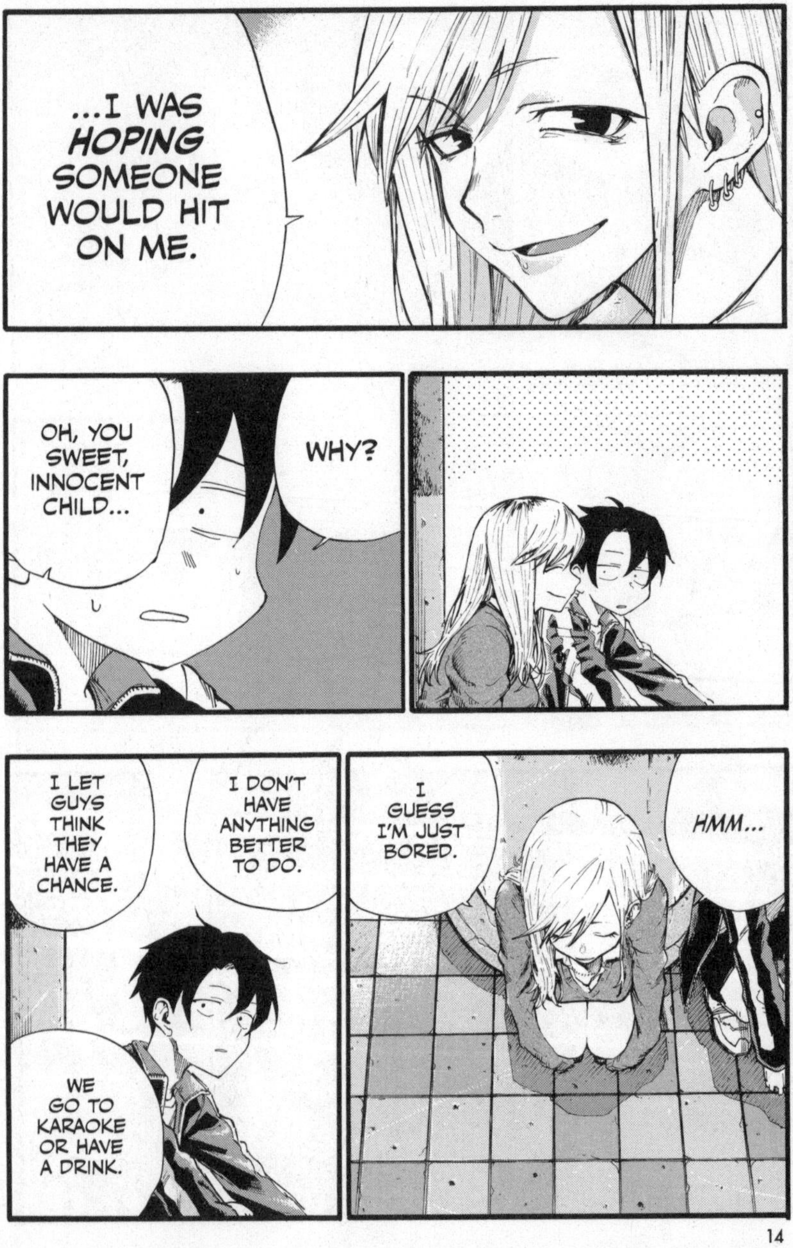
...I WAS *HOPING* SOMEONE WOULD HIT ON ME.
WHY?
OH, YOU SWEET, INNOCENT CHILD...
HMM...
I GUESS I'M JUST BORED.
I DON'T HAVE ANYTHING BETTER TO DO.
I LET GUYS THINK THEY HAVE A CHANCE.
WE GO TO KARAOKE OR HAVE A DRINK.

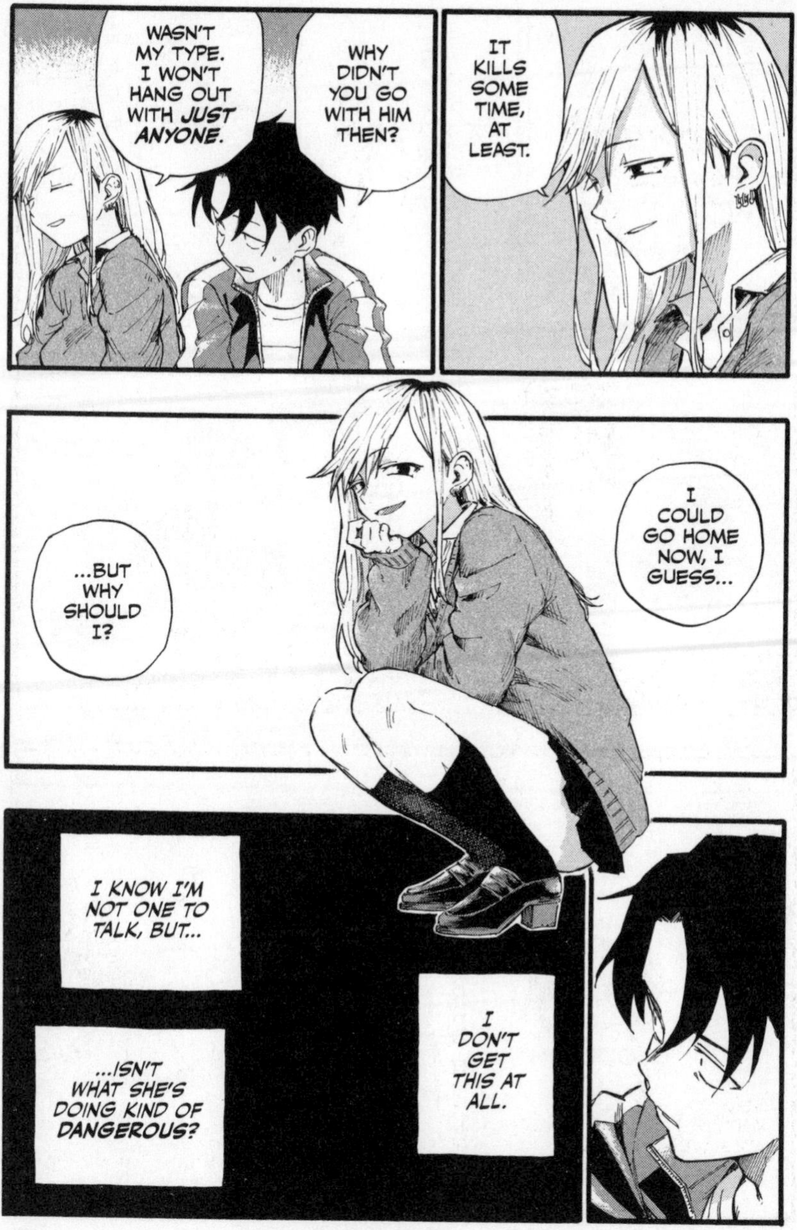
IT KILLS SOME TIME, AT LEAST.
WHY DIDN'T YOU GO WITH HIM THEN?
WASN'T MY TYPE. I WON'T HANG OUT WITH ***JUST ANYONE***.
I COULD GO HOME NOW, I GUESS...
...BUT WHY SHOULD I?
I KNOW I'M NOT ONE TO TALK, BUT...
*...ISN'T WHAT SHE'S DOING KIND OF **DANGEROUS**?*
I DON'T GET THIS AT ALL.

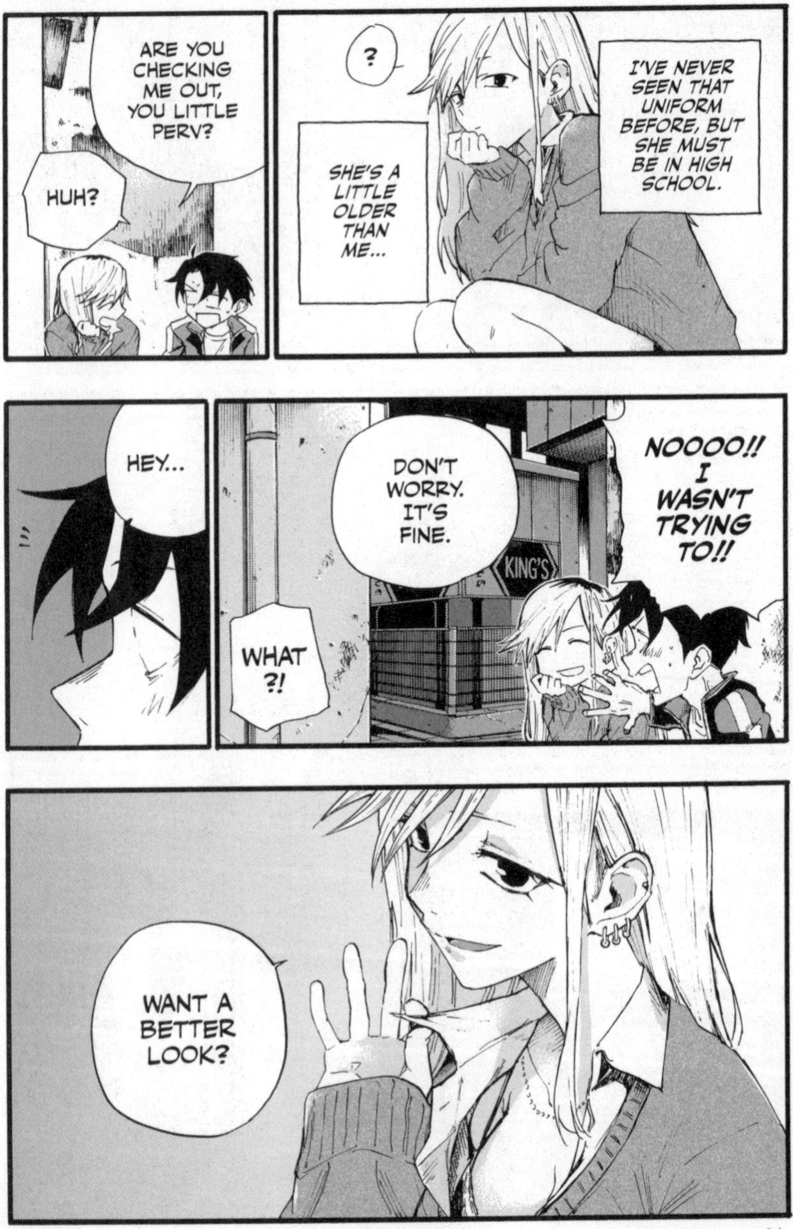
?
I'VE NEVER SEEN THAT UNIFORM BEFORE, BUT SHE MUST BE IN HIGH SCHOOL.
SHE'S A LITTLE OLDER THAN ME...
ARE YOU CHECKING ME OUT, YOU LITTLE PERV?
HUH?
NOOOO!! I WASN'T TRYING TO!!
DON'T WORRY. IT'S FINE.
KING'S
WHAT?!
HEY...
WANT A BETTER LOOK?

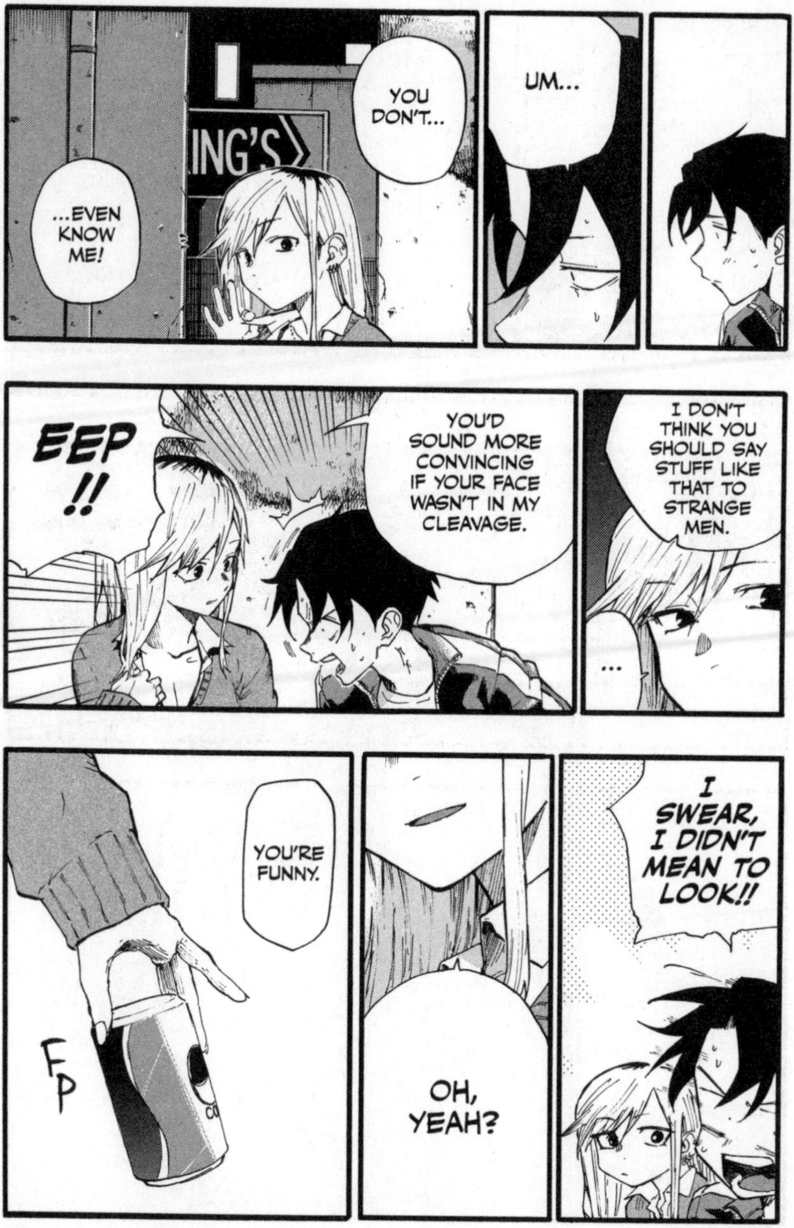
UM...
YOU DON'T...
...EVEN KNOW ME!
I DON'T THINK YOU SHOULD SAY STUFF LIKE THAT TO STRANGE MEN.
...
YOU'D SOUND MORE CONVINCING IF YOUR FACE WASN'T IN MY CLEAVAGE.
EEP!!
I SWEAR, I DIDN'T MEAN TO LOOK!!
OH, YEAH?
YOU'RE FUNNY.
FP

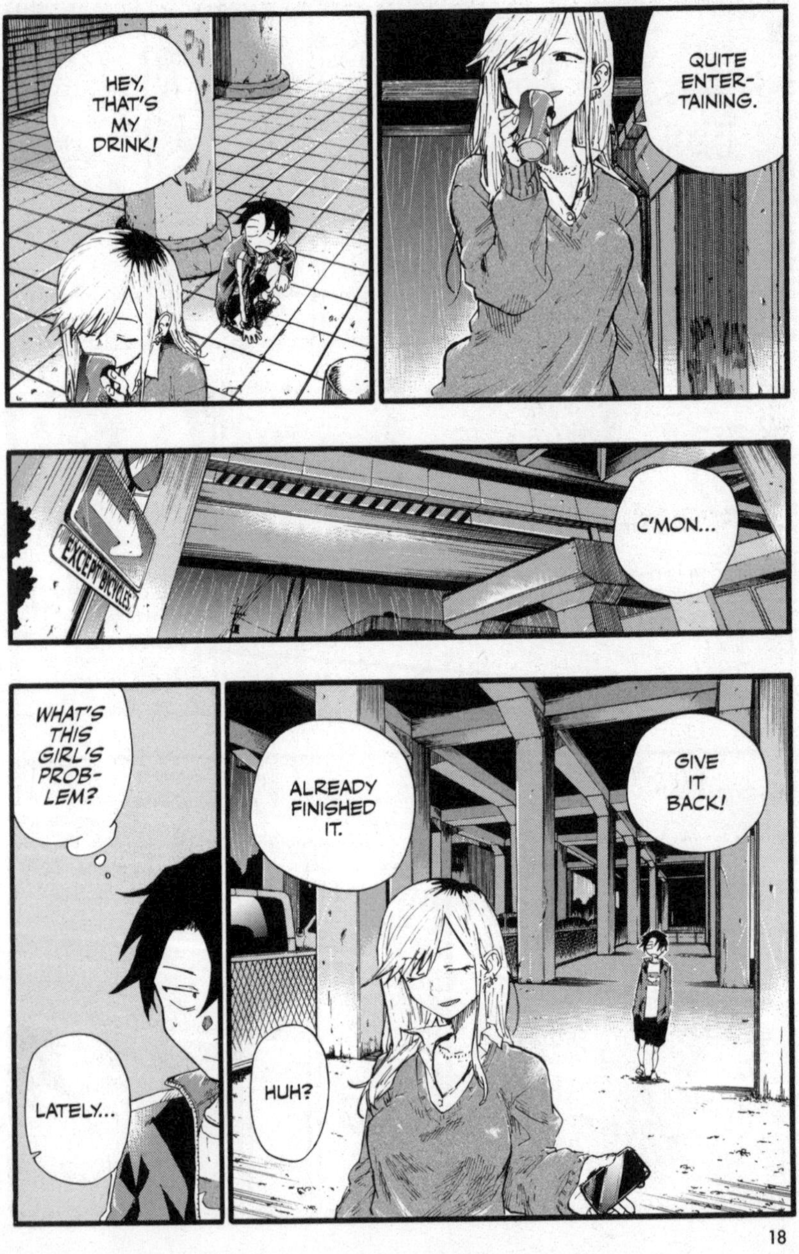
QUITE ENTER-TAINING.
HEY, THAT'S MY DRINK!
C'MON...
EXCEPT BICYCLES
GIVE IT BACK!
ALREADY FINISHED IT.
HUH?
WHAT'S THIS GIRL'S PROB-LEM?
LATELY...

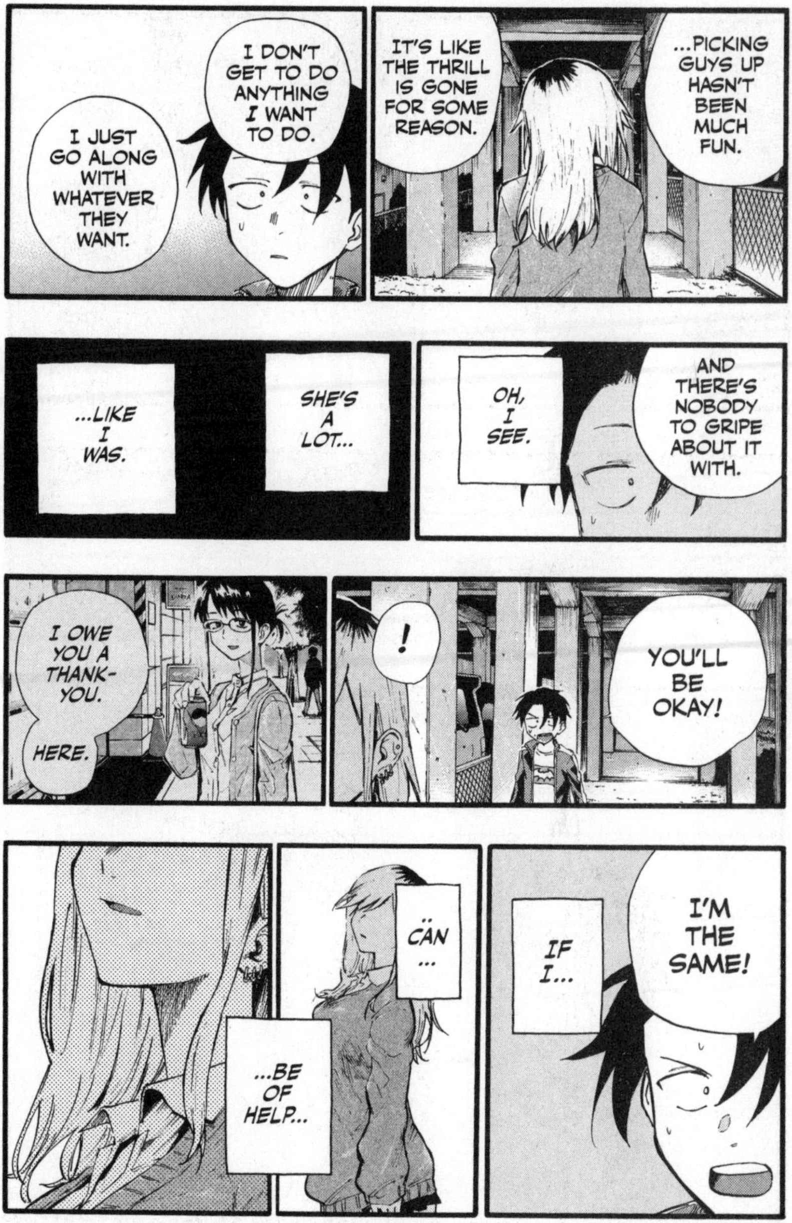

...PICKING GUYS UP HASN'T BEEN MUCH FUN.
IT'S LIKE THE THRILL IS GONE FOR SOME REASON.
I DON'T GET TO DO ANYTHING *I* WANT TO DO.
I JUST GO ALONG WITH WHATEVER THEY WANT.
AND THERE'S NOBODY TO GRIPE ABOUT IT WITH.
OH, I SEE.
SHE'S A LOT...
...LIKE I WAS.
YOU'LL BE OKAY!
!
I OWE YOU A THANK-YOU.
HERE.
I'M THE SAME!
IF I...
CÄN ...
...BE OF HELP...

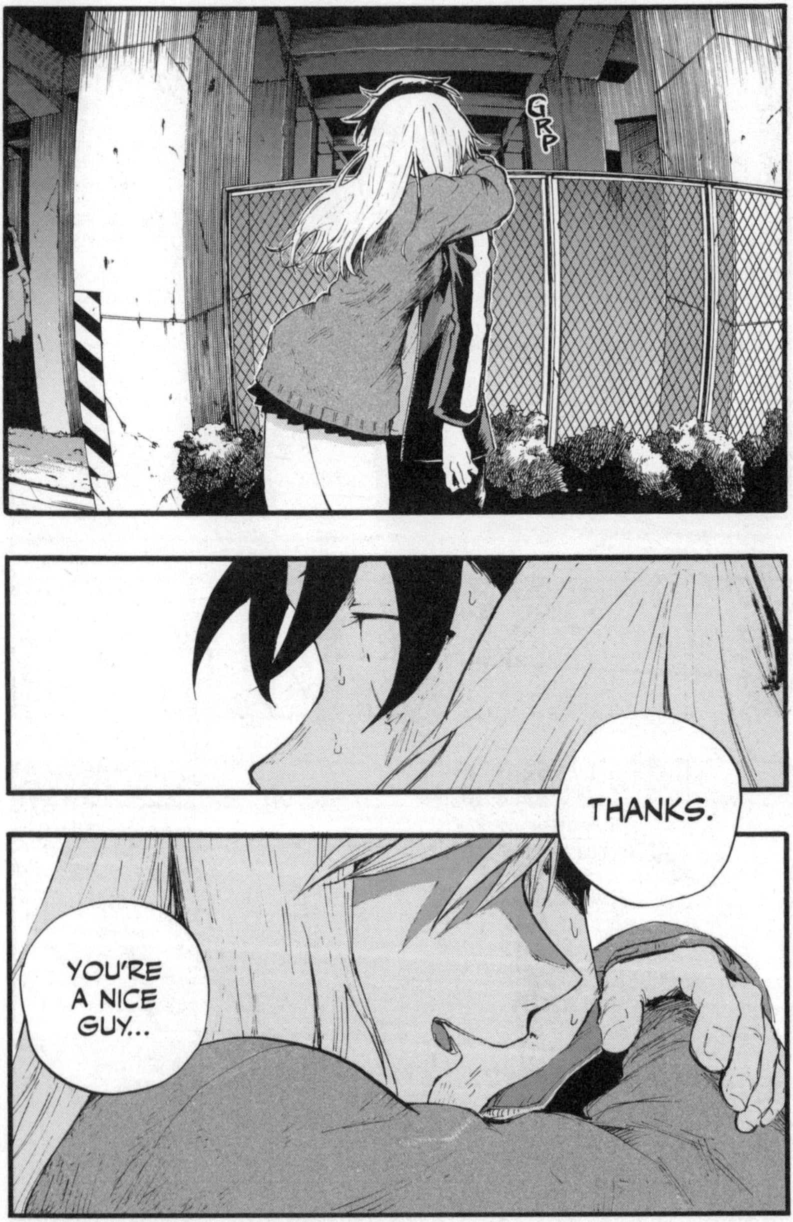
GRP
THANKS.
YOU'RE A NICE GUY...

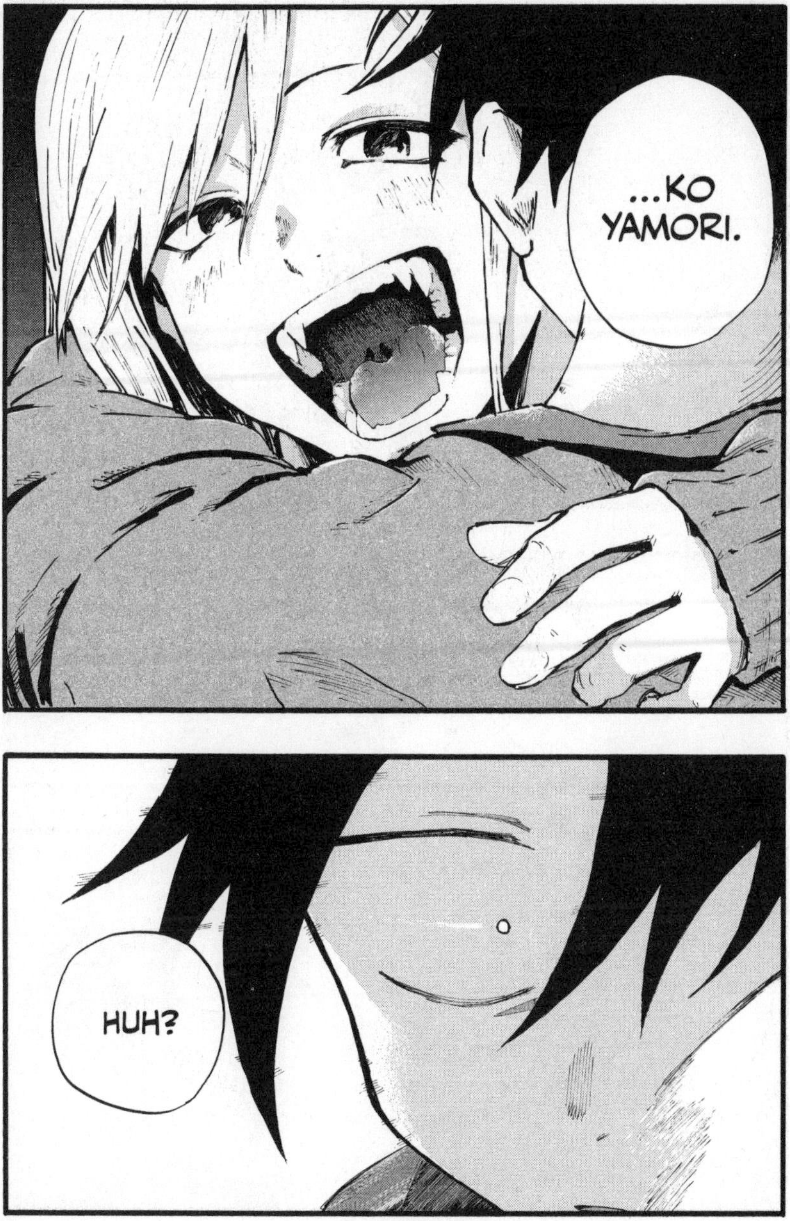
...KO
YAMORI.
HUH?

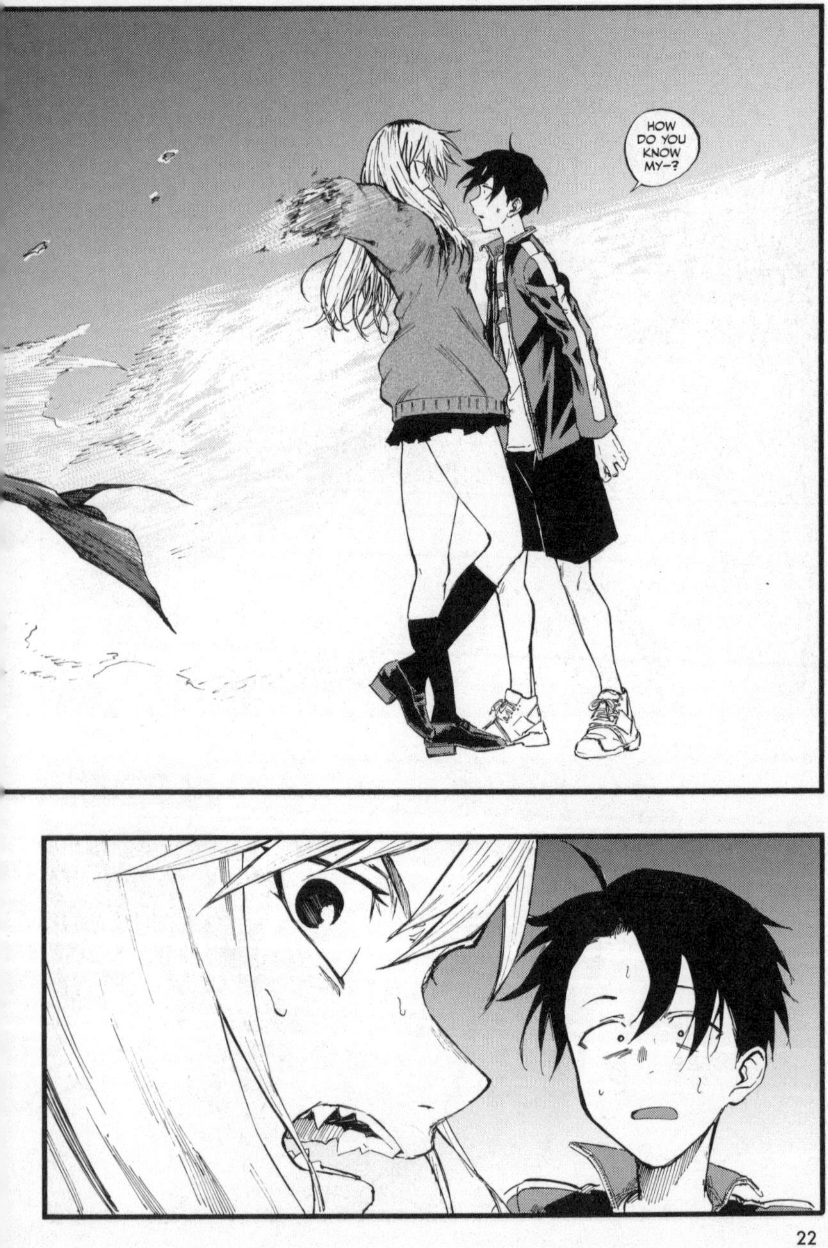
HOW DO YOU KNOW MY--?

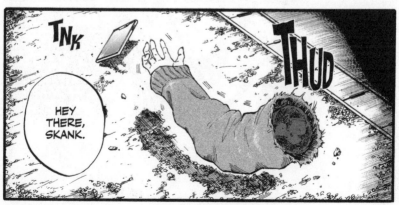

TNK

THUD

HEY
THERE,
SKANK.

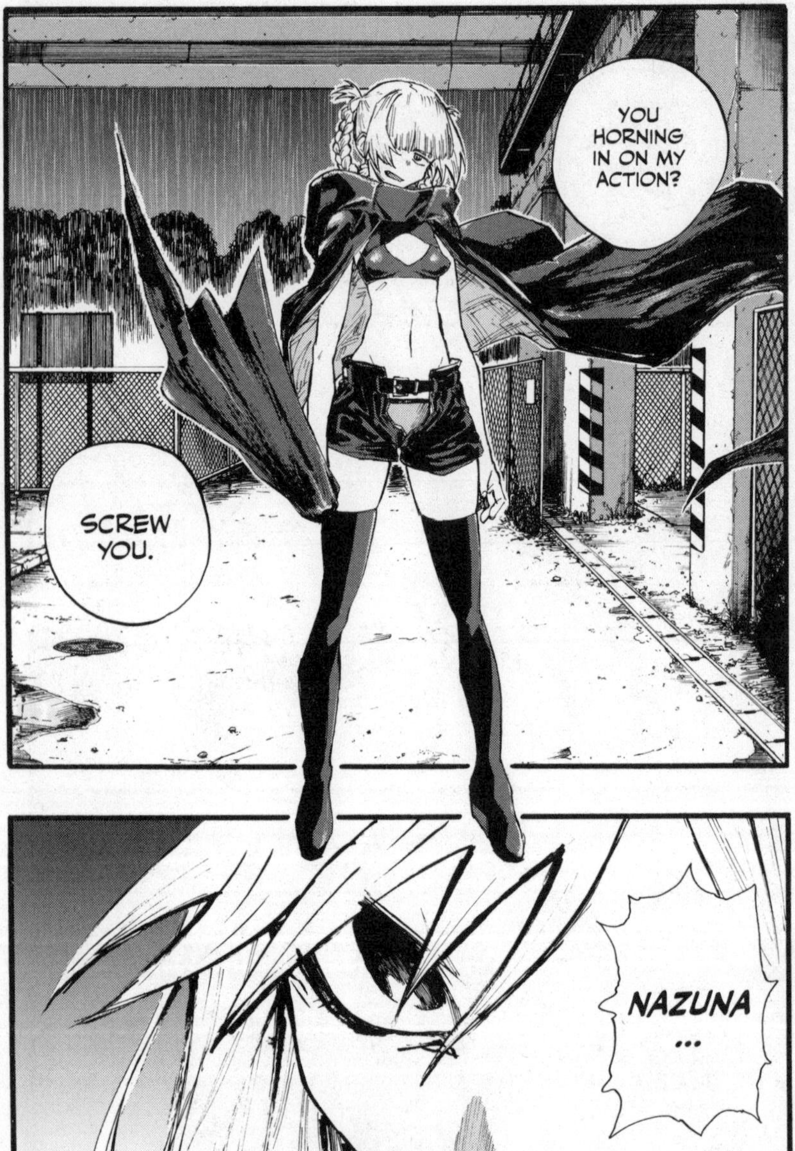
YOU HORNING IN ON MY ACTION?
SCREW YOU.
NAZUNA ...

NIGHT 20: REPRODUCE

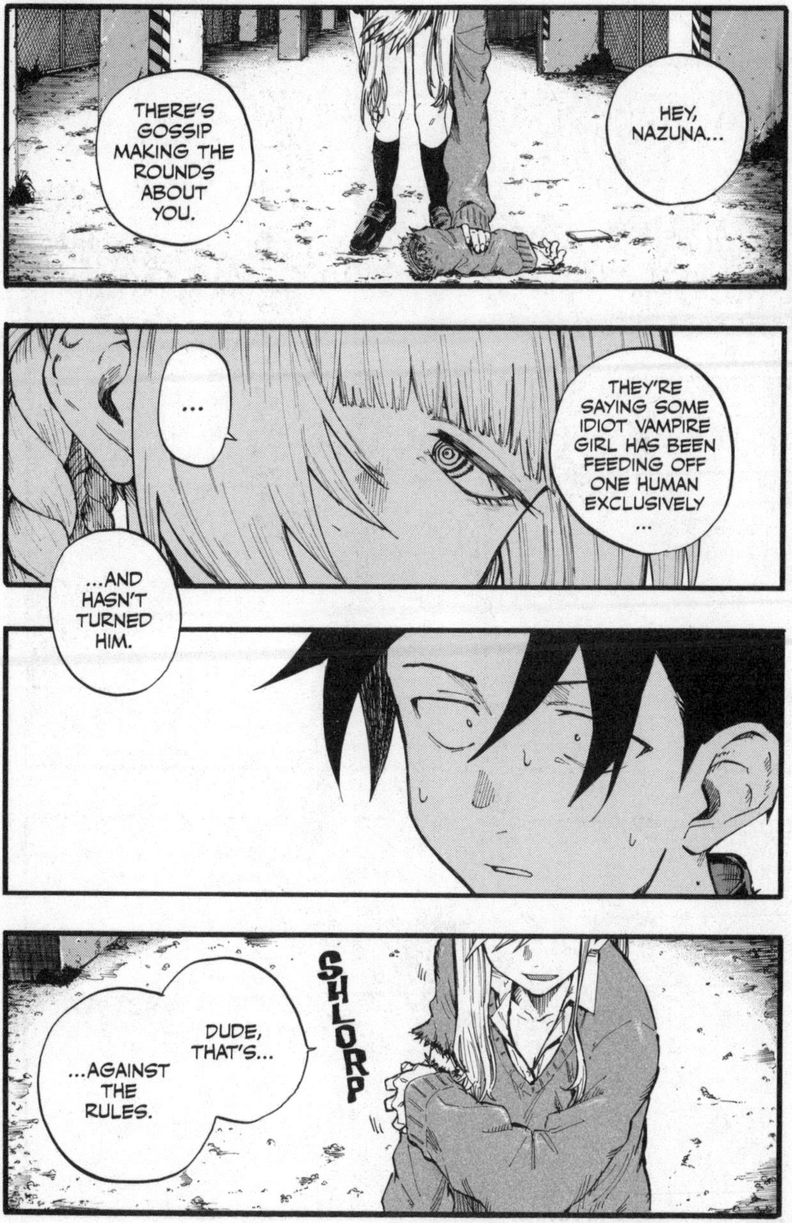
HEY, NAZUNA...
THERE'S GOSSIP MAKING THE ROUNDS ABOUT YOU.
THEY'RE SAYING SOME IDIOT VAMPIRE GIRL HAS BEEN FEEDING OFF ONE HUMAN EXCLUSIVELY...
...
...AND HASN'T TURNED HIM.
SHLORP
DUDE, THAT'S...
...AGAINST THE RULES.

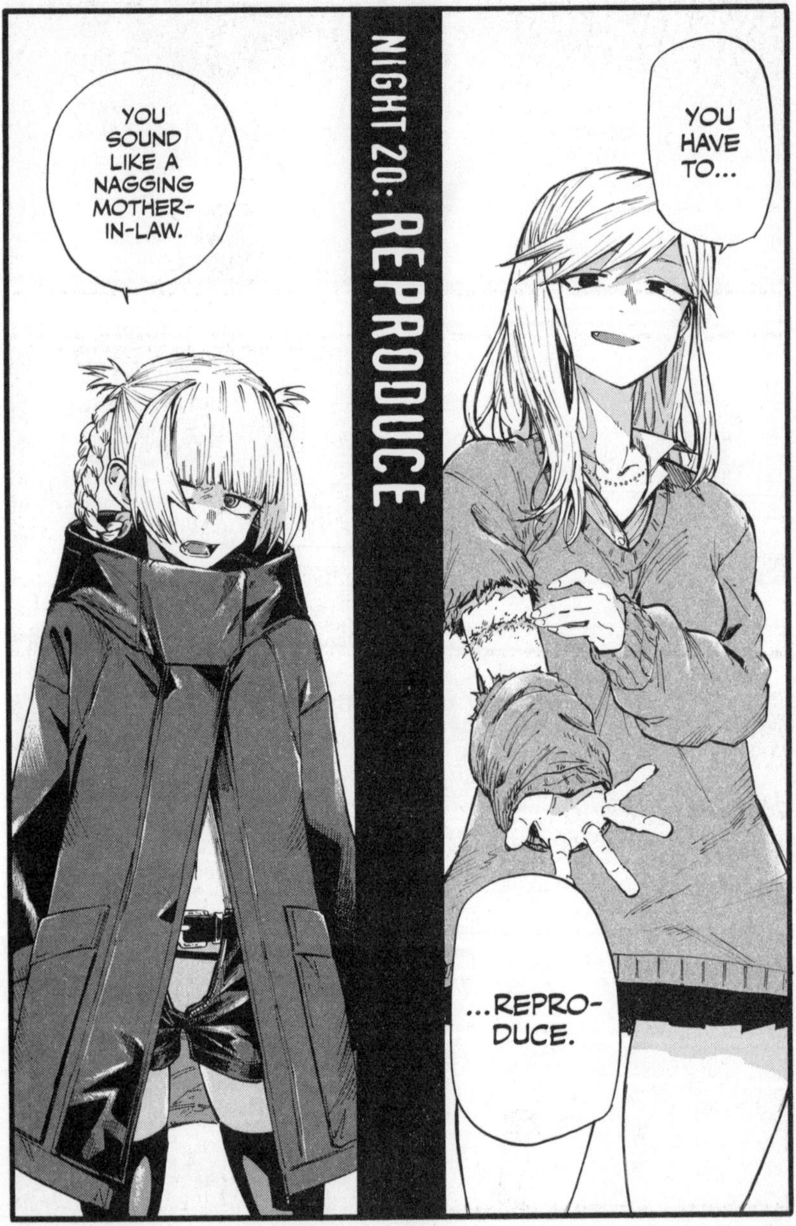
YOU HAVE TO...
...REPRO-DUCE.
NIGHT 20: REPRODUCE
YOU SOUND LIKE A NAGGING MOTHER-IN-LAW.

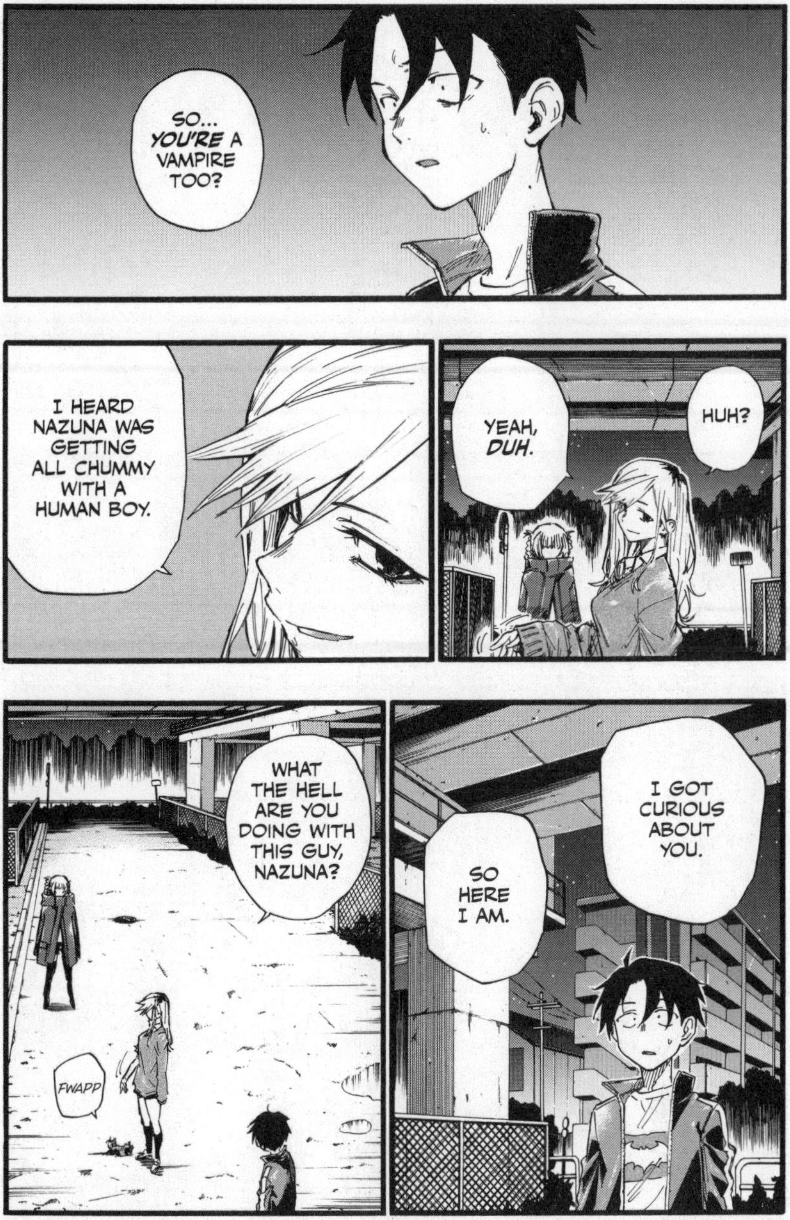
SO... *YOU'RE* A VAMPIRE TOO?
HUH?
YEAH, *DUH*.
I HEARD NAZUNA WAS GETTING ALL CHUMMY WITH A HUMAN BOY.
I GOT CURIOUS ABOUT YOU.
SO HERE I AM.
WHAT THE HELL ARE YOU DOING WITH THIS GUY, NAZUNA?
FWAPP

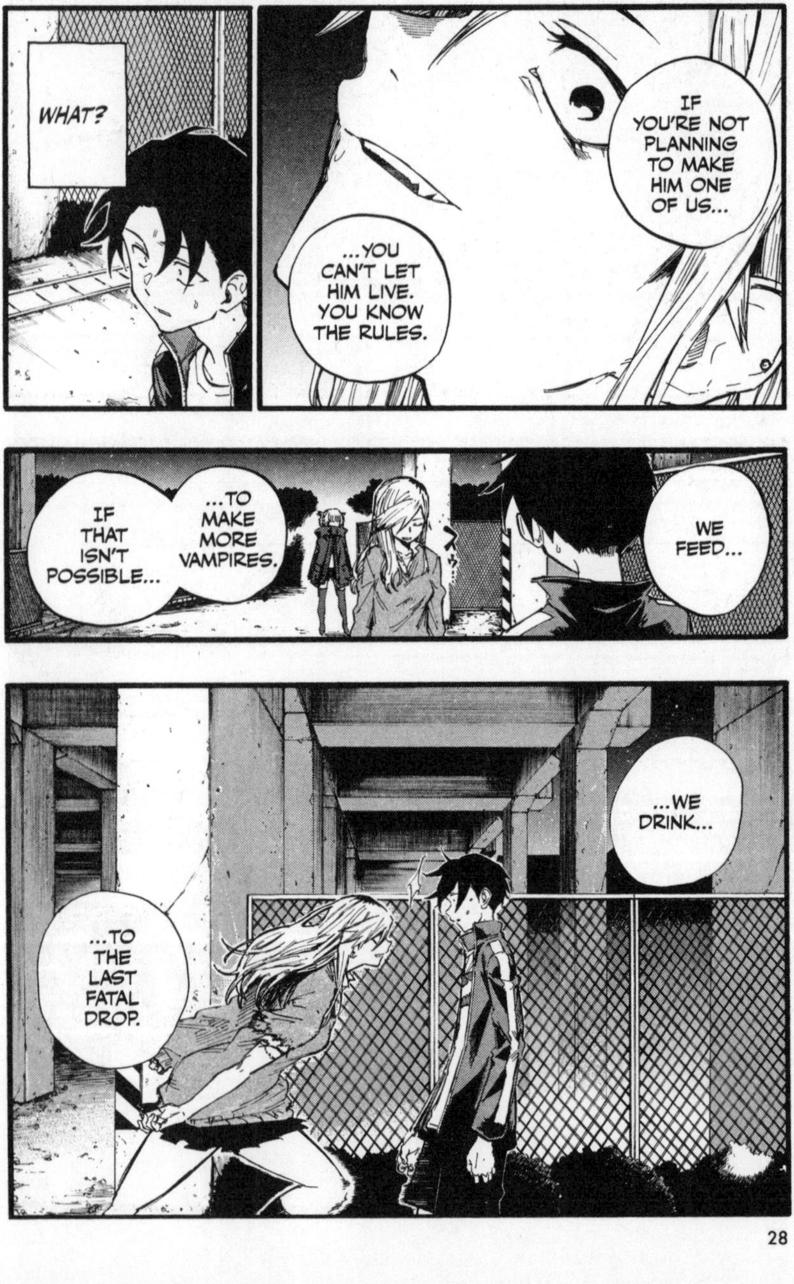
IF YOU'RE NOT PLANNING TO MAKE HIM ONE OF US...
...YOU CAN'T LET HIM LIVE. YOU KNOW THE RULES.
WHAT?
WE FEED...
...TO MAKE MORE VAMPIRES.
IF THAT ISN'T POSSIBLE...
...WE DRINK...
...TO THE LAST FATAL DROP.

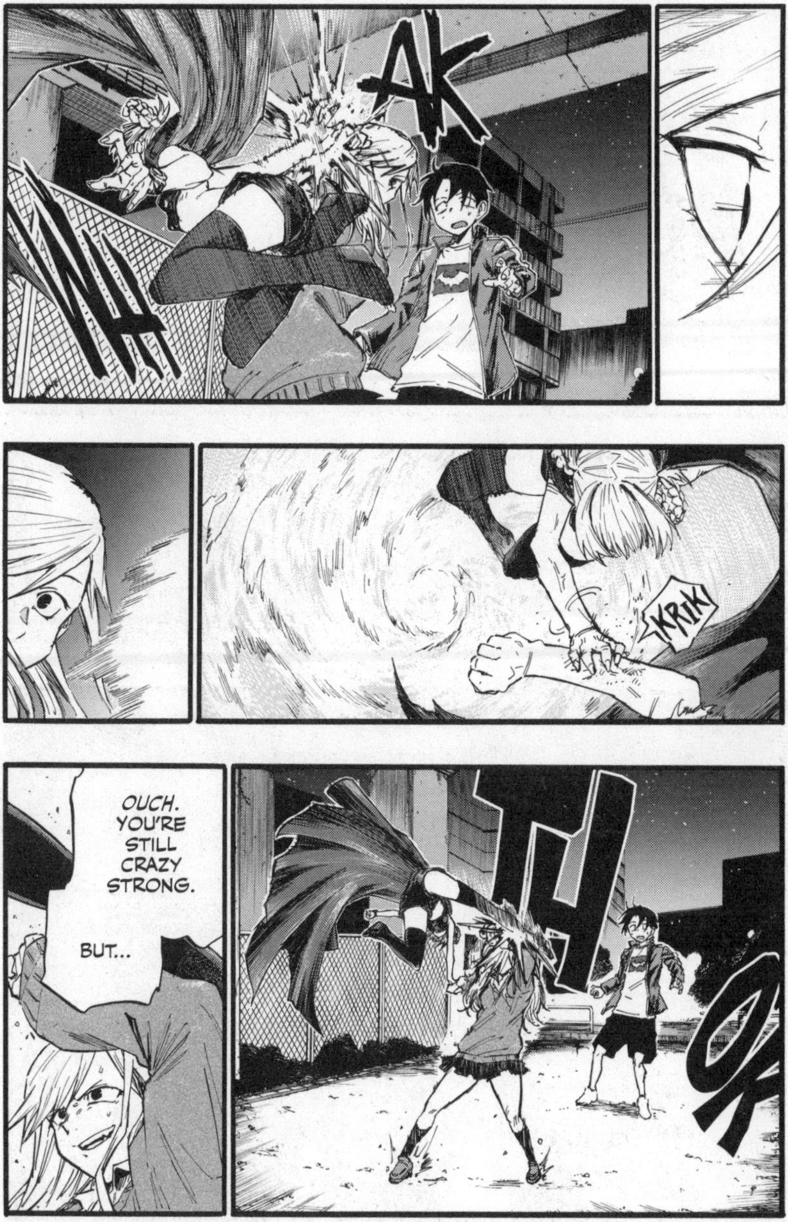
WH
AK
KRIK
TH
OK
OUCH. YOU'RE STILL CRAZY STRONG.
BUT...

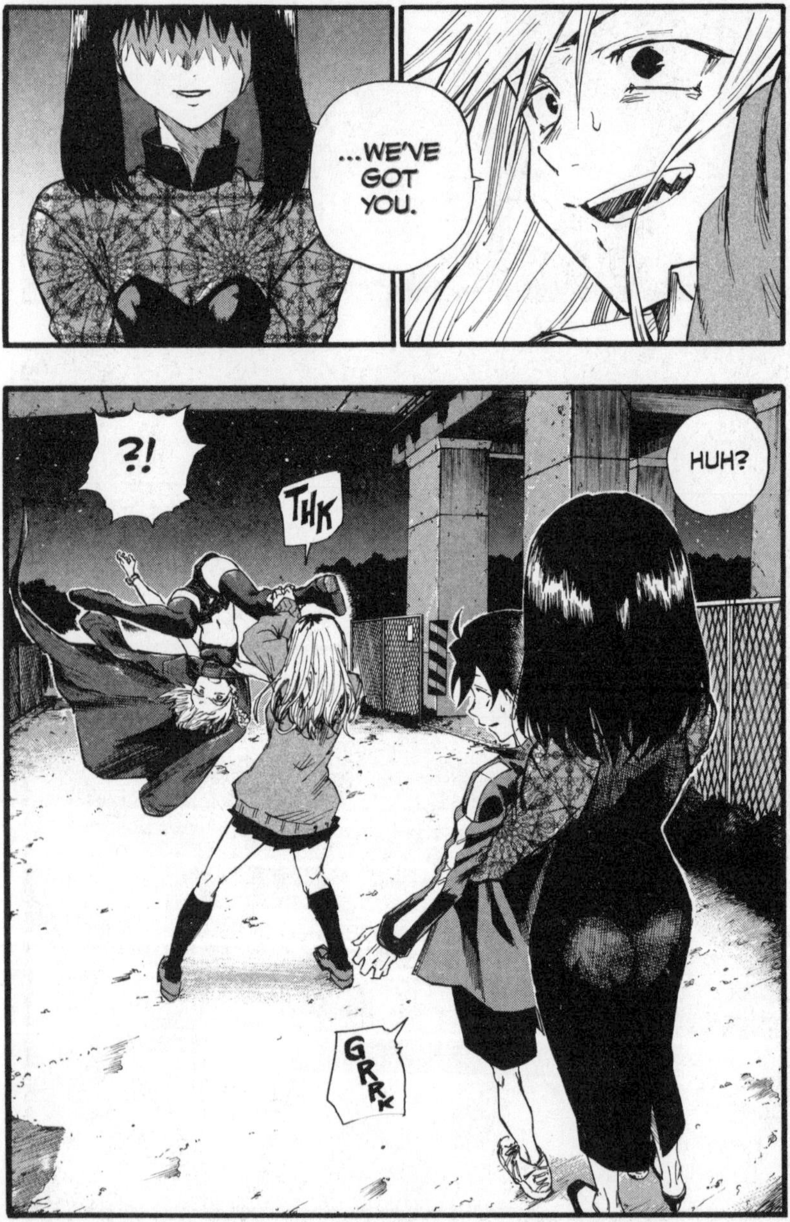
...WE'VE GOT YOU.
HUH?
THK
?!
GRRK

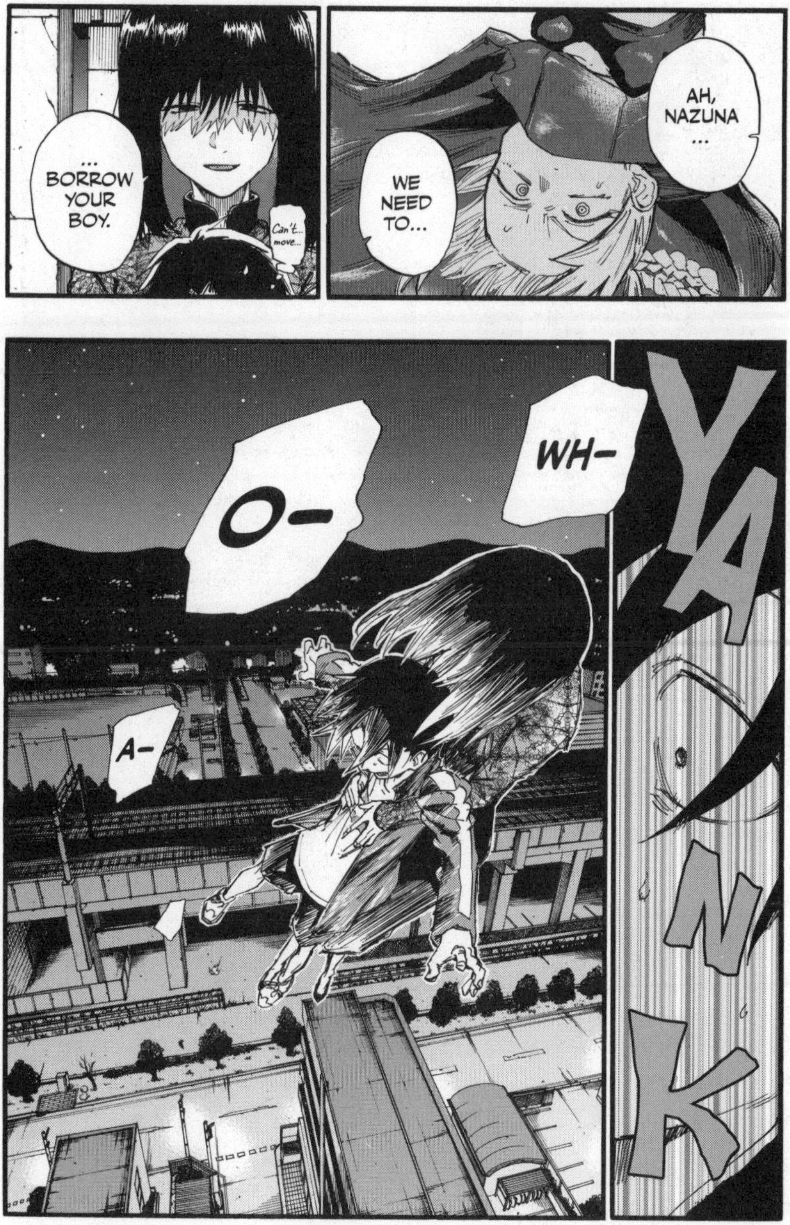
AH, NAZUNA ...
WE NEED TO...
... BORROW YOUR BOY.
Can't... move...
YANK
WH-
O-
A-

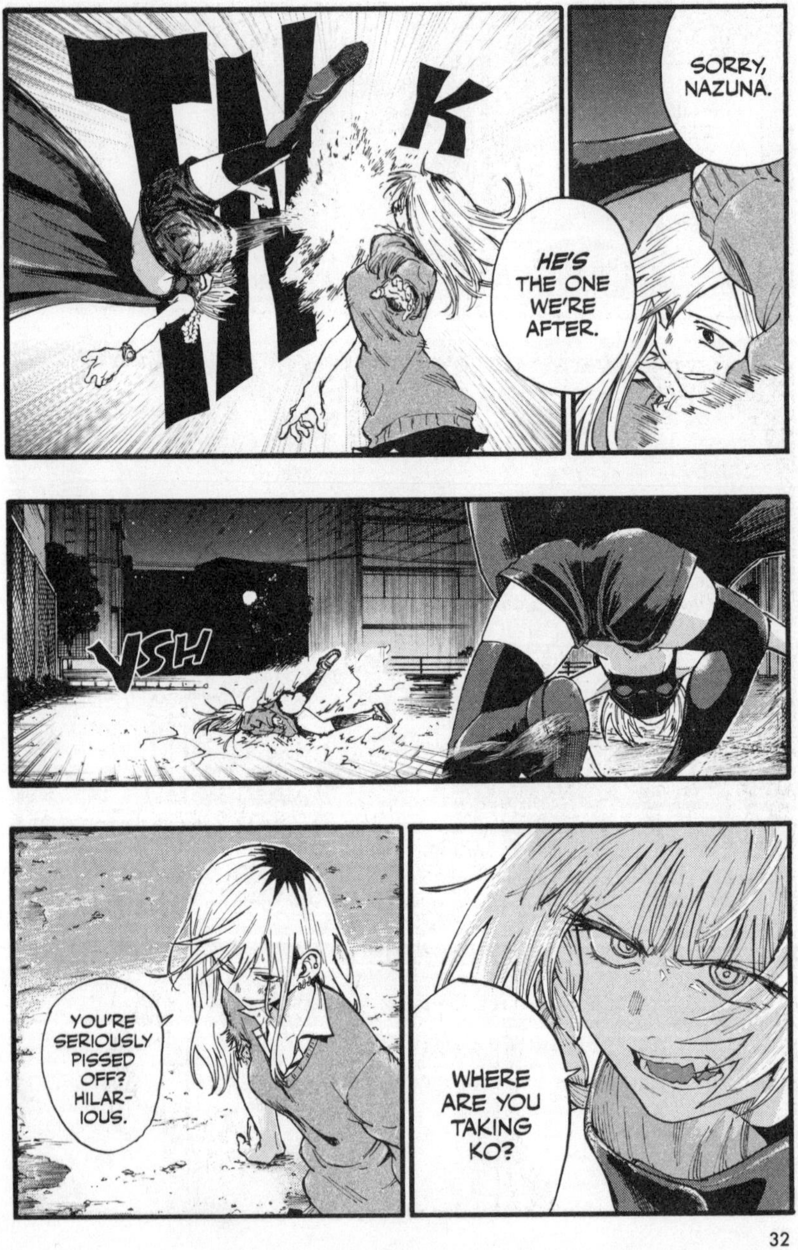
SORRY, NAZUNA.
HE'S THE ONE WE'RE AFTER.
THK
VSH
WHERE ARE YOU TAKING KO?
YOU'RE SERIOUSLY PISSED OFF? HILAR-IOUS.

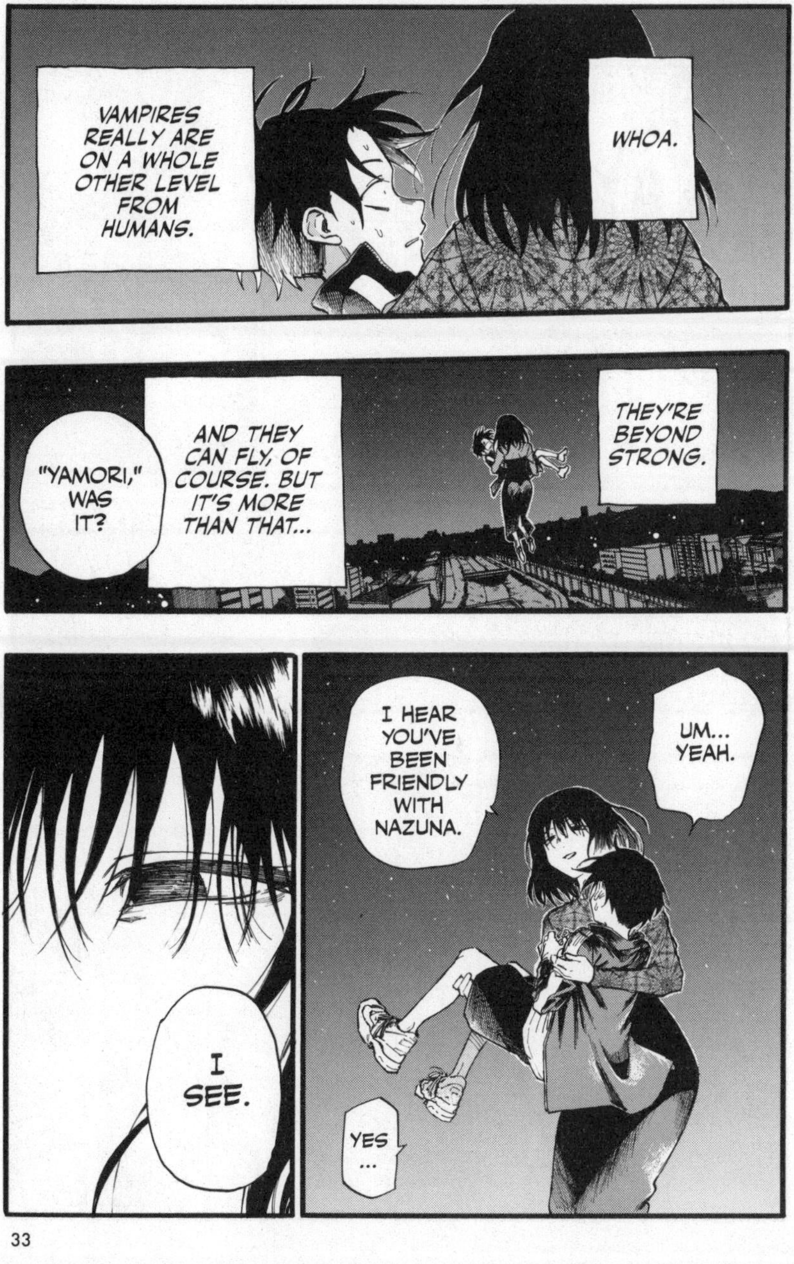
WHOA.
VAMPIRES REALLY ARE ON A WHOLE OTHER LEVEL FROM HUMANS.
THEY'RE BEYOND STRONG.
AND THEY CAN FLY, OF COURSE. BUT IT'S MORE THAN THAT...
"YAMORI," WAS IT?
UM... YEAH.
I HEAR YOU'VE BEEN FRIENDLY WITH NAZUNA.
YES ...
I SEE.

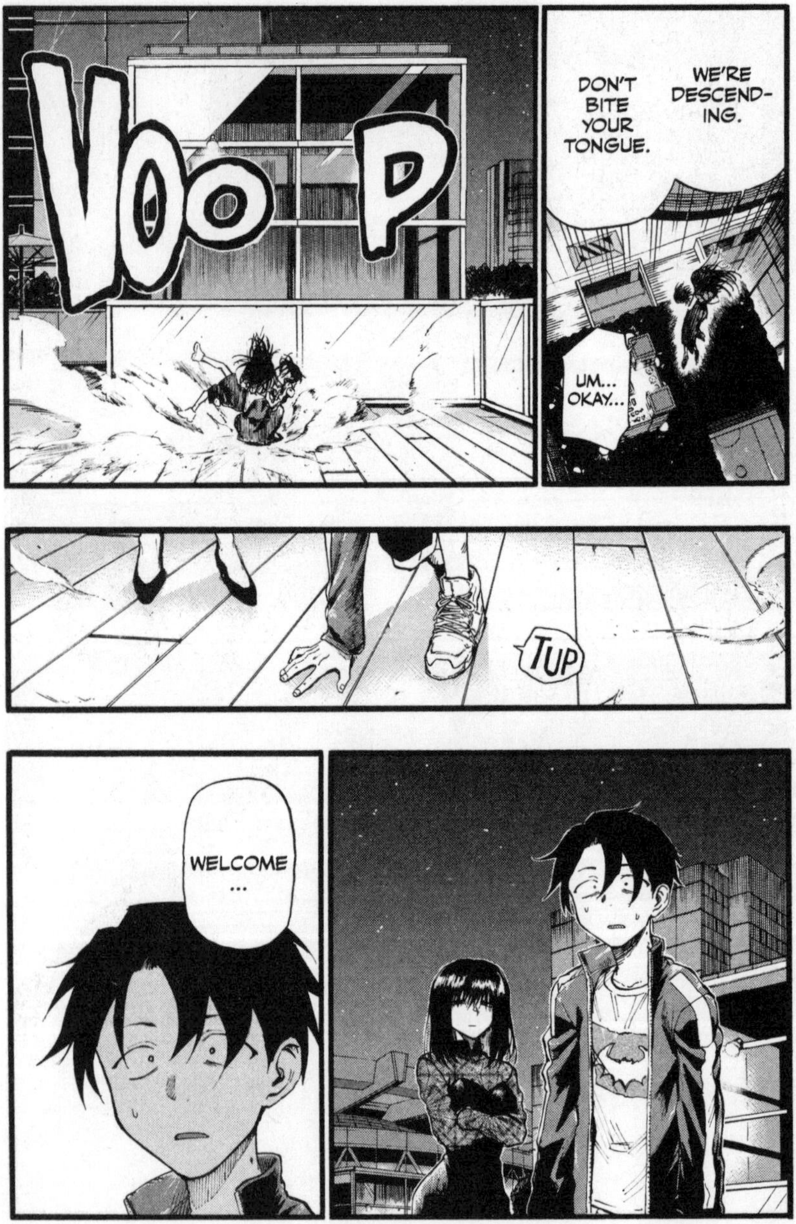
WE'RE DESCENDING.
DON'T BITE YOUR TONGUE.
UM... OKAY...
VOOP
TUP
WELCOME ...

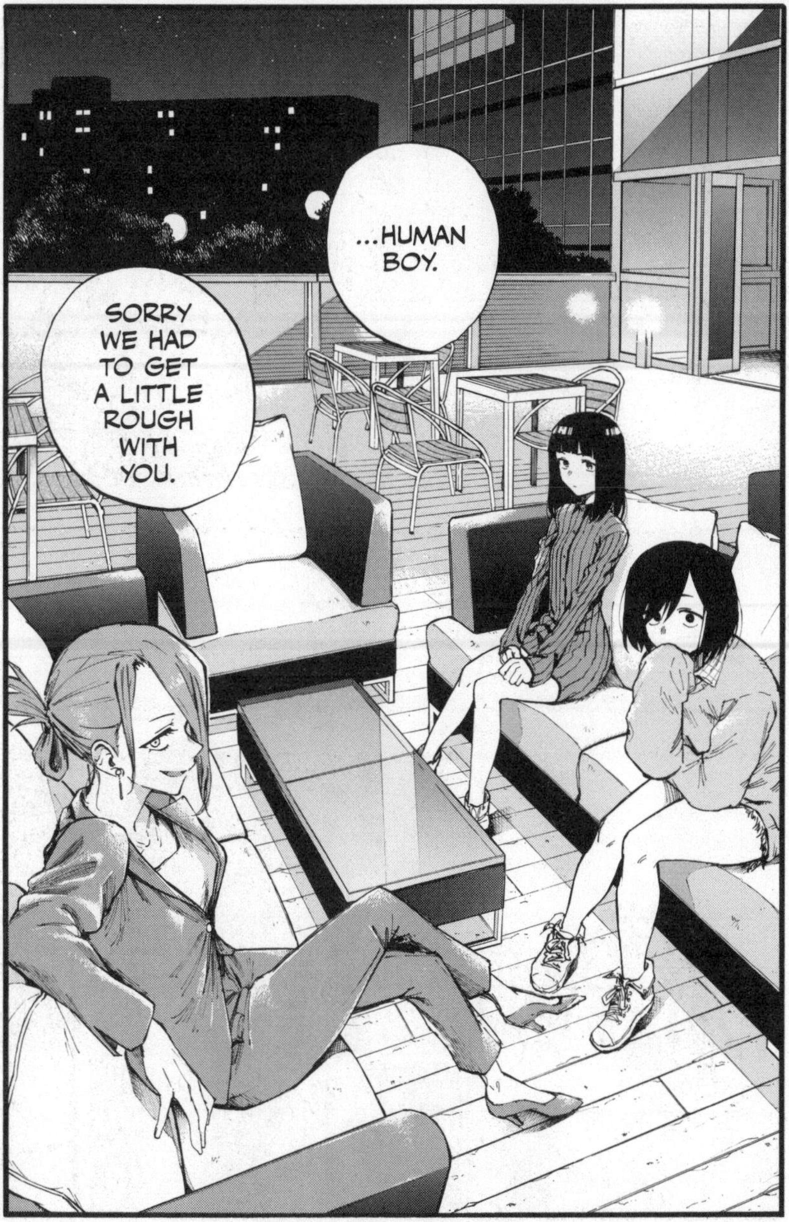
...HUMAN BOY.
SORRY WE HAD TO GET A LITTLE ROUGH WITH YOU.

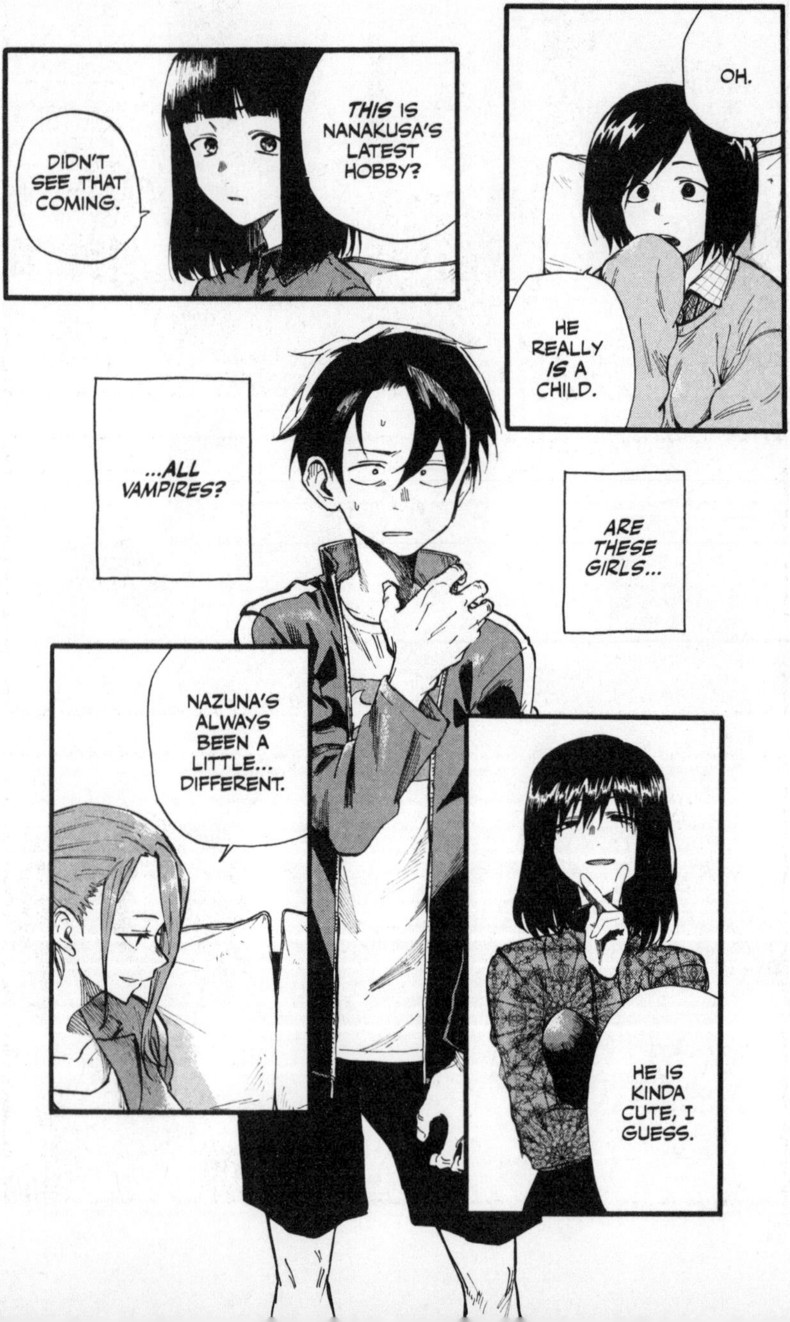
OH.
HE REALLY IS A CHILD.
THIS IS NANAKUSA'S LATEST HOBBY?
DIDN'T SEE THAT COMING.
ARE THESE GIRLS...
...ALL VAMPIRES?
HE IS KINDA CUTE, I GUESS.
NAZUNA'S ALWAYS BEEN A LITTLE... DIFFERENT.

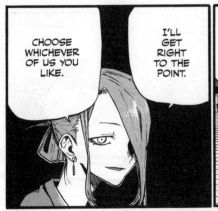

NAZUNA TOLD ME ALL VAMPIRES HAVE A GLAMOUR EFFECT THAT MAKES THEM SUPER ATTRAC-TIVE.
YAMORI, WAS IT...?
SHE WASN'T KIDDING.
I'LL GET RIGHT TO THE POINT.
CHOOSE WHICHEVER OF US YOU LIKE.
WE'LL TURN YOU INTO A VAMPIRE.
THAT WAY, WE CAN SPARE YOUR LIFE.
UH... UM...
DO YOU HAVE A *PROBLEM* WITH THIS DEAL? HOW UNGRATEFUL.
YOU KNOW HOW TO BECOME A VAMPIRE, DON'T YOU?

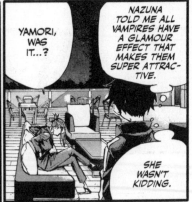

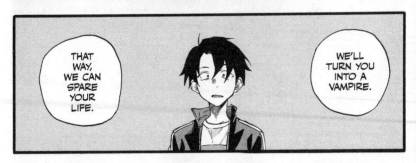

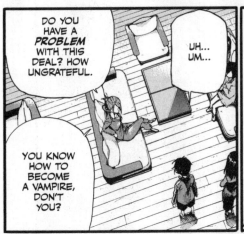

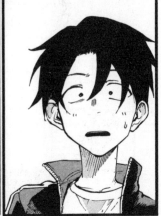

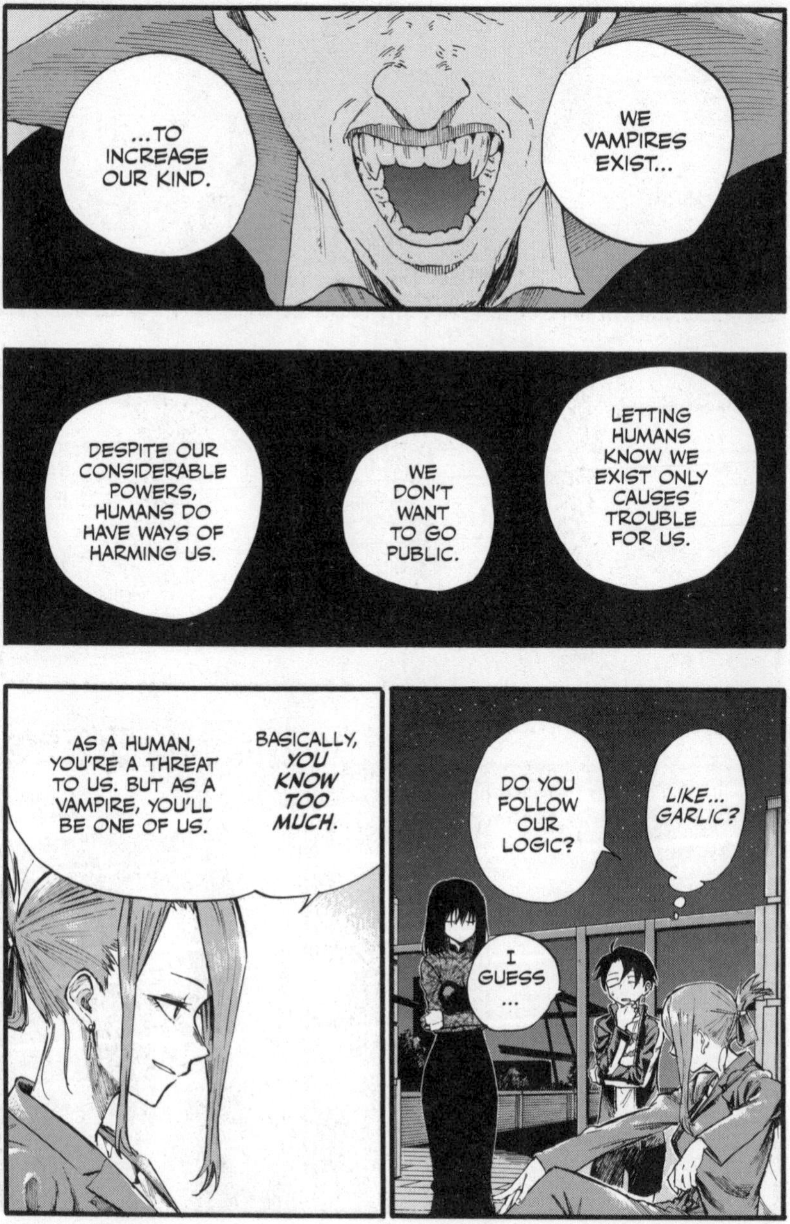
WE VAMPIRES EXIST...
...TO INCREASE OUR KIND.
LETTING HUMANS KNOW WE EXIST ONLY CAUSES TROUBLE FOR US.
WE DON'T WANT TO GO PUBLIC.
DESPITE OUR CONSIDERABLE POWERS, HUMANS DO HAVE WAYS OF HARMING US.
LIKE... GARLIC?
DO YOU FOLLOW OUR LOGIC?
I GUESS ...
BASICALLY, *YOU KNOW TOO MUCH*.
AS A HUMAN, YOU'RE A THREAT TO US. BUT AS A VAMPIRE, YOU'LL BE ONE OF US.

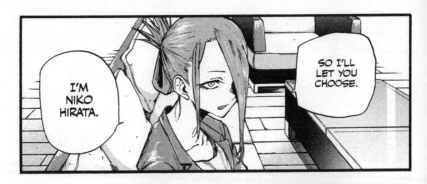

SO I'LL LET YOU CHOOSE.
I'M NIKO HIRATA.
MIDORI KOHA-KOBE.
...
HAKA SUZU-SHIRO.
BEHIND YOU IS...
...KABURA HONDA.
GRIN
THE FIRST ONE OF US YOU MET IS SERI KIKYO. SHE'S AN OPTION TOO.
Seri, huh?

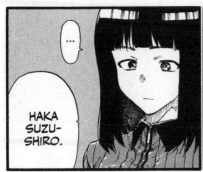

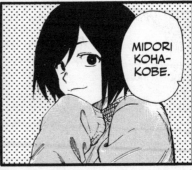

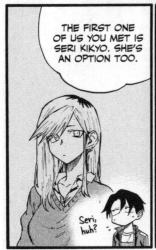

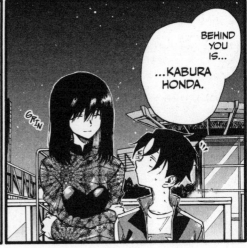

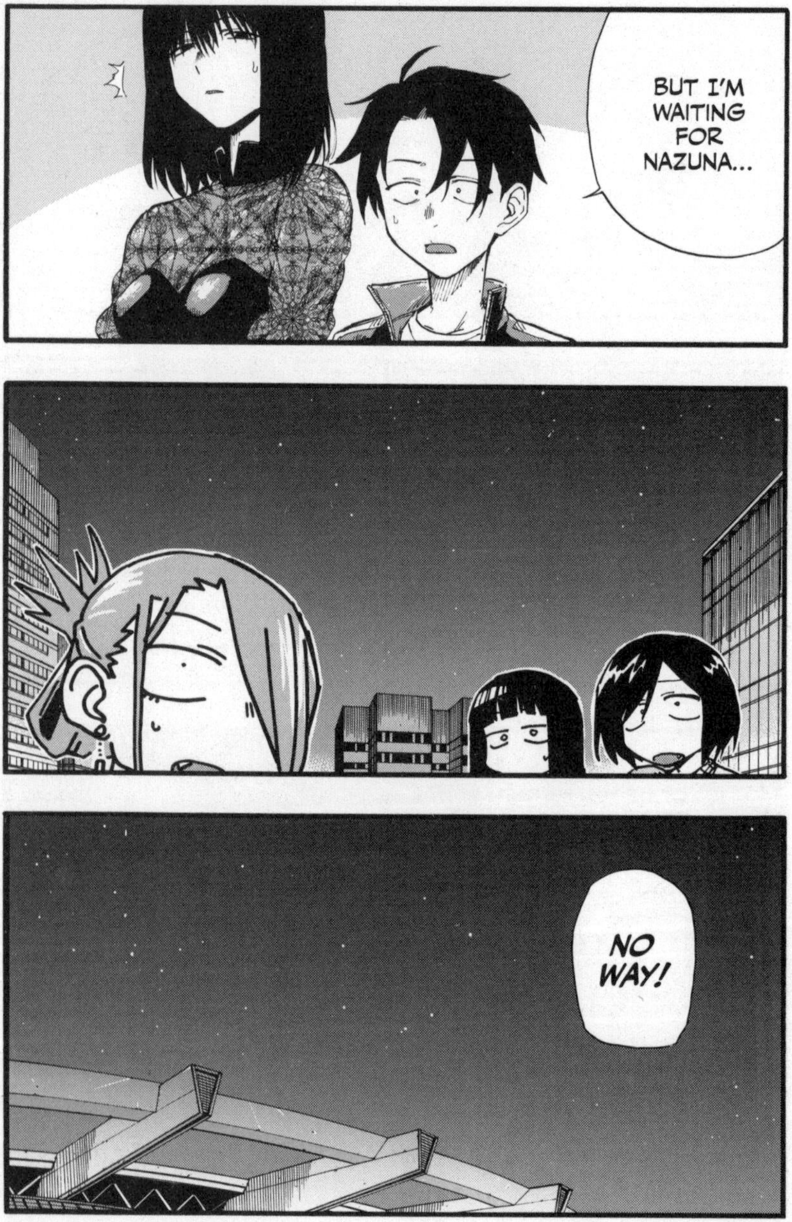
BUT I'M WAITING FOR NAZUNA...
NO WAY!

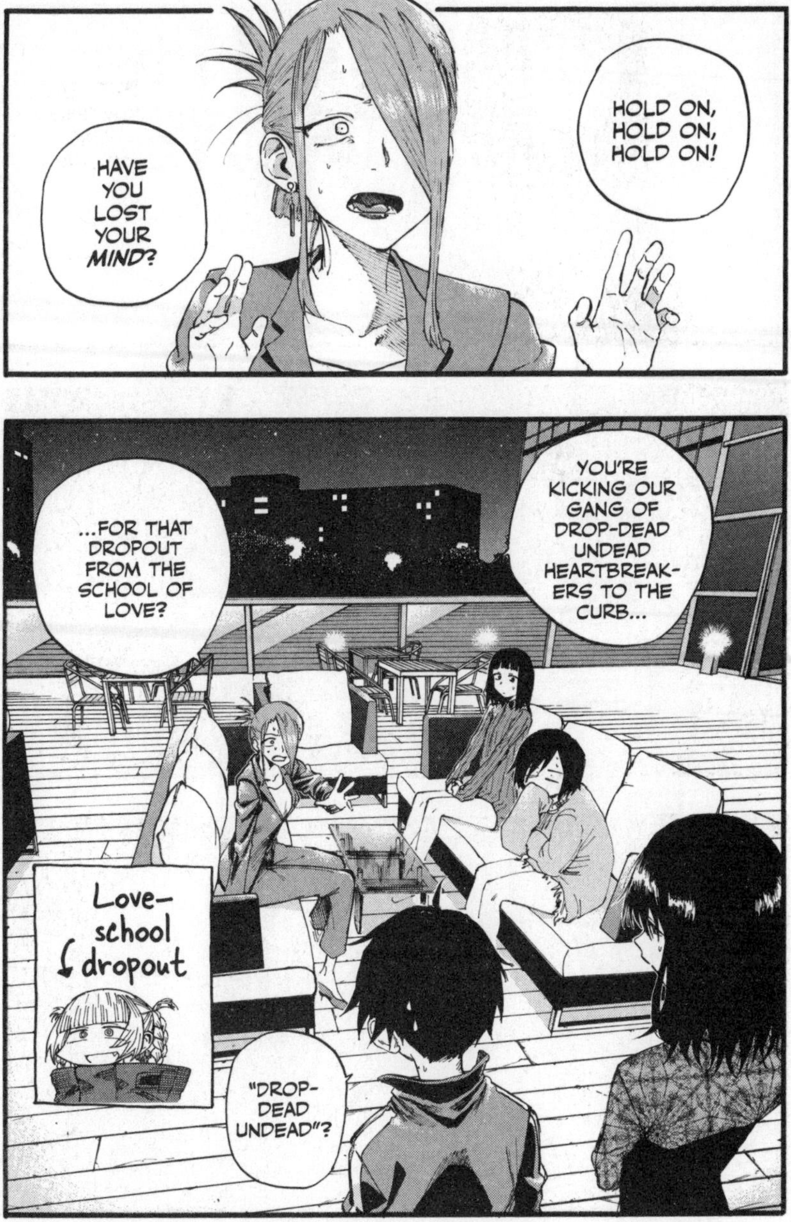
HOLD ON, HOLD ON, HOLD ON!
HAVE YOU LOST YOUR *MIND?*
YOU'RE KICKING OUR GANG OF DROP-DEAD UNDEAD HEARTBREAKERS TO THE CURB...
...FOR THAT DROPOUT FROM THE SCHOOL OF LOVE?
"DROP-DEAD UNDEAD"?
Love-school dropout

NIGHT 21: DROPOUT FROM THE SCHOOL OF LOVE

NIGHT 21:

DROPOUT FROM THE SCHOOL OF LOVE

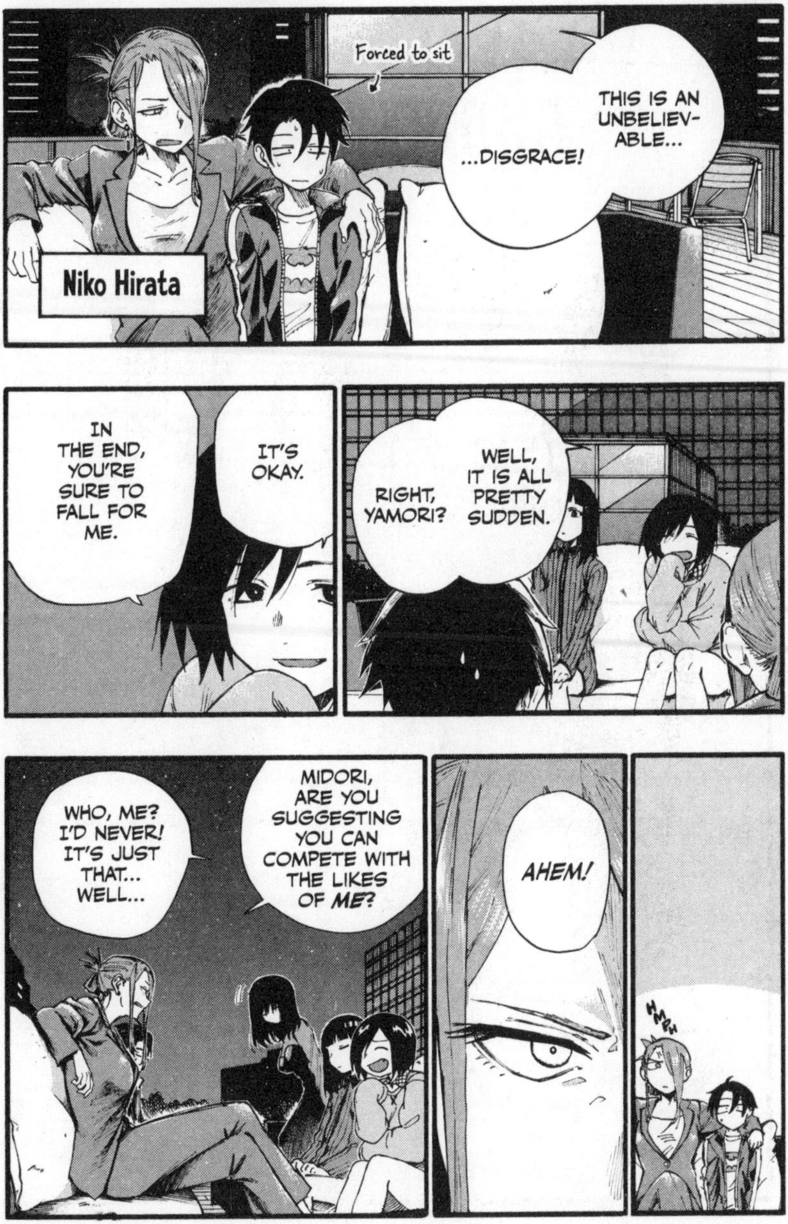
THIS IS AN UNBELIEVABLE...
...DISGRACE!
Forced to sit
Niko Hirata
WELL, IT IS ALL PRETTY SUDDEN.
RIGHT, YAMORI?
IT'S OKAY.
IN THE END, YOU'RE SURE TO FALL FOR ME.
HMPH
AHEM!
MIDORI, ARE YOU SUGGESTING YOU CAN COMPETE WITH THE LIKES OF *ME*?
WHO, ME? I'D NEVER! IT'S JUST THAT... WELL...

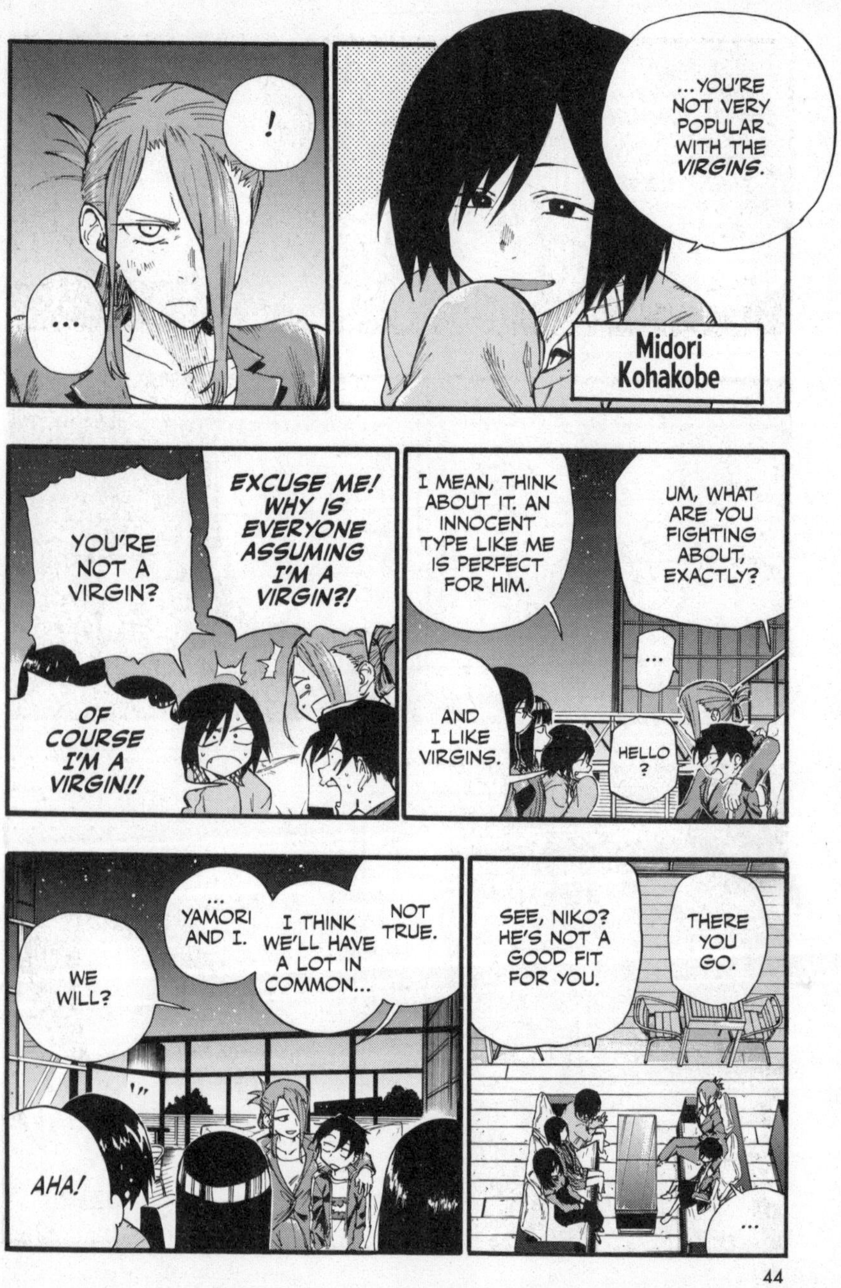
...YOU'RE NOT VERY POPULAR WITH THE VIRGINS.
Midori Kohakobe
!
...
UM, WHAT ARE YOU FIGHTING ABOUT, EXACTLY?
I MEAN, THINK ABOUT IT. AN INNOCENT TYPE LIKE ME IS PERFECT FOR HIM.
...
HELLO ?
AND I LIKE VIRGINS.
EXCUSE ME! WHY IS EVERYONE ASSUMING I'M A VIRGIN?!
YOU'RE NOT A VIRGIN?
OF COURSE I'M A VIRGIN!!
THERE YOU GO.
SEE, NIKO? HE'S NOT A GOOD FIT FOR YOU.
...
NOT TRUE.
I THINK WE'LL HAVE A LOT IN COMMON...
... YAMORI AND I.
WE WILL?
AHA!

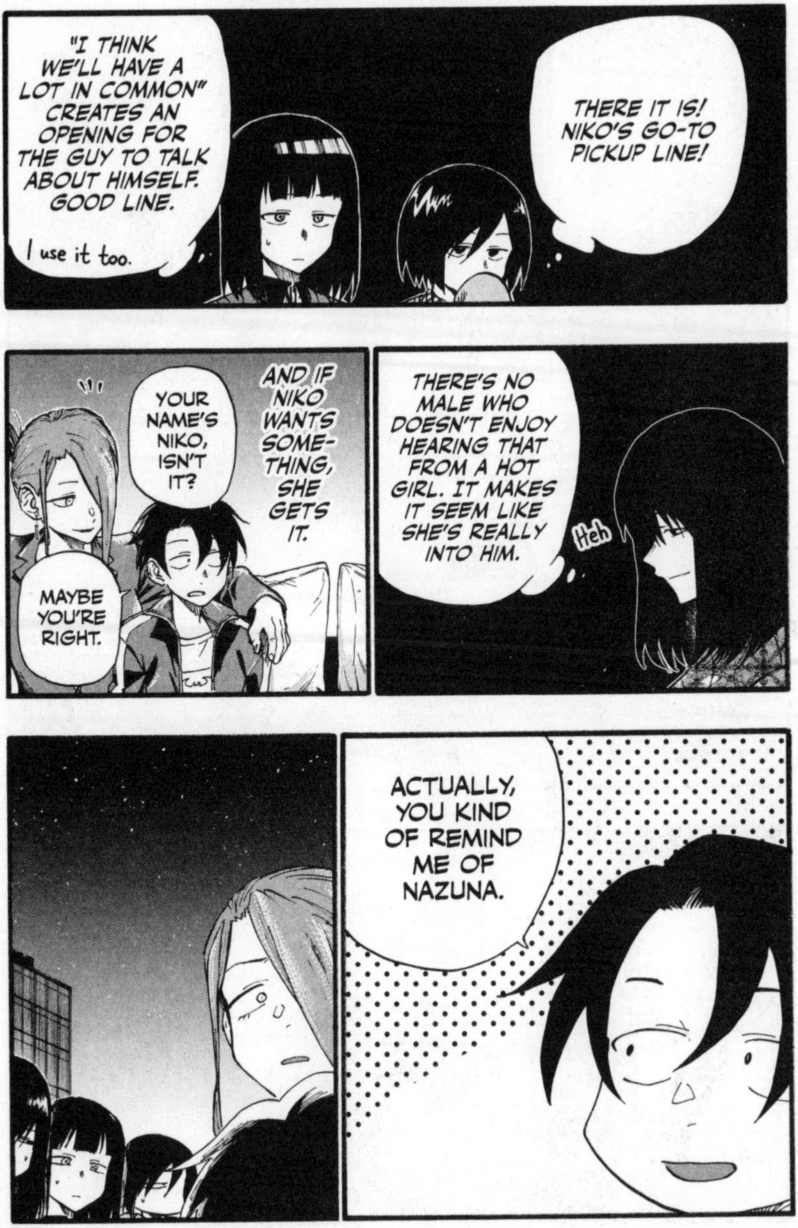
THERE IT IS! NIKO'S GO-TO PICKUP LINE!
"I THINK WE'LL HAVE A LOT IN COMMON" CREATES AN OPENING FOR THE GUY TO TALK ABOUT HIMSELF. GOOD LINE.
I use it too.
THERE'S NO MALE WHO DOESN'T ENJOY HEARING THAT FROM A HOT GIRL. IT MAKES IT SEEM LIKE SHE'S REALLY INTO HIM.
Heh
AND IF NIKO WANTS SOMETHING, SHE GETS IT.
YOUR NAME'S NIKO, ISN'T IT?
MAYBE YOU'RE RIGHT.
ACTUALLY, YOU KIND OF REMIND ME OF NAZUNA.

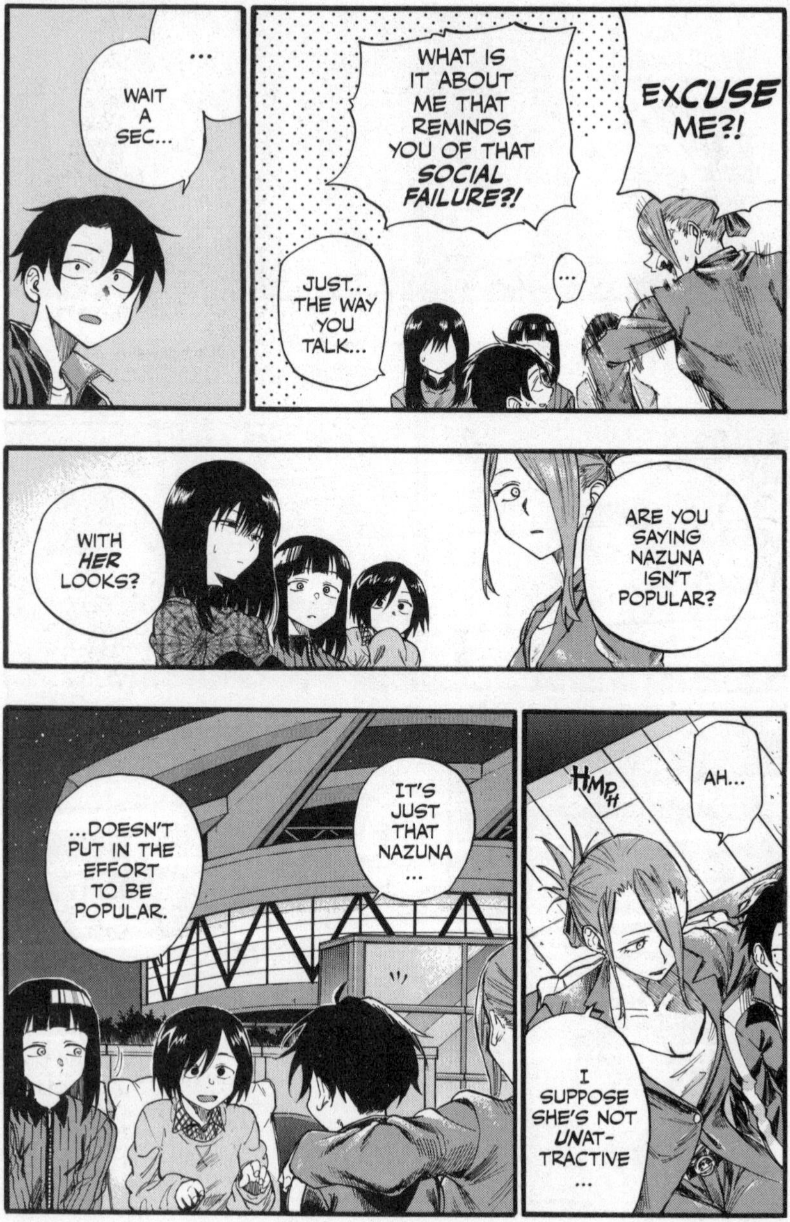

EXCUSE ME?!
WHAT IS IT ABOUT ME THAT REMINDS YOU OF THAT *SOCIAL FAILURE?!*
...
JUST... THE WAY YOU TALK...
...
WAIT A SEC...
ARE YOU SAYING NAZUNA ISN'T POPULAR?
WITH *HER* LOOKS?
HMPH
AH...
I SUPPOSE SHE'S NOT *UN*AT-TRACTIVE ...
IT'S JUST THAT NAZUNA ...
...DOESN'T PUT IN THE EFFORT TO BE POPULAR.

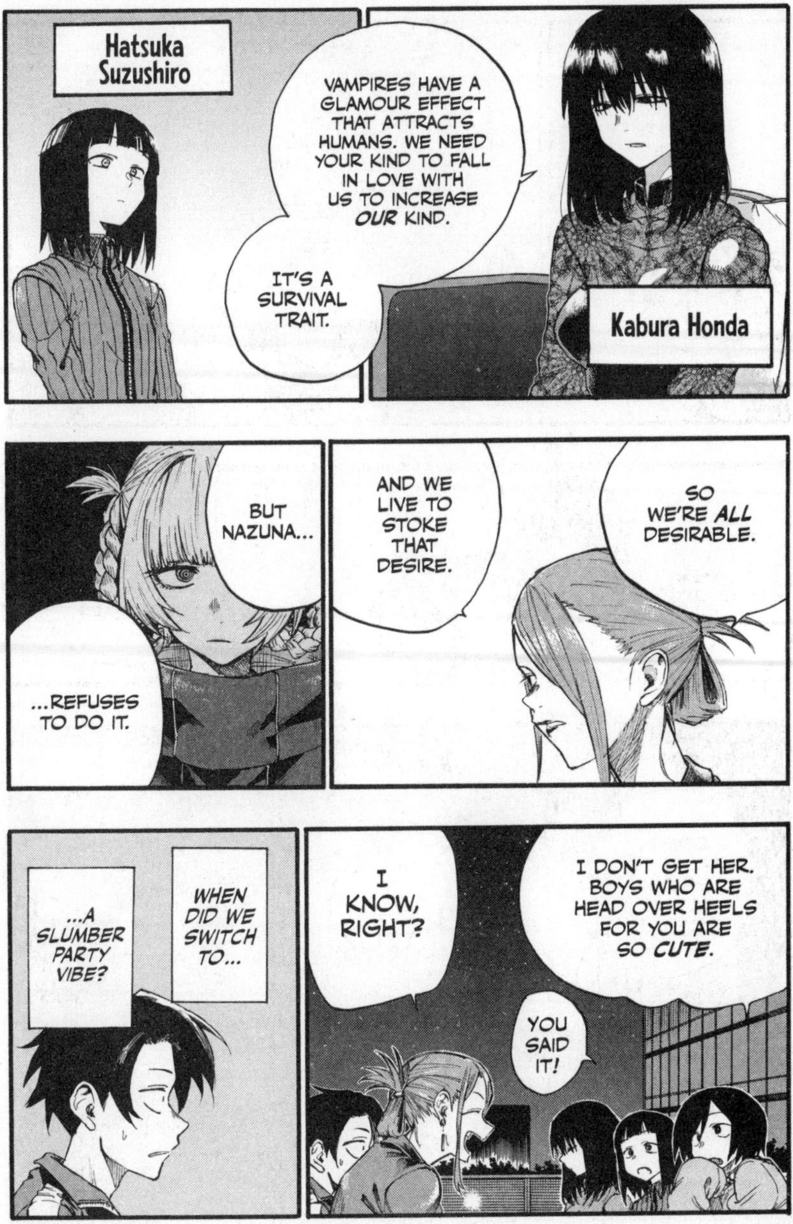
Kabura Honda
VAMPIRES HAVE A GLAMOUR EFFECT THAT ATTRACTS HUMANS. WE NEED YOUR KIND TO FALL IN LOVE WITH US TO INCREASE *OUR* KIND.
IT'S A SURVIVAL TRAIT.
Hatsuka Suzushiro
SO WE'RE *ALL* DESIRABLE.
AND WE LIVE TO STOKE THAT DESIRE.
BUT NAZUNA...
...REFUSES TO DO IT.
I DON'T GET HER. BOYS WHO ARE HEAD OVER HEELS FOR YOU ARE SO *CUTE*.
I KNOW, RIGHT?
YOU SAID IT!
WHEN DID WE SWITCH TO...
...A SLUMBER PARTY VIBE?

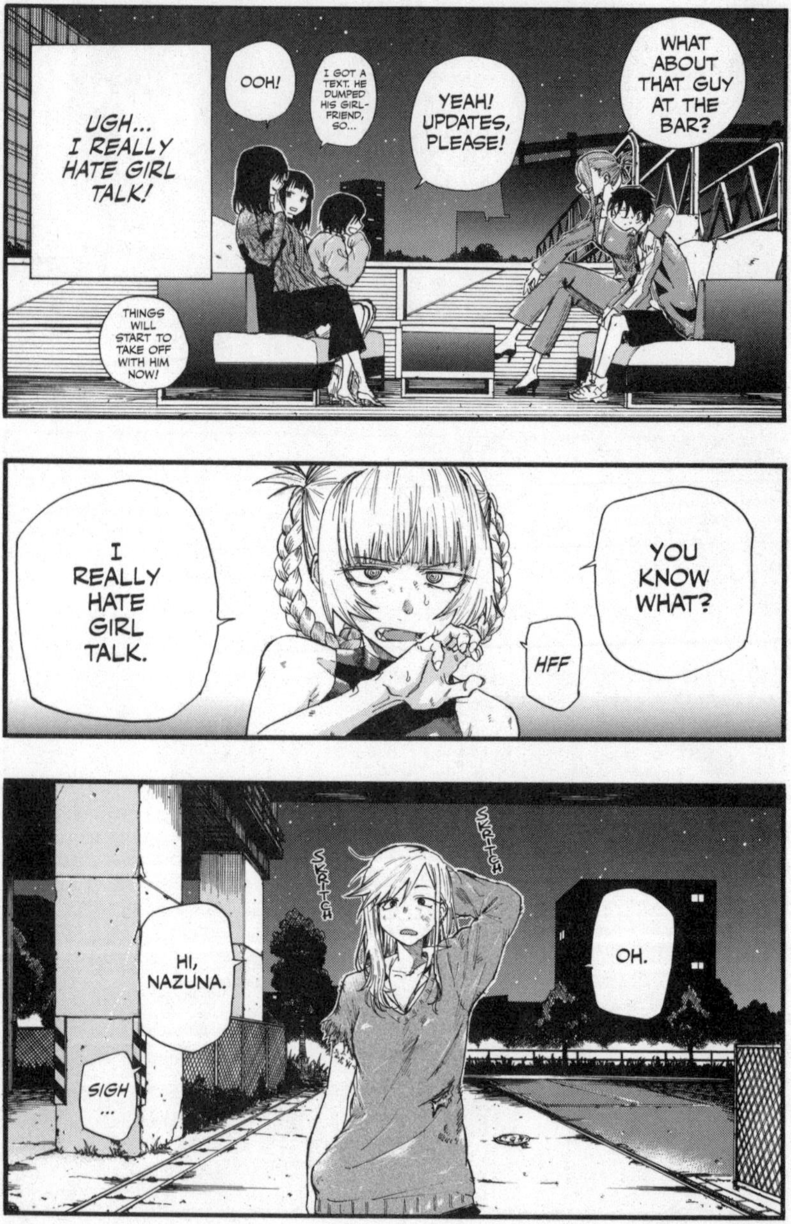
WHAT ABOUT THAT GUY AT THE BAR?
YEAH! UPDATES, PLEASE!
I GOT A TEXT. HE DUMPED HIS GIRL-FRIEND, SO...
OOH!
UGH... I REALLY HATE GIRL TALK!
THINGS WILL START TO TAKE OFF WITH HIM NOW!
YOU KNOW WHAT?
HFF
I REALLY HATE GIRL TALK.
SKRITCH
OH.
SKRITCH
HI, NAZUNA.
SIGH...

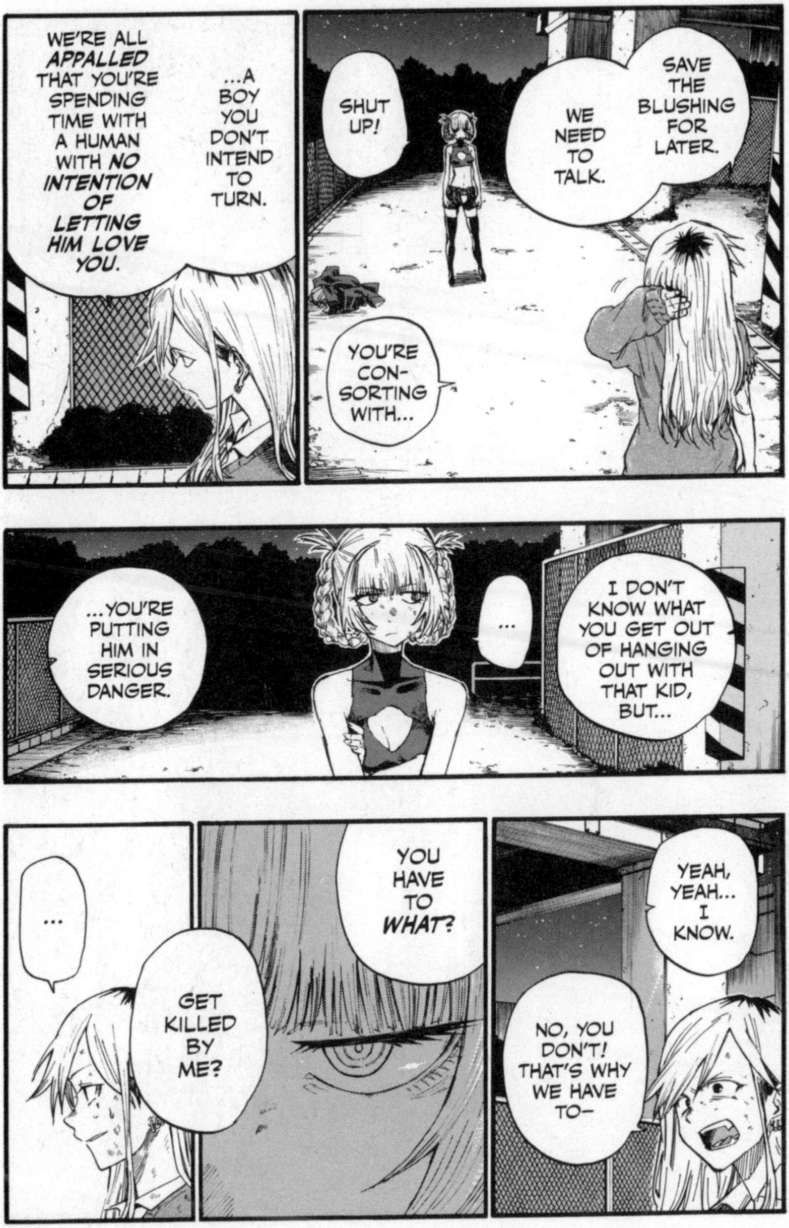
SAVE THE BLUSHING FOR LATER.
WE NEED TO TALK.
SHUT UP!
YOU'RE CON-SORTING WITH...
...A BOY YOU DON'T INTEND TO TURN.
WE'RE ALL *APPALLED* THAT YOU'RE SPENDING TIME WITH A HUMAN WITH *NO INTENTION OF LETTING HIM LOVE YOU.*
I DON'T KNOW WHAT YOU GET OUT OF HANGING OUT WITH THAT KID, BUT...
...
...YOU'RE PUTTING HIM IN SERIOUS DANGER.
YEAH, YEAH... I KNOW.
NO, YOU DON'T! THAT'S WHY WE HAVE TO–
YOU HAVE TO *WHAT?*
GET KILLED BY ME?
...

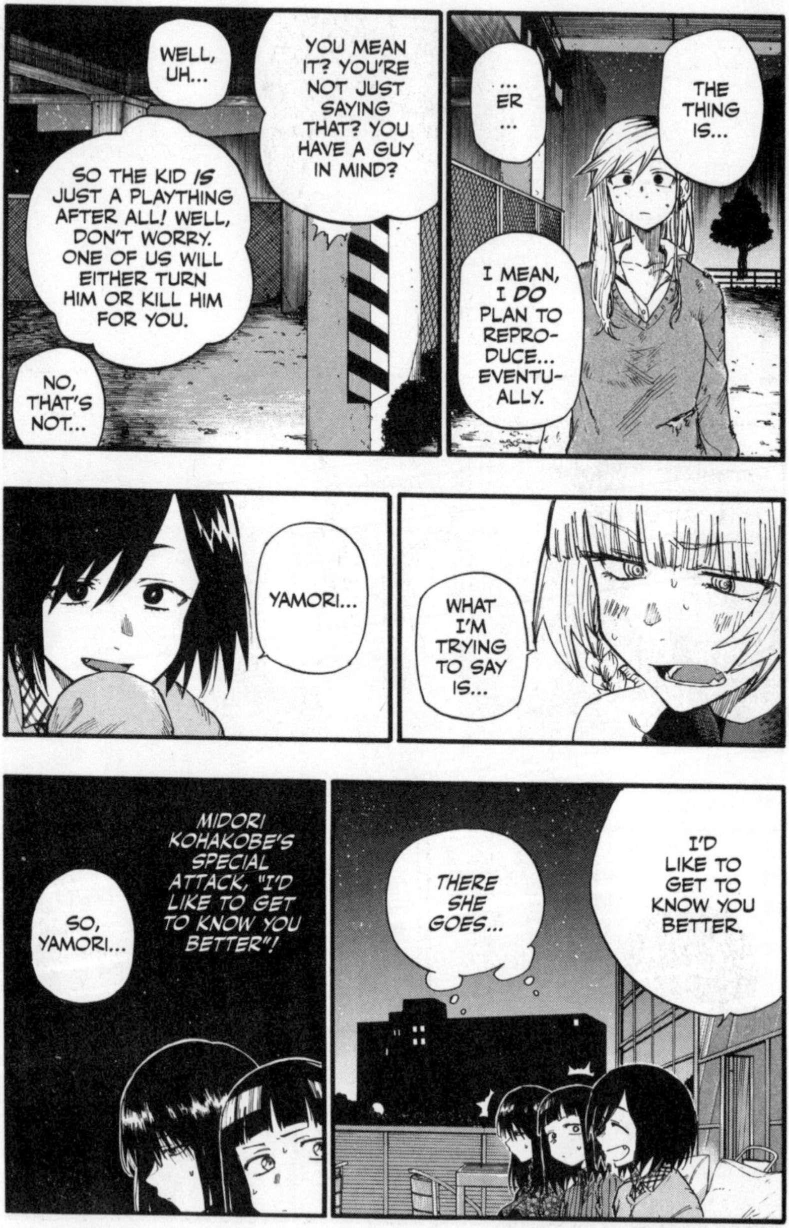
THE THING IS...
... ER ...
I MEAN, I *DO* PLAN TO REPRODUCE... EVENTUALLY.
YOU MEAN IT? YOU'RE NOT JUST SAYING THAT? YOU HAVE A GUY IN MIND?
WELL, UH...
SO THE KID *IS* JUST A PLAYTHING AFTER ALL! WELL, DON'T WORRY. ONE OF US WILL EITHER TURN HIM OR KILL HIM FOR YOU.
NO, THAT'S NOT...
WHAT I'M TRYING TO SAY IS...
YAMORI...
I'D LIKE TO GET TO KNOW YOU BETTER.
THERE SHE GOES...
MIDORI KOHAKOBE'S SPECIAL ATTACK, "I'D LIKE TO GET TO KNOW YOU BETTER"!
SO, YAMORI...

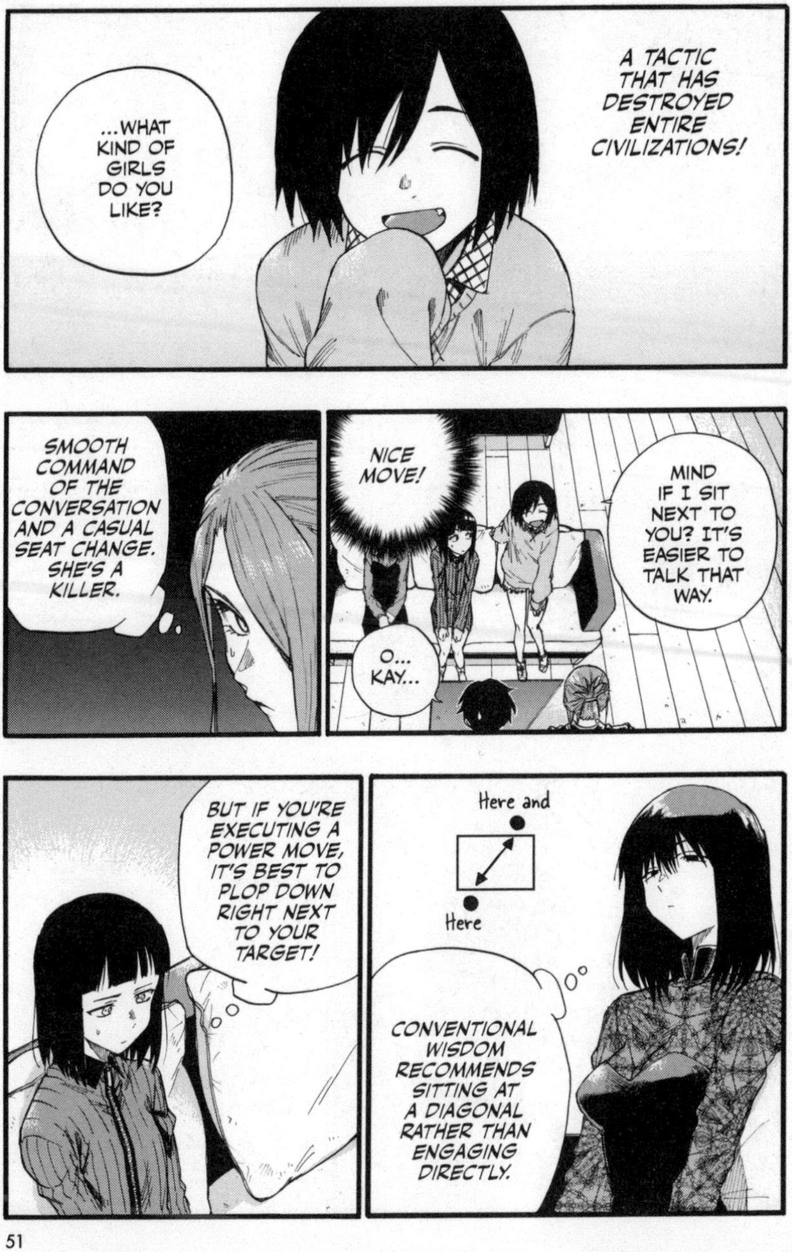
A TACTIC THAT HAS DESTROYED ENTIRE CIVILIZATIONS!
...WHAT KIND OF GIRLS DO YOU LIKE?
MIND IF I SIT NEXT TO YOU? IT'S EASIER TO TALK THAT WAY.
NICE MOVE!
O... KAY...
SMOOTH COMMAND OF THE CONVERSATION AND A CASUAL SEAT CHANGE. SHE'S A KILLER.
Here and
Here
CONVENTIONAL WISDOM RECOMMENDS SITTING AT A DIAGONAL RATHER THAN ENGAGING DIRECTLY.
BUT IF YOU'RE EXECUTING A POWER MOVE, IT'S BEST TO PLOP DOWN RIGHT NEXT TO YOUR TARGET!

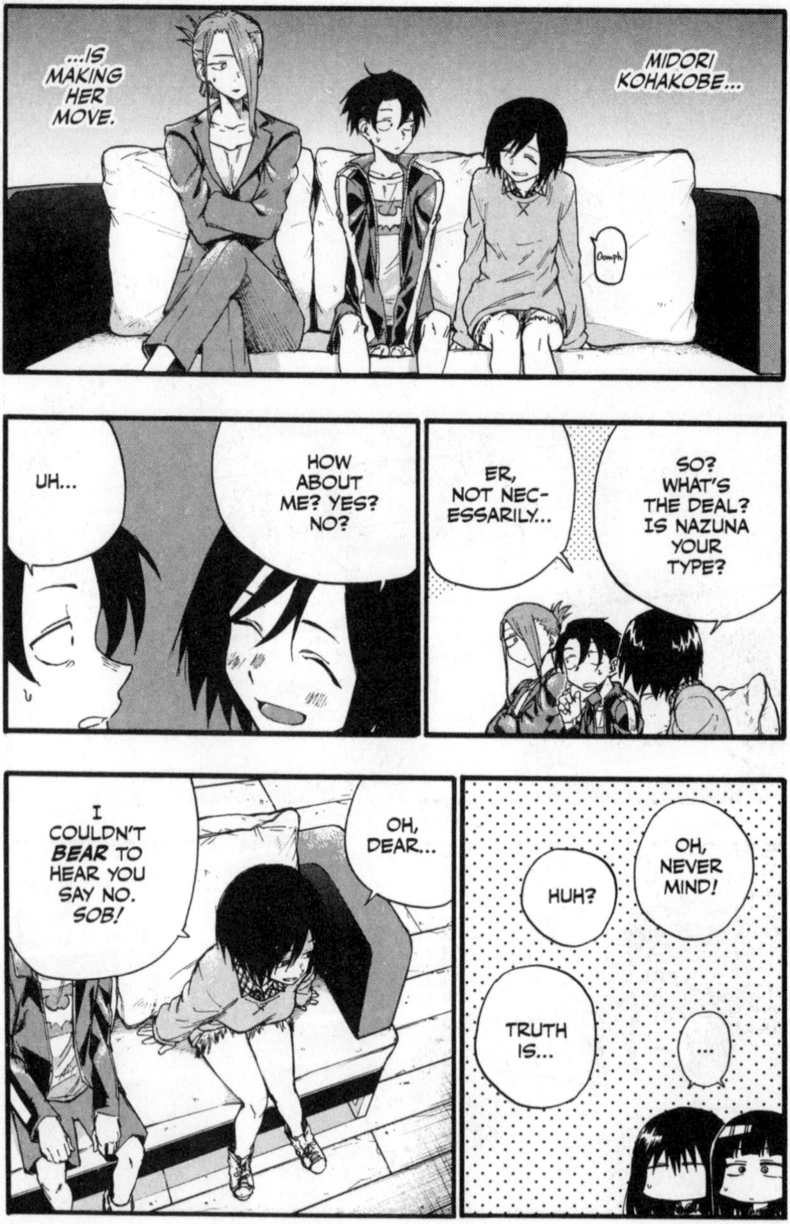
MIDORI KOHAKOBE...
...IS MAKING HER MOVE.
Oomph.
SO? WHAT'S THE DEAL? IS NAZUNA YOUR TYPE?
ER, NOT NEC-ESSARILY...
HOW ABOUT ME? YES? NO?
UH...
OH, NEVER MIND!
HUH?
...
TRUTH IS...
OH, DEAR...
I COULDN'T *BEAR* TO HEAR YOU SAY NO. SOB!

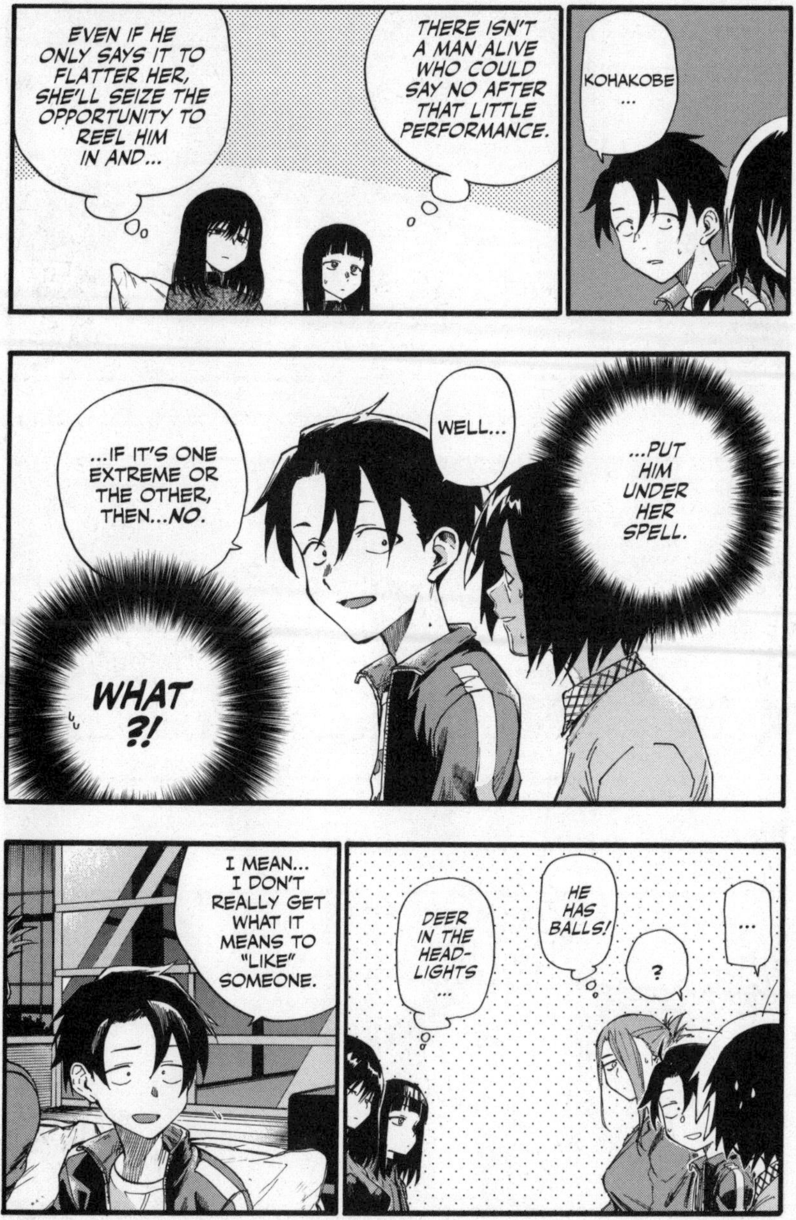
KOHAKOBE...
THERE ISN'T A MAN ALIVE WHO COULD SAY NO AFTER THAT LITTLE PERFORMANCE.
EVEN IF HE ONLY SAYS IT TO FLATTER HER, SHE'LL SEIZE THE OPPORTUNITY TO REEL HIM IN AND...
...PUT HIM UNDER HER SPELL.
WELL...
...IF IT'S ONE EXTREME OR THE OTHER, THEN...NO.
WHAT?!
...
?
HE HAS BALLS!
DEER IN THE HEADLIGHTS...
I MEAN... I DON'T REALLY GET WHAT IT MEANS TO "LIKE" SOMEONE.

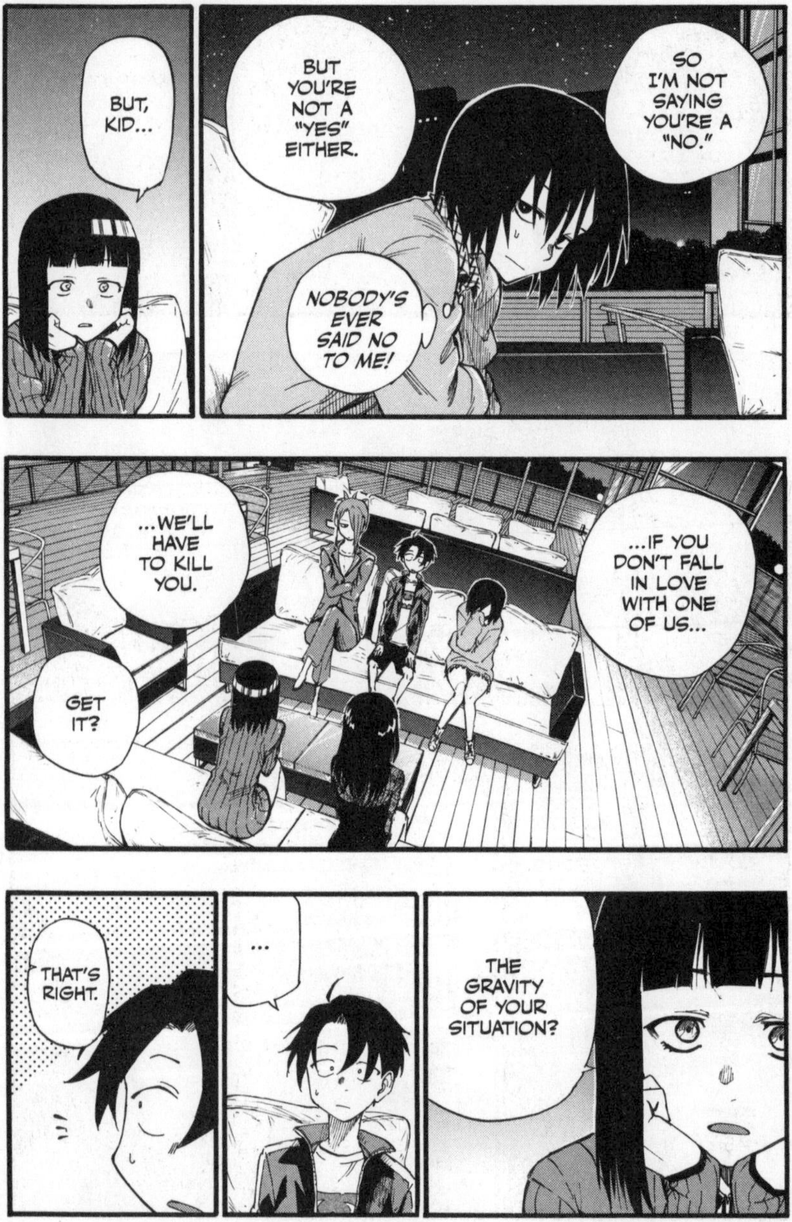
SO I'M NOT SAYING YOU'RE A "NO."
BUT YOU'RE NOT A "YES" EITHER.
NOBODY'S EVER SAID NO TO ME!
BUT, KID...
...IF YOU DON'T FALL IN LOVE WITH ONE OF US...
...WE'LL HAVE TO KILL YOU.
GET IT?
THE GRAVITY OF YOUR SITUATION?
...
THAT'S RIGHT.

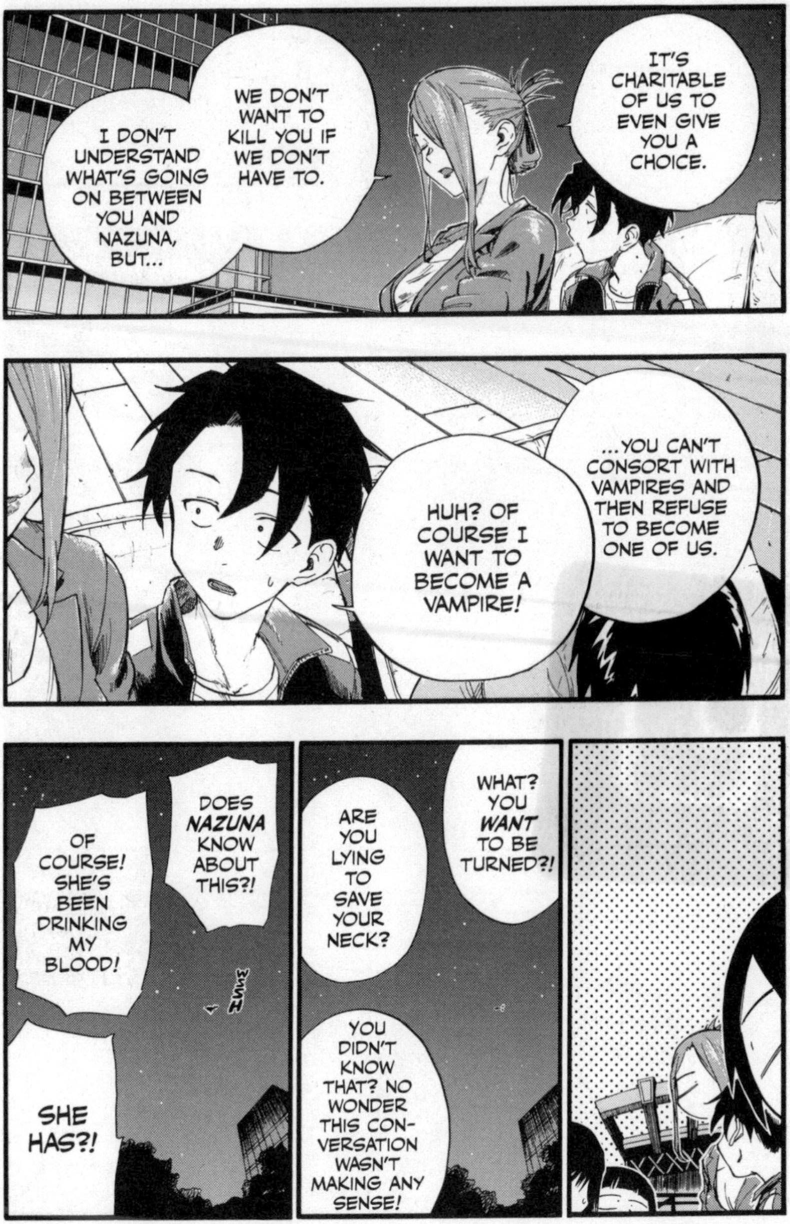
IT'S CHARITABLE OF US TO EVEN GIVE YOU A CHOICE.
WE DON'T WANT TO KILL YOU IF WE DON'T HAVE TO.
I DON'T UNDERSTAND WHAT'S GOING ON BETWEEN YOU AND NAZUNA, BUT...
...YOU CAN'T CONSORT WITH VAMPIRES AND THEN REFUSE TO BECOME ONE OF US.
HUH? OF COURSE I WANT TO BECOME A VAMPIRE!
WHAT? YOU *WANT* TO BE TURNED?!
ARE YOU LYING TO SAVE YOUR NECK?
YOU DIDN'T KNOW THAT? NO WONDER THIS CON-VERSATION WASN'T MAKING ANY SENSE!
DOES *NAZUNA* KNOW ABOUT THIS?!
OF COURSE! SHE'S BEEN DRINKING MY BLOOD!
WHSH
SHE HAS?!

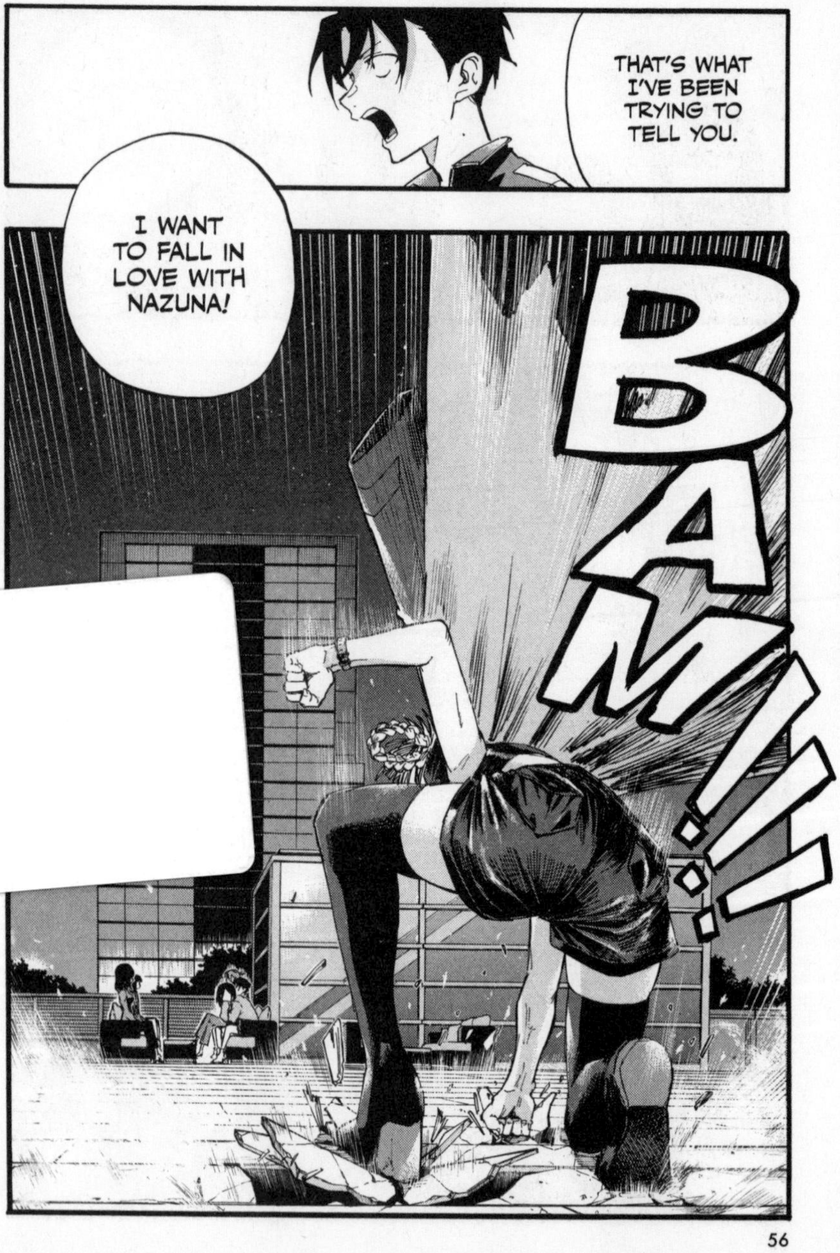
THAT'S WHAT I'VE BEEN TRYING TO TELL YOU.
I WANT TO FALL IN LOVE WITH NAZUNA!
BAM!!!!

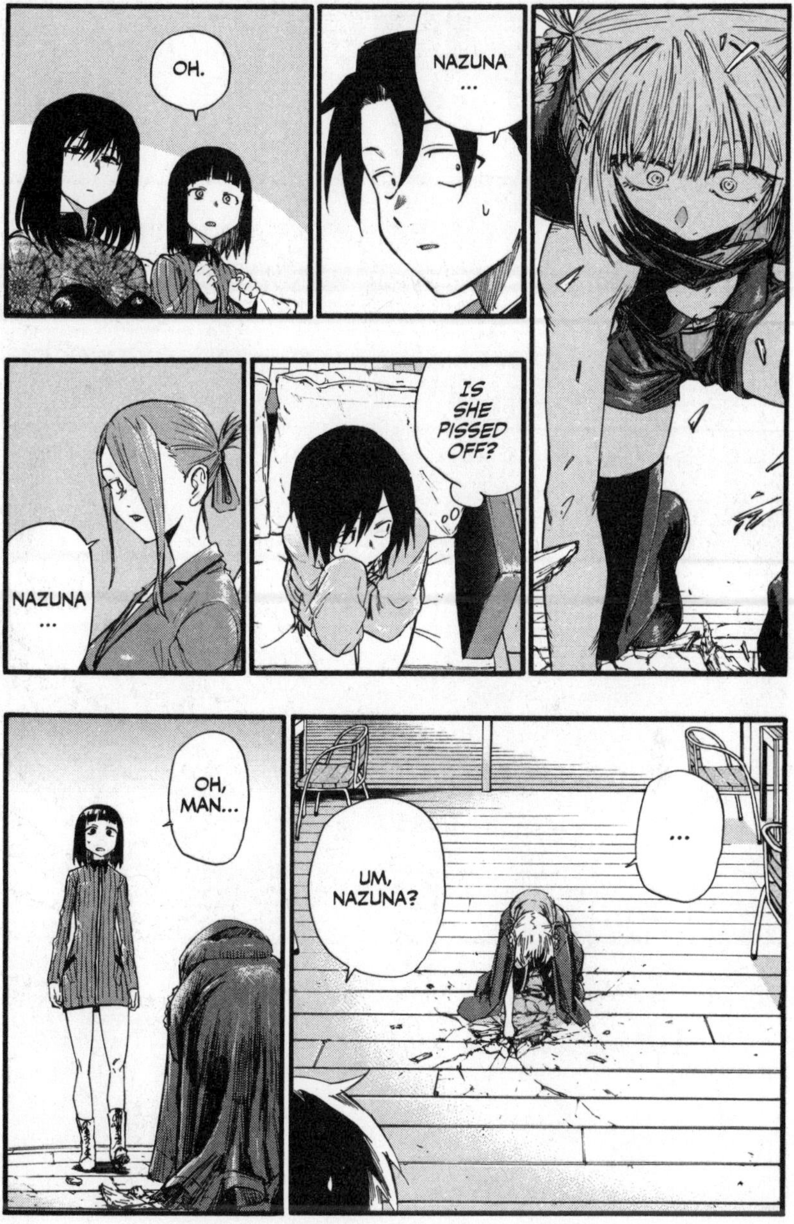
NAZUNA ...
OH.
IS SHE PISSED OFF?
NAZUNA ...
...
UM, NAZUNA?
OH, MAN...

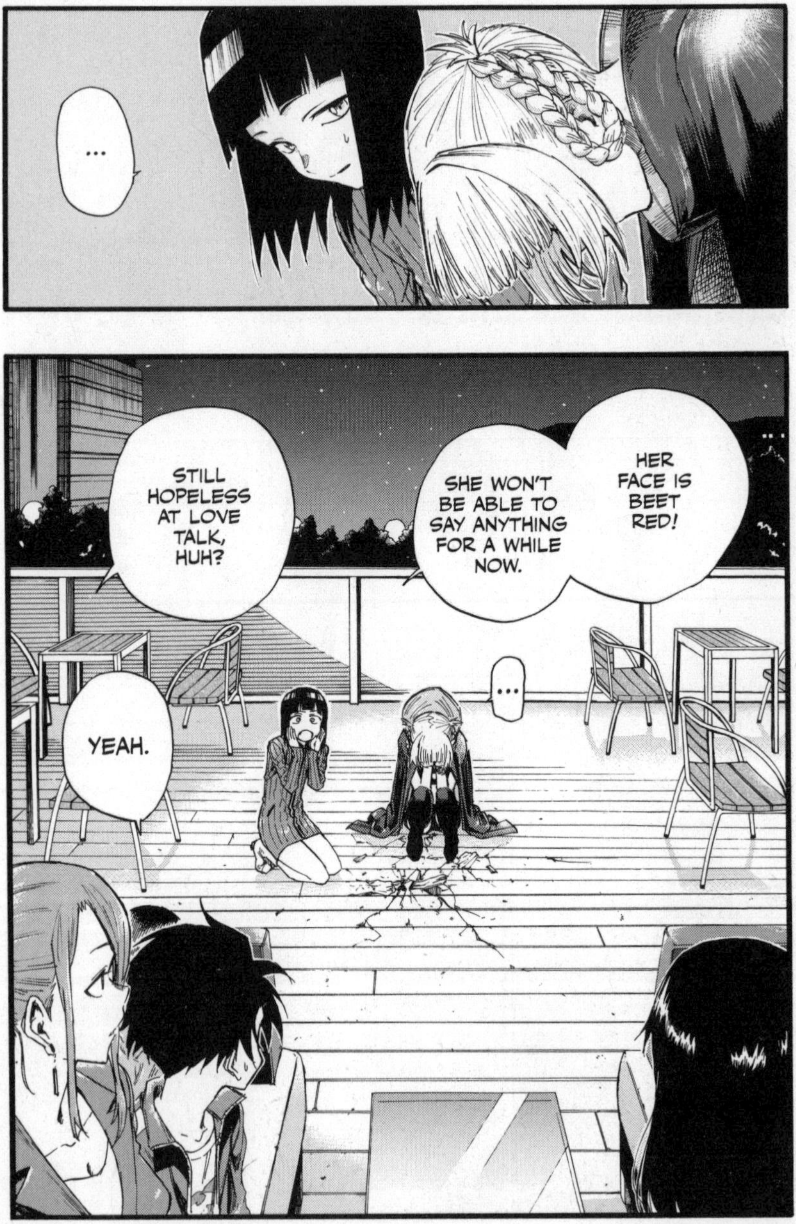
...
HER FACE IS BEET RED!
SHE WON'T BE ABLE TO SAY ANYTHING FOR A WHILE NOW.
STILL HOPELESS AT LOVE TALK, HUH?
...
YEAH.

NIGHT 22: CHEERS!

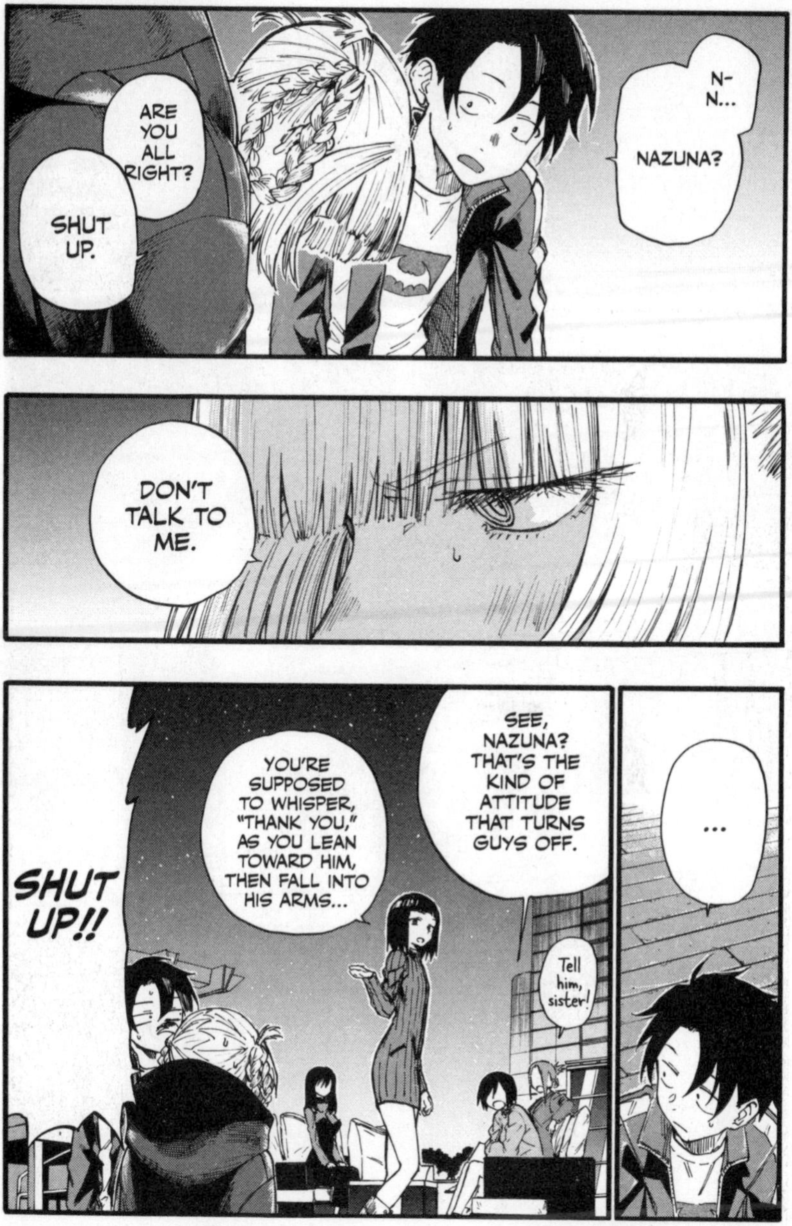
N- N... NAZUNA?
ARE YOU ALL RIGHT?
SHUT UP.
DON'T TALK TO ME.
...
SEE, NAZUNA? THAT'S THE KIND OF ATTITUDE THAT TURNS GUYS OFF.
YOU'RE SUPPOSED TO WHISPER, "THANK YOU," AS YOU LEAN TOWARD HIM, THEN FALL INTO HIS ARMS...
SHUT UP!!
Tell him, sister!

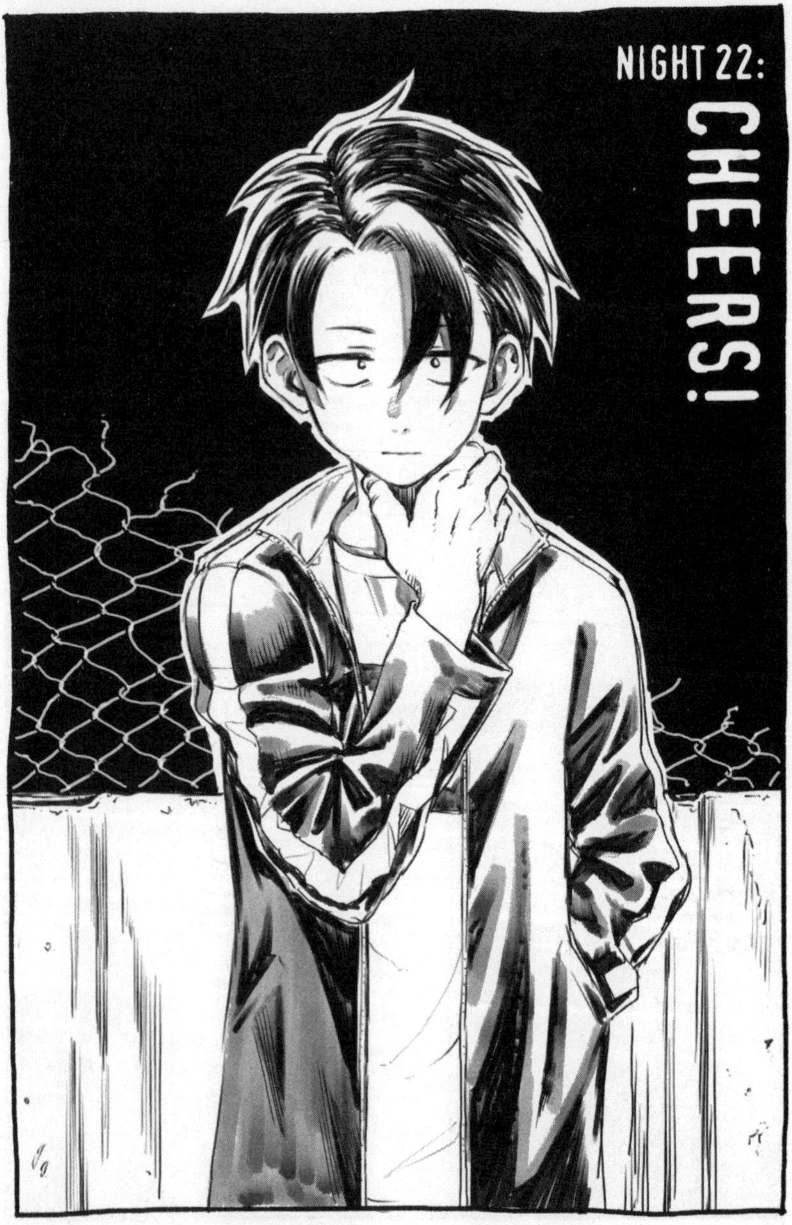
NIGHT 22:
CHEERS!

WHEW.
LET'S GET OUT OF HERE, KO.
UH...
UM...
HEY, HEY!
THAT'S NOT HOW IT WORKS, NAZUNA!
YOU THINK YOU CAN JUST TROT ON HOME?
DON'T YOU HAVE SOME-THING...
...TO SAY TO US?
LIKE WHAT, NIKO?
KRKL
SORRY TO RUIN YOUR *KIDNAP-PING PARTY*?
KRKL

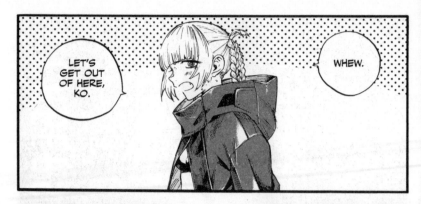

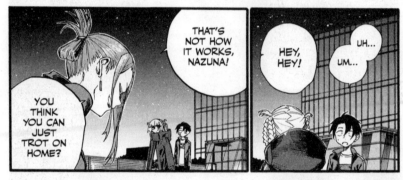

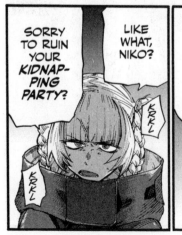

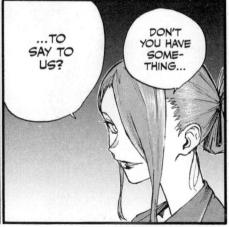

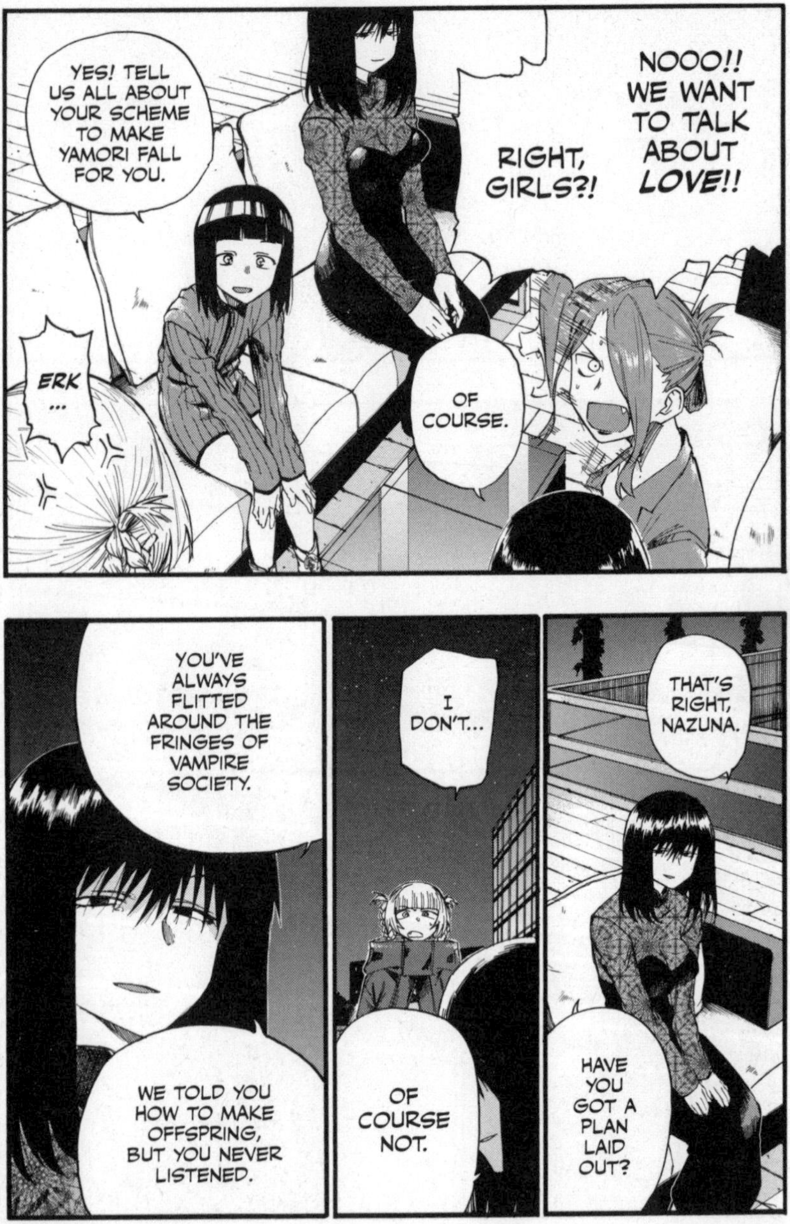
NOOO!! WE WANT TO TALK ABOUT *LOVE!!*
RIGHT, GIRLS?!
YES! TELL US ALL ABOUT YOUR SCHEME TO MAKE YAMORI FALL FOR YOU.
OF COURSE.
ERK ...
THAT'S RIGHT, NAZUNA.
HAVE YOU GOT A PLAN LAID OUT?
I DON'T...
OF COURSE NOT.
YOU'VE ALWAYS FLITTED AROUND THE FRINGES OF VAMPIRE SOCIETY.
WE TOLD YOU HOW TO MAKE OFFSPRING, BUT YOU NEVER LISTENED.

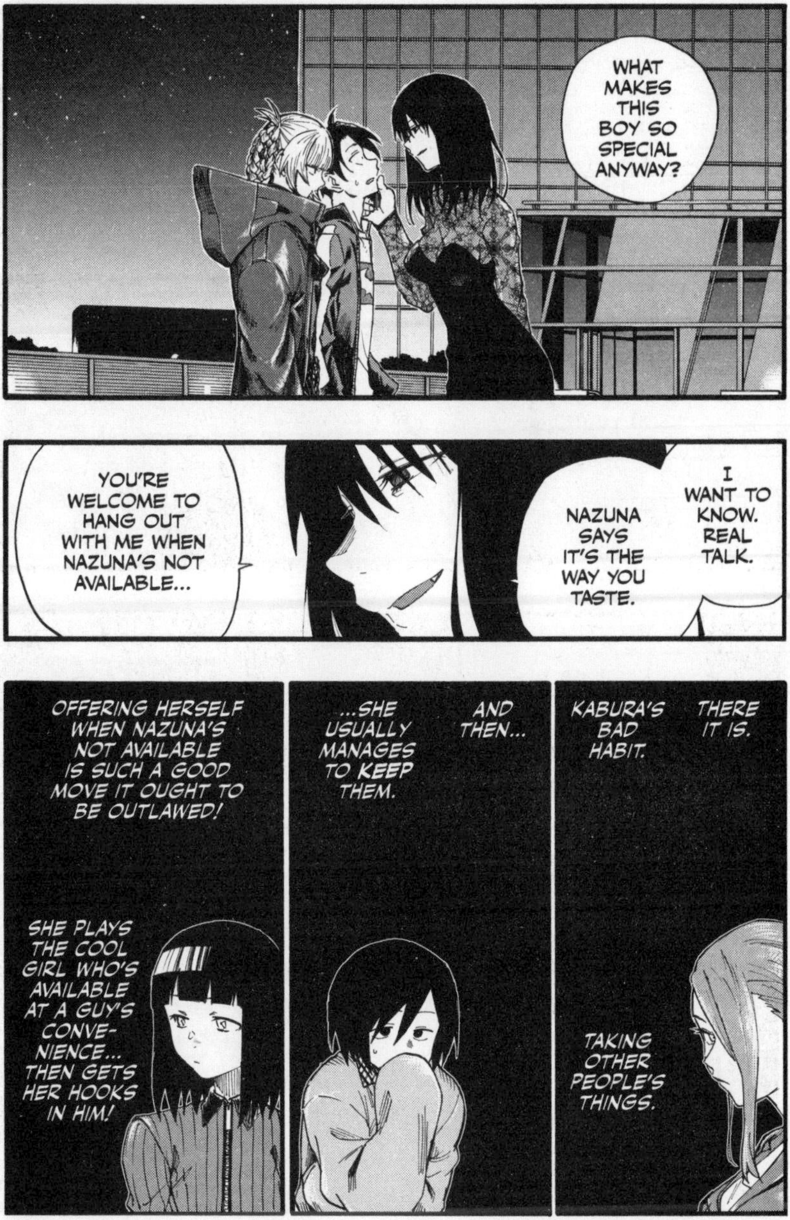
WHAT MAKES THIS BOY SO SPECIAL ANYWAY?
I WANT TO KNOW. REAL TALK.
NAZUNA SAYS IT'S THE WAY YOU TASTE.
YOU'RE WELCOME TO HANG OUT WITH ME WHEN NAZUNA'S NOT AVAILABLE...
THERE IT IS.
KABURA'S BAD HABIT.
TAKING OTHER PEOPLE'S THINGS.
AND THEN...
...SHE USUALLY MANAGES TO **KEEP** THEM.
OFFERING HERSELF WHEN NAZUNA'S NOT AVAILABLE IS SUCH A GOOD MOVE IT OUGHT TO BE OUTLAWED!
SHE PLAYS THE COOL GIRL WHO'S AVAILABLE AT A GUY'S CONVE-NIENCE... THEN GETS HER HOOKS IN HIM!

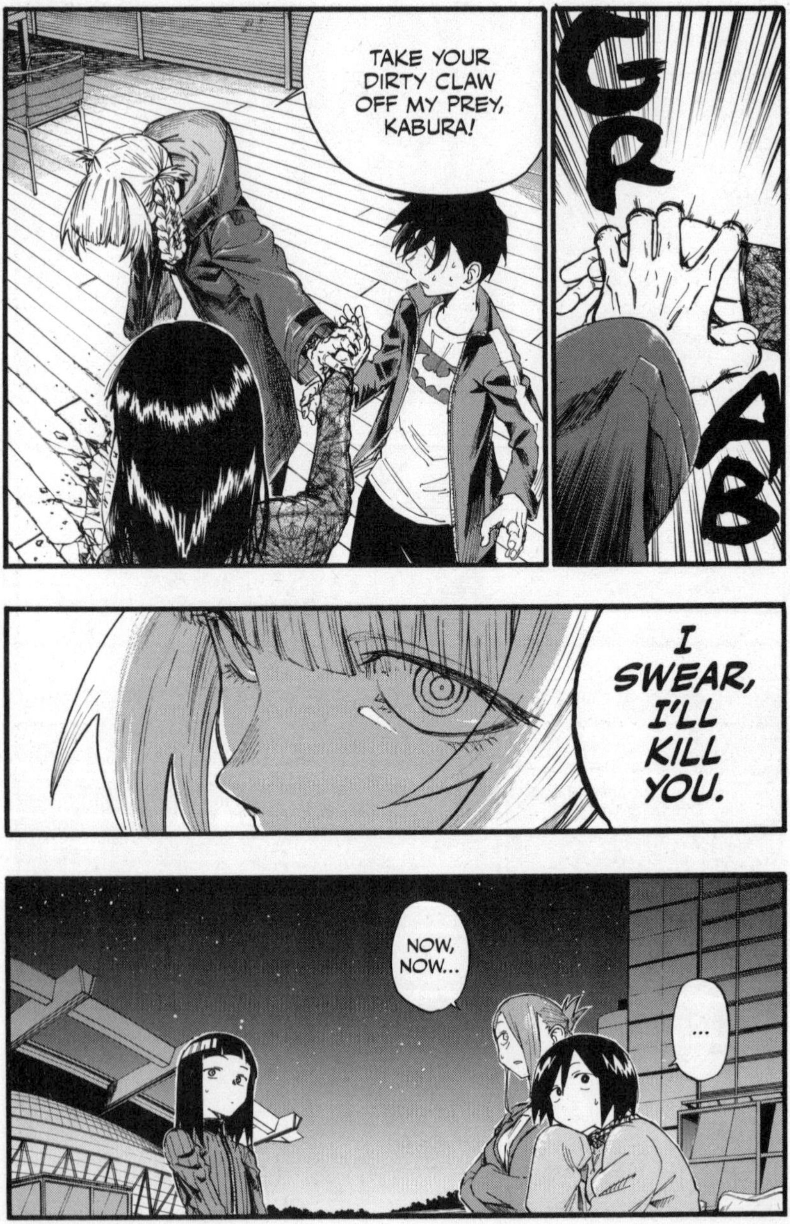
GRAB
TAKE YOUR DIRTY CLAW OFF MY PREY, KABURA!
I SWEAR, I'LL KILL YOU.
...
NOW, NOW...

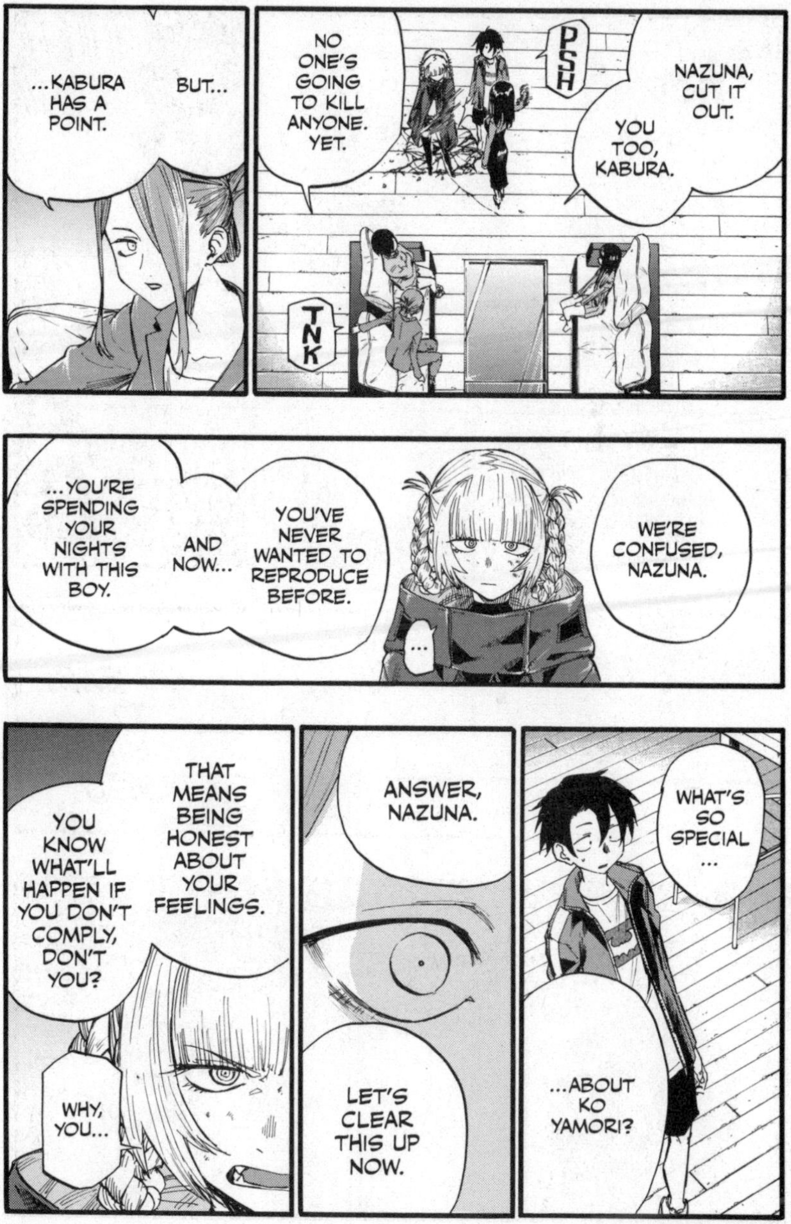
NAZUNA, CUT IT OUT.
YOU TOO, KABURA.
PSH
NO ONE'S GOING TO KILL ANYONE. YET.
TNK
BUT...
...KABURA HAS A POINT.
WE'RE CONFUSED, NAZUNA.
...
YOU'VE NEVER WANTED TO REPRODUCE BEFORE.
AND NOW...
...YOU'RE SPENDING YOUR NIGHTS WITH THIS BOY.
WHAT'S SO SPECIAL...
...ABOUT KO YAMORI?
ANSWER, NAZUNA.
LET'S CLEAR THIS UP NOW.
THAT MEANS BEING HONEST ABOUT YOUR FEELINGS.
YOU KNOW WHAT'LL HAPPEN IF YOU DON'T COMPLY, DON'T YOU?
WHY, YOU...

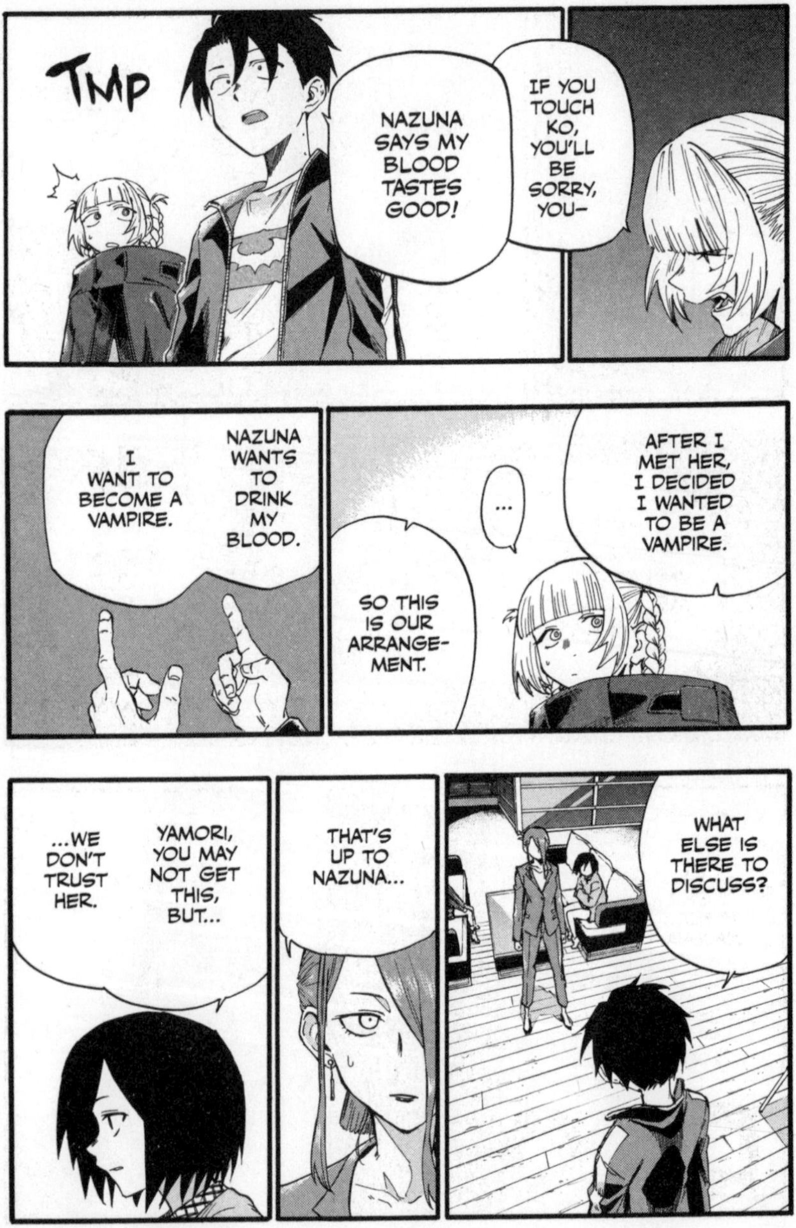
IF YOU TOUCH KO, YOU'LL BE SORRY, YOU–
NAZUNA SAYS MY BLOOD TASTES GOOD!
TMP
AFTER I MET HER, I DECIDED I WANTED TO BE A VAMPIRE.
...
SO THIS IS OUR ARRANGE-MENT.
NAZUNA WANTS TO DRINK MY BLOOD.
I WANT TO BECOME A VAMPIRE.
WHAT ELSE IS THERE TO DISCUSS?
THAT'S UP TO NAZUNA...
YAMORI, YOU MAY NOT GET THIS, BUT...
...WE DON'T TRUST HER.

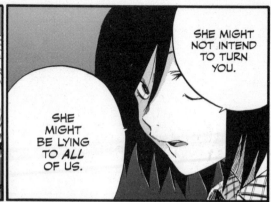

SHE MIGHT NOT INTEND TO TURN YOU.
SHE MIGHT BE LYING TO *ALL* OF US.
HEY...
SHUT UP!
NAZUNA TOLD ME...
..."IF YOU WANNA FALL IN LOVE WITH ME, GO RIGHT AHEAD."
HEH.
HEH ... HA HA HA!
HA HA... I GET IT NOW, NAZUNA.
?
...

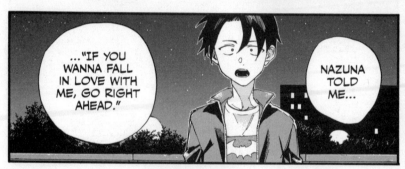

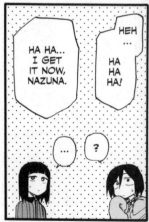

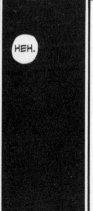

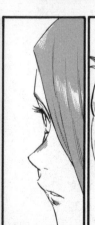

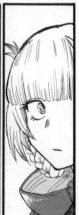

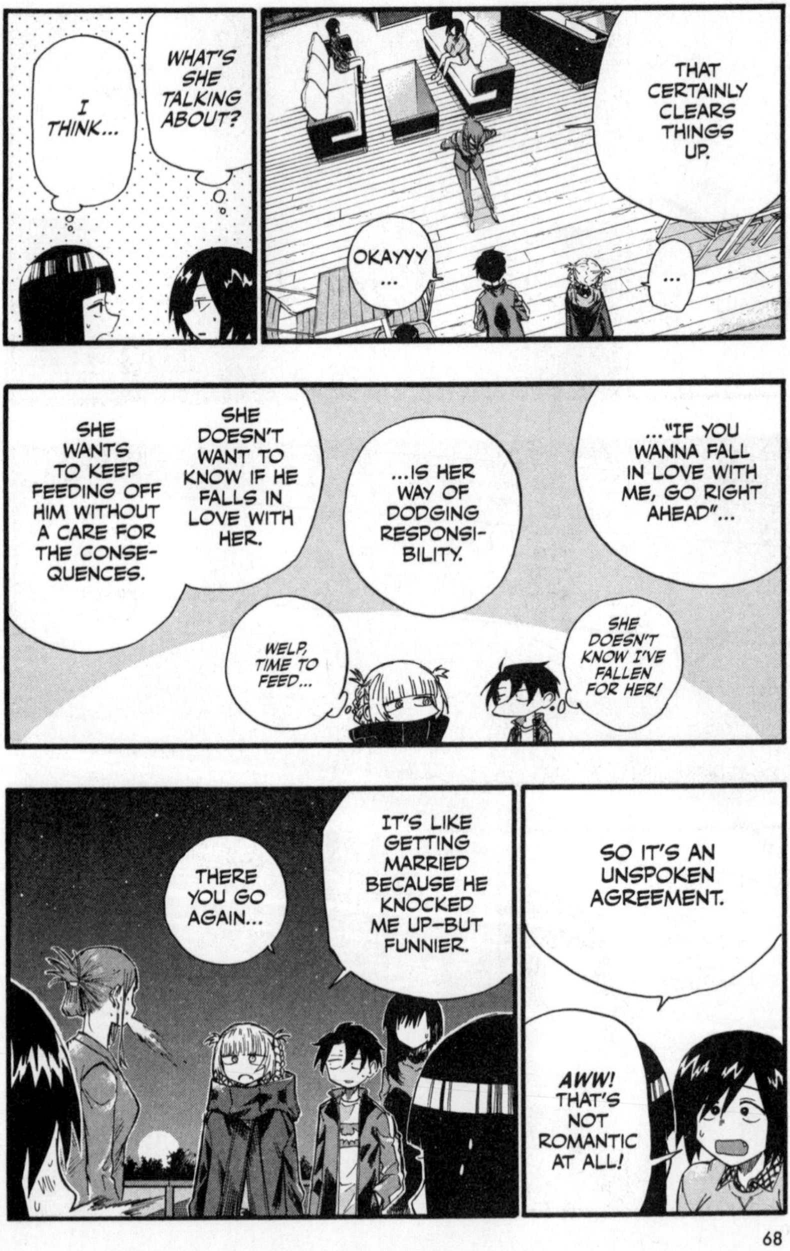
THAT CERTAINLY CLEARS THINGS UP.
...
OKAYYY...
WHAT'S SHE TALKING ABOUT?
I THINK...
..."IF YOU WANNA FALL IN LOVE WITH ME, GO RIGHT AHEAD"...
...IS HER WAY OF DODGING RESPONSIBILITY.
SHE DOESN'T WANT TO KNOW IF HE FALLS IN LOVE WITH HER.
SHE WANTS TO KEEP FEEDING OFF HIM WITHOUT A CARE FOR THE CONSEQUENCES.
SHE DOESN'T KNOW I'VE FALLEN FOR HER!
WELP, TIME TO FEED...
SO IT'S AN UNSPOKEN AGREEMENT.
AWW! THAT'S NOT ROMANTIC AT ALL!
IT'S LIKE GETTING MARRIED BECAUSE HE KNOCKED ME UP—BUT FUNNIER.
THERE YOU GO AGAIN...

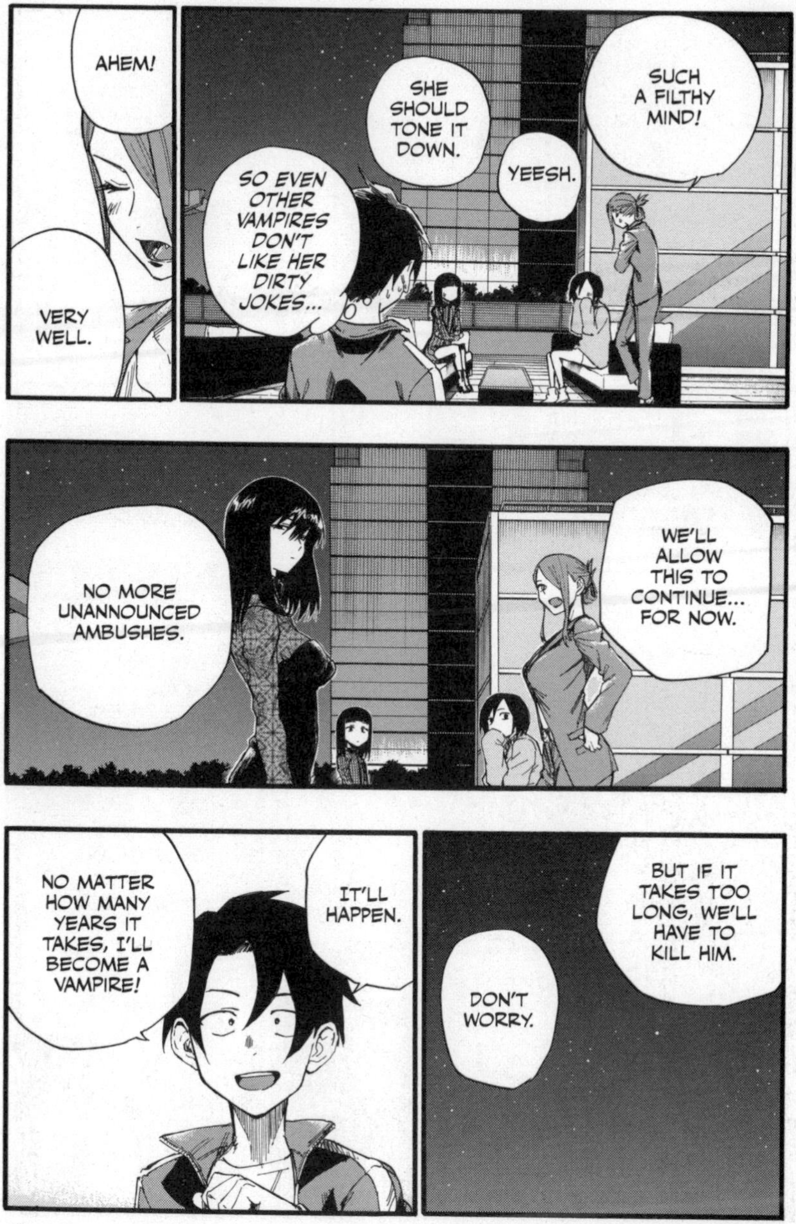
SUCH A FILTHY MIND!
YEESH.
SHE SHOULD TONE IT DOWN.
SO EVEN OTHER VAMPIRES DON'T LIKE HER DIRTY JOKES...
AHEM!
VERY WELL.
WE'LL ALLOW THIS TO CONTINUE... FOR NOW.
NO MORE UNANNOUNCED AMBUSHES.
BUT IF IT TAKES TOO LONG, WE'LL HAVE TO KILL HIM.
DON'T WORRY.
IT'LL HAPPEN.
NO MATTER HOW MANY YEARS IT TAKES, I'LL BECOME A VAMPIRE!

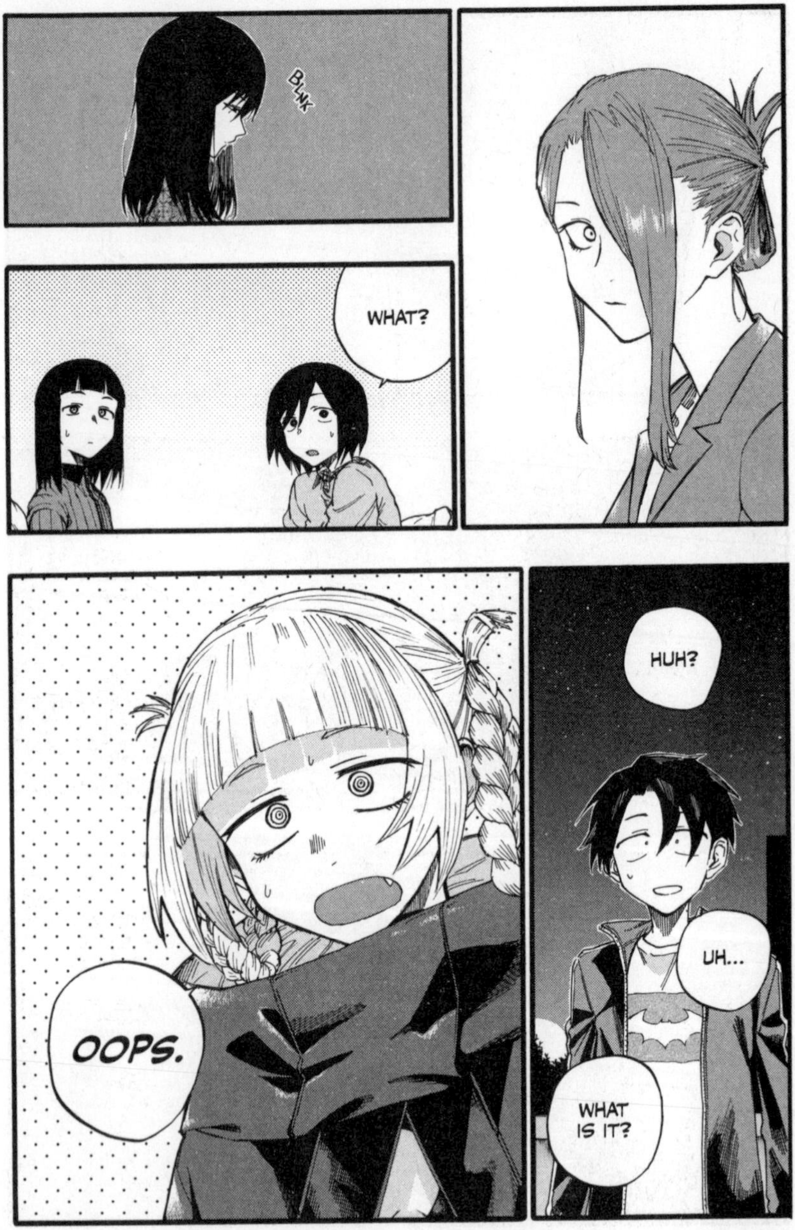
BLNK
WHAT?
HUH?
UH...
WHAT IS IT?
OOPS.

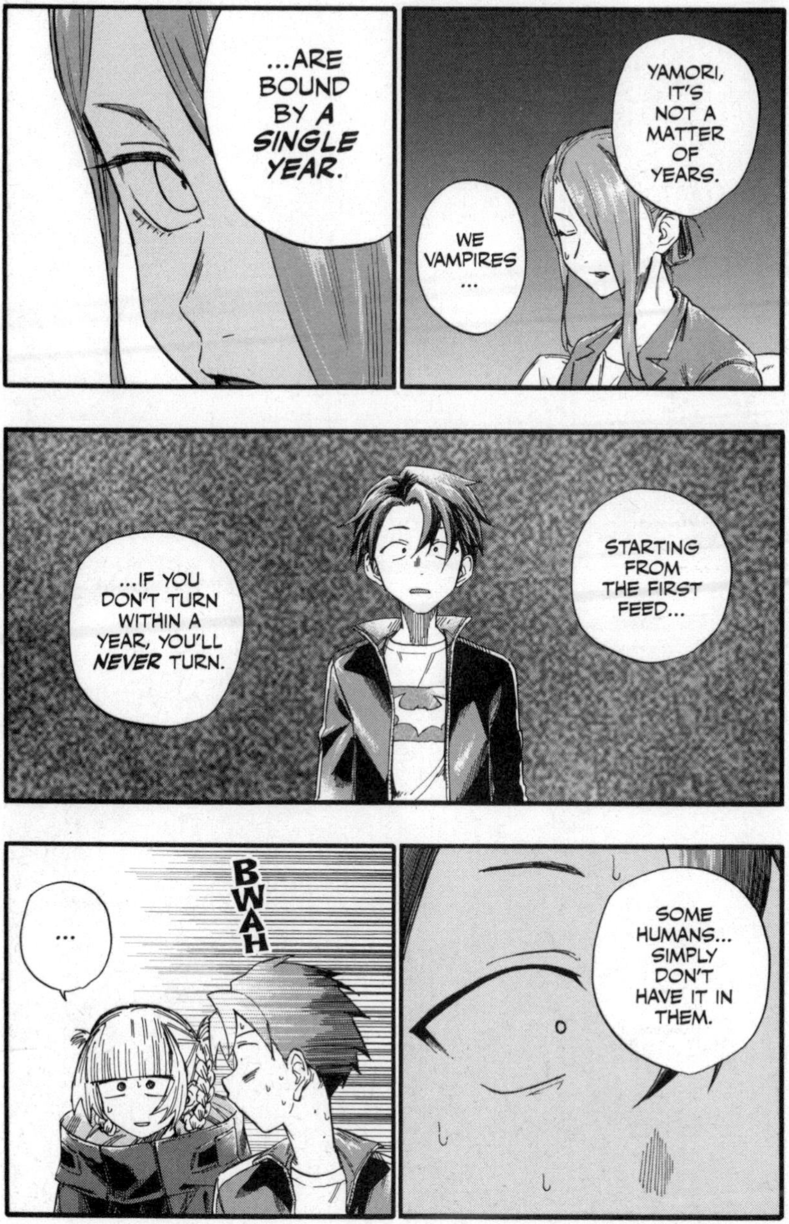
YAMORI, IT'S NOT A MATTER OF YEARS.
WE VAMPIRES ...
...ARE BOUND BY *A SINGLE YEAR.*
STARTING FROM THE FIRST FEED...
...IF YOU DON'T TURN WITHIN A YEAR, YOU'LL *NEVER* TURN.
SOME HUMANS... SIMPLY DON'T HAVE IT IN THEM.
BWAH
...

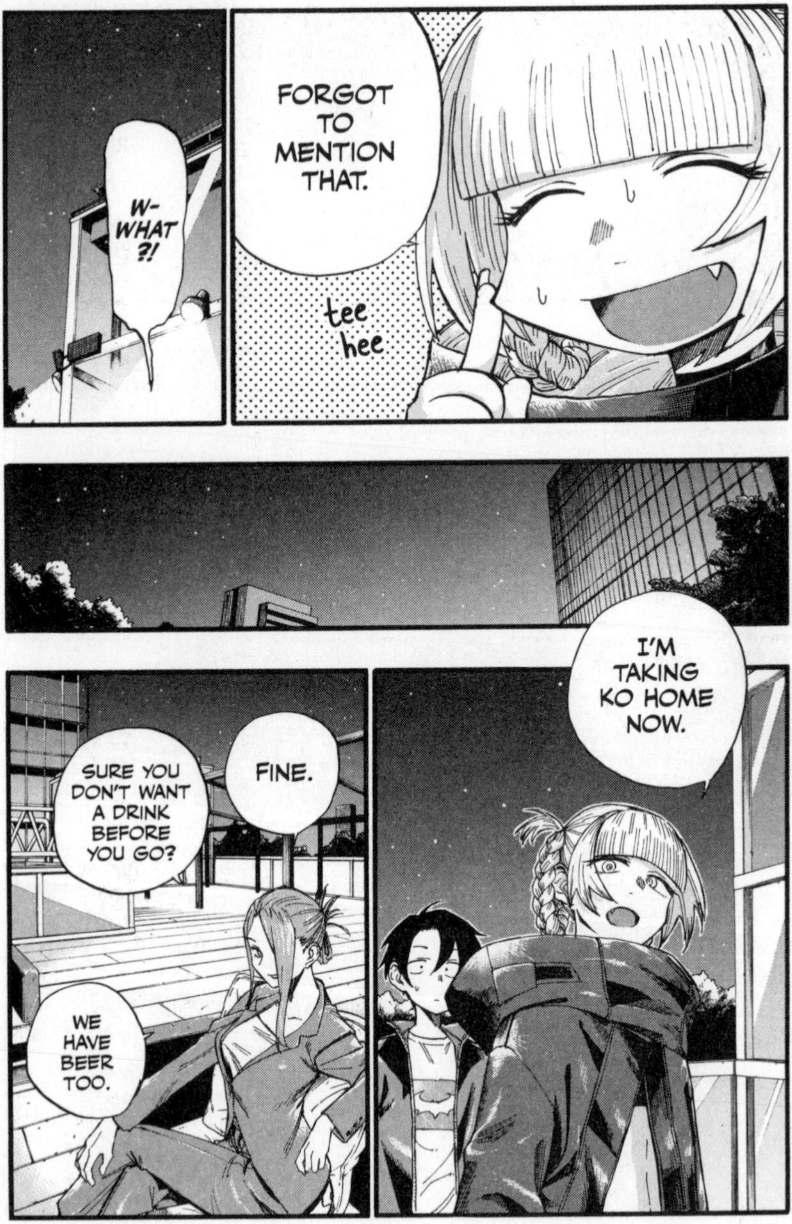
FORGOT TO MENTION THAT.
tee hee
W-WHAT?!
I'M TAKING KO HOME NOW.
FINE.
SURE YOU DON'T WANT A DRINK BEFORE YOU GO?
WE HAVE BEER TOO.

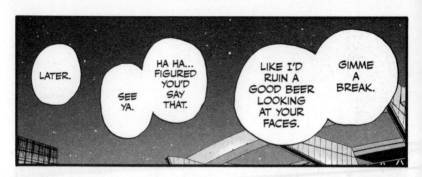

GIMME A BREAK.
LIKE I'D RUIN A GOOD BEER LOOKING AT YOUR FACES.
HA HA... FIGURED YOU'D SAY THAT.
SEE YA.
LATER.
Heck, yeah!
Beer time!
OH, KO... THERE'S ONE MORE THING I FORGOT.
THERE'S *MORE*?
THAT MESSAGE THE OTHER DAY...
OH, THE ONE FOR KIYOSUMI?
WHAT WAS IT?
UH... UM... NAZUNA?
TOK

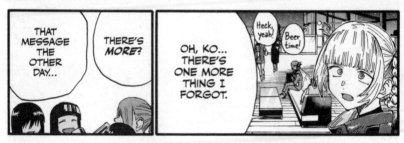

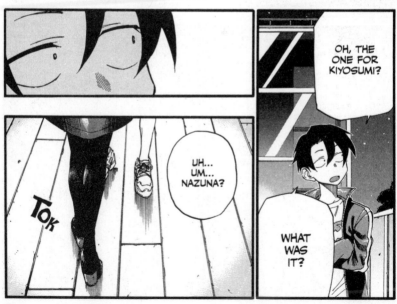

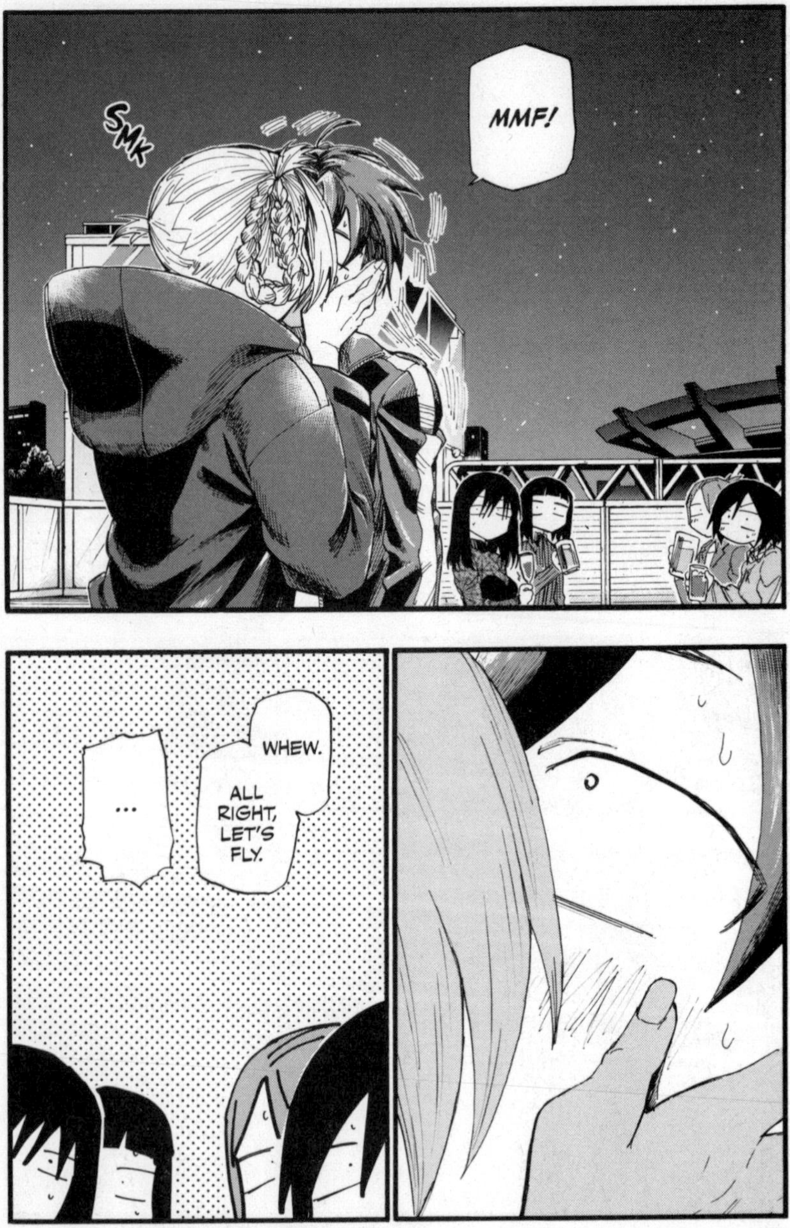
SMK
MMF!
WHEW.
ALL RIGHT, LET'S FLY.
...

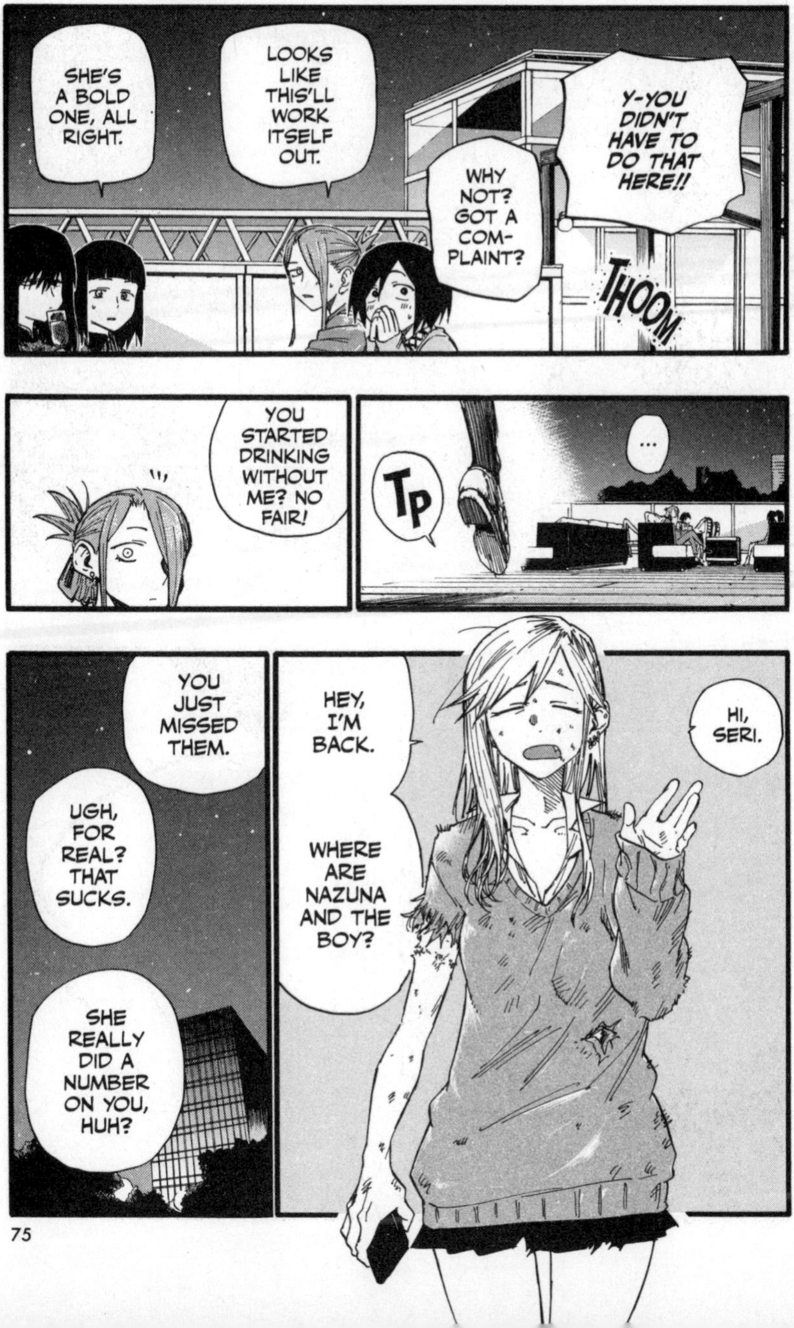
Y-YOU DIDN'T HAVE TO DO THAT HERE!!
THOOM
WHY NOT? GOT A COM-PLAINT?
LOOKS LIKE THIS'LL WORK ITSELF OUT.
SHE'S A BOLD ONE, ALL RIGHT.
...
TP
YOU STARTED DRINKING WITHOUT ME? NO FAIR!
HI, SERI.
HEY, I'M BACK.
WHERE ARE NAZUNA AND THE BOY?
YOU JUST MISSED THEM.
UGH, FOR REAL? THAT SUCKS.
SHE REALLY DID A NUMBER ON YOU, HUH?

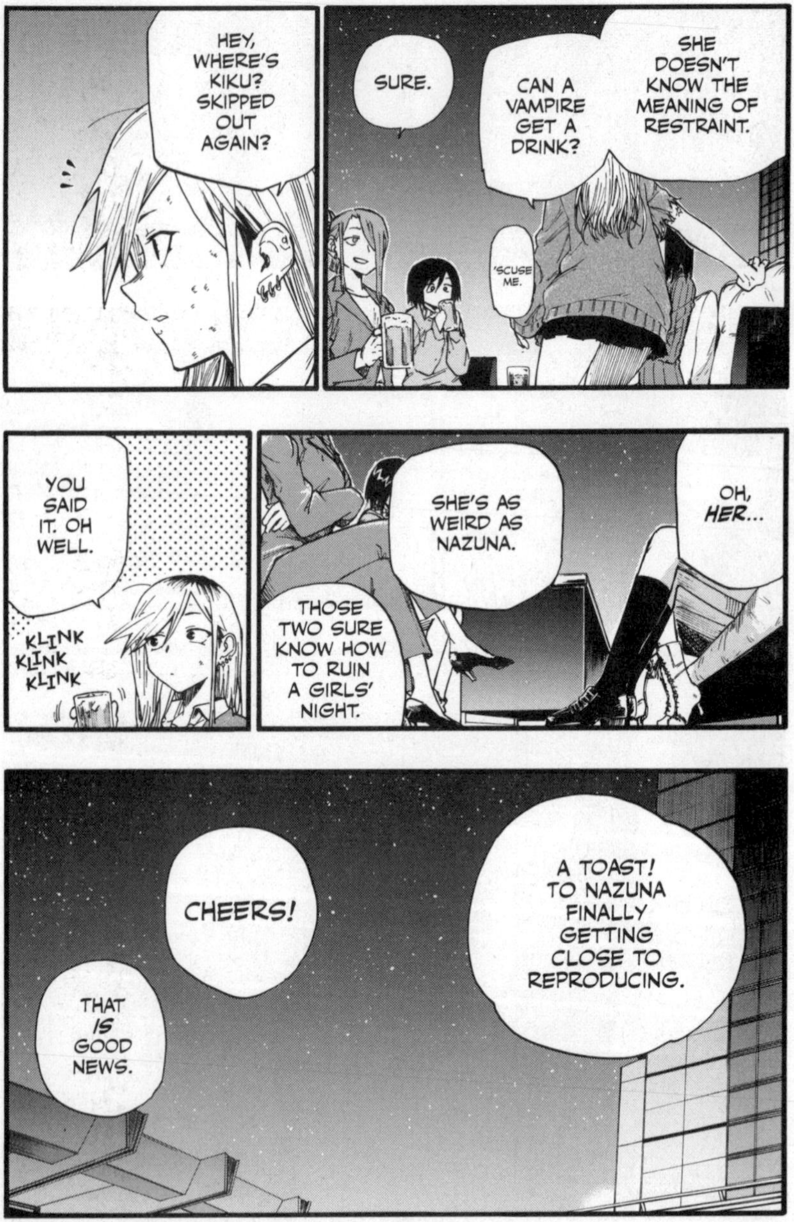
SHE DOESN'T KNOW THE MEANING OF RESTRAINT.
CAN A VAMPIRE GET A DRINK?
SURE.
'SCUSE ME.
HEY, WHERE'S KIKU? SKIPPED OUT AGAIN?
OH, *HER*...
SHE'S AS WEIRD AS NAZUNA.
THOSE TWO SURE KNOW HOW TO RUIN A GIRLS' NIGHT.
YOU SAID IT. OH WELL.
KLINK KLINK KLINK
A TOAST! TO NAZUNA FINALLY GETTING CLOSE TO REPRODUCING.
CHEERS!
THAT *IS* GOOD NEWS.

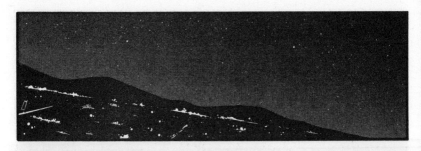

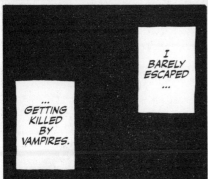

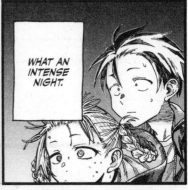

WHAT AN INTENSE NIGHT.
I BARELY ESCAPED...
...GETTING KILLED BY VAMPIRES.
THANKS TO NAZUNA, I WASN'T TOO SCARED TO TALK BACK TO THEM, BUT...
...
BRRR
SIGH...
? WHAT'S UP?

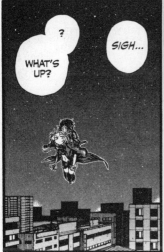

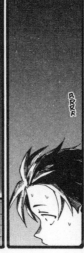

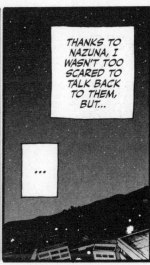

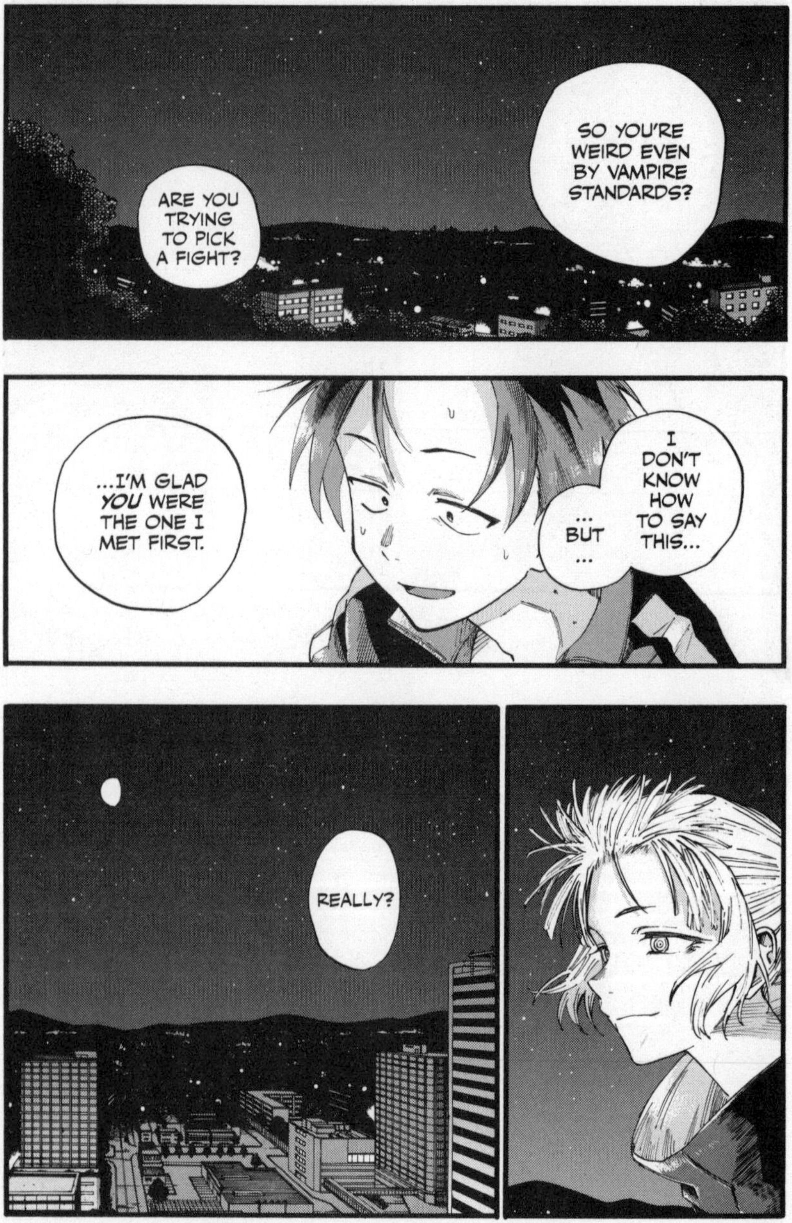
SO YOU'RE WEIRD EVEN BY VAMPIRE STANDARDS?
ARE YOU TRYING TO PICK A FIGHT?
I DON'T KNOW HOW TO SAY THIS...
...BUT...
...I'M GLAD *YOU* WERE THE ONE I MET FIRST.
REALLY?

NIGHT 23: ALL OF US

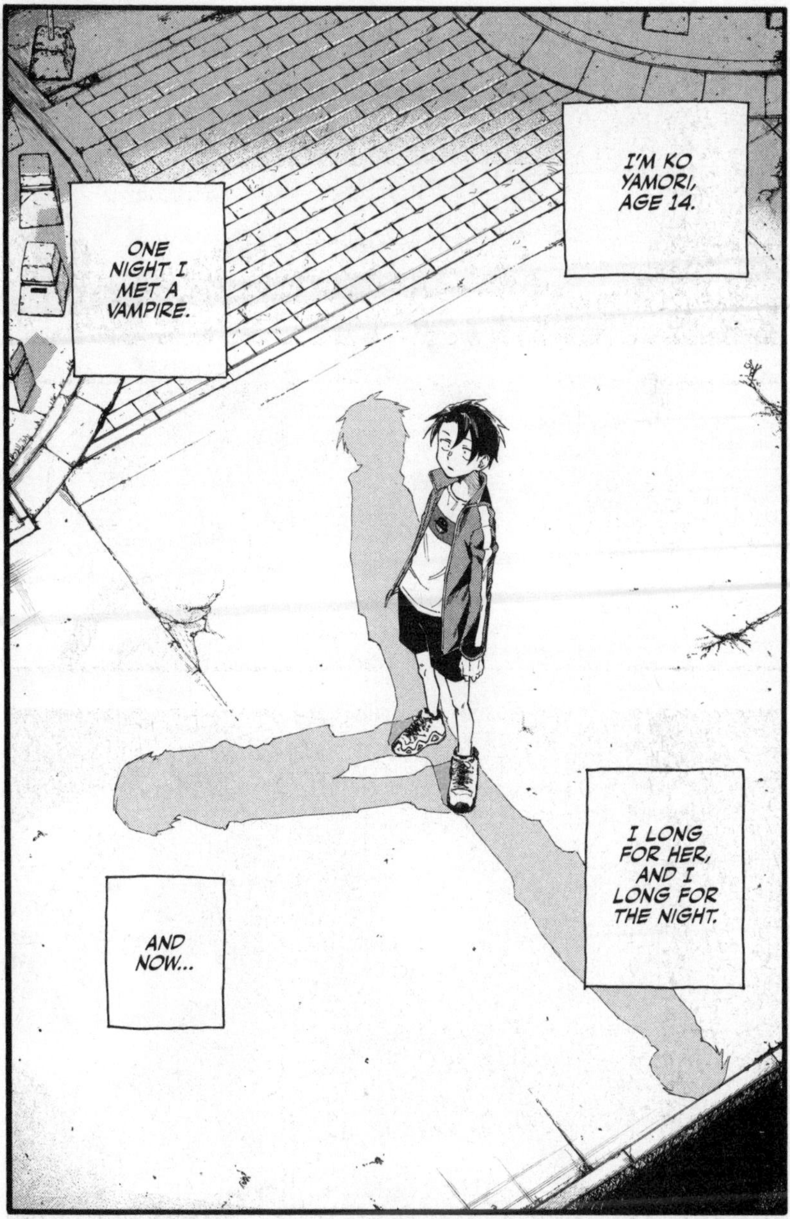
I'M KO YAMORI, AGE 14.
ONE NIGHT I MET A VAMPIRE.
I LONG FOR HER, AND I LONG FOR THE NIGHT.
AND NOW...

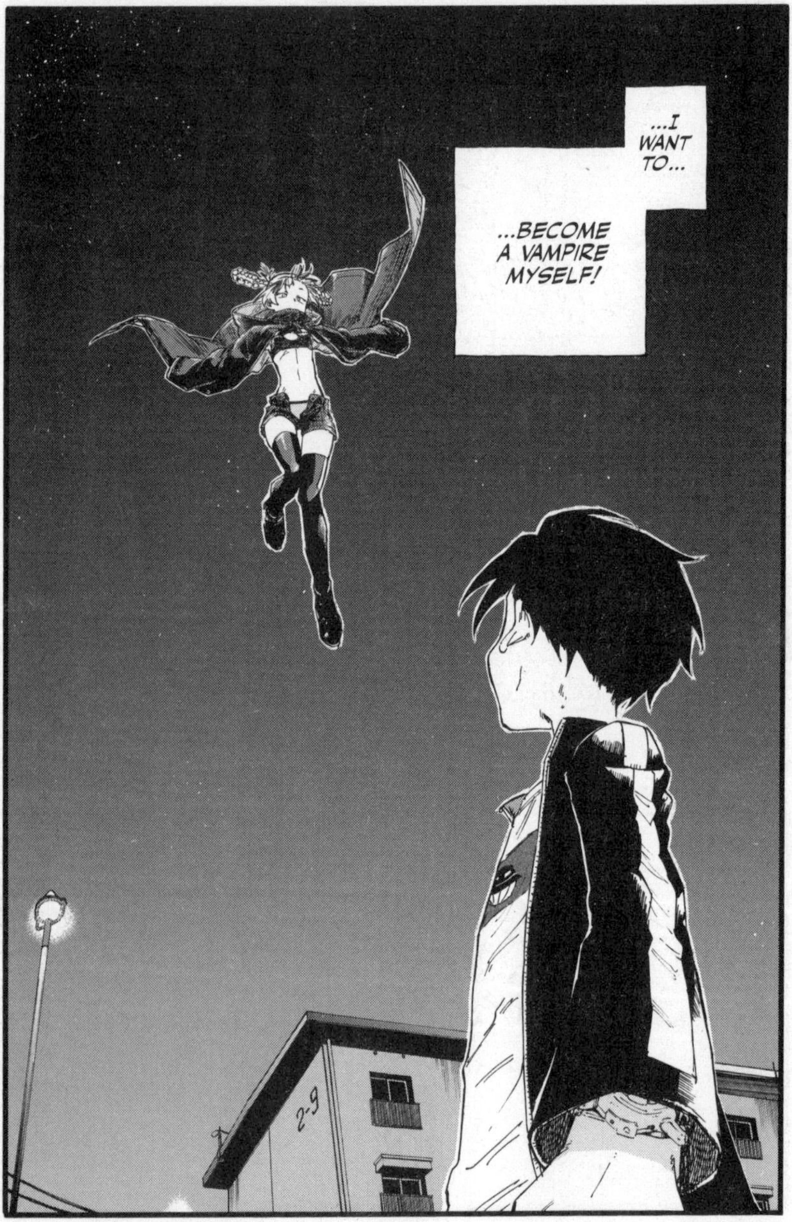
...I WANT TO...
...BECOME A VAMPIRE MYSELF!
2-9

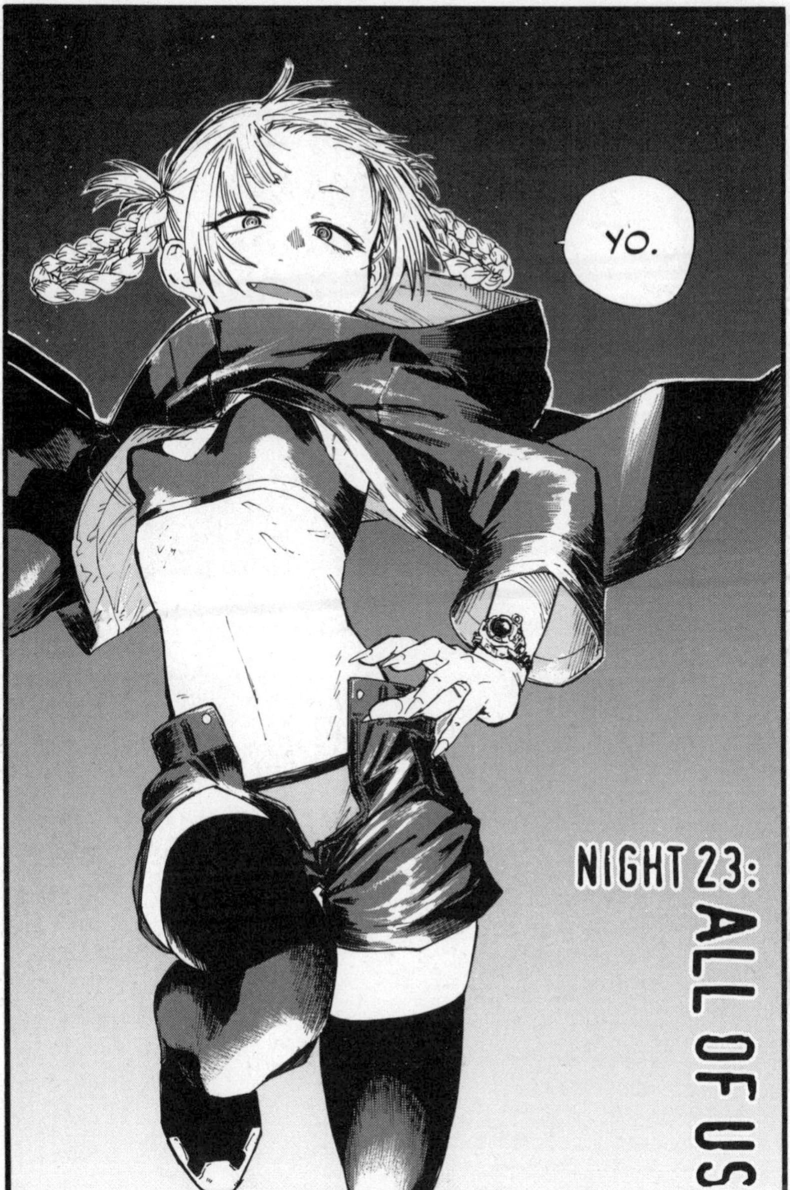
YO.
NIGHT 23:
ALL OF US

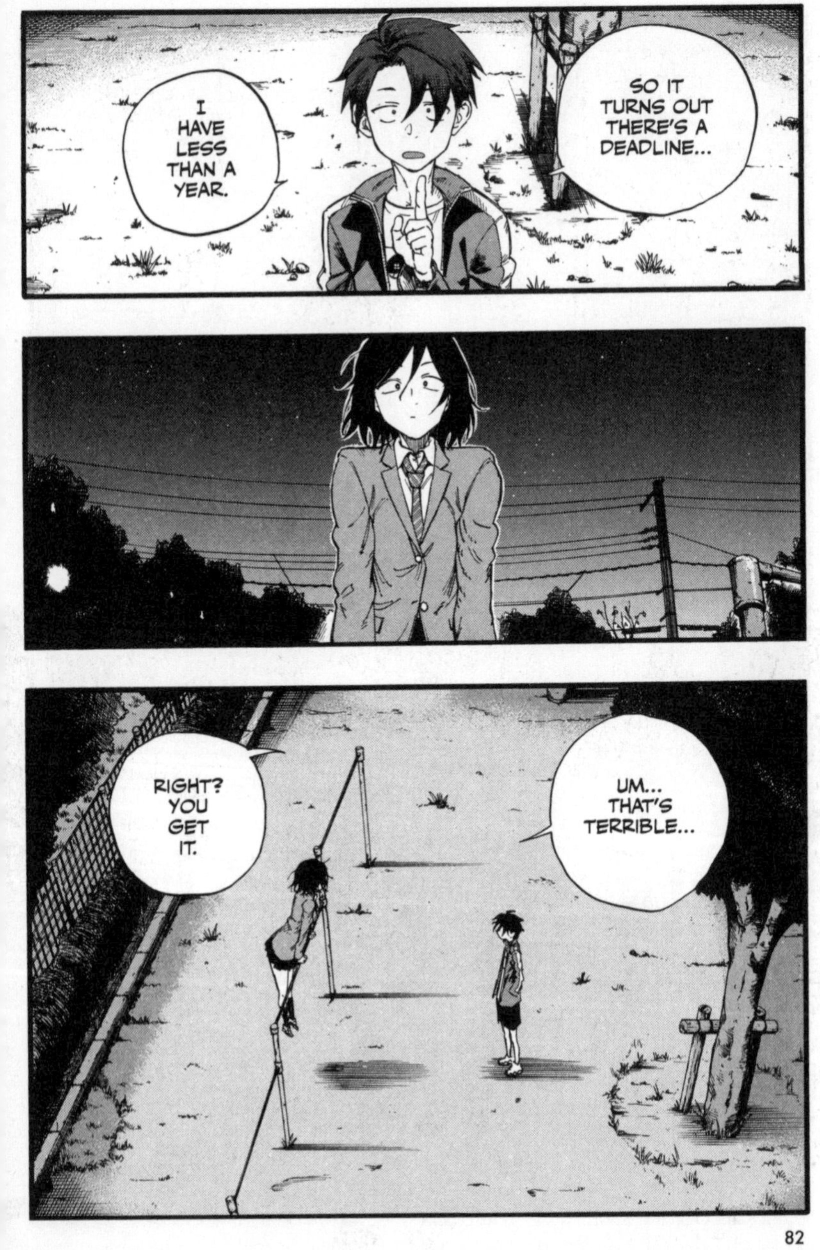
SO IT TURNS OUT THERE'S A DEADLINE...
I HAVE LESS THAN A YEAR.
UM... THAT'S TERRIBLE...
RIGHT? YOU GET IT.

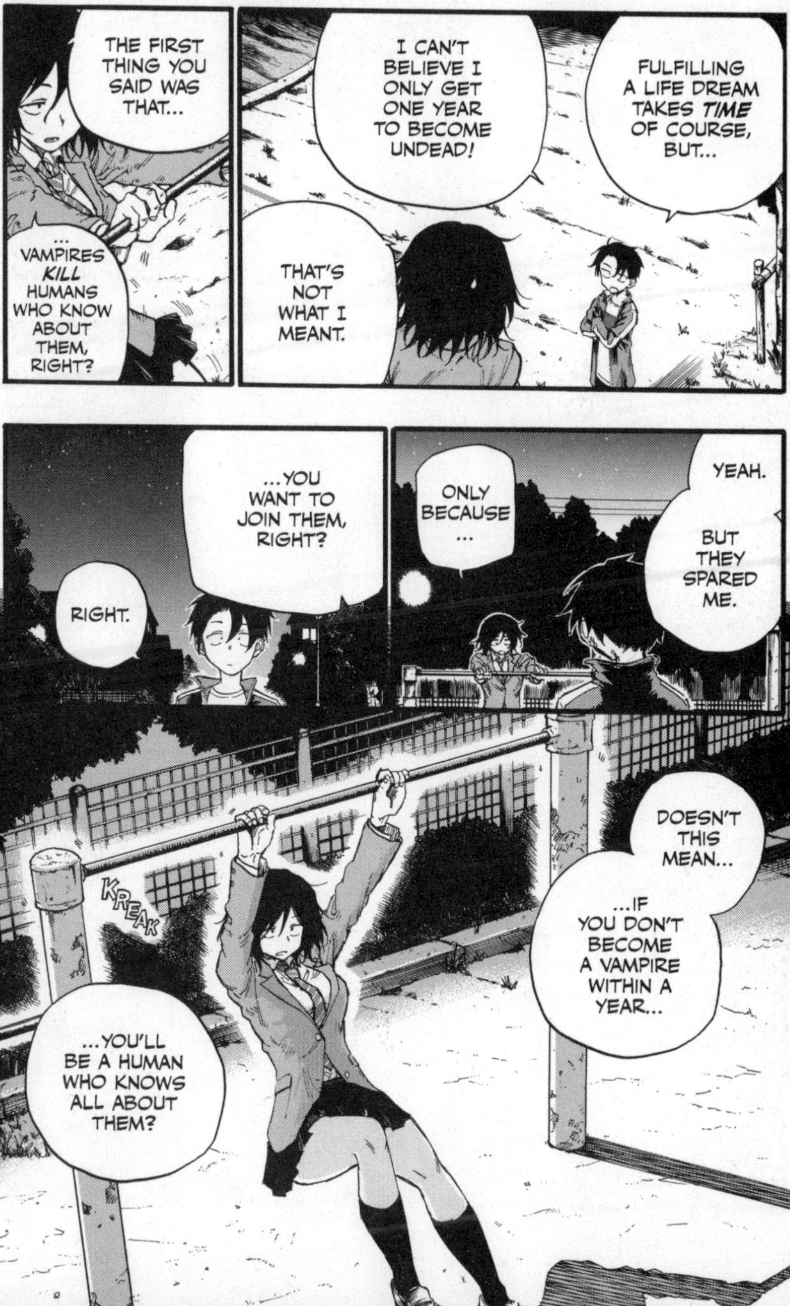
FULFILLING A LIFE DREAM TAKES *TIME* OF COURSE, BUT...
I CAN'T BELIEVE I ONLY GET ONE YEAR TO BECOME UNDEAD!
THAT'S NOT WHAT I MEANT.
THE FIRST THING YOU SAID WAS THAT...
...VAMPIRES *KILL* HUMANS WHO KNOW ABOUT THEM, RIGHT?
YEAH.
BUT THEY SPARED ME.
ONLY BECAUSE...
...YOU WANT TO JOIN THEM, RIGHT?
RIGHT.
DOESN'T THIS MEAN...
...IF YOU DON'T BECOME A VAMPIRE WITHIN A YEAR...
KREAK
...YOU'LL BE A HUMAN WHO KNOWS ALL ABOUT THEM?

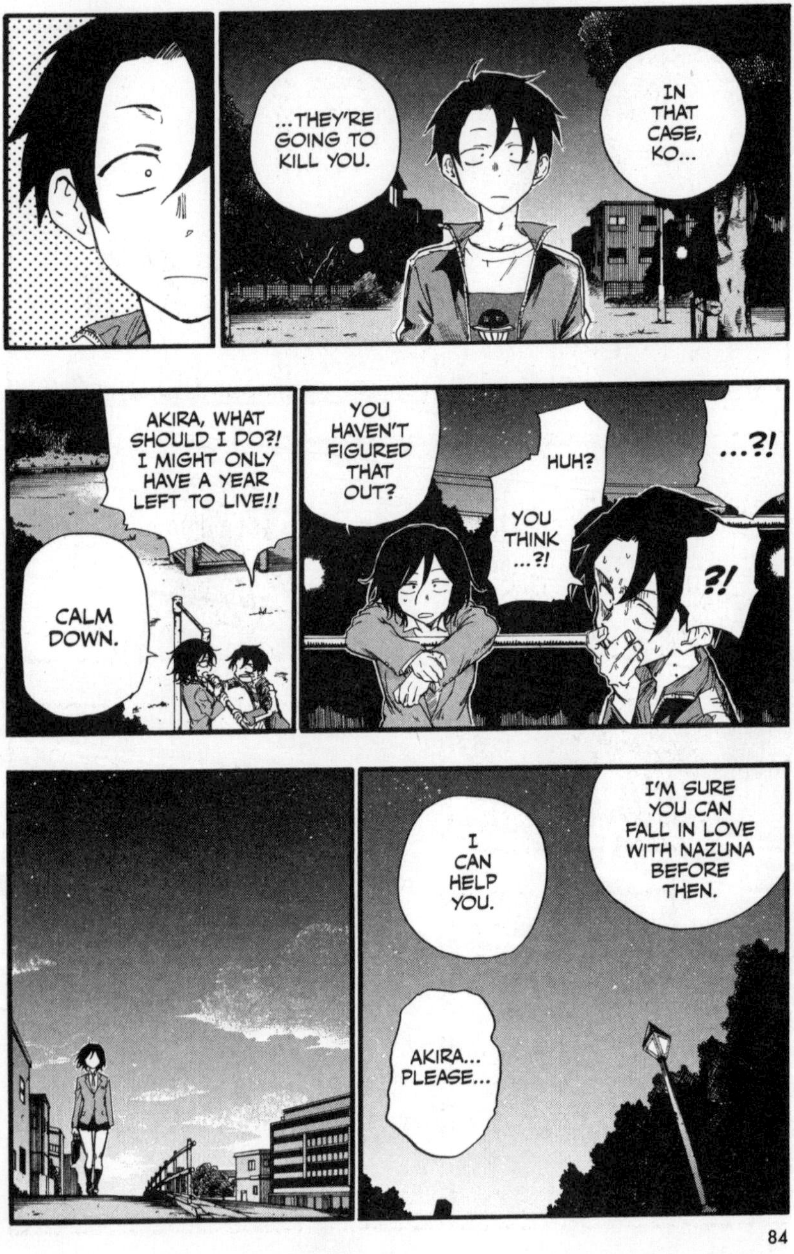
IN THAT CASE, KO...
...THEY'RE GOING TO KILL YOU.
...?!
HUH? YOU THINK...?!
YOU HAVEN'T FIGURED THAT OUT?
?!
AKIRA, WHAT SHOULD I DO?! I MIGHT ONLY HAVE A YEAR LEFT TO LIVE!!
CALM DOWN.
I'M SURE YOU CAN FALL IN LOVE WITH NAZUNA BEFORE THEN.
I CAN HELP YOU.
AKIRA... PLEASE...

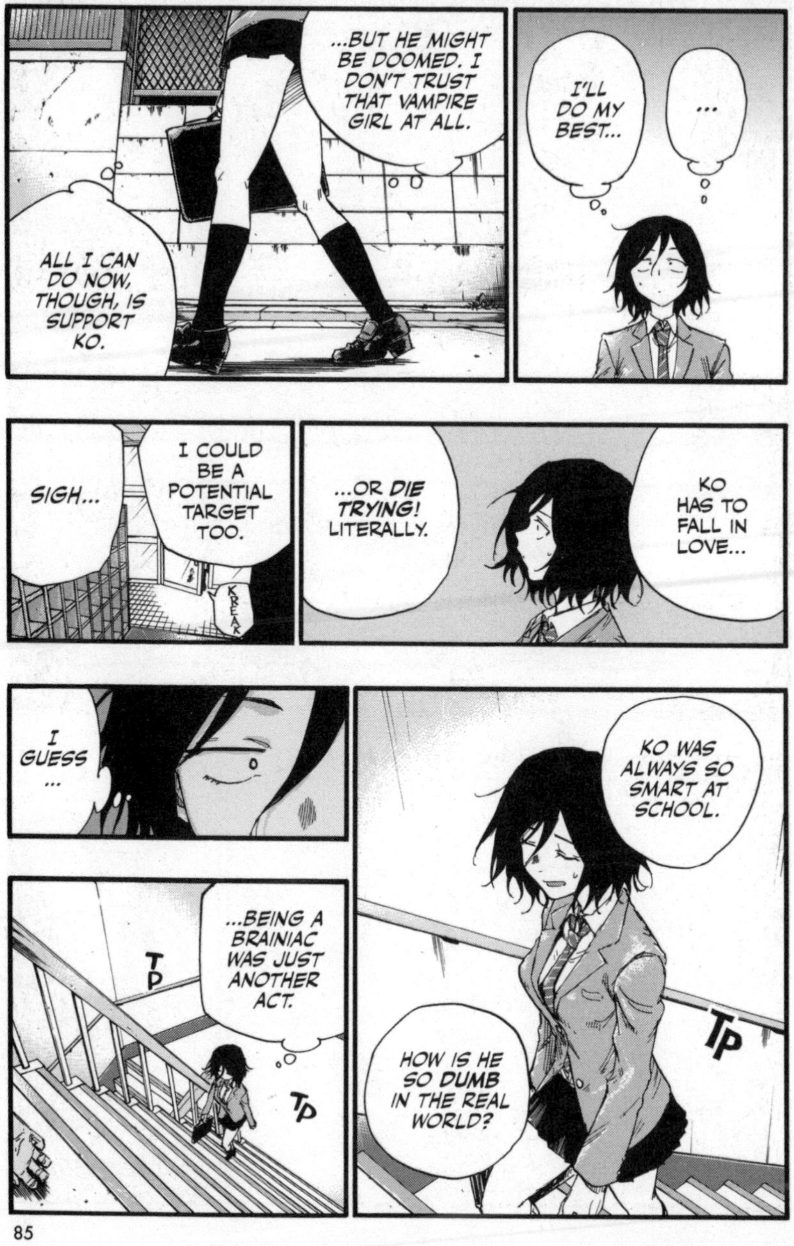
...
I'LL DO MY BEST...
...BUT HE MIGHT BE DOOMED. I DON'T TRUST THAT VAMPIRE GIRL AT ALL.
ALL I CAN DO NOW, THOUGH, IS SUPPORT KO.
KO HAS TO FALL IN LOVE...
...OR DIE TRYING! LITERALLY.
I COULD BE A POTENTIAL TARGET TOO.
SIGH...
KREAK
KO WAS ALWAYS SO SMART AT SCHOOL.
TP
HOW IS HE SO DUMB IN THE REAL WORLD?
I GUESS...
...BEING A BRAINIAC WAS JUST ANOTHER ACT.
TP
TP

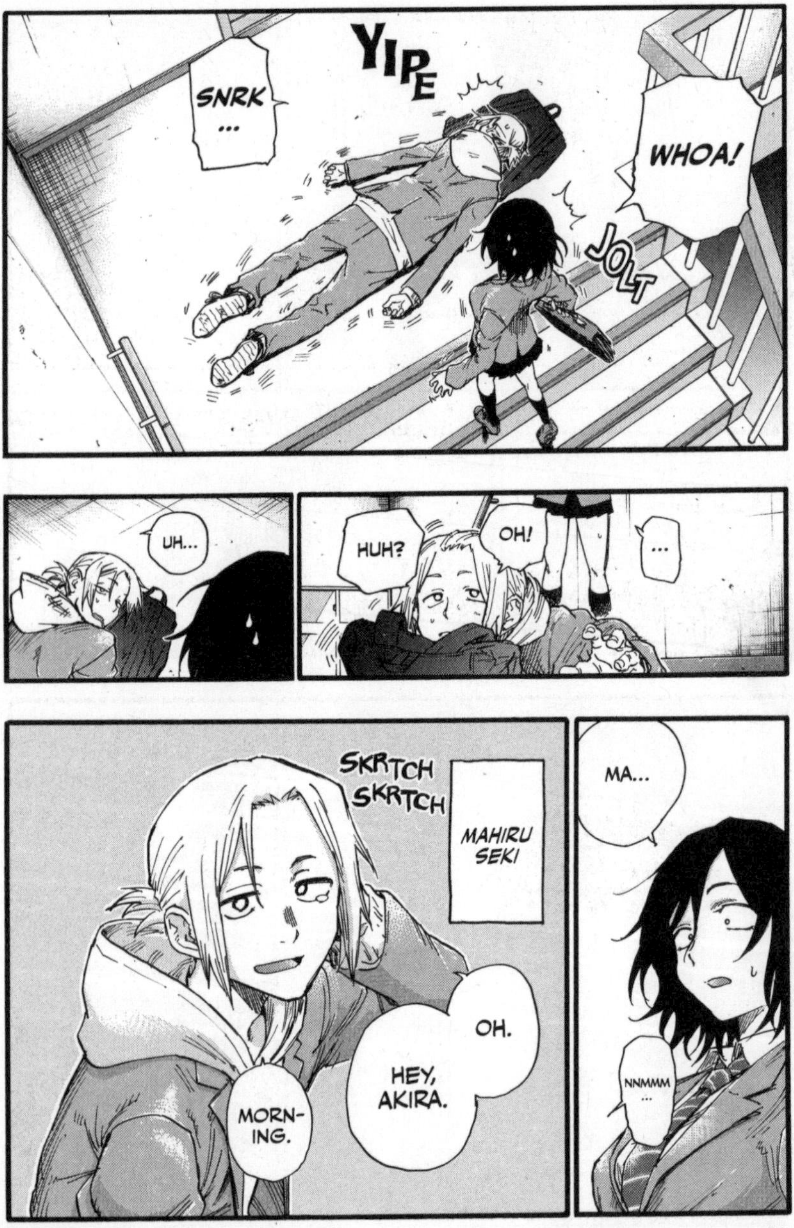
WHOA!
JOLT
YIPE
SNRK ...
...
OH!
HUH?
UH...
MA...
NNMMM ...
SKRTCH SKRTCH
MAHIRU SEKI
OH.
HEY, AKIRA.
MORN-ING.

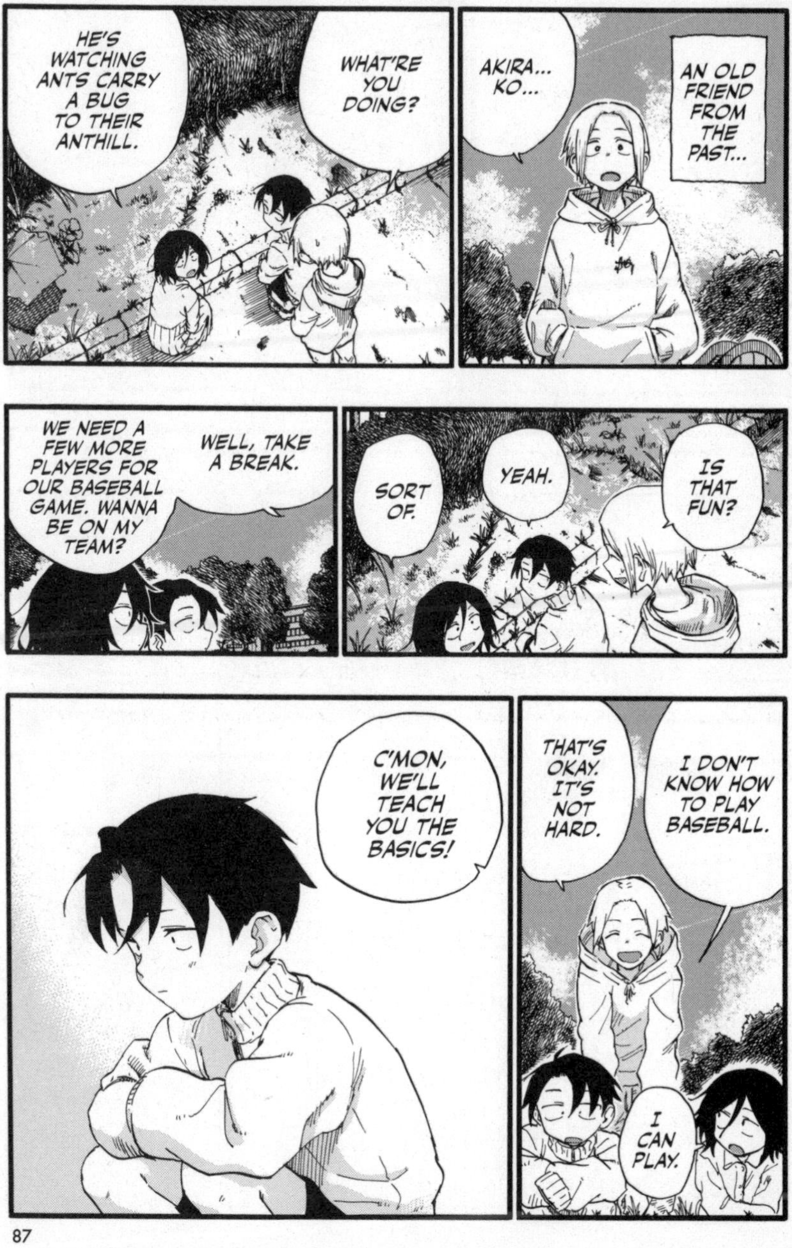
AN OLD FRIEND FROM THE PAST...
AKIRA... KO...
WHAT'RE YOU DOING?
HE'S WATCHING ANTS CARRY A BUG TO THEIR ANTHILL.
IS THAT FUN?
YEAH.
SORT OF.
WELL, TAKE A BREAK.
WE NEED A FEW MORE PLAYERS FOR OUR BASEBALL GAME. WANNA BE ON MY TEAM?
I DON'T KNOW HOW TO PLAY BASEBALL.
THAT'S OKAY. IT'S NOT HARD.
I CAN PLAY.
C'MON, WE'LL TEACH YOU THE BASICS!

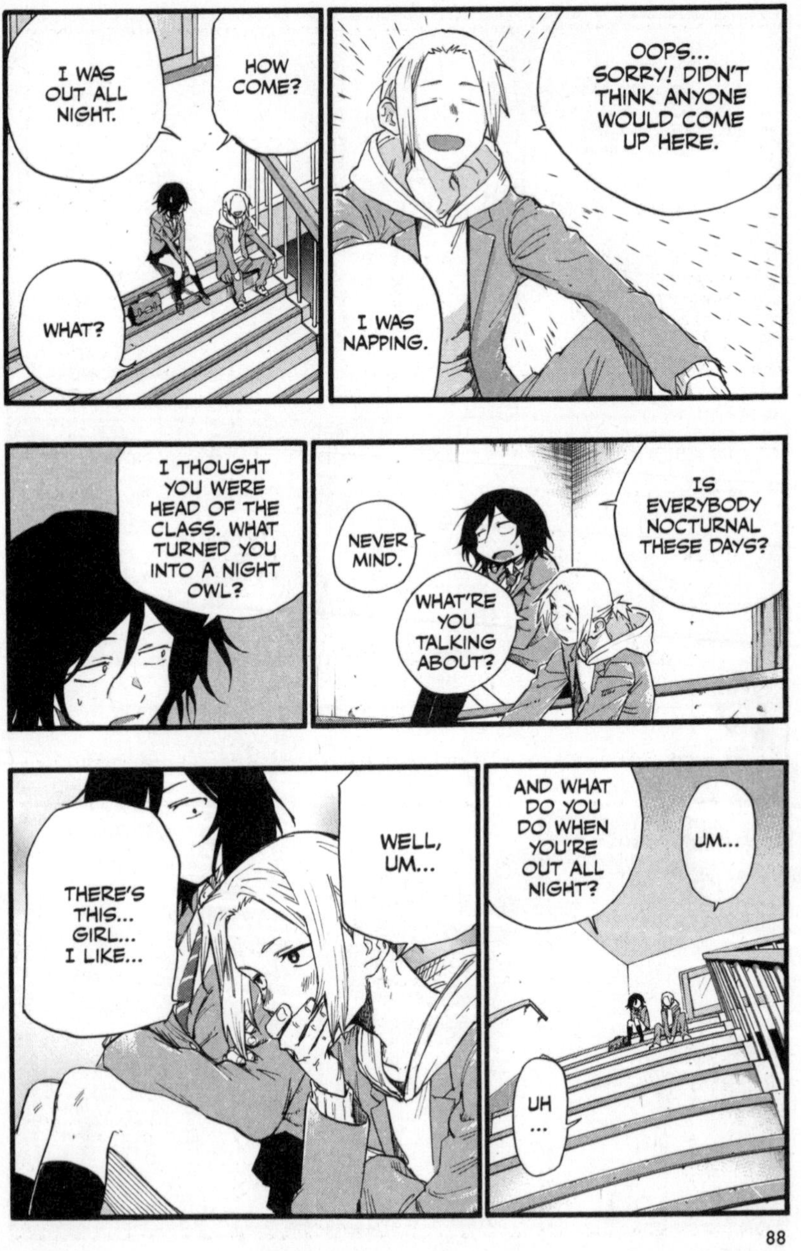
OOPS... SORRY! DIDN'T THINK ANYONE WOULD COME UP HERE.
I WAS NAPPING.
HOW COME?
I WAS OUT ALL NIGHT.
WHAT?
IS EVERYBODY NOCTURNAL THESE DAYS?
NEVER MIND.
WHAT'RE YOU TALKING ABOUT?
I THOUGHT YOU WERE HEAD OF THE CLASS. WHAT TURNED YOU INTO A NIGHT OWL?
UM...
AND WHAT DO YOU DO WHEN YOU'RE OUT ALL NIGHT?
UH ...
WELL, UM...
THERE'S THIS... GIRL... I LIKE...

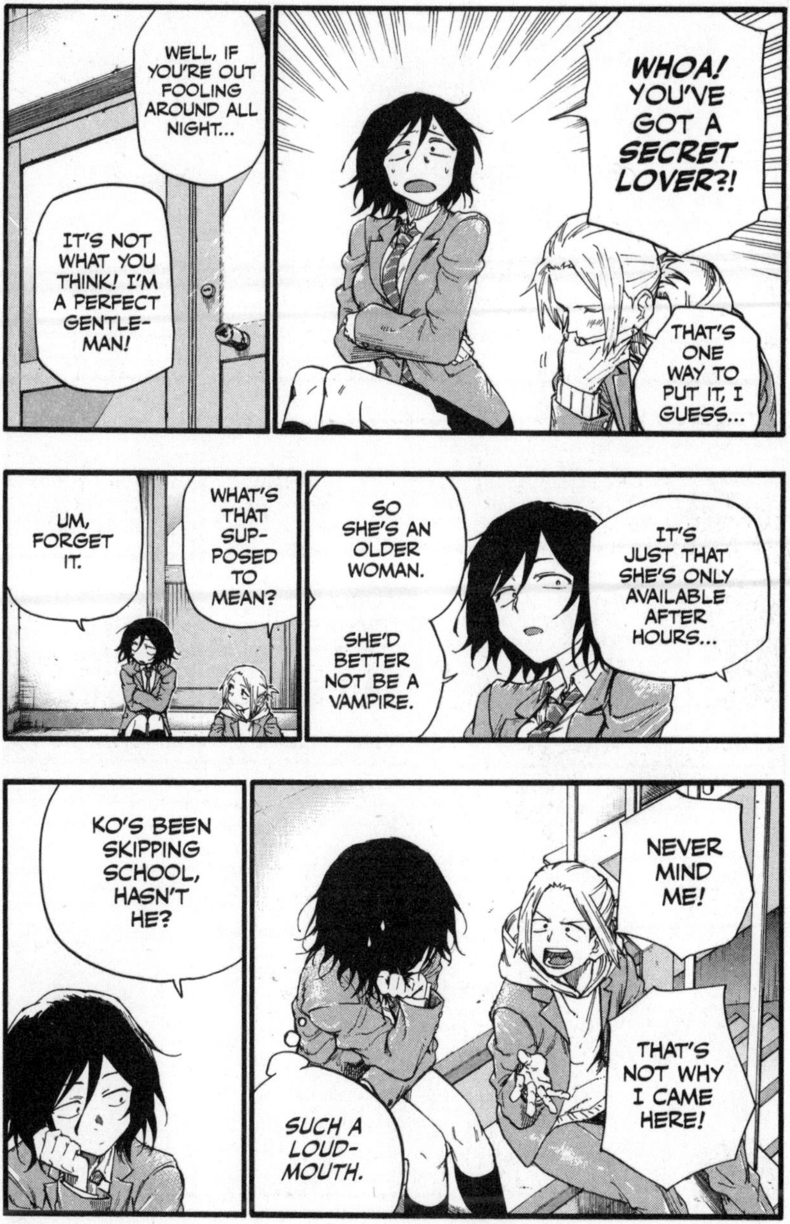
WHOA! YOU'VE GOT A SECRET LOVER?!
THAT'S ONE WAY TO PUT IT, I GUESS...
WELL, IF YOU'RE OUT FOOLING AROUND ALL NIGHT...
IT'S NOT WHAT YOU THINK! I'M A PERFECT GENTLE-MAN!
IT'S JUST THAT SHE'S ONLY AVAILABLE AFTER HOURS...
SO SHE'S AN OLDER WOMAN.
SHE'D BETTER NOT BE A VAMPIRE.
WHAT'S THAT SUP-POSED TO MEAN?
UM, FORGET IT.
NEVER MIND ME!
THAT'S NOT WHY I CAME HERE!
SUCH A LOUD-MOUTH.
KO'S BEEN SKIPPING SCHOOL, HASN'T HE?

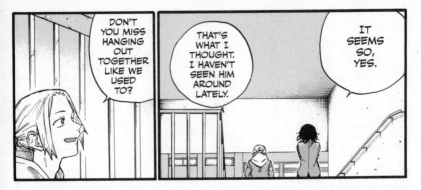

IT SEEMS SO, YES.
THAT'S WHAT I THOUGHT. I HAVEN'T SEEN HIM AROUND LATELY.
DON'T YOU MISS HANGING OUT TOGETHER LIKE WE USED TO?
WE DIDN'T HANG OUT THAT MUCH...
I CAN'T BELIEVE YOU'D SAY THAT! AM I THE ONLY ONE WHO THOUGHT WE WERE THE DYNAMIC TRIO?
IT'S JUST THAT YOU HAVE SO *MANY* FRIENDS.
THERE'S ALWAYS A CROWD AROUND YOU, SO I DON'T HAVE MANY MEMORIES OF JUST THE THREE OF US.
WELL, THIS IS EMBAR-RASSING...
SORRY.

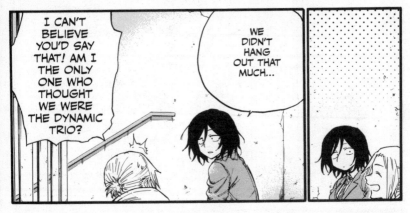

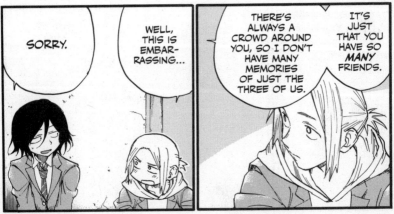

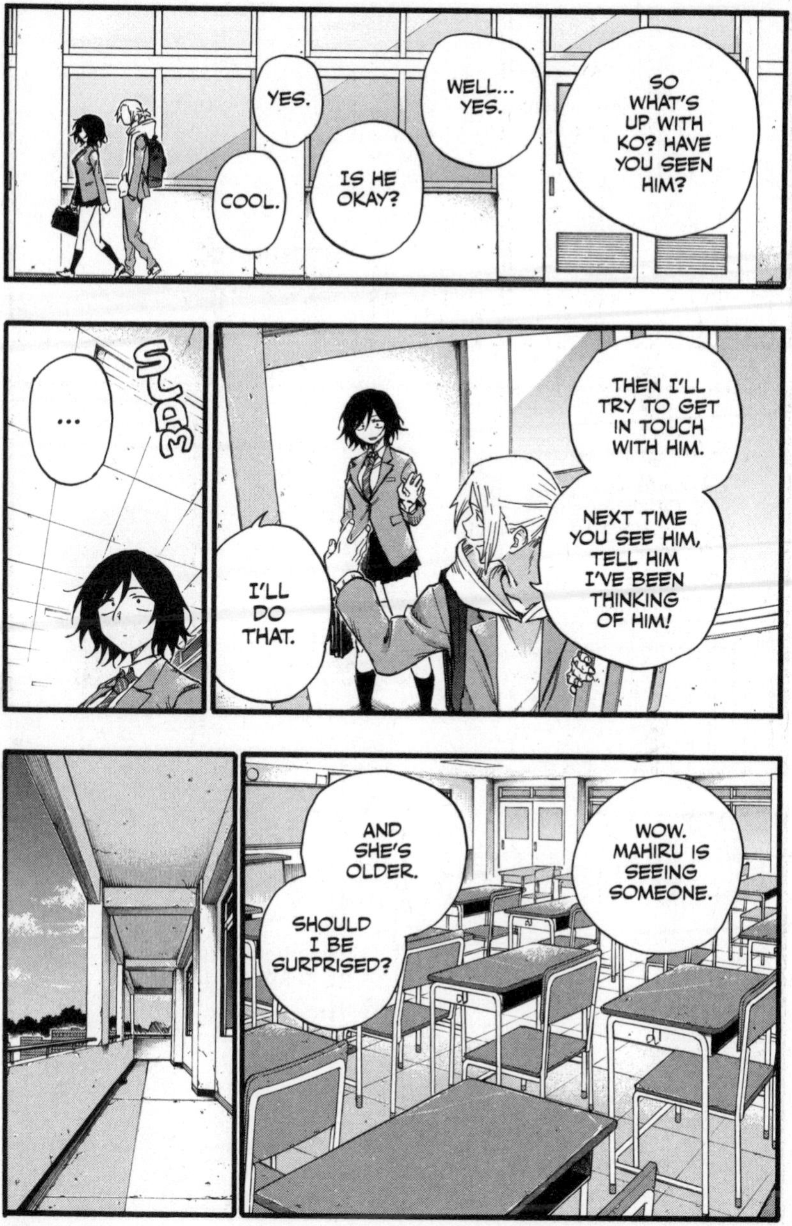
SO WHAT'S UP WITH KO? HAVE YOU SEEN HIM?
WELL... YES.
IS HE OKAY?
YES.
COOL.
THEN I'LL TRY TO GET IN TOUCH WITH HIM.
NEXT TIME YOU SEE HIM, TELL HIM I'VE BEEN THINKING OF HIM!
I'LL DO THAT.
SLAM
...
WOW. MAHIRU IS SEEING SOMEONE.
AND SHE'S OLDER.
SHOULD I BE SURPRISED?

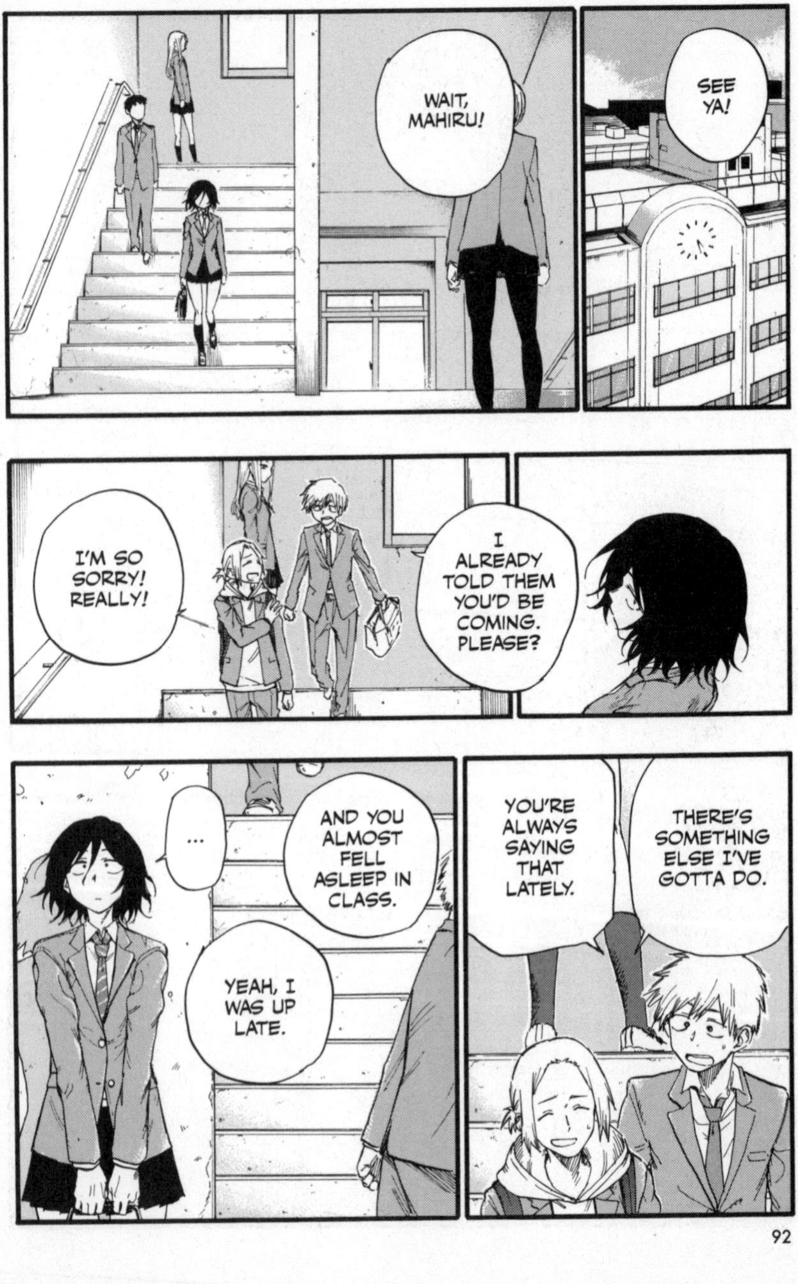
SEE YA!
WAIT, MAHIRU!
I ALREADY TOLD THEM YOU'D BE COMING. PLEASE?
I'M SO SORRY! REALLY!
THERE'S SOMETHING ELSE I'VE GOTTA DO.
YOU'RE ALWAYS SAYING THAT LATELY.
AND YOU ALMOST FELL ASLEEP IN CLASS.
...
YEAH, I WAS UP LATE.

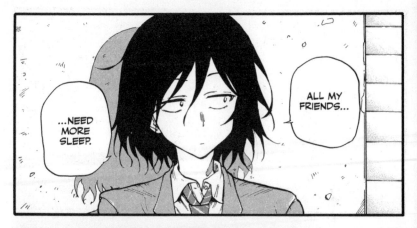

ALL MY FRIENDS...
...NEED MORE SLEEP.
SIGH... I'M SO TIRED...
HFF
HFF
TP
TP
TP
HFF
OH!

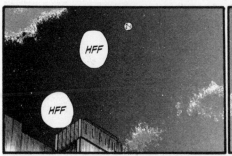

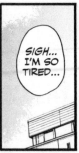

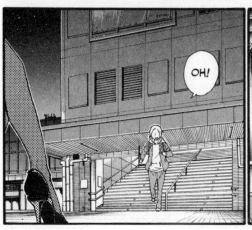

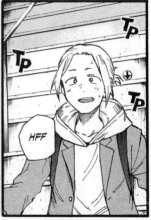

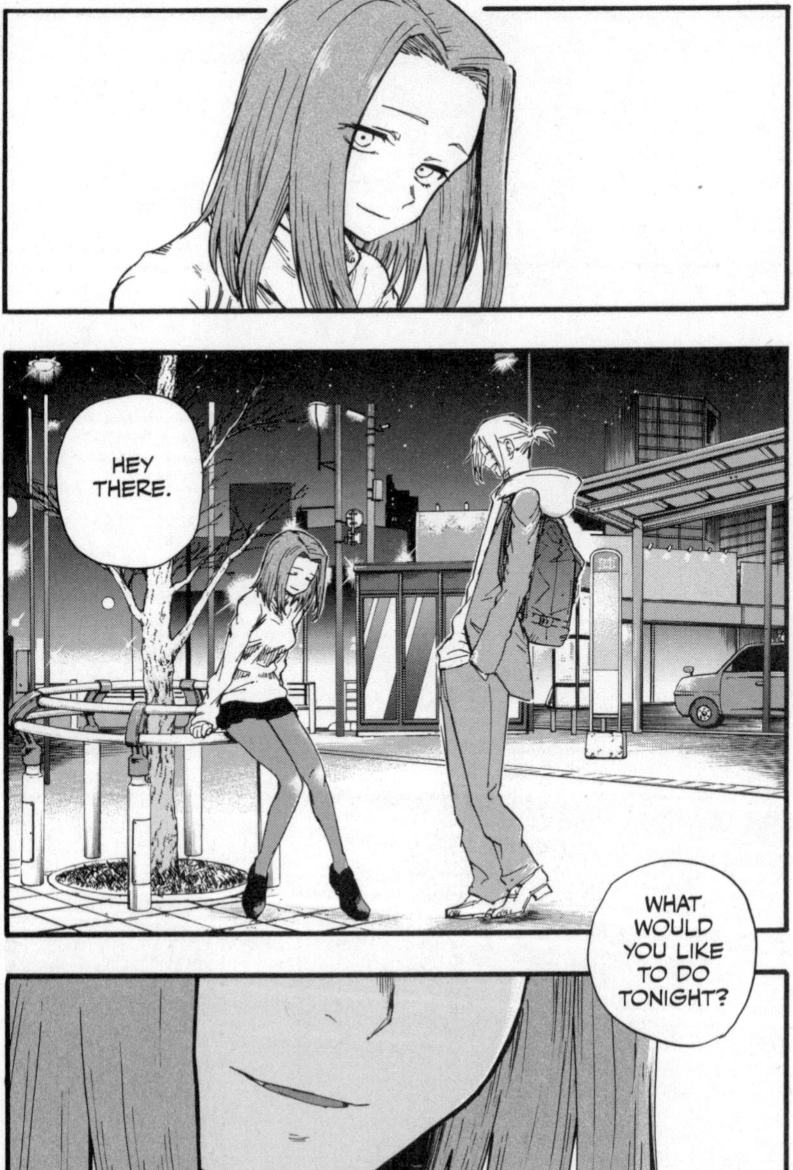
HEY THERE.
WHAT WOULD YOU LIKE TO DO TONIGHT?

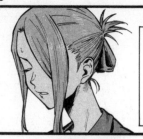

NIGHT 24: VAMPIRE LOVE GURU

"YAMORI, IT'S NOT A MATTER OF YEARS."
"WE VAMPIRES ARE BOUND BY A SINGLE YEAR."
"STARTING FROM THE FIRST FEED..."
"...IF YOU DON'T TURN WITHIN A YEAR, YOU'LL NEVER TURN."
"IN THAT CASE, KO..."
"...THEY'RE GOING TO KILL YOU."

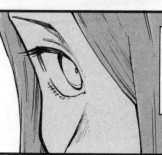

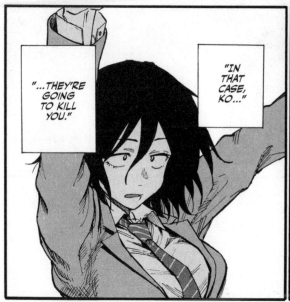

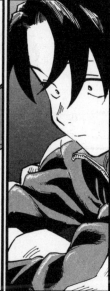

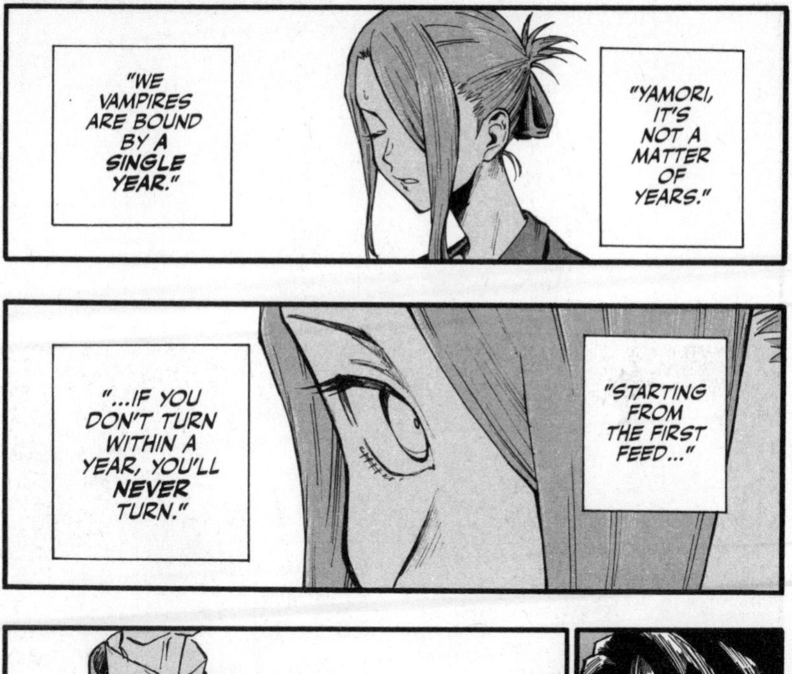

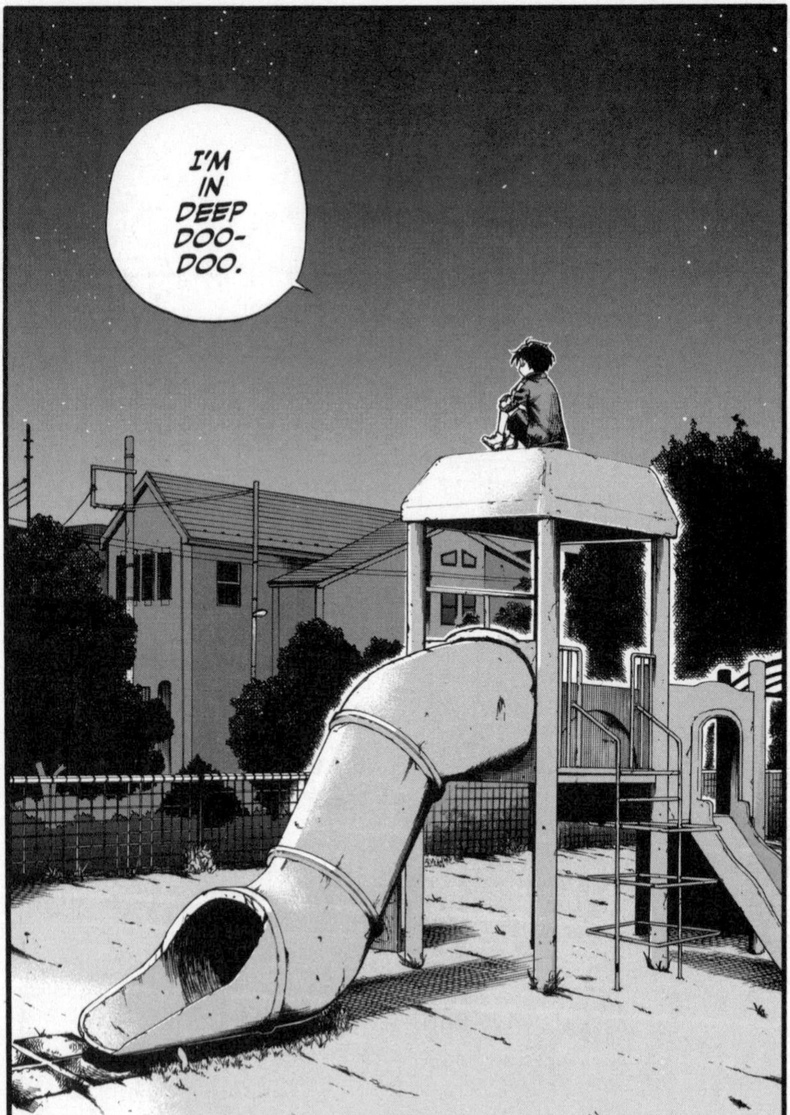
I'M IN DEEP DOO-DOO.

NIGHT 24: VAMPIRE LOVE GURU

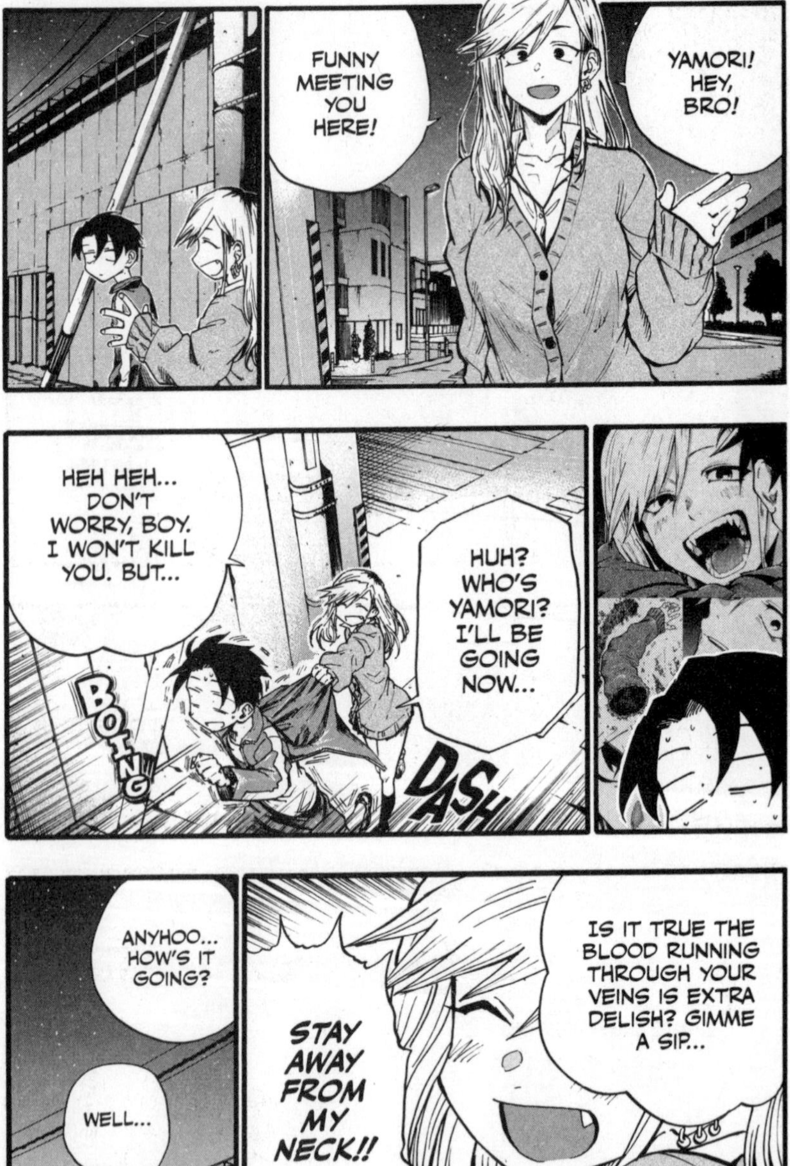
YAMORI! HEY, BRO!
FUNNY MEETING YOU HERE!
HUH? WHO'S YAMORI? I'LL BE GOING NOW...
DASH
HEH HEH... DON'T WORRY, BOY. I WON'T KILL YOU. BUT...
BOING
IS IT TRUE THE BLOOD RUNNING THROUGH YOUR VEINS IS EXTRA DELISH? GIMME A SIP...
STAY AWAY FROM MY NECK!!
ANYHOO... HOW'S IT GOING?
WELL...

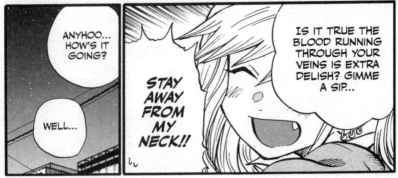

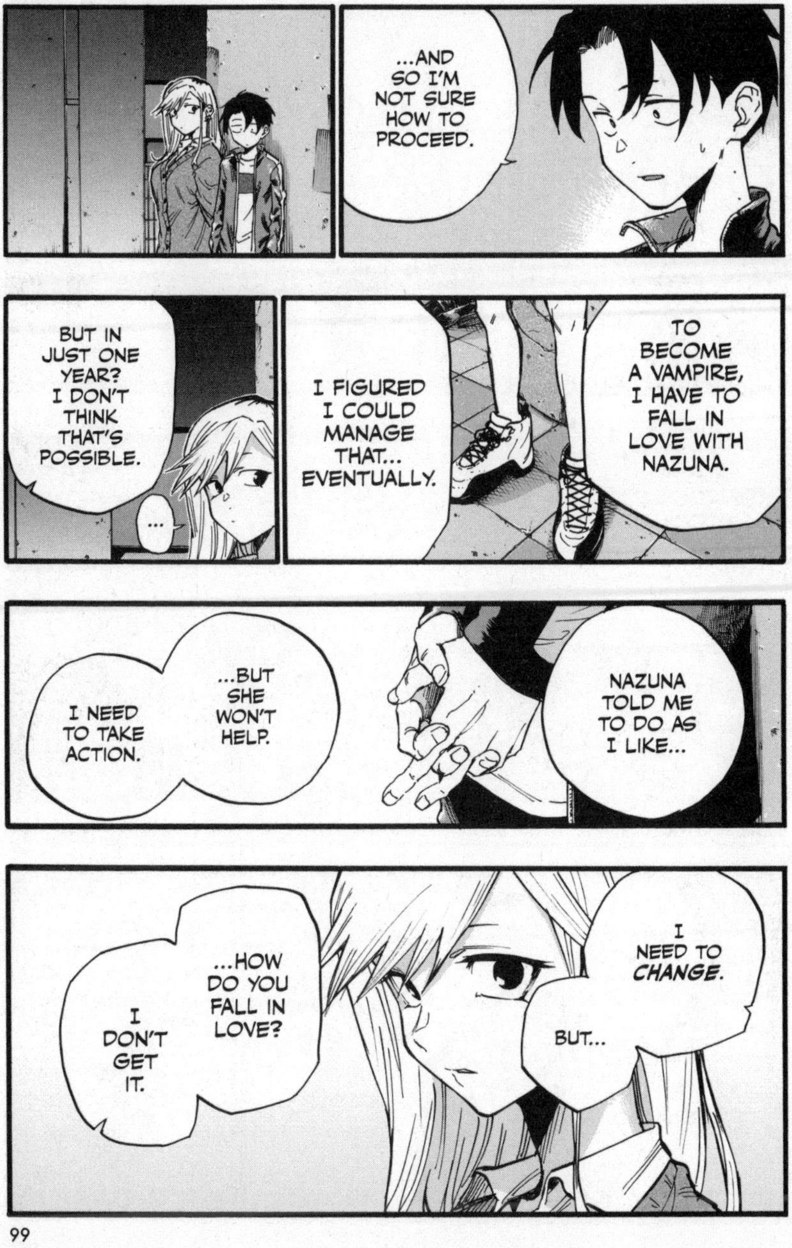
...AND SO I'M NOT SURE HOW TO PROCEED.
TO BECOME A VAMPIRE, I HAVE TO FALL IN LOVE WITH NAZUNA.
I FIGURED I COULD MANAGE THAT... EVENTUALLY.
BUT IN JUST ONE YEAR? I DON'T THINK THAT'S POSSIBLE.
...
NAZUNA TOLD ME TO DO AS I LIKE...
...BUT SHE WON'T HELP.
I NEED TO TAKE ACTION.
I NEED TO *CHANGE*.
BUT...
...HOW DO YOU FALL IN LOVE?
I DON'T GET IT.

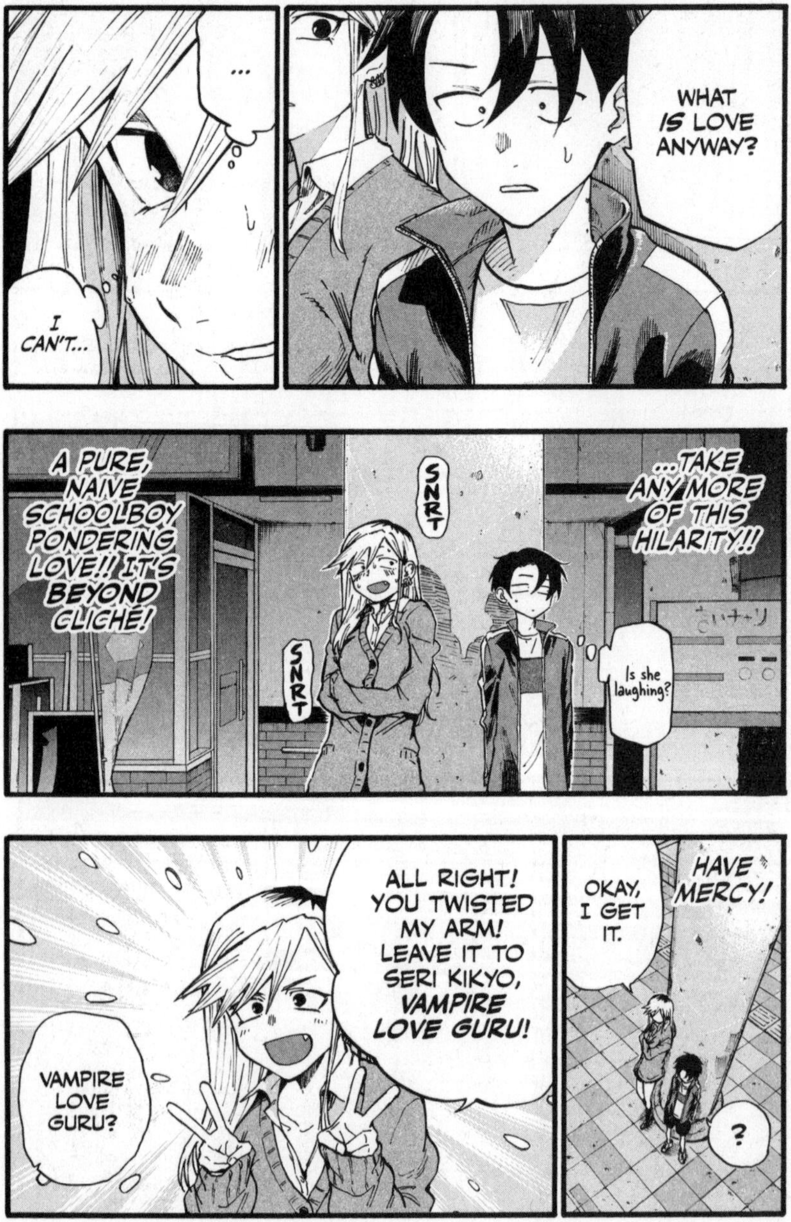
WHAT *IS* LOVE ANYWAY?
...
I CAN'T...
...TAKE ANY MORE OF THIS HILARITY!!
SNRT
A PURE, NAIVE SCHOOLBOY PONDERING LOVE!! IT'S BEYOND CLICHÉ!
Is she laughing?
SNRT
HAVE MERCY!
OKAY, I GET IT.
?
ALL RIGHT! YOU TWISTED MY ARM! LEAVE IT TO SERI KIKYO, *VAMPIRE LOVE GURU!*
VAMPIRE LOVE GURU?

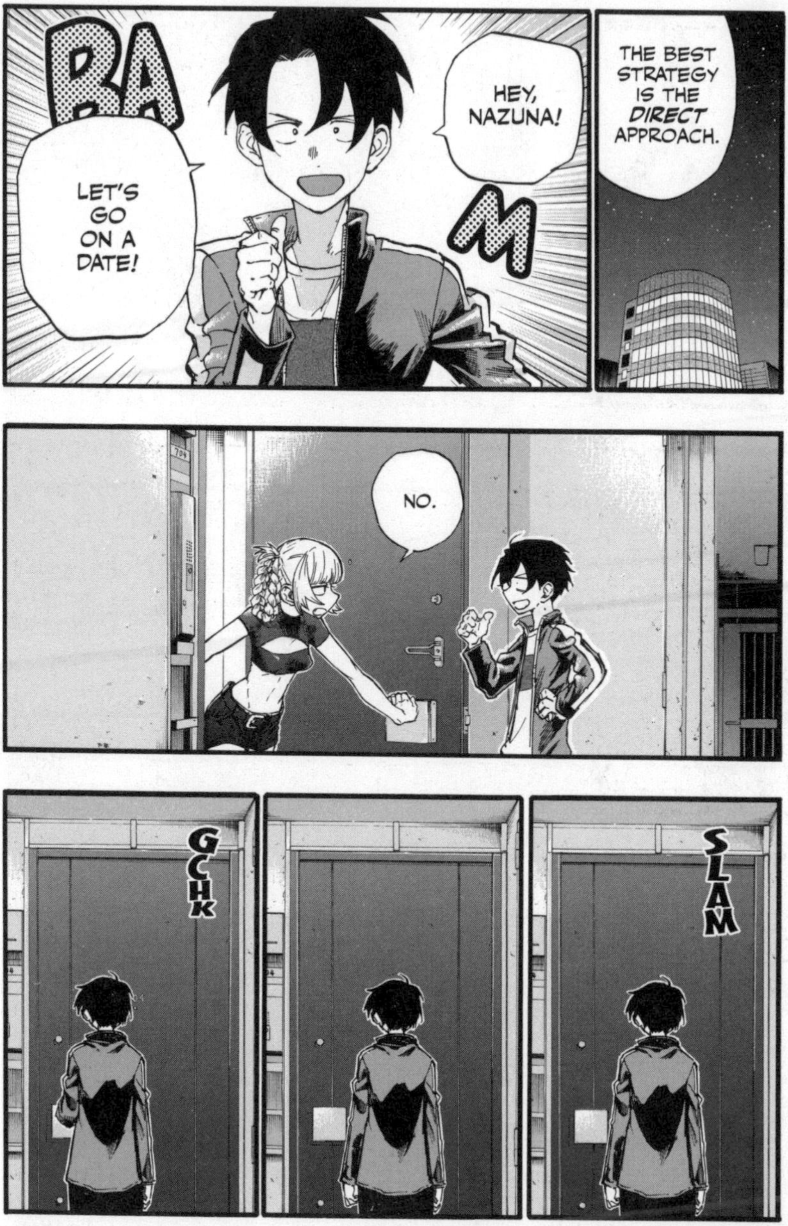
THE BEST STRATEGY IS THE *DIRECT* APPROACH.
HEY, NAZUNA!
BAM
LET'S GO ON A DATE!
NO.
SLAM
GCHK

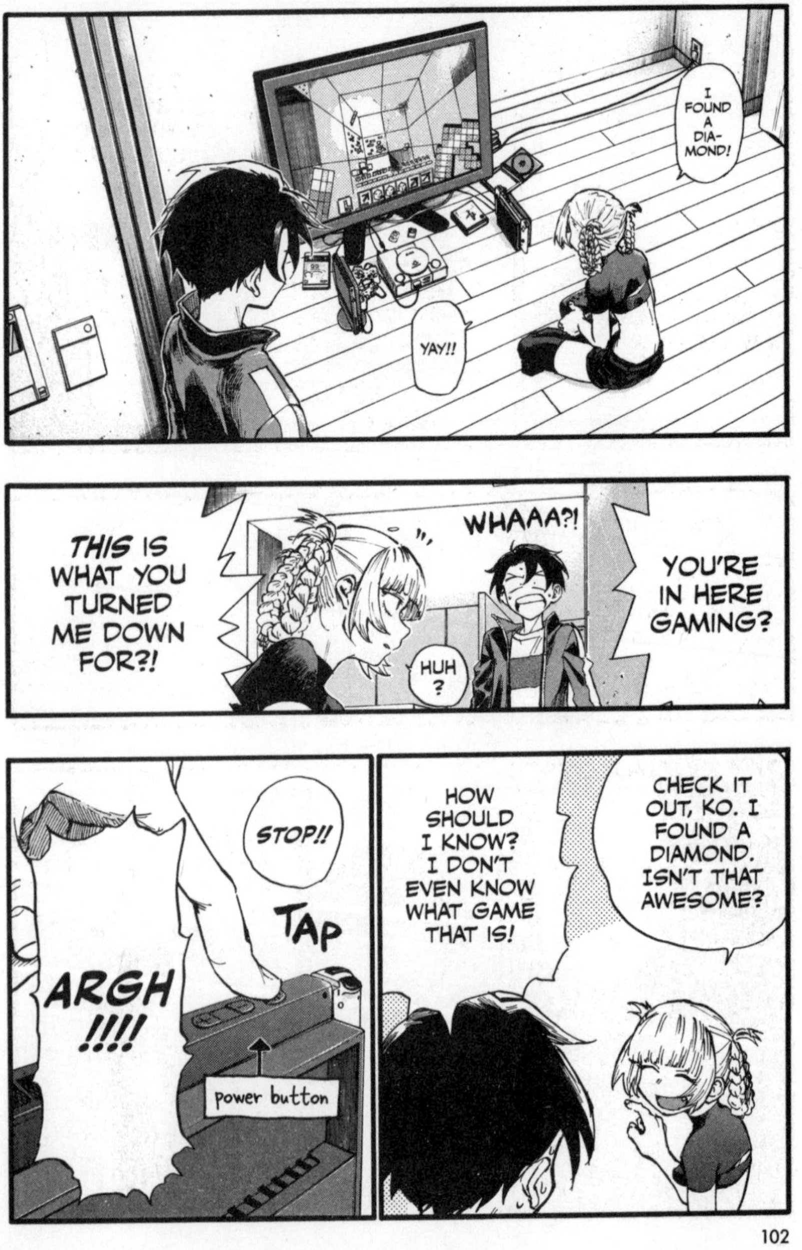
I FOUND A DIA-MOND!
YAY!!
YOU'RE IN HERE GAMING?
WHAAA?!
HUH?
THIS IS WHAT YOU TURNED ME DOWN FOR?!
CHECK IT OUT, KO. I FOUND A DIAMOND. ISN'T THAT AWESOME?
HOW SHOULD I KNOW? I DON'T EVEN KNOW WHAT GAME THAT IS!
STOP!!
TAP
ARGH!!!!
power button

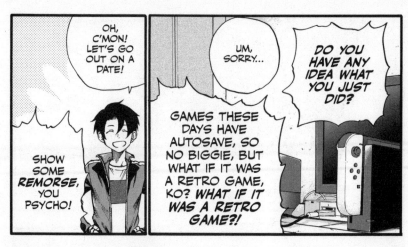

DO YOU HAVE ANY IDEA WHAT YOU JUST DID?
UM, SORRY...
GAMES THESE DAYS HAVE AUTOSAVE, SO NO BIGGIE, BUT WHAT IF IT WAS A RETRO GAME, KO? WHAT IF IT WAS A RETRO GAME?!
OH, C'MON! LET'S GO OUT ON A DATE!
SHOW SOME REMORSE, YOU PSYCHO!
ANYWAY, I'M NOT INTO DATING.
DON'T KNOCK IT TILL YOU'VE TRIED IT.
SO FAR, SO GOOD.
ACCORDING TO SERI, THE NEXT STEP IS...
...
FWP
COME ON! THIS WAY, NAZUNA!
SHEESH.

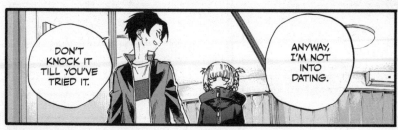

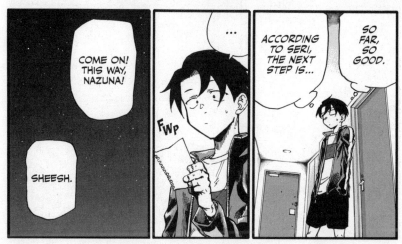

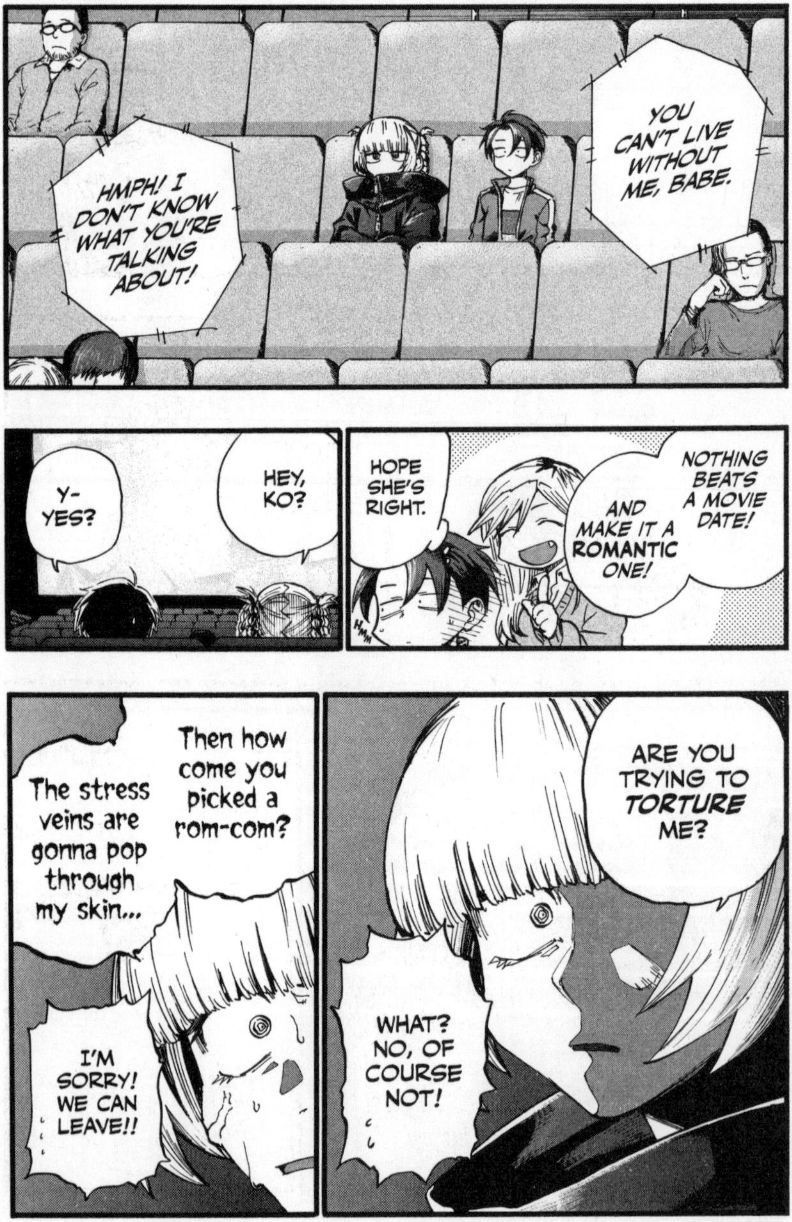
YOU CAN'T LIVE WITHOUT ME, BABE.
HMPH! I DON'T KNOW WHAT YOU'RE TALKING ABOUT!
NOTHING BEATS A MOVIE DATE!
AND MAKE IT A ROMANTIC ONE!
HOPE SHE'S RIGHT.
HMM
HEY, KO?
Y-YES?
ARE YOU TRYING TO *TORTURE* ME?
WHAT? NO, OF COURSE NOT!
Then how come you picked a rom-com?
The stress veins are gonna pop through my skin...
I'M SORRY! WE CAN LEAVE!!

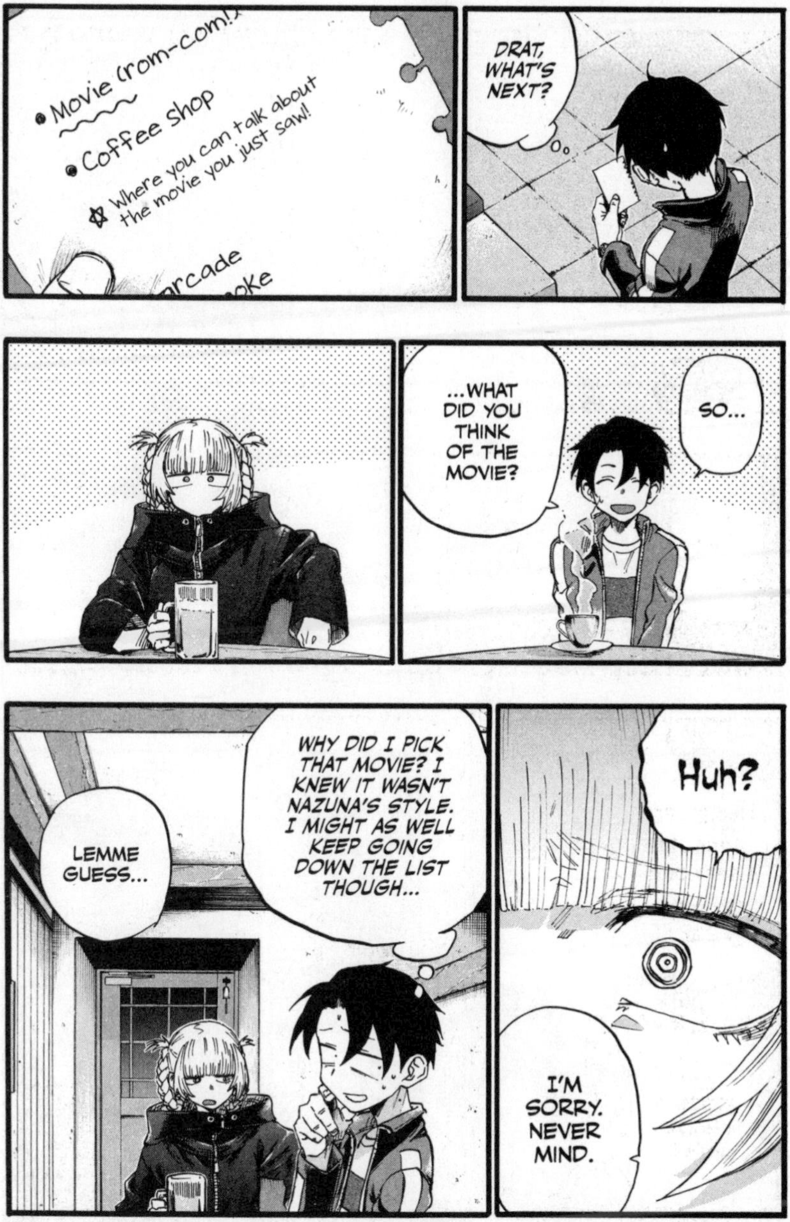
DRAT, WHAT'S NEXT?
Movie (rom-com!)
Coffee Shop
Where you can talk about the movie you just saw!
SO...
...WHAT DID YOU THINK OF THE MOVIE?
Huh?
I'M SORRY. NEVER MIND.
WHY DID I PICK THAT MOVIE? I KNEW IT WASN'T NAZUNA'S STYLE. I MIGHT AS WELL KEEP GOING DOWN THE LIST THOUGH...
LEMME GUESS...

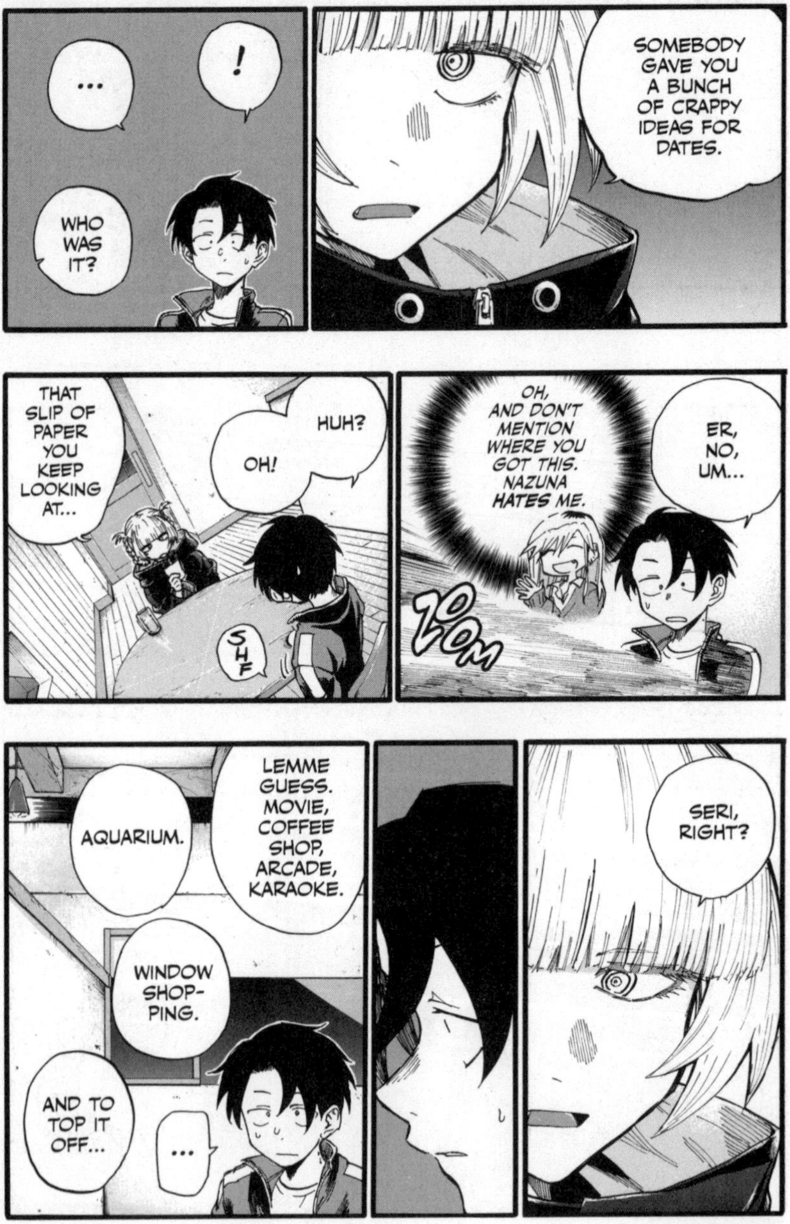
SOMEBODY GAVE YOU A BUNCH OF CRAPPY IDEAS FOR DATES.
!
...
WHO WAS IT?
ER, NO, UM...
OH, AND DON'T MENTION WHERE YOU GOT THIS. NAZUNA HATES ME.
ZOOM
HUH?
OH!
THAT SLIP OF PAPER YOU KEEP LOOKING AT...
SHF
SERI, RIGHT?
LEMME GUESS. MOVIE, COFFEE SHOP, ARCADE, KARAOKE.
AQUARIUM.
WINDOW SHOP-PING.
...
AND TO TOP IT OFF...

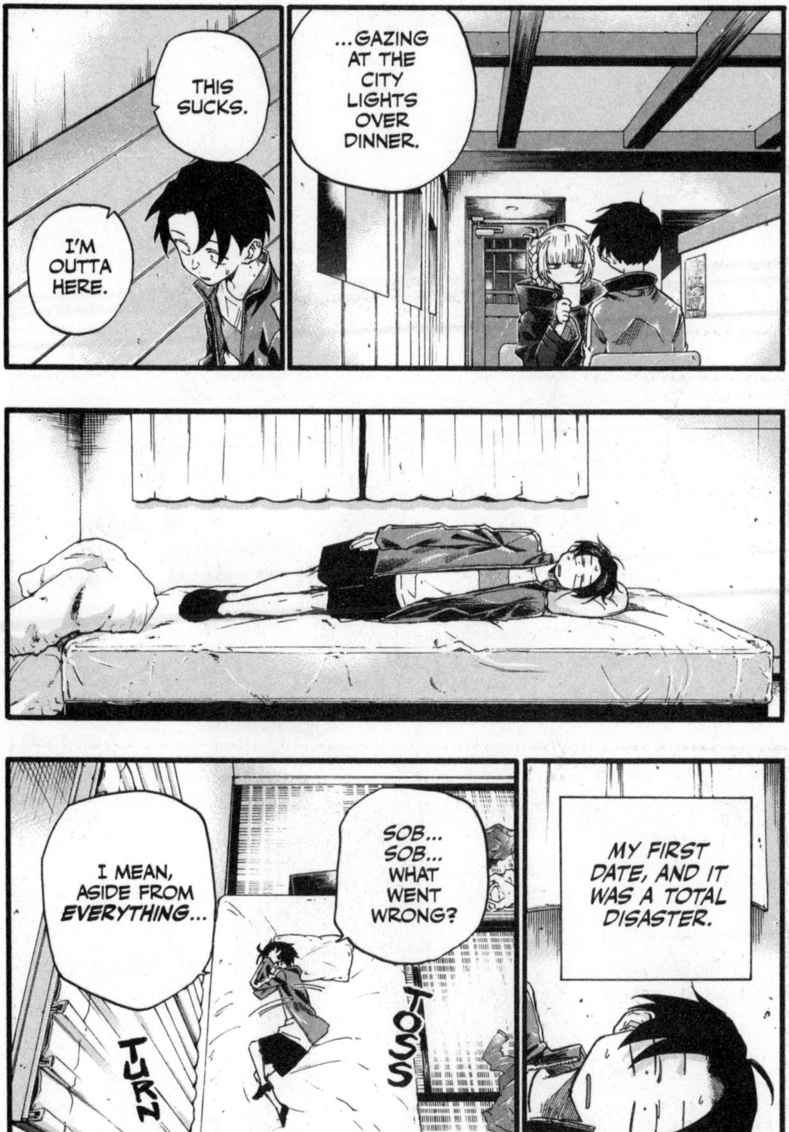
...GAZING AT THE CITY LIGHTS OVER DINNER.
THIS SUCKS.
I'M OUTTA HERE.
MY FIRST DATE, AND IT WAS A TOTAL DISASTER.
SOB... SOB... WHAT WENT WRONG?
TOSS
I MEAN, ASIDE FROM *EVERYTHING*...
TURN

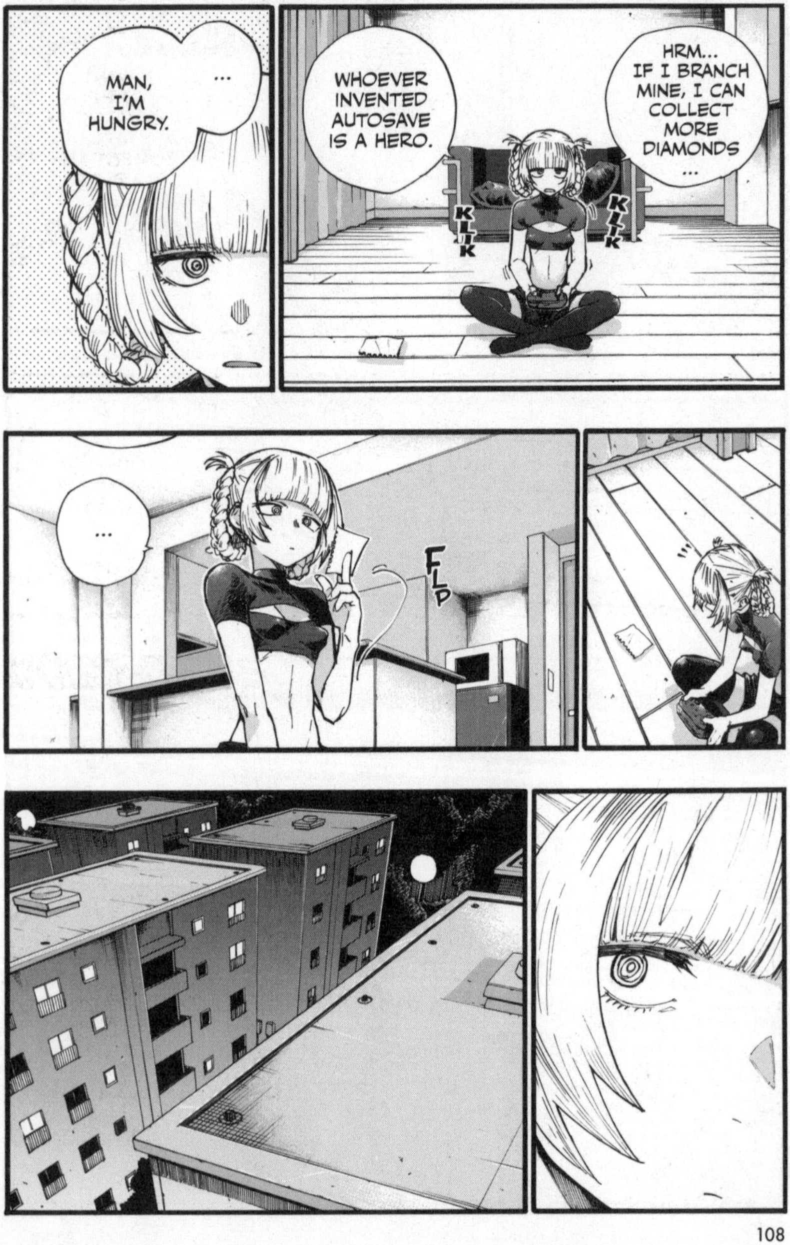
HRM... IF I BRANCH MINE, I CAN COLLECT MORE DIAMONDS ...
WHOEVER INVENTED AUTOSAVE IS A HERO.
KLIK
KLIK
...
MAN, I'M HUNGRY.
...
FLP

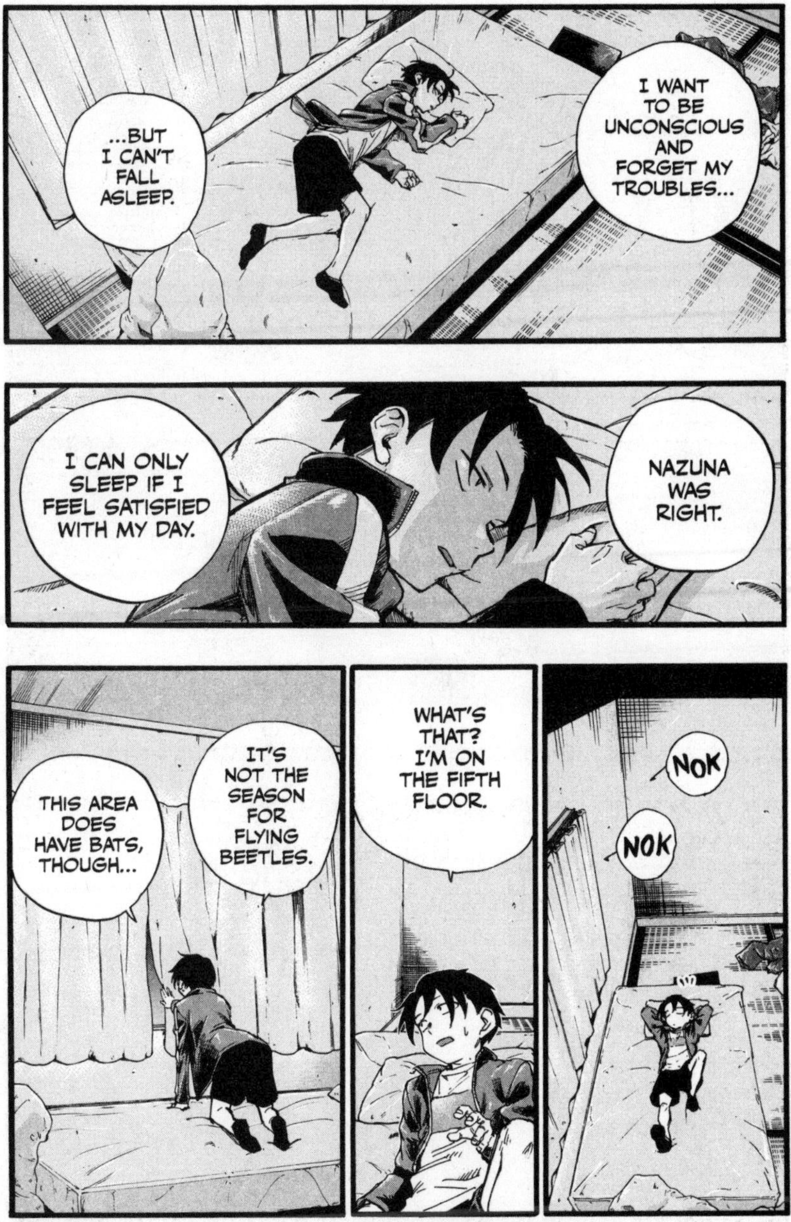
I WANT TO BE UNCONSCIOUS AND FORGET MY TROUBLES...
...BUT I CAN'T FALL ASLEEP.
NAZUNA WAS RIGHT.
I CAN ONLY SLEEP IF I FEEL SATISFIED WITH MY DAY.
NOK
NOK
WHAT'S THAT? I'M ON THE FIFTH FLOOR.
IT'S NOT THE SEASON FOR FLYING BEETLES.
THIS AREA DOES HAVE BATS, THOUGH...

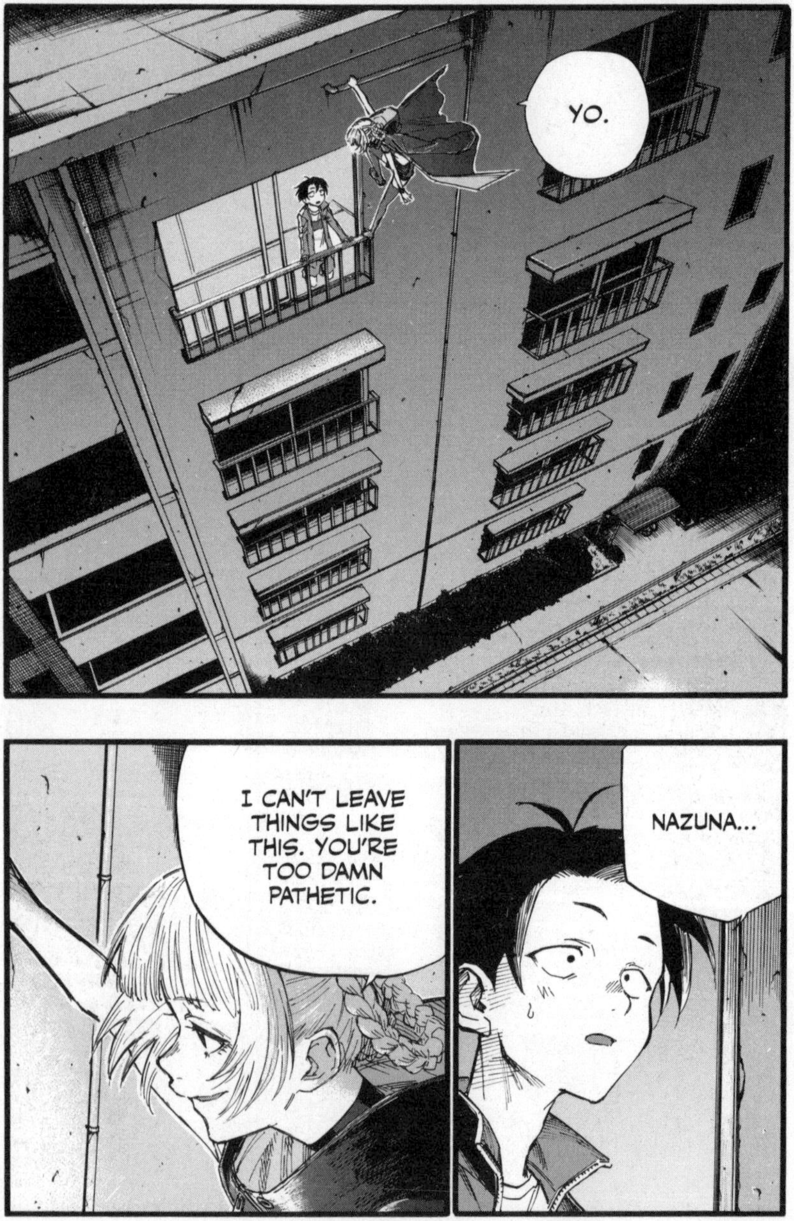
YO.
NAZUNA...
I CAN'T LEAVE THINGS LIKE THIS. YOU'RE TOO DAMN PATHETIC.

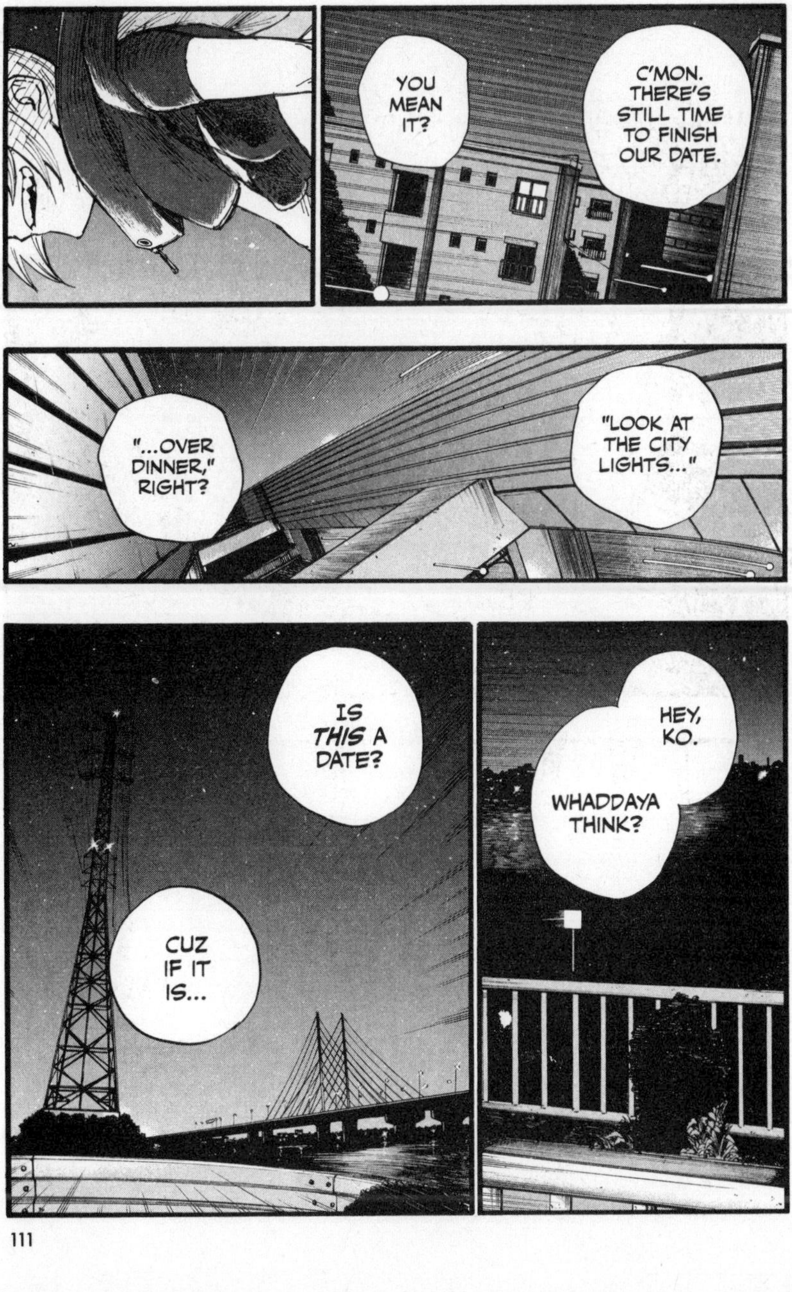
C'MON. THERE'S STILL TIME TO FINISH OUR DATE.
YOU MEAN IT?
"LOOK AT THE CITY LIGHTS..."
"...OVER DINNER," RIGHT?
HEY, KO.
WHADDAYA THINK?
IS *THIS* A DATE?
CUZ IF IT IS...

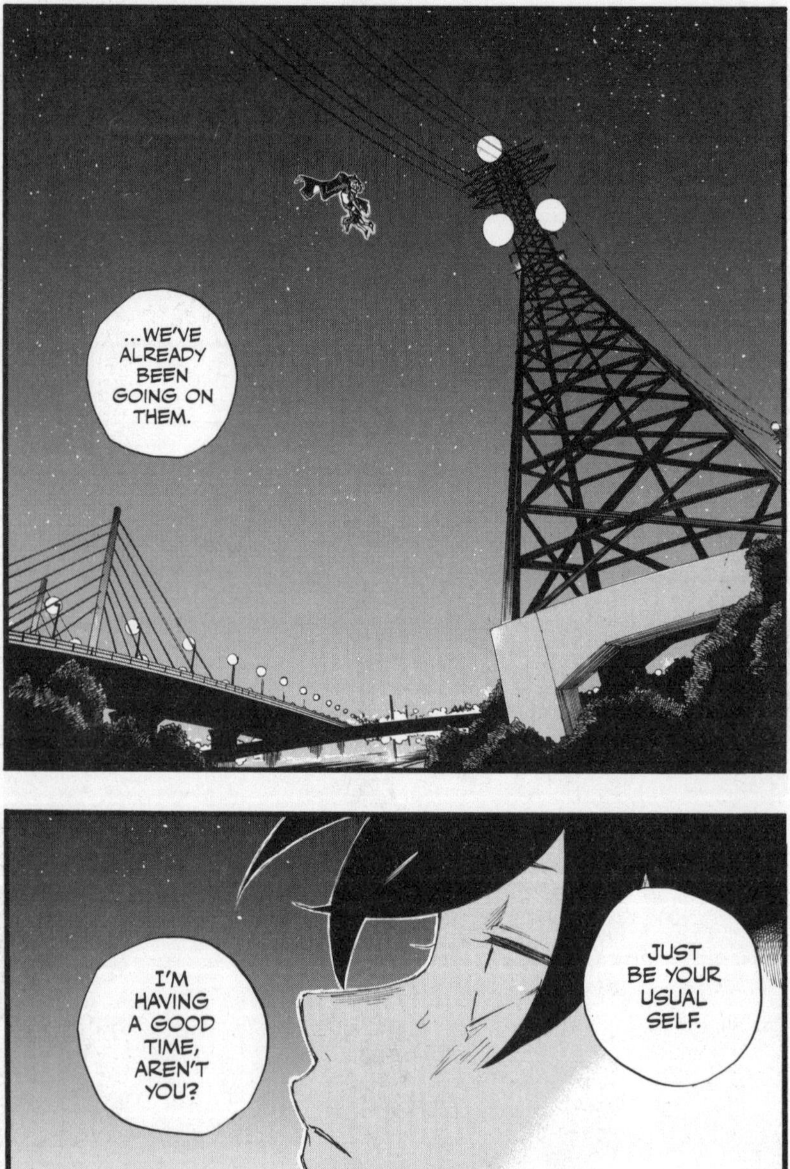
...WE'VE ALREADY BEEN GOING ON THEM.
JUST BE YOUR USUAL SELF.
I'M HAVING A GOOD TIME, AREN'T YOU?

NIGHT 25: SHE'S BEEN BUSY

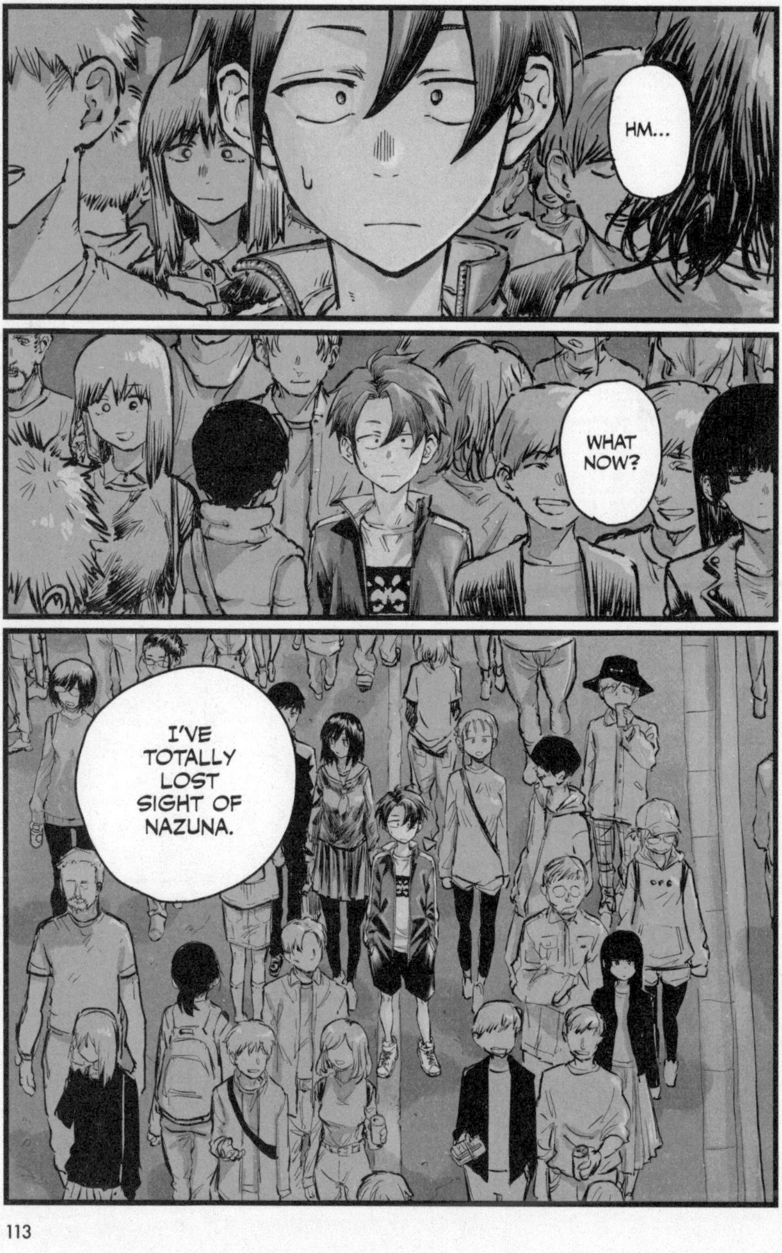
HM...
WHAT NOW?
I'VE TOTALLY LOST SIGHT OF NAZUNA.

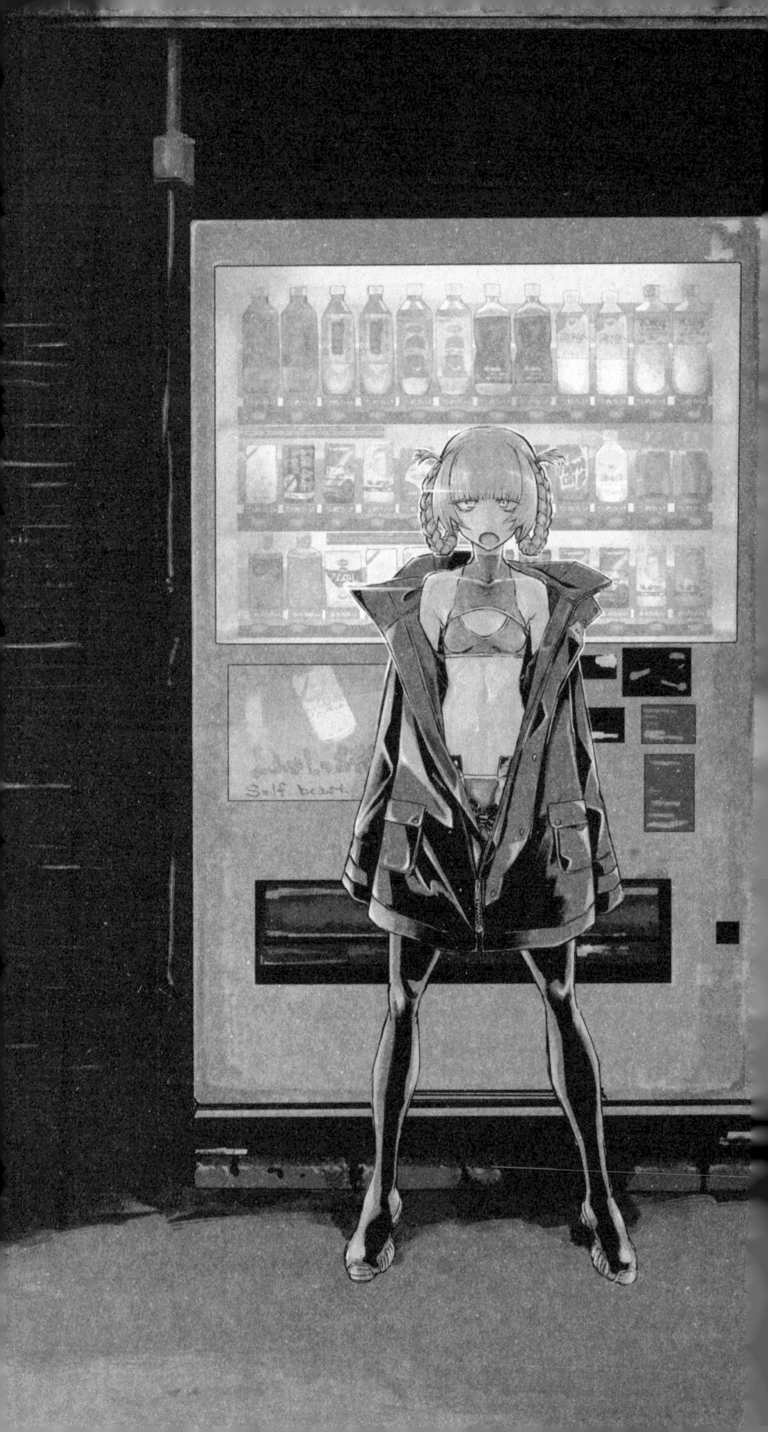
Self beast

NIGHT 25:
SHE'S
BEEN
BUSY

Call of the Night

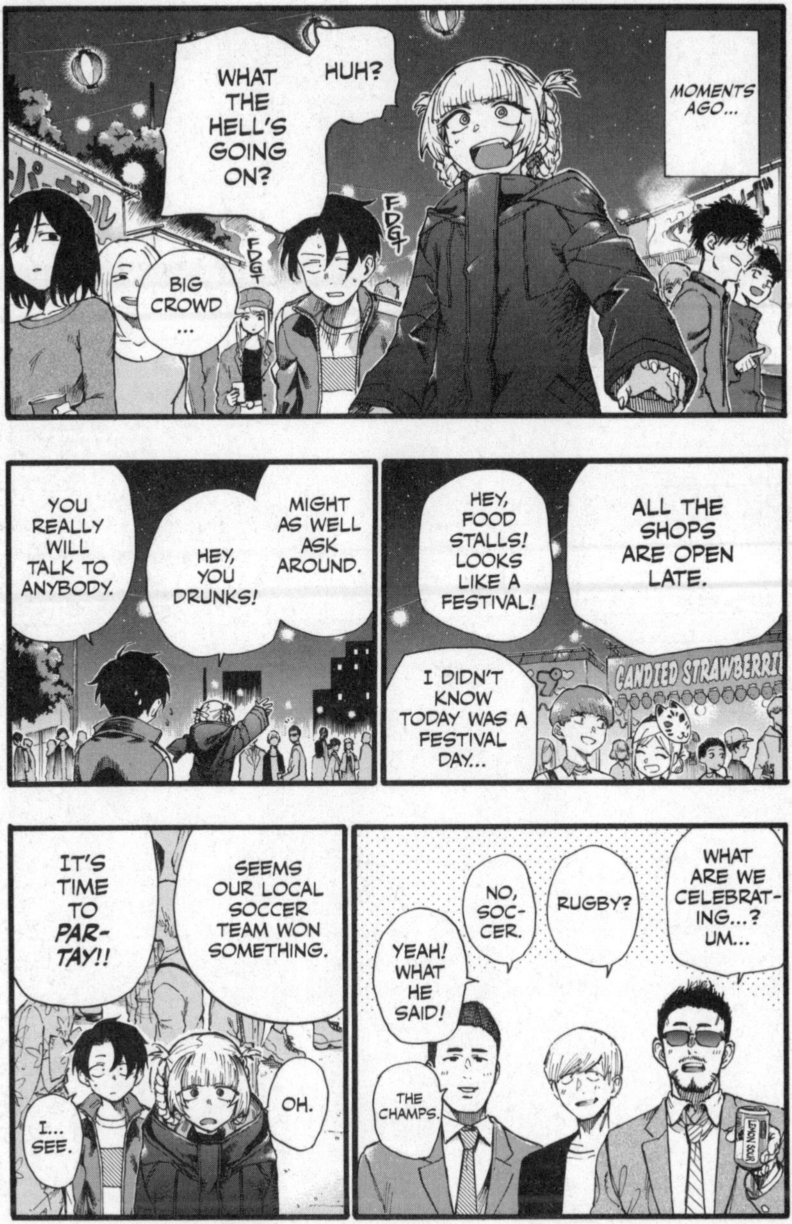
MOMENTS AGO...
HUH?
WHAT THE HELL'S GOING ON?
FDGT
FDGT
BIG CROWD...
ALL THE SHOPS ARE OPEN LATE.
HEY, FOOD STALLS! LOOKS LIKE A FESTIVAL!
I DIDN'T KNOW TODAY WAS A FESTIVAL DAY...
MIGHT AS WELL ASK AROUND.
HEY, YOU DRUNKS!
YOU REALLY WILL TALK TO ANYBODY.
WHAT ARE WE CELEBRATING...? UM...
RUGBY?
NO, SOCCER.
YEAH! WHAT HE SAID!
THE CHAMPS.
LEMON SOUR
SEEMS OUR LOCAL SOCCER TEAM WON SOMETHING.
IT'S TIME TO *PARTAY*!!
OH.
I... SEE.

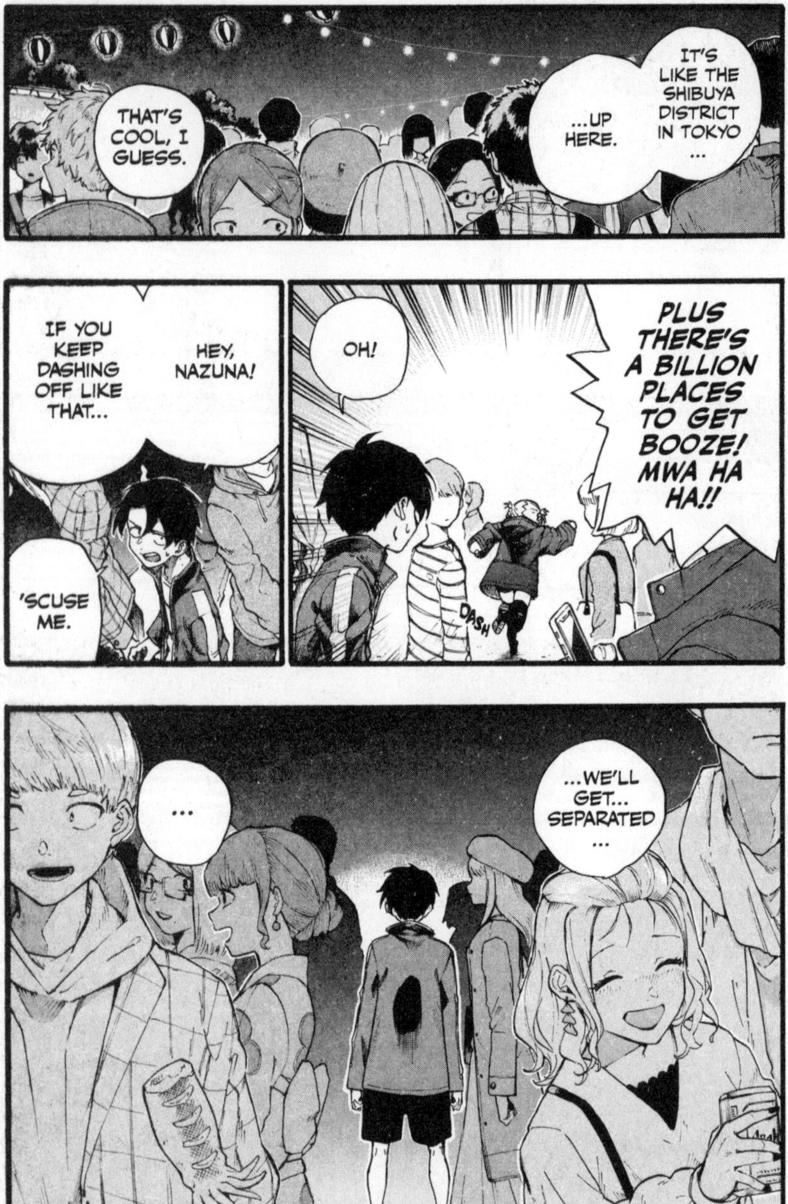
IT'S LIKE THE SHIBUYA DISTRICT IN TOKYO ...
...UP HERE.
THAT'S COOL, I GUESS.
PLUS THERE'S A BILLION PLACES TO GET BOOZE! MWA HA HA!!
DASH
OH!
HEY, NAZUNA!
IF YOU KEEP DASHING OFF LIKE THAT...
'SCUSE ME.
...WE'LL GET... SEPARATED ...
...

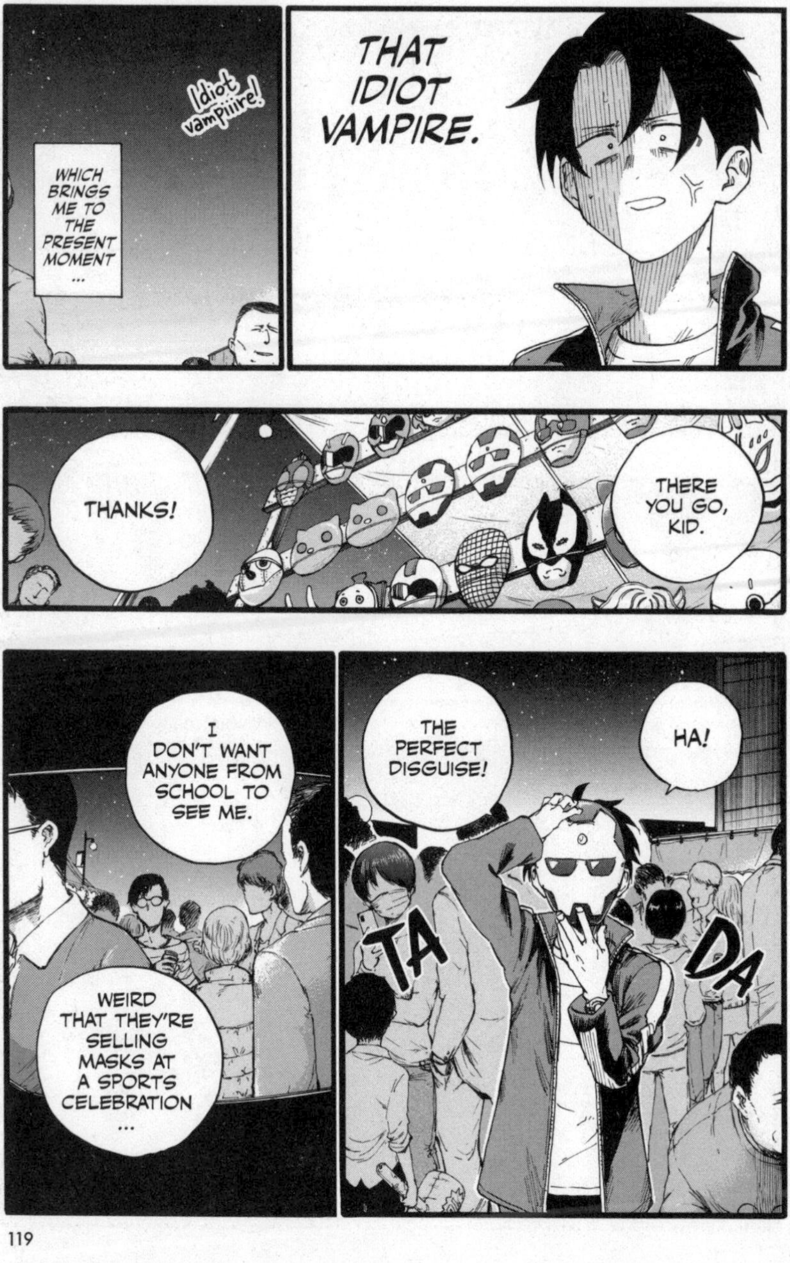
THAT IDIOT VAMPIRE.
Idiot vampiiire!
WHICH BRINGS ME TO THE PRESENT MOMENT ...
THERE YOU GO, KID.
THANKS!
HA!
THE PERFECT DISGUISE!
TA
DA
I DON'T WANT ANYONE FROM SCHOOL TO SEE ME.
WEIRD THAT THEY'RE SELLING MASKS AT A SPORTS CELEBRATION ...

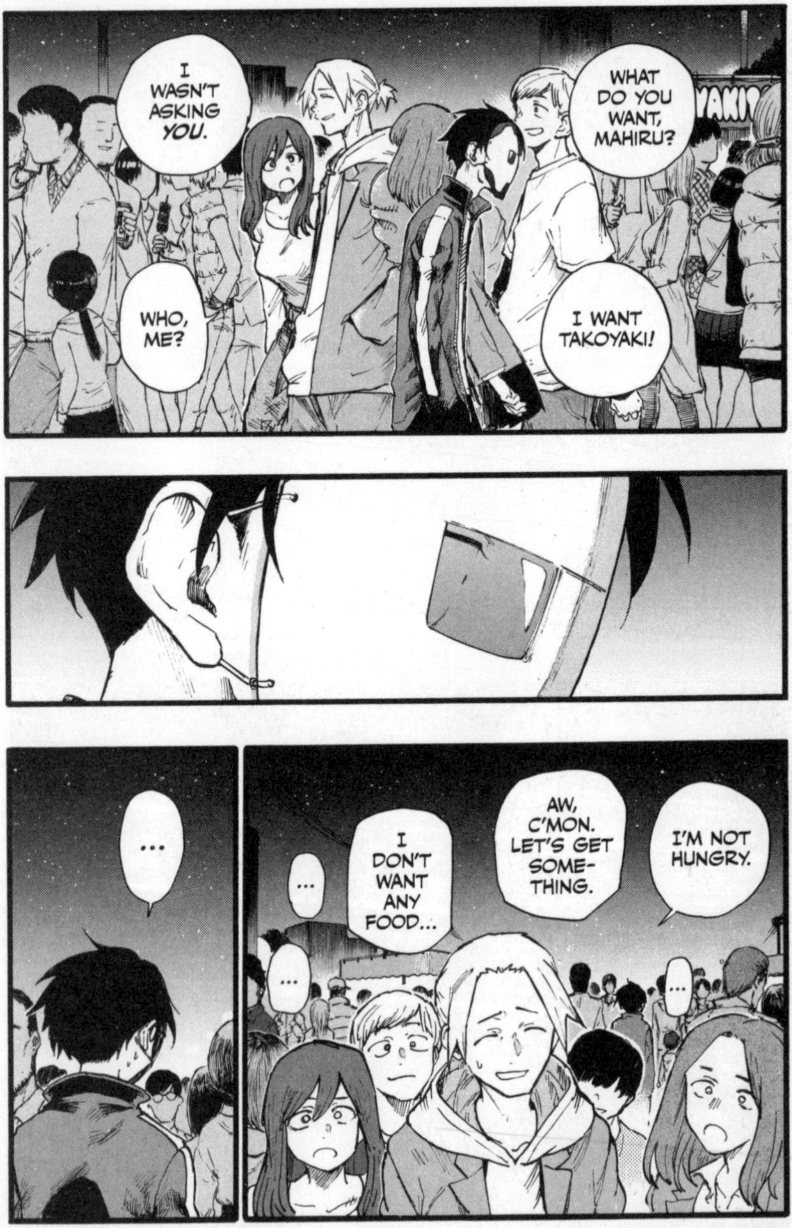
WHAT DO YOU WANT, MAHIRU?
I WANT TAKOYAKI!
I WASN'T ASKING *YOU*.
WHO, ME?
I'M NOT HUNGRY.
AW, C'MON. LET'S GET SOME-THING.
I DON'T WANT ANY FOOD...
...
...
...
...

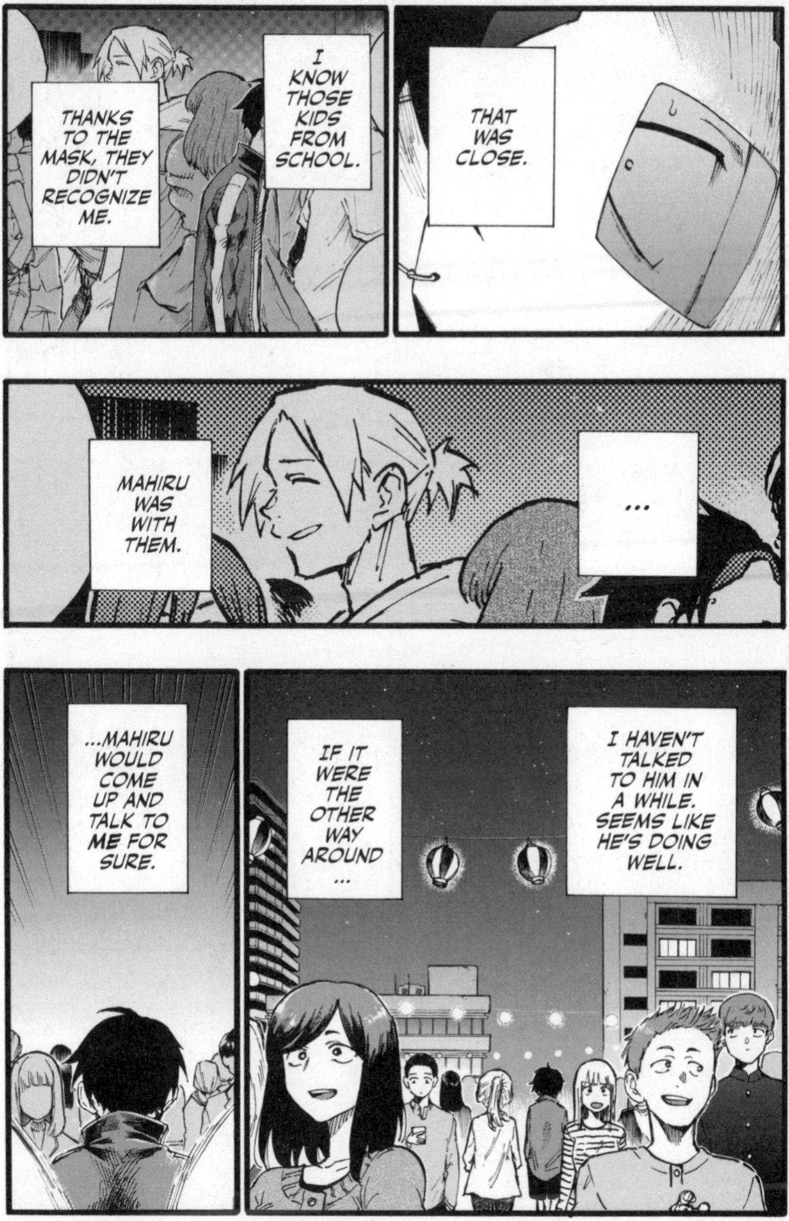
THAT WAS CLOSE.
I KNOW THOSE KIDS FROM SCHOOL.
THANKS TO THE MASK, THEY DIDN'T RECOGNIZE ME.
...
MAHIRU WAS WITH THEM.
I HAVEN'T TALKED TO HIM IN A WHILE. SEEMS LIKE HE'S DOING WELL.
IF IT WERE THE OTHER WAY AROUND...
...MAHIRU WOULD COME UP AND TALK TO ME FOR SURE.

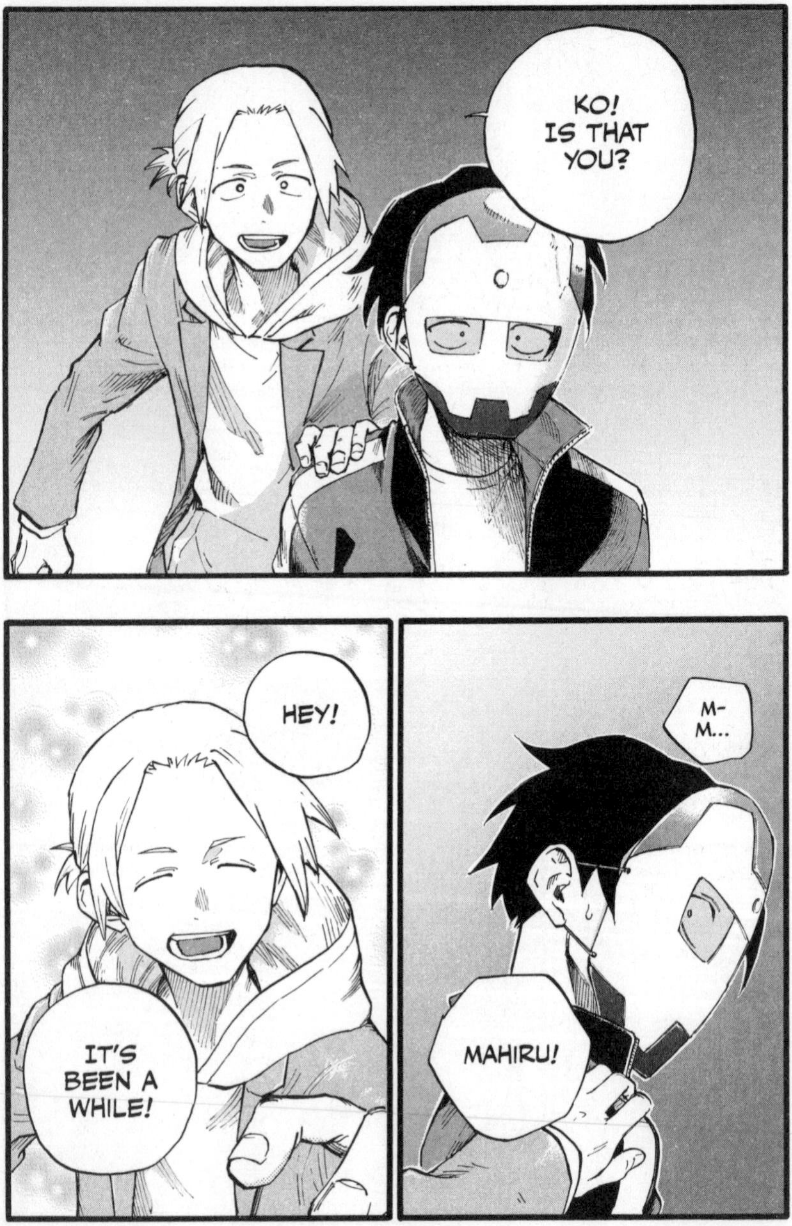
KO! IS THAT YOU?
M- M...
MAHIRU!
HEY!
IT'S BEEN A WHILE!

UGH.
UM.
HEY!
AH.
OH, IT'S NAZUNA.
YOU CHICKS? SIGH.
DON'T BE RUDE.
STOP MAKING THAT FACE!

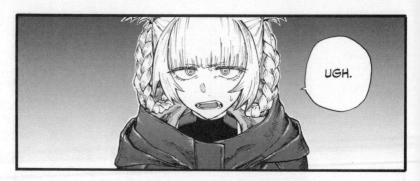

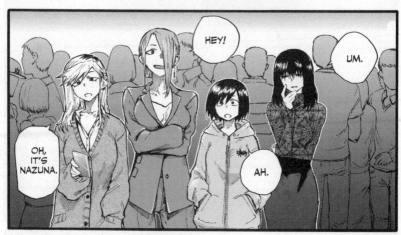

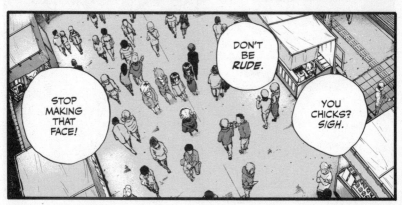

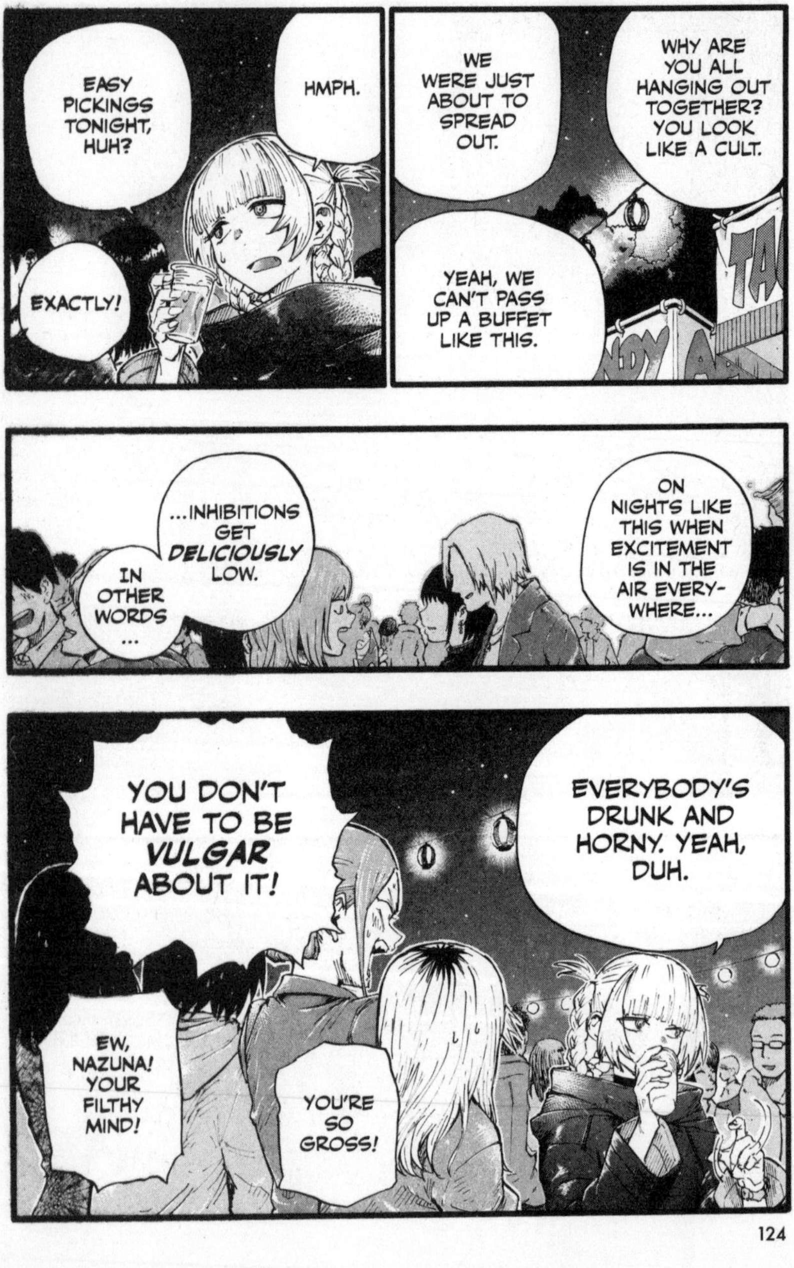
WHY ARE YOU ALL HANGING OUT TOGETHER? YOU LOOK LIKE A CULT.
WE WERE JUST ABOUT TO SPREAD OUT.
YEAH, WE CAN'T PASS UP A BUFFET LIKE THIS.
HMPH.
EASY PICKINGS TONIGHT, HUH?
EXACTLY!
ON NIGHTS LIKE THIS WHEN EXCITEMENT IS IN THE AIR EVERY-WHERE...
...INHIBITIONS GET DELICIOUSLY LOW.
IN OTHER WORDS...
EVERYBODY'S DRUNK AND HORNY. YEAH, DUH.
YOU DON'T HAVE TO BE VULGAR ABOUT IT!
YOU'RE SO GROSS!
EW, NAZUNA! YOUR FILTHY MIND!

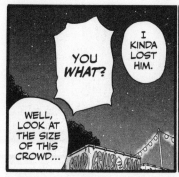

HEY.
WHERE'S YAMORI? ISN'T HE WITH YOU?
I KINDA LOST HIM.
YOU *WHAT?*
WELL, LOOK AT THE SIZE OF THIS CROWD...
IDIOT!! YOU'RE SUPPOSED TO HOLD HANDS SO YOU DON'T GET SEPARATED!
THAT'S RIGHT, NAZUNA. MAKE AN EFFORT.
YOU DOPE.
LAY OFF!
WHEW.
JUST ONE BLOCK OVER, IT'S SO MUCH QUIETER.
YEAH.
Y'KNOW, WE DON'T HAVE TO HANG OUT RIGHT NOW. WEREN'T YOU HERE WITH FRIENDS?
HUH? OH, I JUST BUMPED INTO THEM. WE DIDN'T COME TOGETHER.
OH, OKAY.
I CAN'T BELIEVE YOU RECOGNIZED ME!
I WAS WEARING THIS TO STAY INCOGNITO.

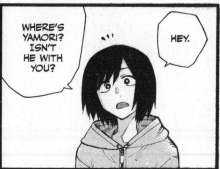

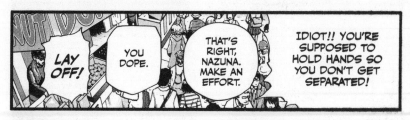

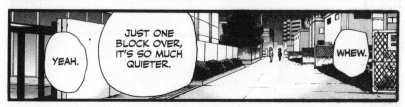

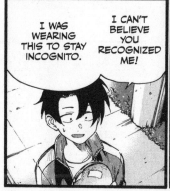

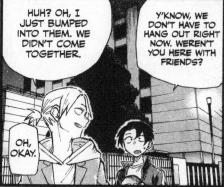

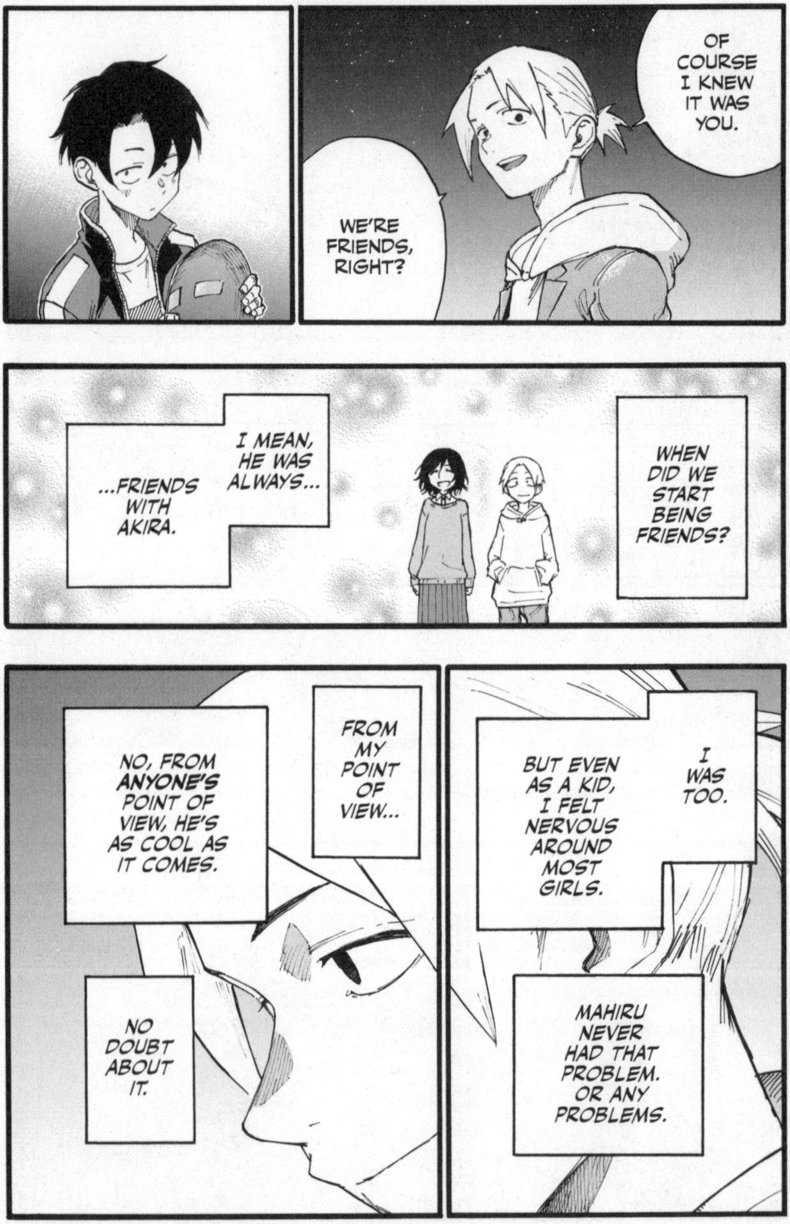
OF COURSE I KNEW IT WAS YOU.
WE'RE FRIENDS, RIGHT?
WHEN DID WE START BEING FRIENDS?
I MEAN, HE WAS ALWAYS...
...FRIENDS WITH AKIRA.
I WAS TOO.
BUT EVEN AS A KID, I FELT NERVOUS AROUND MOST GIRLS.
MAHIRU NEVER HAD THAT PROBLEM. OR ANY PROBLEMS.
FROM MY POINT OF VIEW...
NO, FROM ANYONE'S POINT OF VIEW, HE'S AS COOL AS IT COMES.
NO DOUBT ABOUT IT.

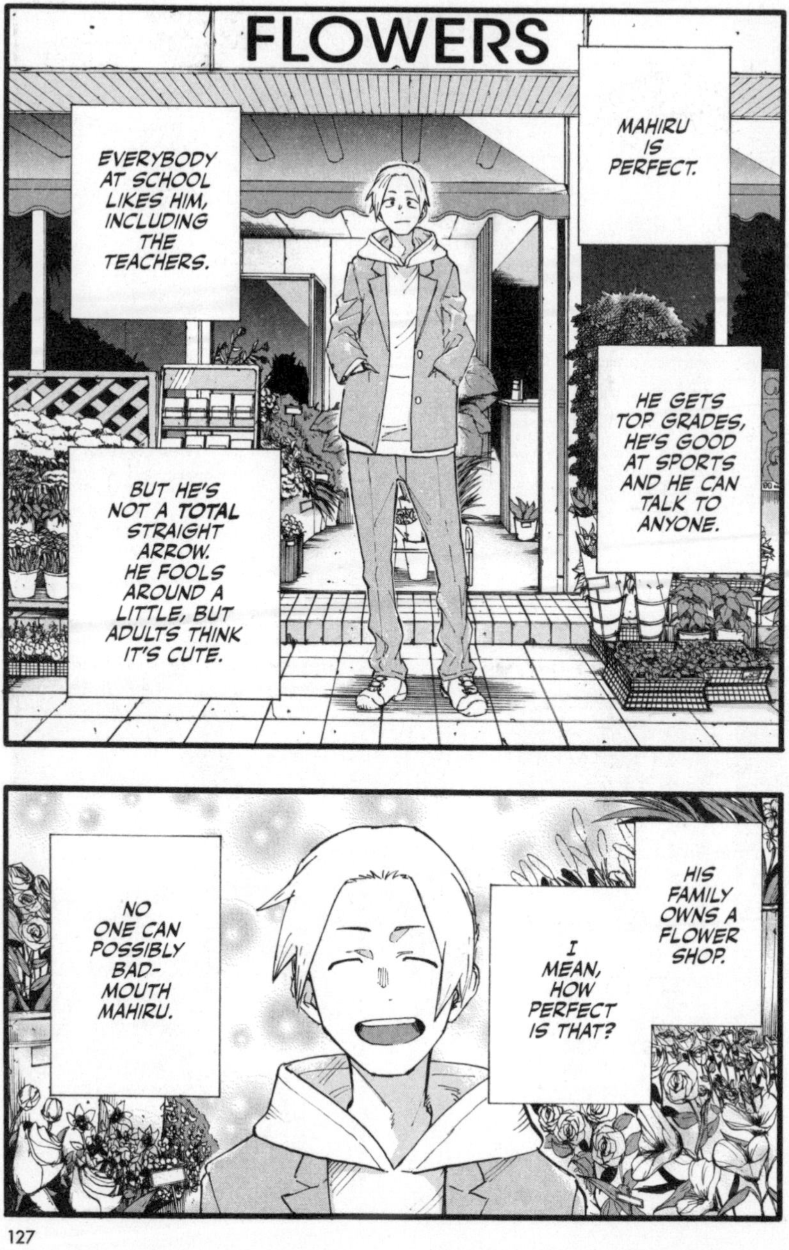
FLOWERS
MAHIRU IS PERFECT.
EVERYBODY AT SCHOOL LIKES HIM, INCLUDING THE TEACHERS.
HE GETS TOP GRADES, HE'S GOOD AT SPORTS AND HE CAN TALK TO ANYONE.
BUT HE'S NOT A **TOTAL** STRAIGHT ARROW. HE FOOLS AROUND A LITTLE, BUT ADULTS THINK IT'S CUTE.
HIS FAMILY OWNS A FLOWER SHOP.
I MEAN, HOW PERFECT IS THAT?
NO ONE CAN POSSIBLY BAD-MOUTH MAHIRU.

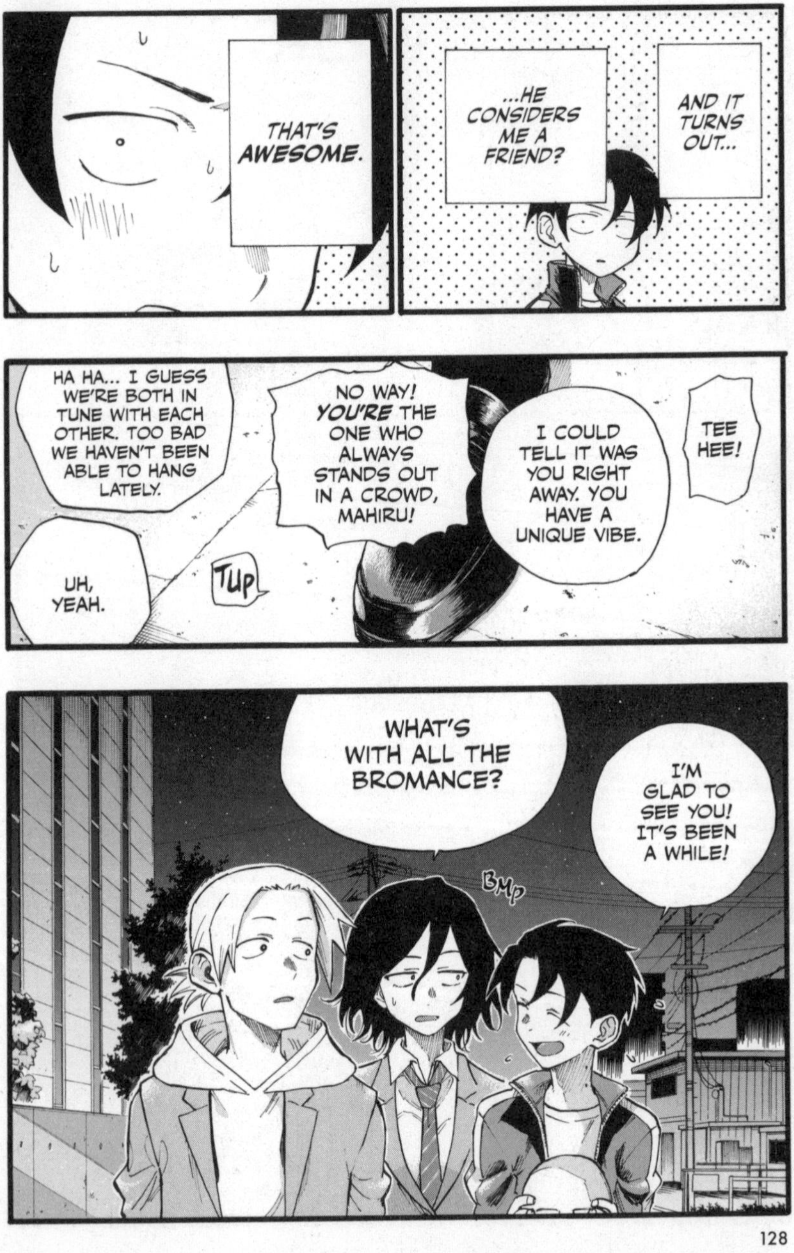

AND IT TURNS OUT...
...HE CONSIDERS ME A FRIEND?
THAT'S AWESOME.
TEE HEE!
I COULD TELL IT WAS YOU RIGHT AWAY. YOU HAVE A UNIQUE VIBE.
NO WAY! YOU'RE THE ONE WHO ALWAYS STANDS OUT IN A CROWD, MAHIRU!
TUP
HA HA... I GUESS WE'RE BOTH IN TUNE WITH EACH OTHER. TOO BAD WE HAVEN'T BEEN ABLE TO HANG LATELY.
UH, YEAH.
I'M GLAD TO SEE YOU! IT'S BEEN A WHILE!
BMP
WHAT'S WITH ALL THE BROMANCE?

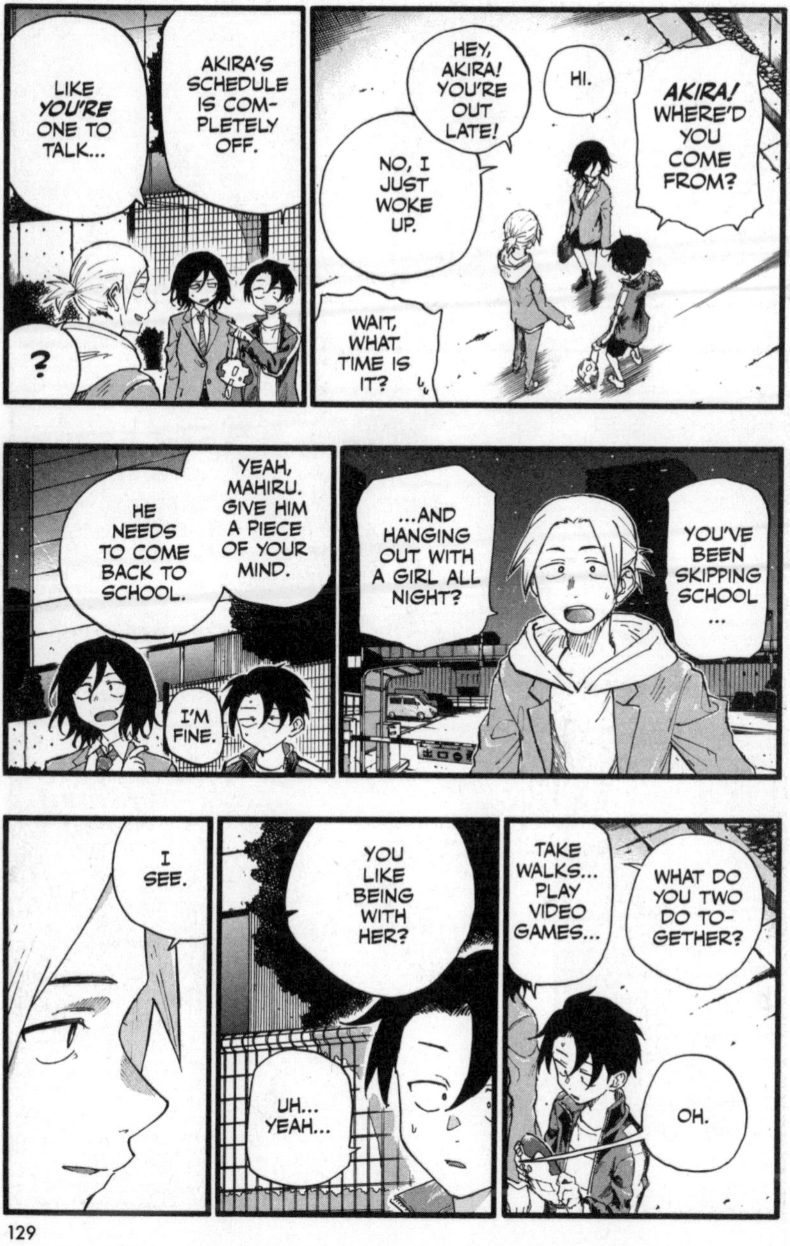
AKIRA! WHERE'D YOU COME FROM?
HI.
HEY, AKIRA! YOU'RE OUT LATE!
NO, I JUST WOKE UP.
WAIT, WHAT TIME IS IT?
AKIRA'S SCHEDULE IS COMPLETELY OFF.
LIKE *YOU'RE* ONE TO TALK...
?
YOU'VE BEEN SKIPPING SCHOOL...
...AND HANGING OUT WITH A GIRL ALL NIGHT?
YEAH, MAHIRU. GIVE HIM A PIECE OF YOUR MIND.
HE NEEDS TO COME BACK TO SCHOOL.
I'M FINE.
WHAT DO YOU TWO DO TOGETHER?
TAKE WALKS... PLAY VIDEO GAMES...
OH.
YOU LIKE BEING WITH HER?
UH... YEAH...
I SEE.

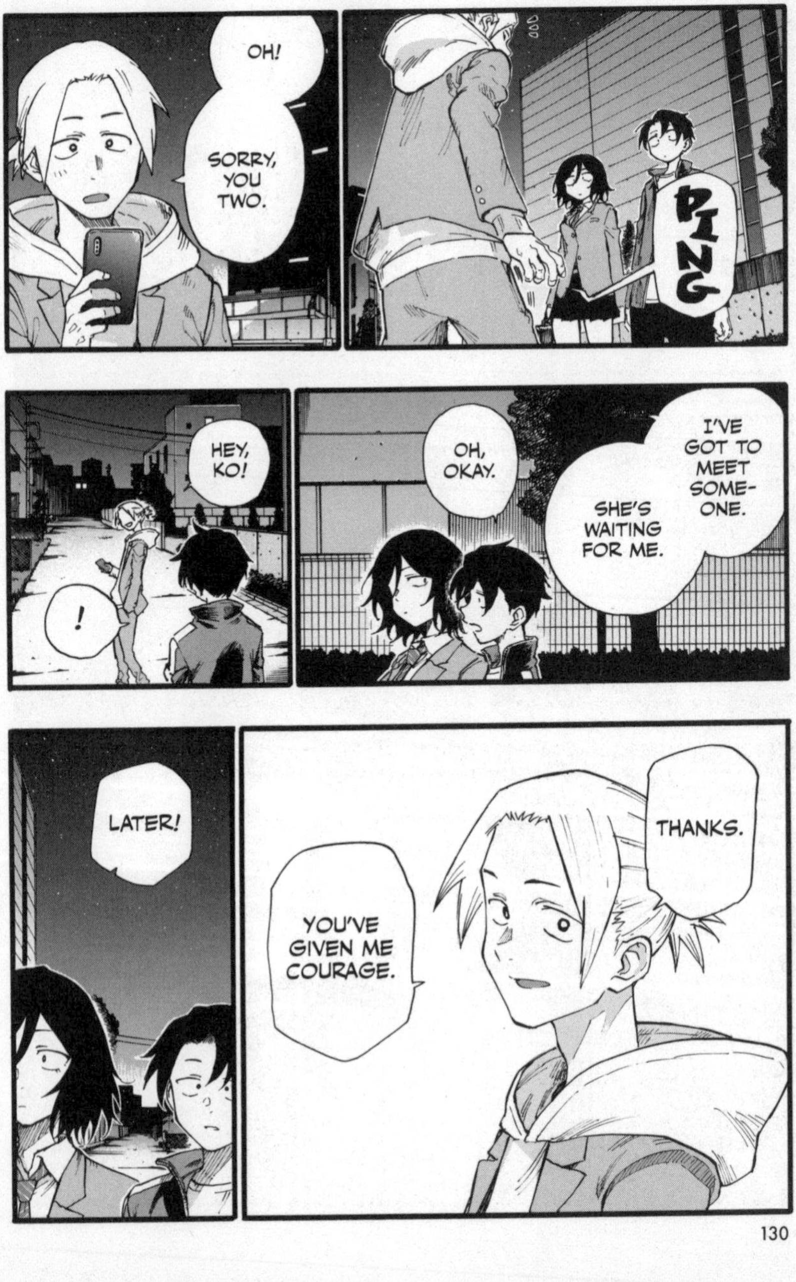
PING
OH!
SORRY, YOU TWO.
I'VE GOT TO MEET SOME-ONE.
SHE'S WAITING FOR ME.
OH, OKAY.
HEY, KO!
!
THANKS.
YOU'VE GIVEN ME COURAGE.
LATER!

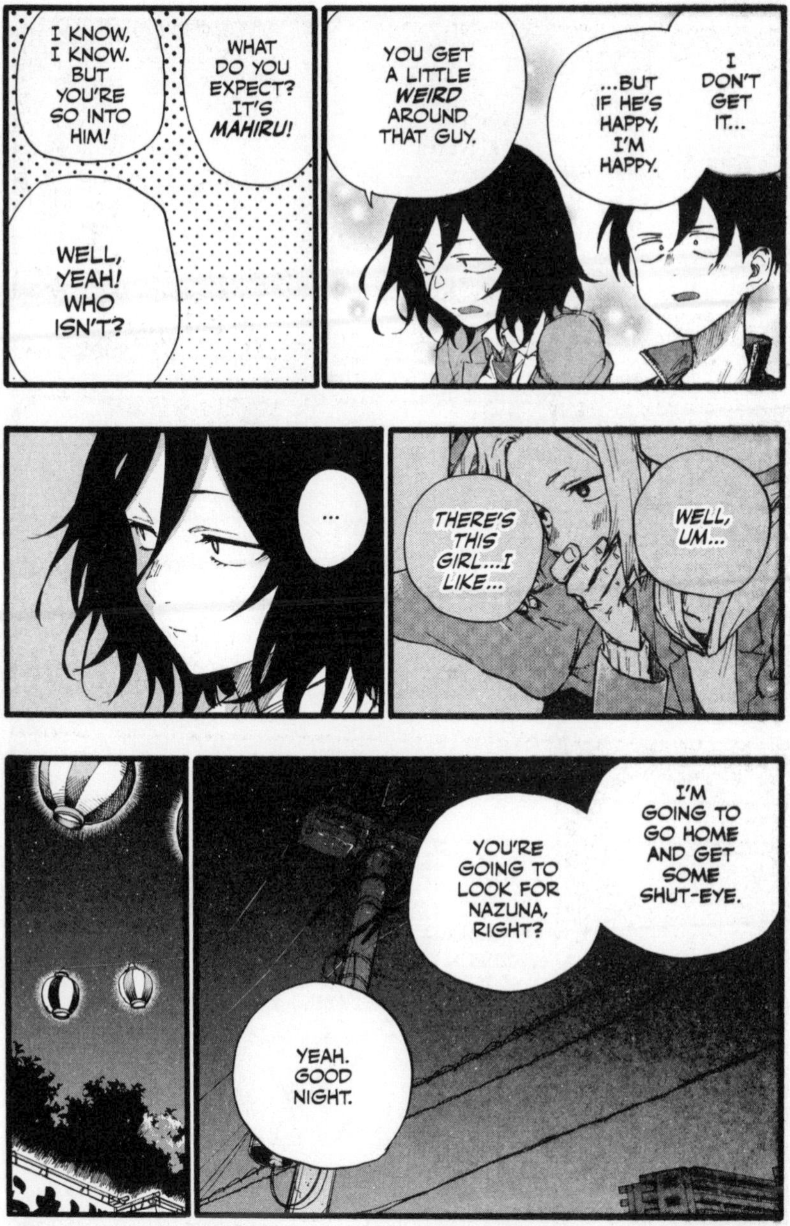
I DON'T GET IT...
...BUT IF HE'S HAPPY, I'M HAPPY.
YOU GET A LITTLE WEIRD AROUND THAT GUY.
WHAT DO YOU EXPECT? IT'S MAHIRU!
I KNOW, I KNOW. BUT YOU'RE SO INTO HIM!
WELL, YEAH! WHO ISN'T?
WELL, UM...
THERE'S THIS GIRL...I LIKE...
...
I'M GOING TO GO HOME AND GET SOME SHUT-EYE.
YOU'RE GOING TO LOOK FOR NAZUNA, RIGHT?
YEAH. GOOD NIGHT.

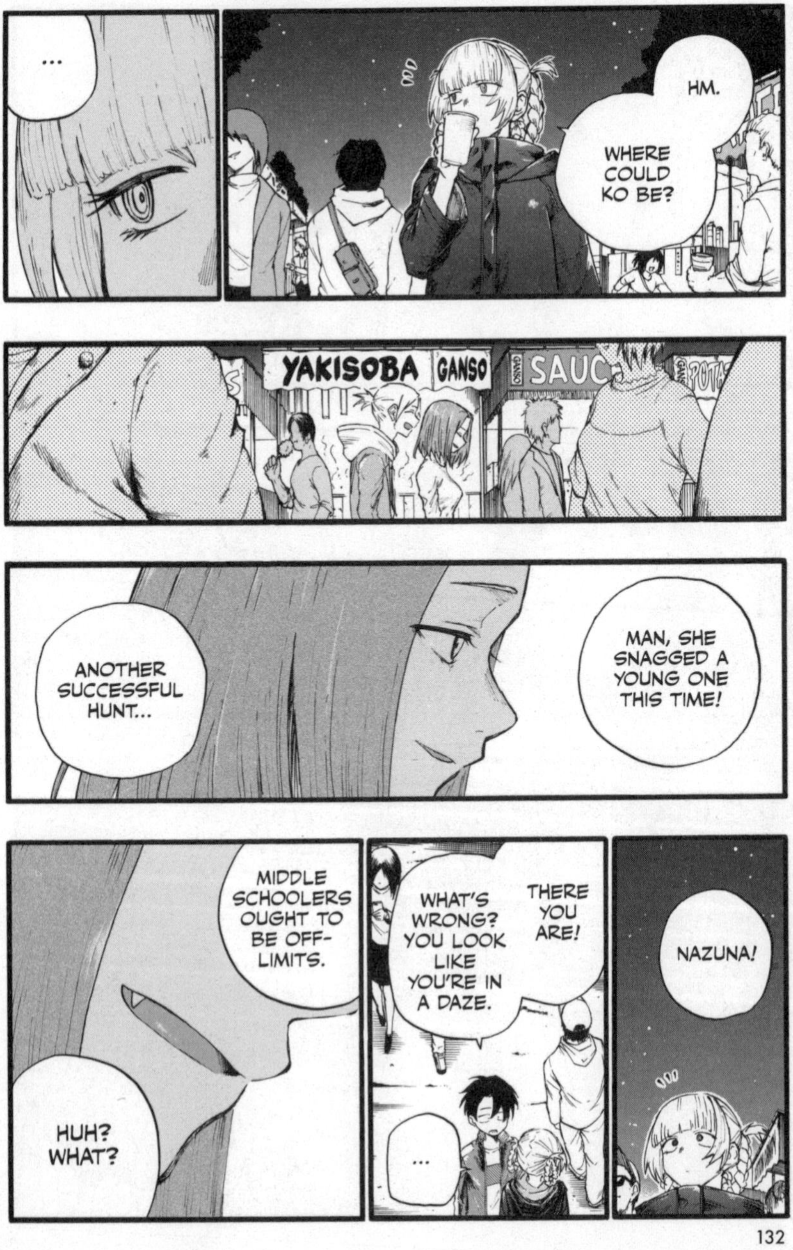
HM.
WHERE COULD KO BE?
...
YAKISOBA
GANSO
MAN, SHE SNAGGED A YOUNG ONE THIS TIME!
ANOTHER SUCCESSFUL HUNT...
NAZUNA!
THERE YOU ARE!
WHAT'S WRONG? YOU LOOK LIKE YOU'RE IN A DAZE.
...
MIDDLE SCHOOLERS OUGHT TO BE OFF-LIMITS.
HUH? WHAT?

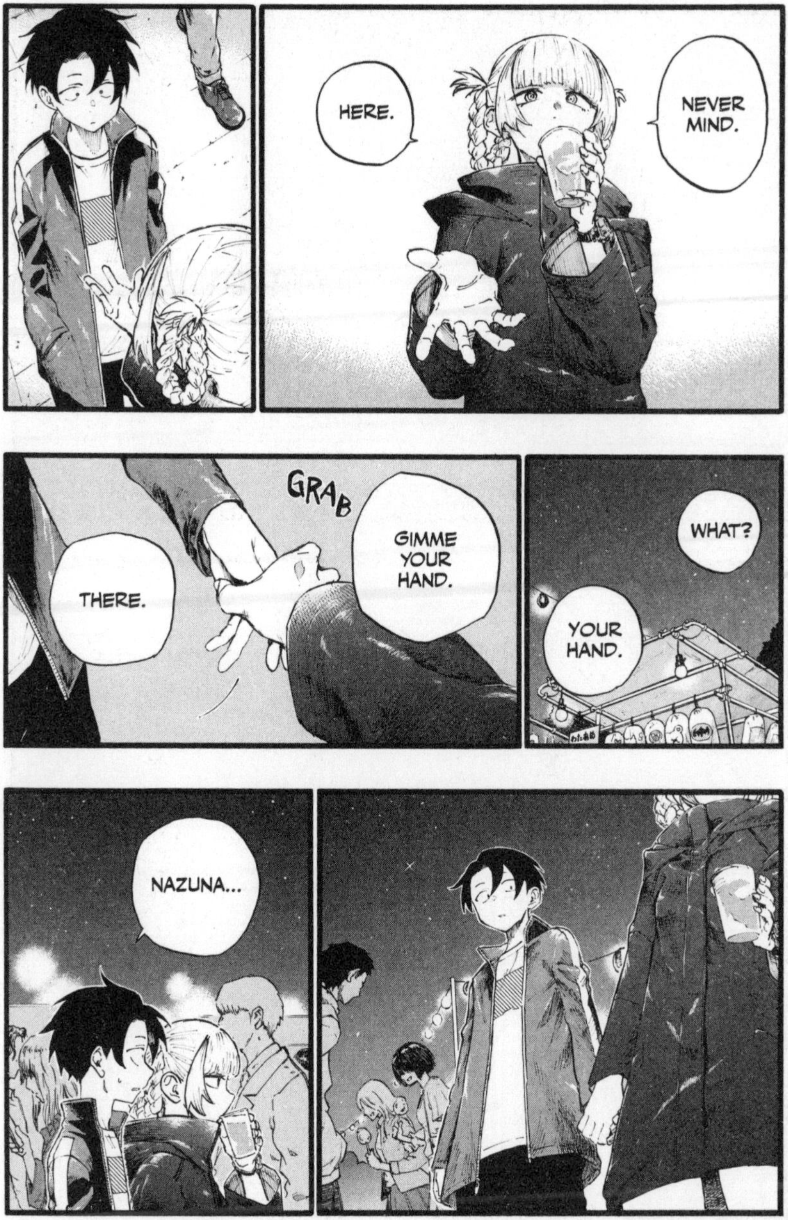
NEVER MIND.
HERE.
WHAT?
YOUR HAND.
GRAB
GIMME YOUR HAND.
THERE.
NAZUNA...

I CAN'T TAKE MY EYES OFF YOU FOR A MINUTE, CAN I?

YOU'RE THE ONE WHO GOT LOST!

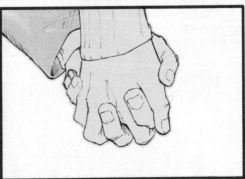

NIGHT 26: YOU KNOW THOSE HAREM MANGA?

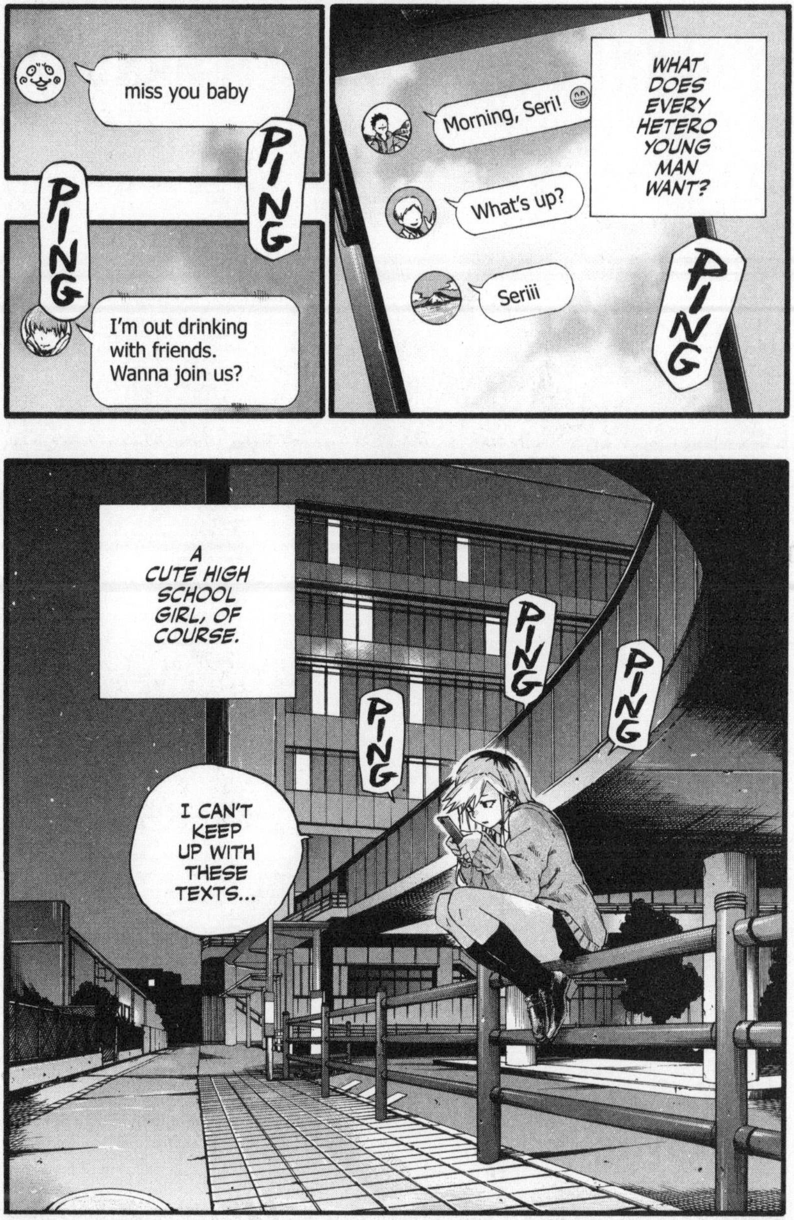
WHAT DOES EVERY HETERO YOUNG MAN WANT?
Morning, Seri!
What's up?
Seriii
PING
miss you baby
PING
PING
I'm out drinking with friends. Wanna join us?
A CUTE HIGH SCHOOL GIRL, OF COURSE.
PING
PING
PING
I CAN'T KEEP UP WITH THESE TEXTS...

NIGHT 26:

YOU KNOW THOSE HAREM MANGA?

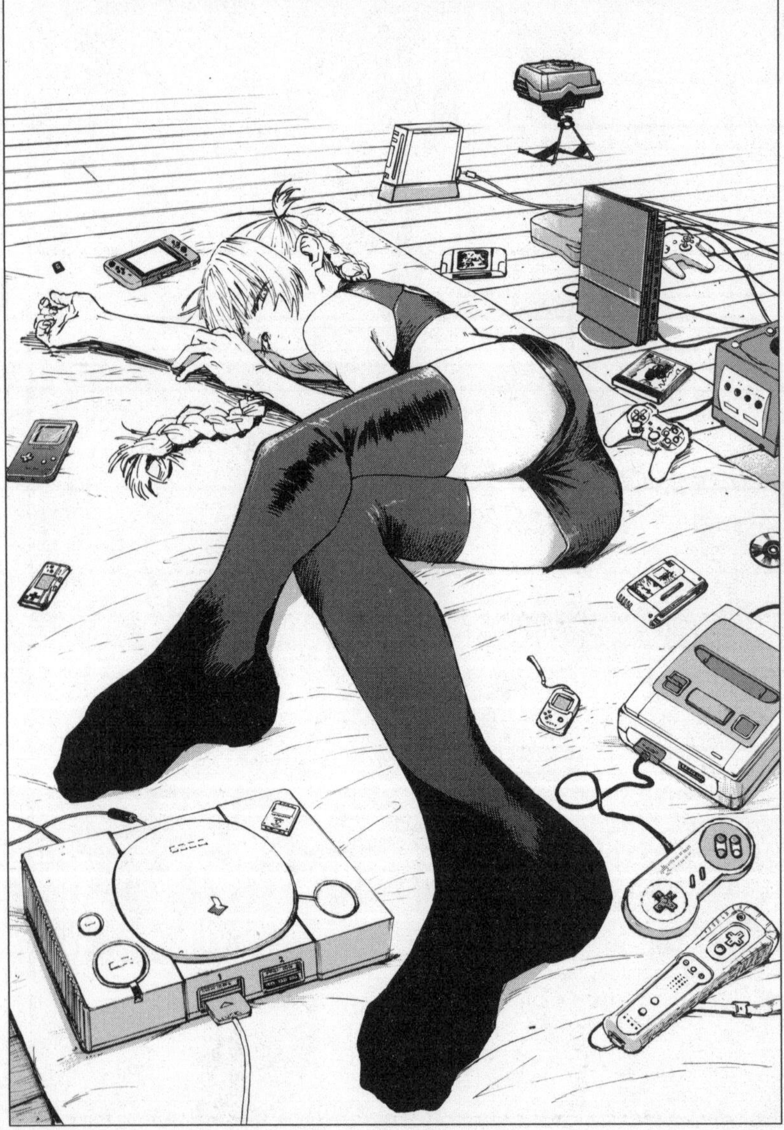

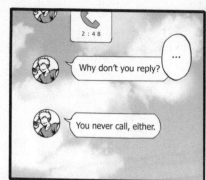

PING
!
2:48
...
Why don't you reply?
You never call, either.
...
UGH, I HATE IT WHEN THEY GET ALL CLINGY.
I CAN'T BELIEVE I CONSIDERED *TURNING* THAT LOSER.
GUYS LIKE THAT SEEM GREAT AT THE START.
I'm not like this with everyone.
I feel like I can really open up to you, LOL...
THEN THEY GO TOTALLY **MENTAL.**
AND YOU HAVE TO DUMP 'EM. **SUCH A DRAG.**
I'm not crazy, am I? Who keeps texting you?
Are you seeing other guys? It's okay. You can tell me.

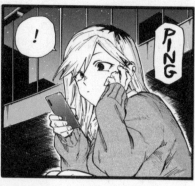

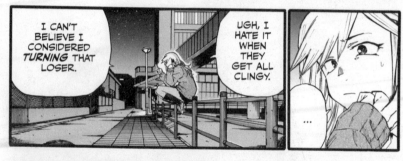

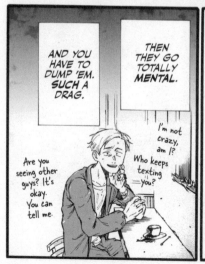

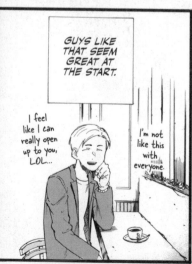

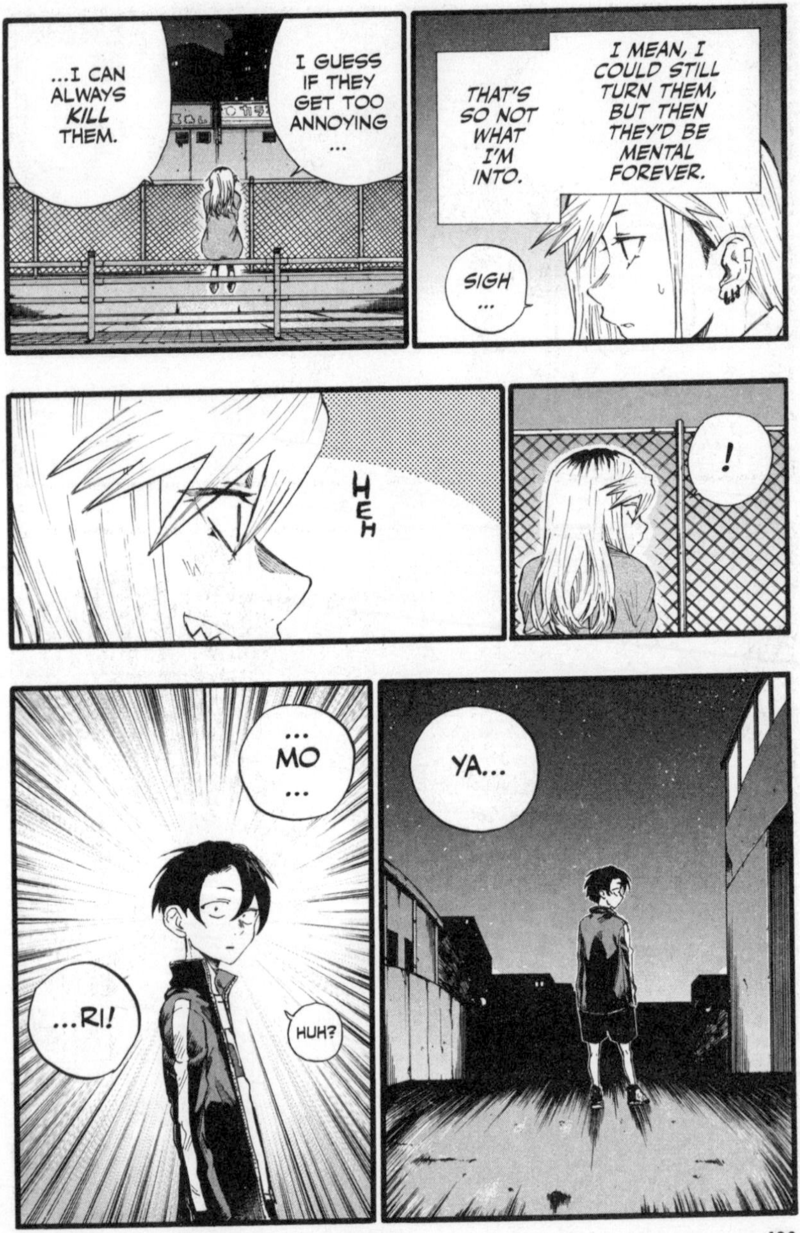
I MEAN, I COULD STILL TURN THEM, BUT THEN THEY'D BE MENTAL FOREVER.
THAT'S SO NOT WHAT I'M INTO.
SIGH ...
I GUESS IF THEY GET TOO ANNOYING ...
...I CAN ALWAYS KILL THEM.
!
HEH
YA...
... MO ...
HUH?
...RI!

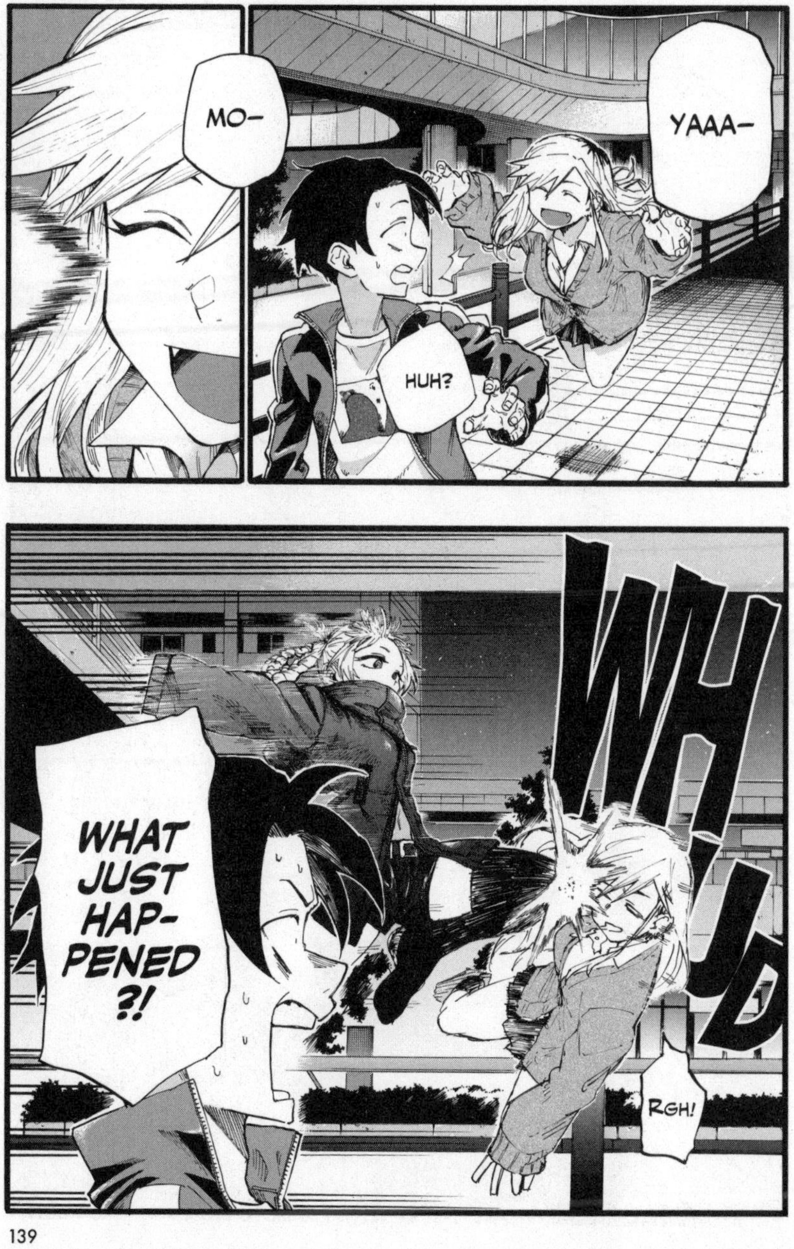
YAAA-
HUH?
MO-
WHUD
RGH!
WHAT JUST HAP-PENED?!

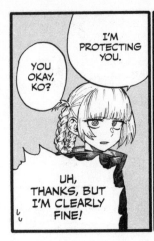

Nngh... koff koff...
Na... zuna...
WHAT WAS THAT ALL ABOUT?
...
You are so dead...
SHE DIDN'T DO ANY-THING!
I'M PROTECTING YOU.
YOU OKAY, KO?
UH, THANKS, BUT I'M CLEARLY FINE!
SORRY. EVERY TIME I GET A LOOK AT HER FACE, I SEE RED AND I GET THE KICKY LEGS...
SO IT'S NOT ABOUT PROTECTING ME AT ALL!
SHE'LL BE FINE. FOR A VAMPIRE, THIS IS NOTH-
UM.
-ING.
THOK

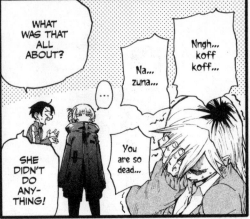

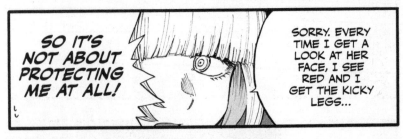

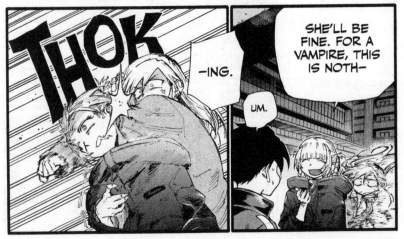

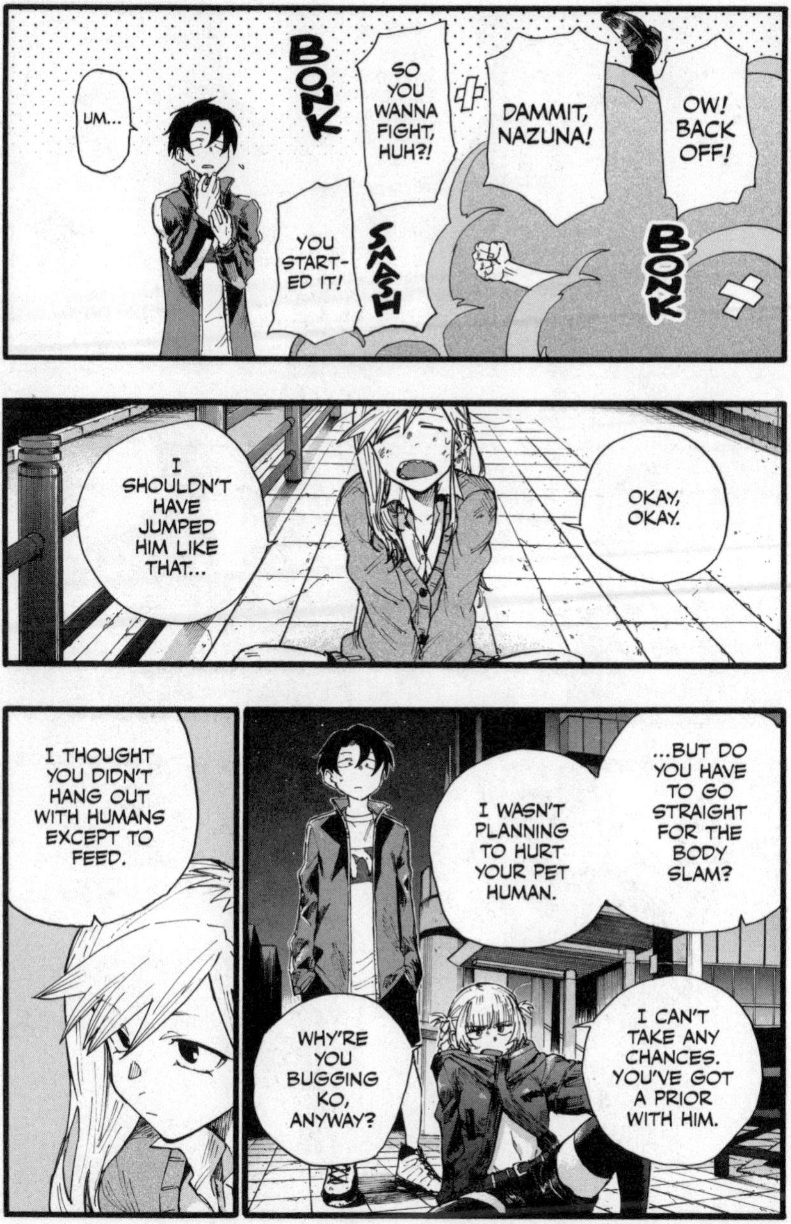
OW! BACK OFF!
BONK
DAMMIT, NAZUNA!
SO YOU WANNA FIGHT, HUH?!
BONK
SMASH
YOU START-ED IT!
UM...
OKAY, OKAY.
I SHOULDN'T HAVE JUMPED HIM LIKE THAT...
...BUT DO YOU HAVE TO GO STRAIGHT FOR THE BODY SLAM?
I WASN'T PLANNING TO HURT YOUR PET HUMAN.
I CAN'T TAKE ANY CHANCES. YOU'VE GOT A PRIOR WITH HIM.
WHY'RE YOU BUGGING KO, ANYWAY?
I THOUGHT YOU DIDN'T HANG OUT WITH HUMANS EXCEPT TO FEED.

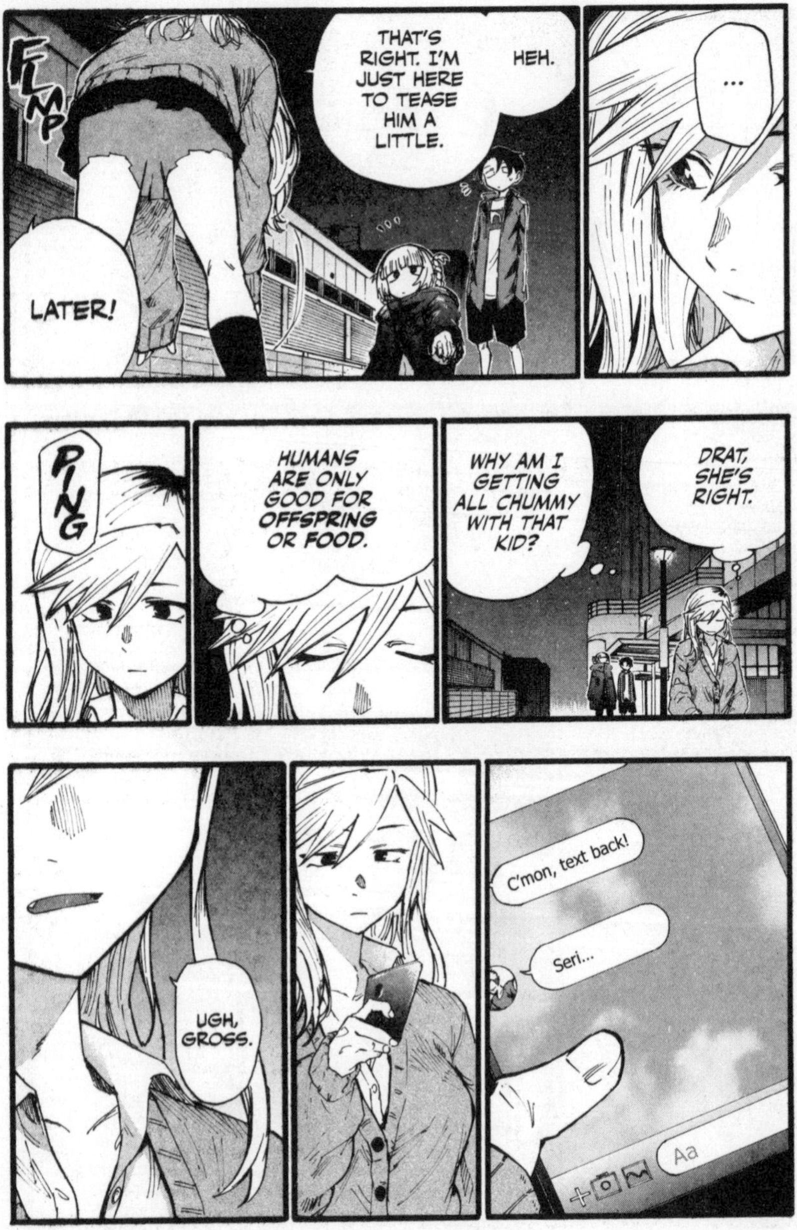
...
HEH.
THAT'S RIGHT. I'M JUST HERE TO TEASE HIM A LITTLE.
FLMP
LATER!
DRAT, SHE'S RIGHT.
WHY AM I GETTING ALL CHUMMY WITH THAT KID?
HUMANS ARE ONLY GOOD FOR OFFSPRING OR FOOD.
PING
C'mon, text back!
Seri...
Aa
UGH, GROSS.

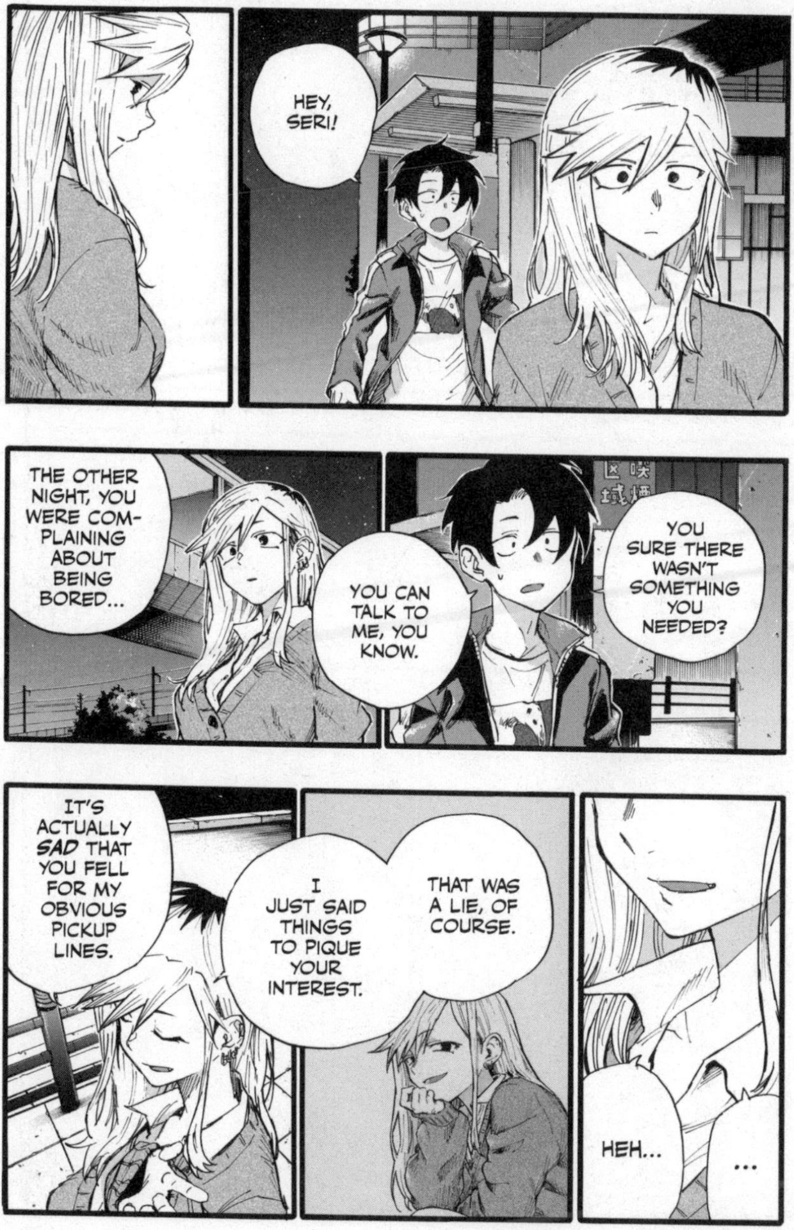
HEY, SERI!
YOU SURE THERE WASN'T SOMETHING YOU NEEDED?
YOU CAN TALK TO ME, YOU KNOW.
THE OTHER NIGHT, YOU WERE COM-PLAINING ABOUT BEING BORED...
...
HEH...
THAT WAS A LIE, OF COURSE.
I JUST SAID THINGS TO PIQUE YOUR INTEREST.
IT'S ACTUALLY *SAD* THAT YOU FELL FOR MY OBVIOUS PICKUP LINES.

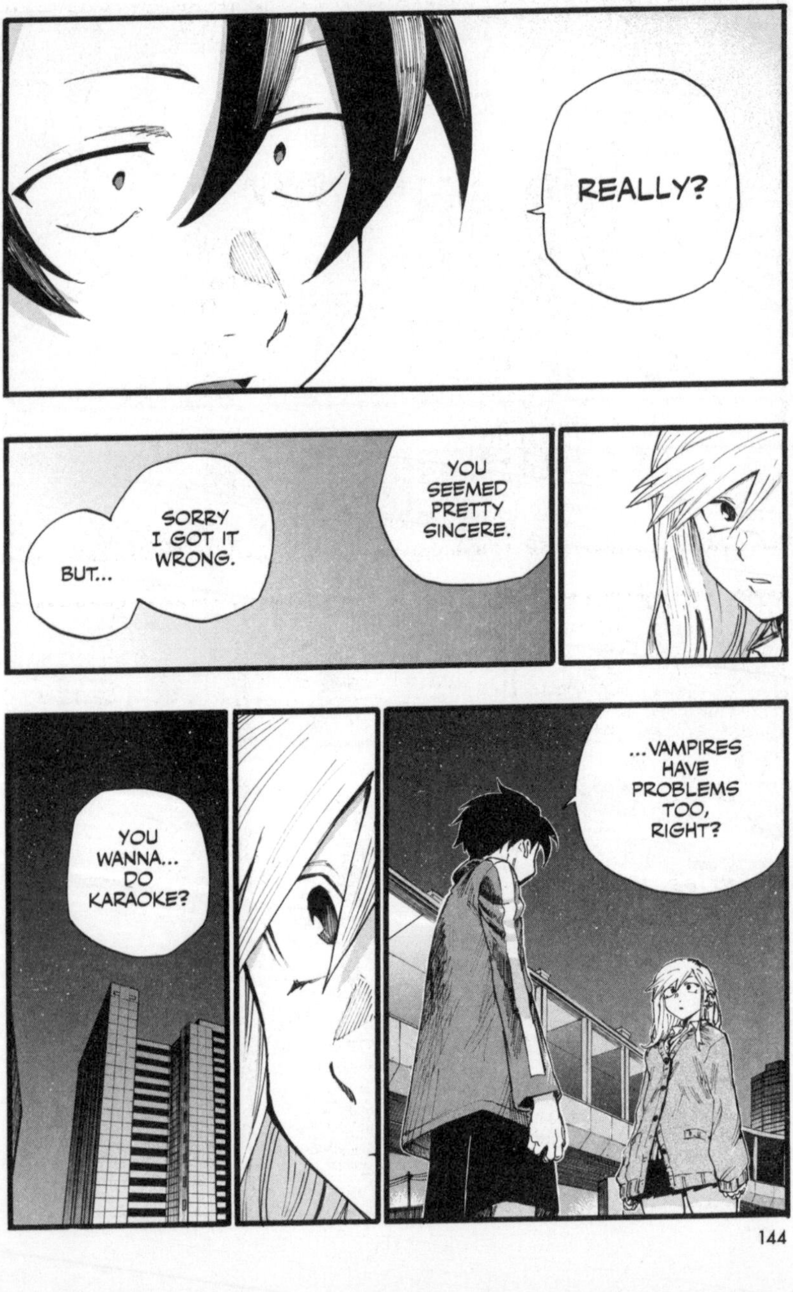
REALLY?
YOU SEEMED PRETTY SINCERE.
SORRY I GOT IT WRONG. BUT...
...VAMPIRES HAVE PROBLEMS TOO, RIGHT?
YOU WANNA... DO KARAOKE?

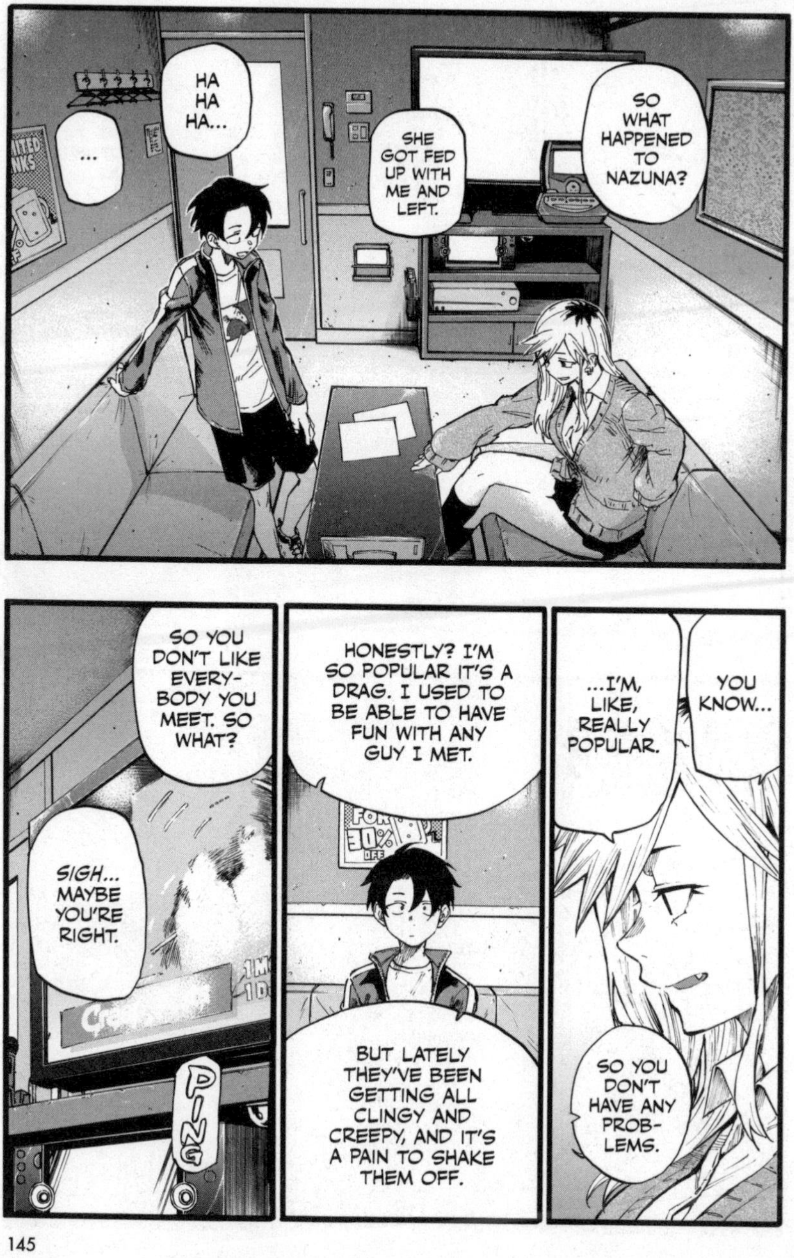
SO WHAT HAPPENED TO NAZUNA?
SHE GOT FED UP WITH ME AND LEFT.
HA HA HA...
...
YOU KNOW...
...I'M, LIKE, REALLY POPULAR.
SO YOU DON'T HAVE ANY PROB-LEMS.
HONESTLY? I'M SO POPULAR IT'S A DRAG. I USED TO BE ABLE TO HAVE FUN WITH ANY GUY I MET.
BUT LATELY THEY'VE BEEN GETTING ALL CLINGY AND CREEPY, AND IT'S A PAIN TO SHAKE THEM OFF.
SO YOU DON'T LIKE EVERY-BODY YOU MEET. SO WHAT?
SIGH... MAYBE YOU'RE RIGHT.
PING

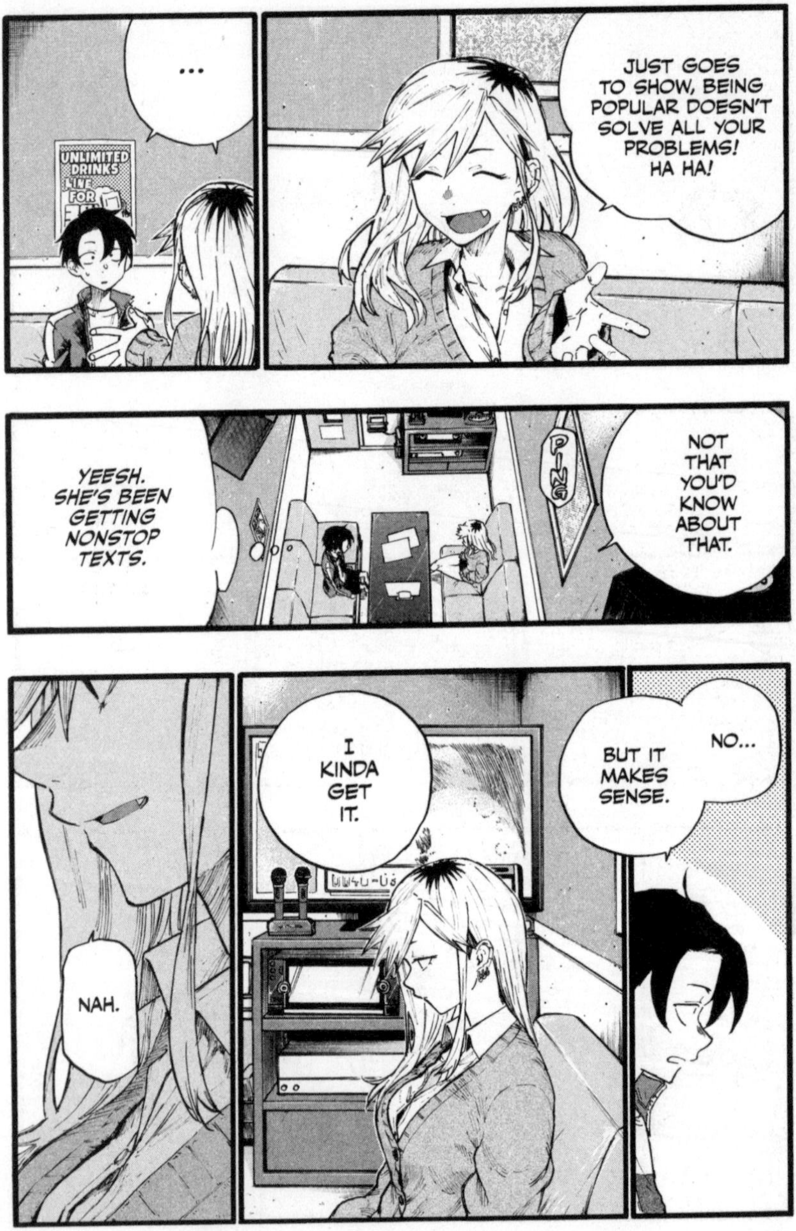
JUST GOES TO SHOW, BEING POPULAR DOESN'T SOLVE ALL YOUR PROBLEMS! HA HA!
UNLIMITED DRINKS
LINE FOR
...
NOT THAT YOU'D KNOW ABOUT THAT.
PING
YEESH. SHE'S BEEN GETTING NONSTOP TEXTS.
NO...
BUT IT MAKES SENSE.
I KINDA GET IT.
NAH.

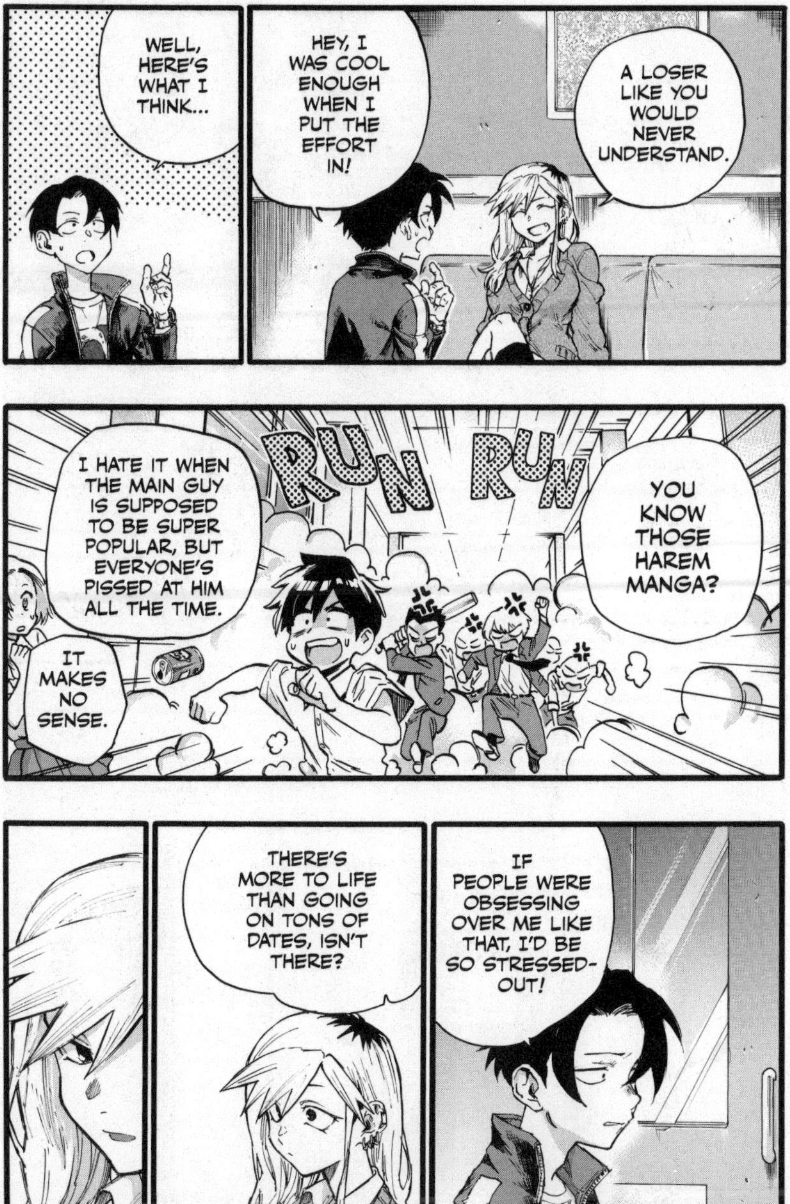
A LOSER LIKE YOU WOULD NEVER UNDERSTAND.
HEY, I WAS COOL ENOUGH WHEN I PUT THE EFFORT IN!
WELL, HERE'S WHAT I THINK...
YOU KNOW THOSE HAREM MANGA?
RUN RUN
I HATE IT WHEN THE MAIN GUY IS SUPPOSED TO BE SUPER POPULAR, BUT EVERYONE'S PISSED AT HIM ALL THE TIME.
IT MAKES NO SENSE.
IF PEOPLE WERE OBSESSING OVER ME LIKE THAT, I'D BE SO STRESSED-OUT!
THERE'S MORE TO LIFE THAN GOING ON TONS OF DATES, ISN'T THERE?

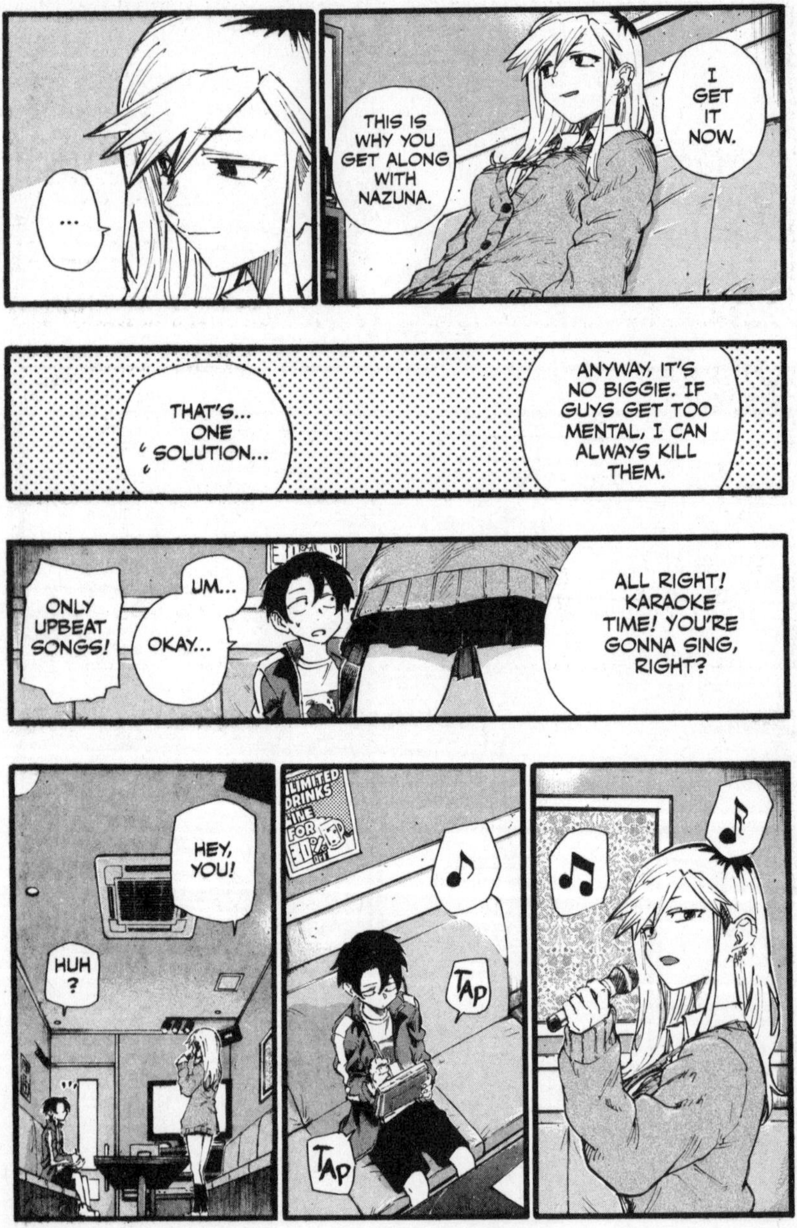
I GET IT NOW.
THIS IS WHY YOU GET ALONG WITH NAZUNA.
...
ANYWAY, IT'S NO BIGGIE. IF GUYS GET TOO MENTAL, I CAN ALWAYS KILL THEM.
THAT'S... ONE SOLUTION...
ALL RIGHT! KARAOKE TIME! YOU'RE GONNA SING, RIGHT?
UM...
OKAY...
ONLY UPBEAT SONGS!
♪
♪
UNLIMITED DRINKS
♪
TAP
TAP
HEY, YOU!
HUH?

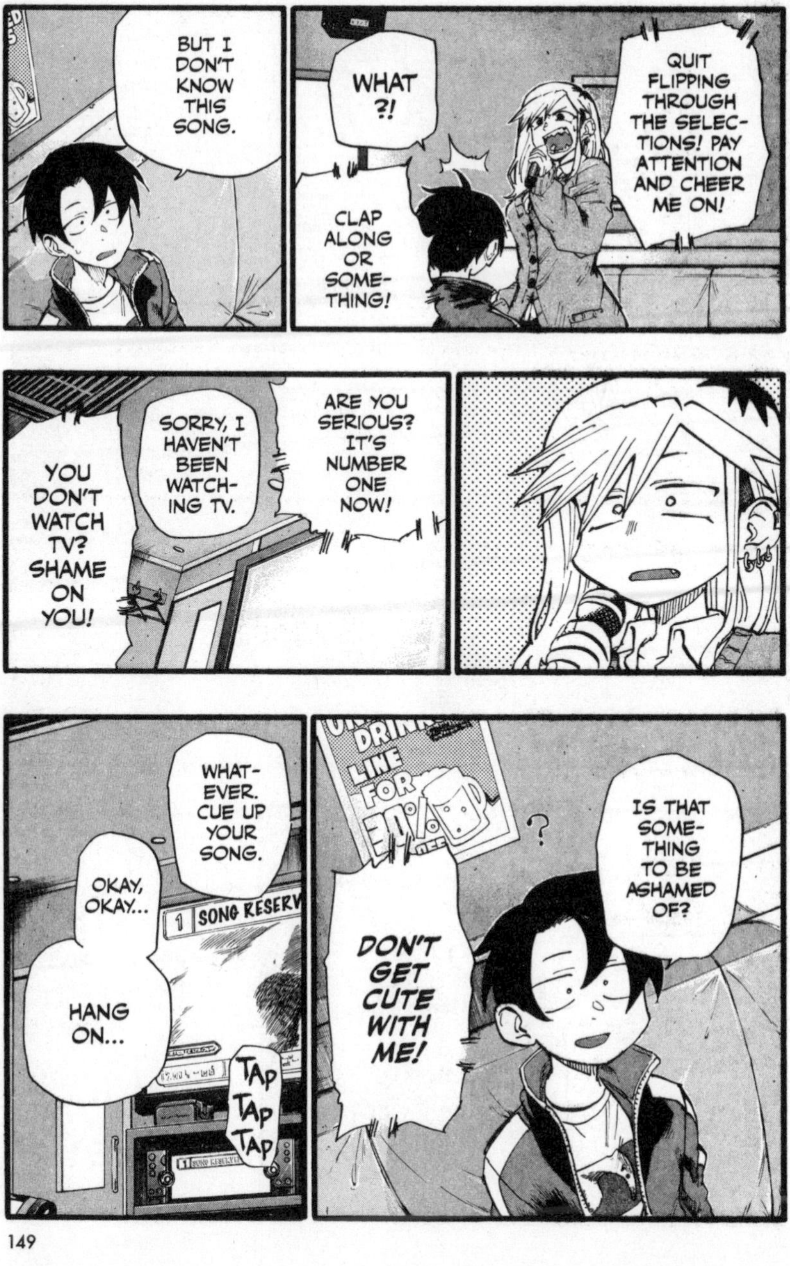
QUIT FLIPPING THROUGH THE SELECTIONS! PAY ATTENTION AND CHEER ME ON!
WHAT?!
CLAP ALONG OR SOMETHING!
BUT I DON'T KNOW THIS SONG.
ARE YOU SERIOUS? IT'S NUMBER ONE NOW!
SORRY, I HAVEN'T BEEN WATCHING TV.
YOU DON'T WATCH TV? SHAME ON YOU!
DRINK
LINE FOR
?
IS THAT SOMETHING TO BE ASHAMED OF?
DON'T GET CUTE WITH ME!
WHATEVER. CUE UP YOUR SONG.
OKAY, OKAY...
SONG RESERV
HANG ON...
TAP TAP TAP

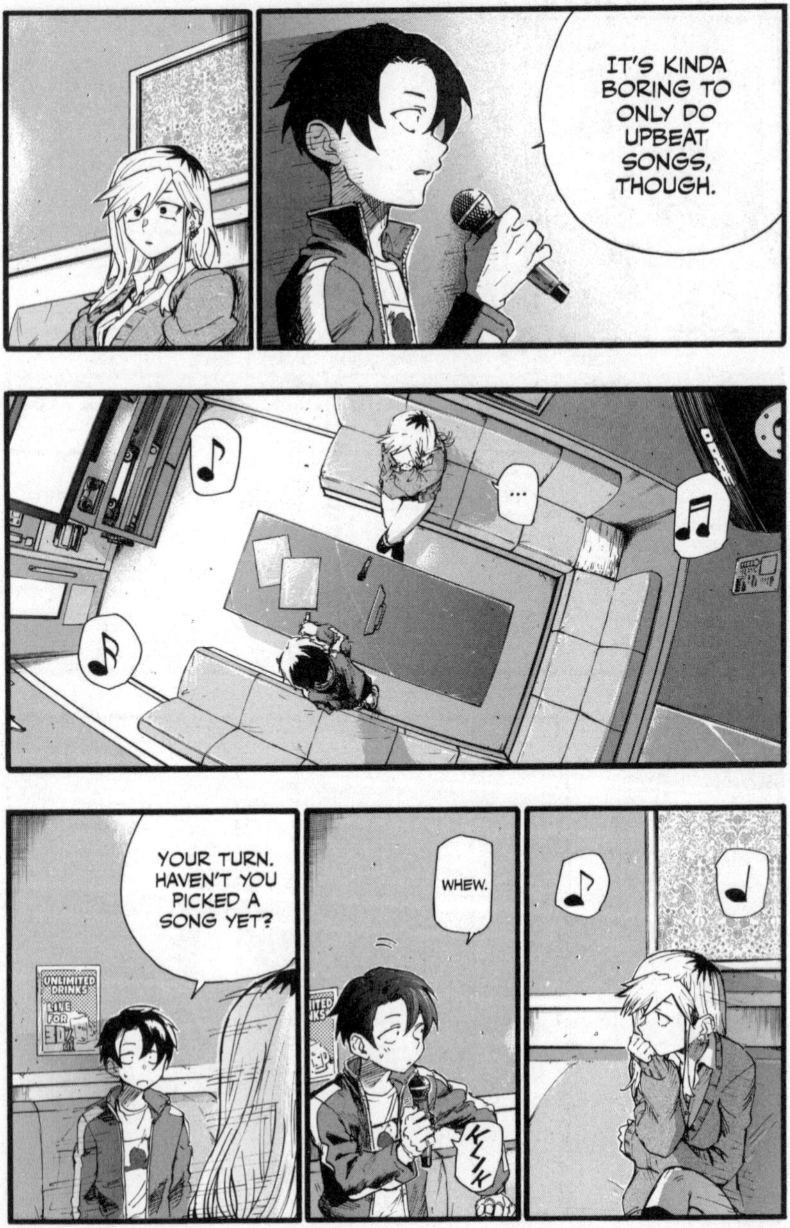
IT'S KINDA BORING TO ONLY DO UPBEAT SONGS, THOUGH.
...
WHEW.
KLIK
YOUR TURN. HAVEN'T YOU PICKED A SONG YET?
UNLIMITED DRINKS

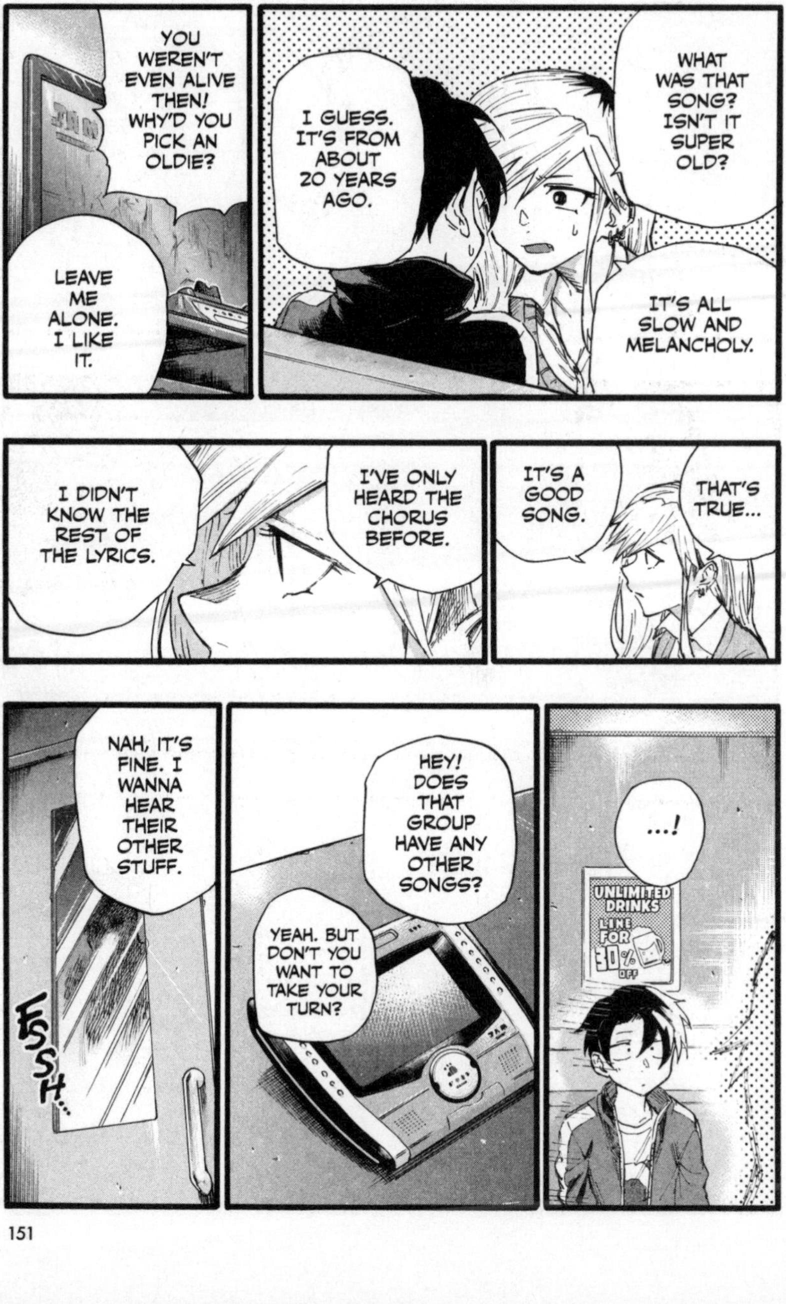
WHAT WAS THAT SONG? ISN'T IT SUPER OLD?
I GUESS. IT'S FROM ABOUT 20 YEARS AGO.
IT'S ALL SLOW AND MELANCHOLY.
YOU WEREN'T EVEN ALIVE THEN! WHY'D YOU PICK AN OLDIE?
LEAVE ME ALONE. I LIKE IT.
THAT'S TRUE...
IT'S A GOOD SONG.
I'VE ONLY HEARD THE CHORUS BEFORE.
I DIDN'T KNOW THE REST OF THE LYRICS.
...!
UNLIMITED DRINKS
LINE FOR 30% OFF
HEY! DOES THAT GROUP HAVE ANY OTHER SONGS?
YEAH. BUT DON'T YOU WANT TO TAKE YOUR TURN?
NAH, IT'S FINE. I WANNA HEAR THEIR OTHER STUFF.
FSSH...

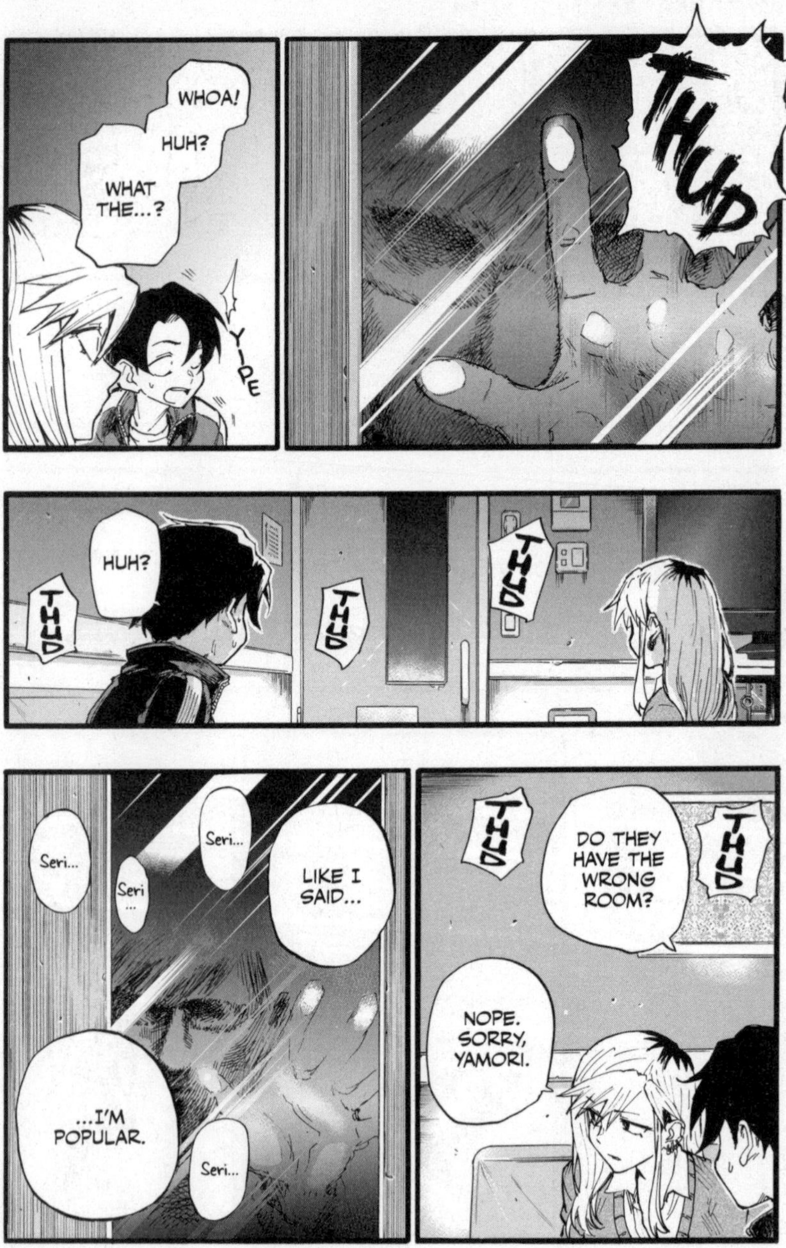
THUD
WHOA!
HUH?
WHAT THE...?
YIPE
THUD
THUD
HUH?
THUD
THUD
DO THEY HAVE THE WRONG ROOM?
THUD
NOPE. SORRY, YAMORI.
LIKE I SAID...
Seri...
Seri...
Seri...
...I'M POPULAR.
Seri...

NIGHT 27: **WHAT ARE YOU TO HER?**

WHAT DOES IT MEAN TO BE "MENTAL"?

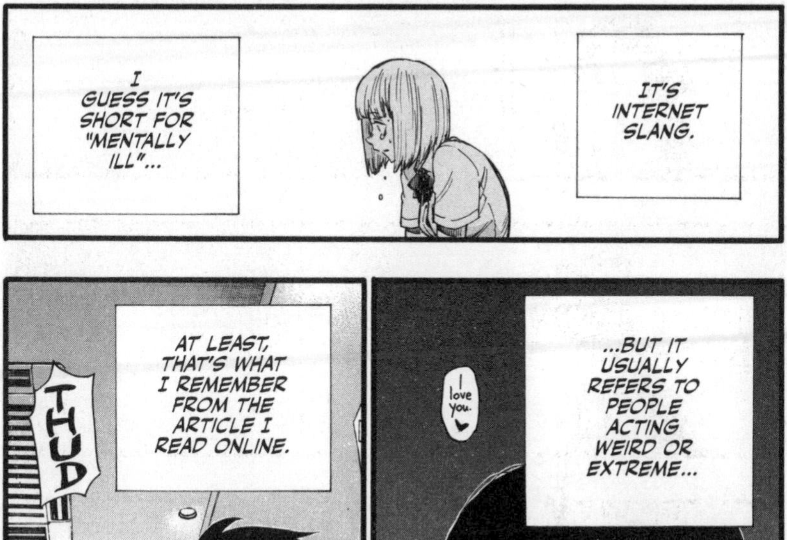

IT'S INTERNET SLANG.
I GUESS IT'S SHORT FOR "MENTALLY ILL"...
...BUT IT USUALLY REFERS TO PEOPLE ACTING WEIRD OR EXTREME...
I love you.
I love you.
I love you.
...BECAUSE THEY'RE LOVESICK.
AT LEAST, THAT'S WHAT I REMEMBER FROM THE ARTICLE I READ ONLINE.
THUD
...
I COULDN'T RELATE TO IT AT ALL.
THUD

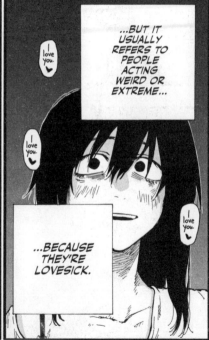

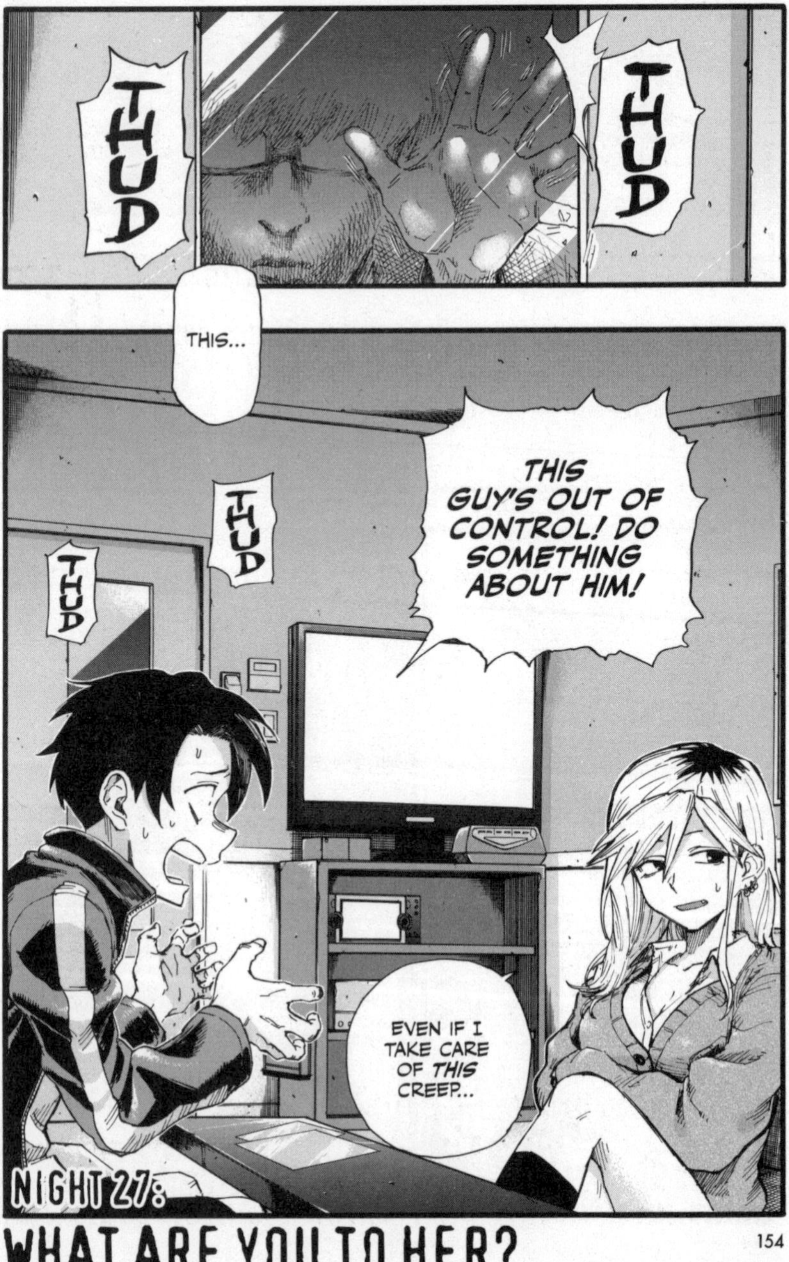
THUD
THUD
THIS...
THUD
THUD
THIS GUY'S OUT OF CONTROL! DO SOMETHING ABOUT HIM!
EVEN IF I TAKE CARE OF *THIS* CREEP...

NIGHT 27: WHAT ARE YOU TO HER?

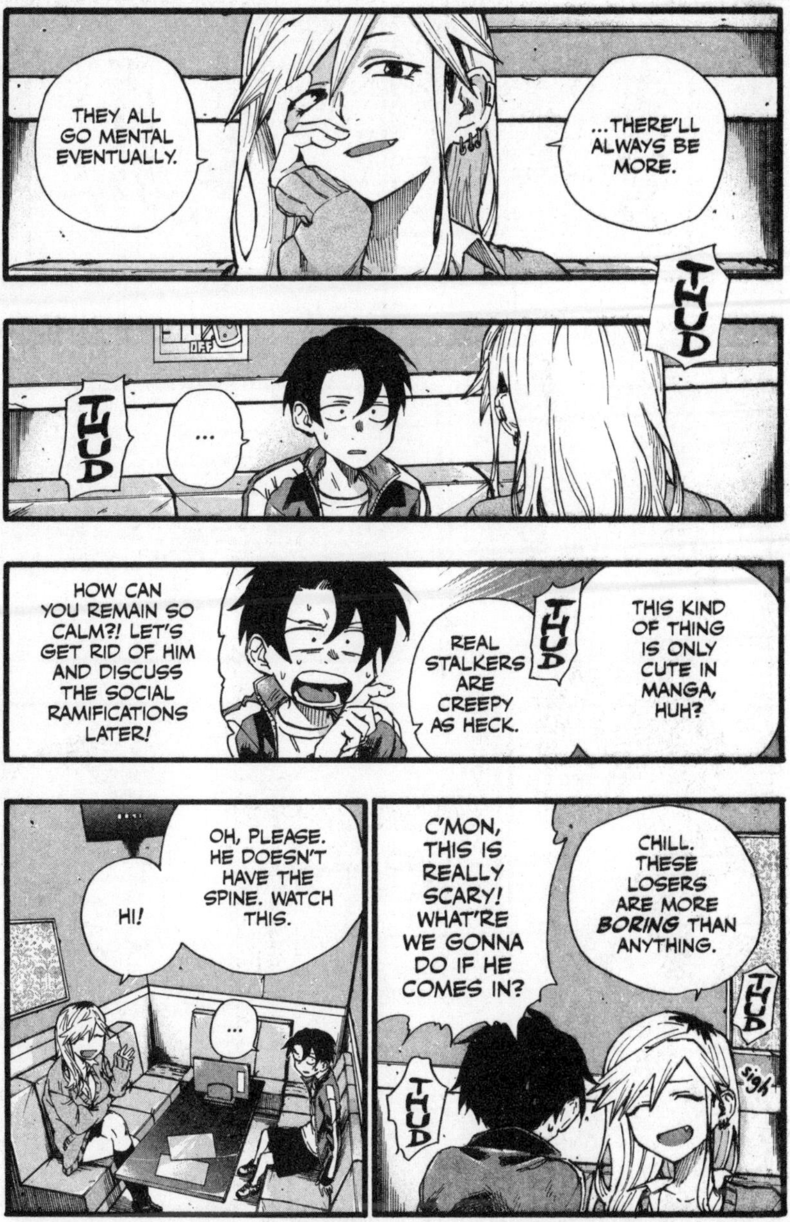

...THERE'LL ALWAYS BE MORE.
THEY ALL GO MENTAL EVENTUALLY.
THUD
...
THUD
THIS KIND OF THING IS ONLY CUTE IN MANGA, HUH?
THUD
REAL STALKERS ARE CREEPY AS HECK.
HOW CAN YOU REMAIN SO CALM?! LET'S GET RID OF HIM AND DISCUSS THE SOCIAL RAMIFICATIONS LATER!
CHILL. THESE LOSERS ARE MORE *BORING* THAN ANYTHING.
C'MON, THIS IS REALLY SCARY! WHAT'RE WE GONNA DO IF HE COMES IN?
THUD
sigh
THUD
OH, PLEASE. HE DOESN'T HAVE THE SPINE. WATCH THIS.
HI!
...

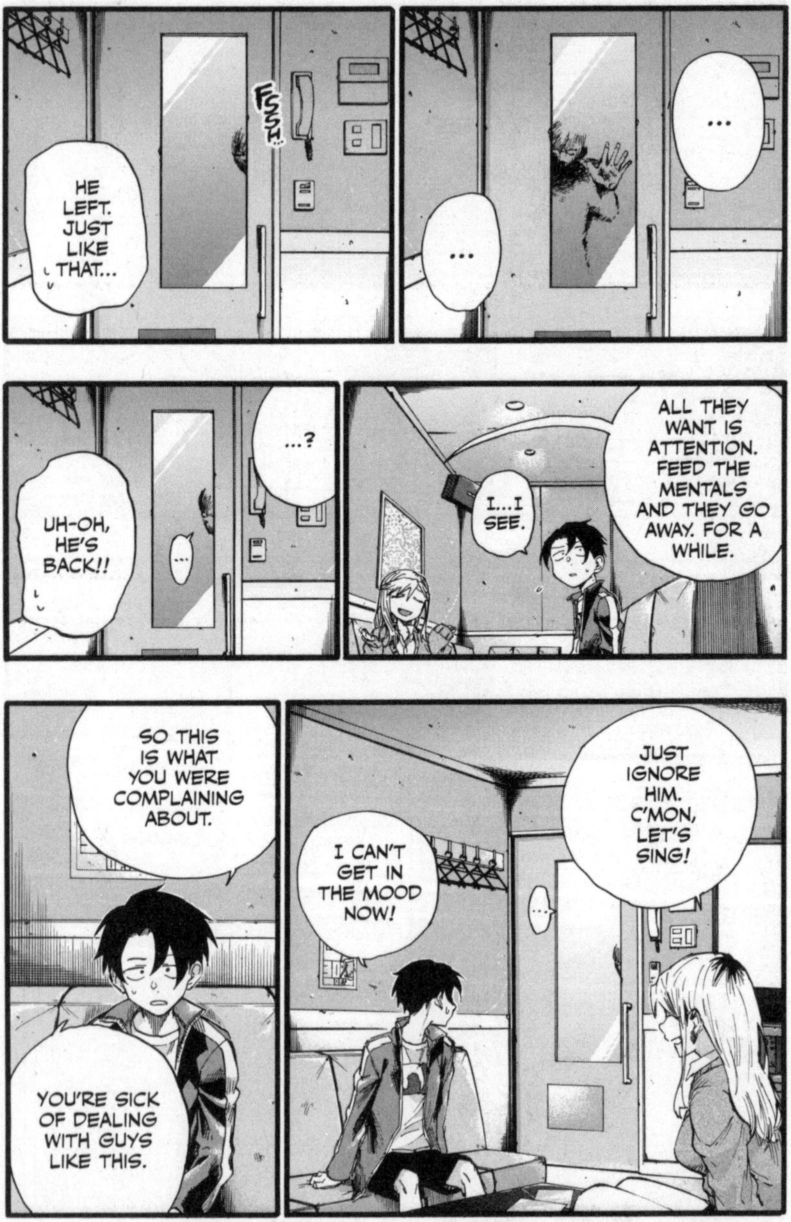
...
...
FSSH..
HE LEFT. JUST LIKE THAT...
ALL THEY WANT IS ATTENTION. FEED THE MENTALS AND THEY GO AWAY. FOR A WHILE.
I...I SEE.
...?
...
UH-OH, HE'S BACK!!
JUST IGNORE HIM. C'MON, LET'S SING!
...
I CAN'T GET IN THE MOOD NOW!
SO THIS IS WHAT YOU WERE COMPLAINING ABOUT.
YOU'RE SICK OF DEALING WITH GUYS LIKE THIS.

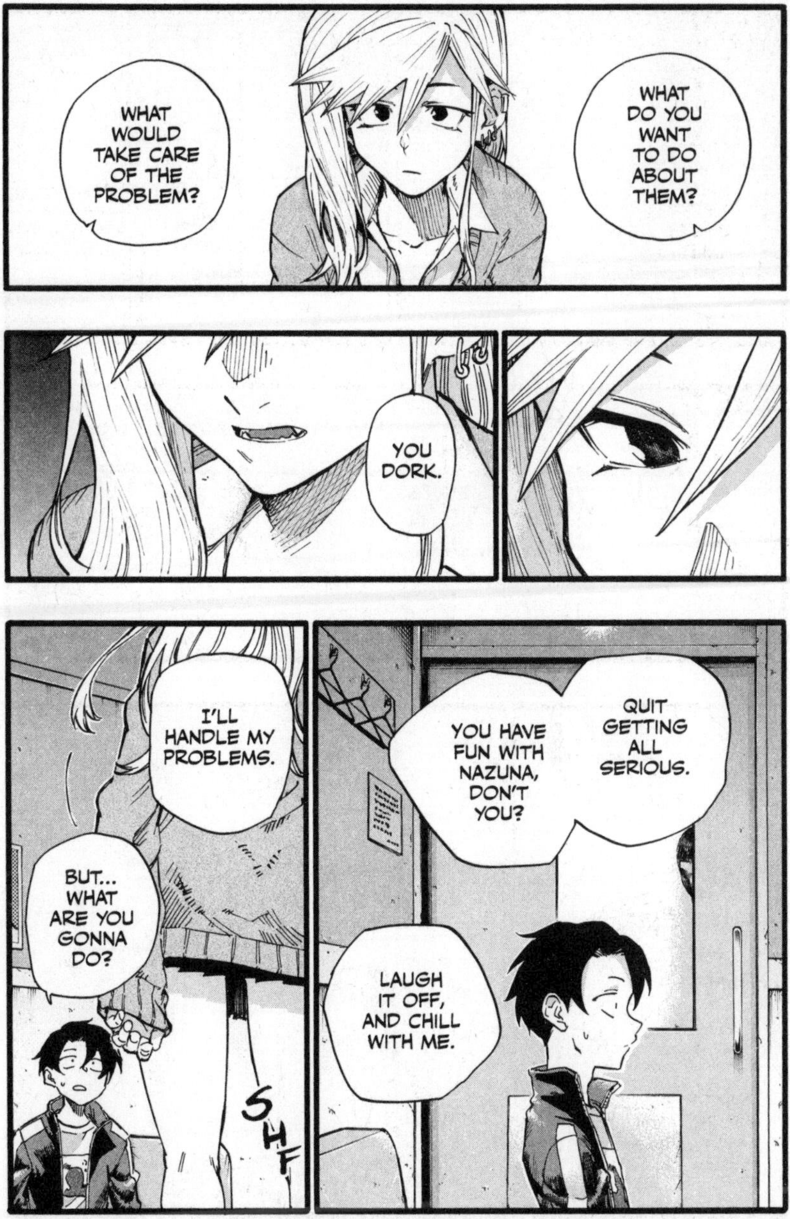
WHAT DO YOU WANT TO DO ABOUT THEM?
WHAT WOULD TAKE CARE OF THE PROBLEM?
YOU DORK.
QUIT GETTING ALL SERIOUS.
YOU HAVE FUN WITH NAZUNA, DON'T YOU?
LAUGH IT OFF, AND CHILL WITH ME.
I'LL HANDLE MY PROBLEMS.
BUT... WHAT ARE YOU GONNA DO?
SHF

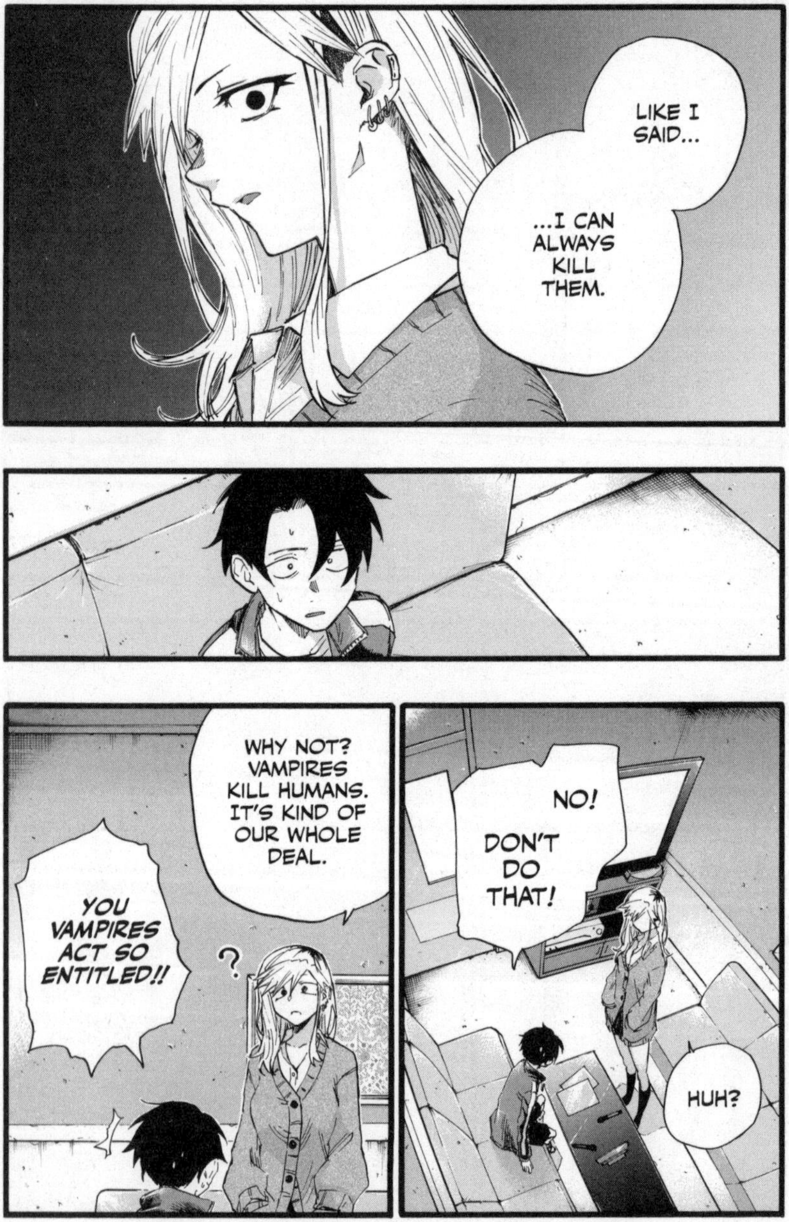
LIKE I SAID...
...I CAN ALWAYS KILL THEM.
NO!
DON'T DO THAT!
HUH?
WHY NOT? VAMPIRES KILL HUMANS. IT'S KIND OF OUR WHOLE DEAL.
YOU VAMPIRES ACT SO ENTITLED!!

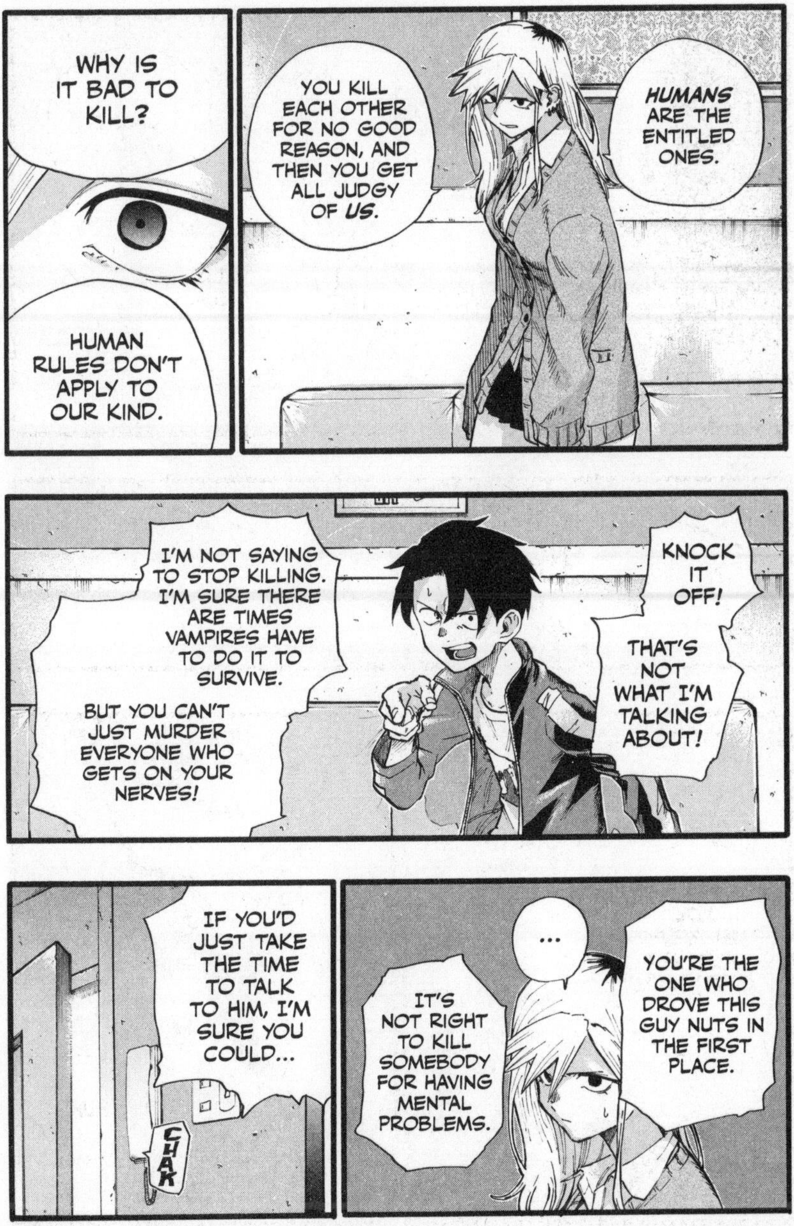
HUMANS ARE THE ENTITLED ONES.
YOU KILL EACH OTHER FOR NO GOOD REASON, AND THEN YOU GET ALL JUDGY OF US.
WHY IS IT BAD TO KILL?
HUMAN RULES DON'T APPLY TO OUR KIND.
KNOCK IT OFF!
THAT'S NOT WHAT I'M TALKING ABOUT!
I'M NOT SAYING TO STOP KILLING. I'M SURE THERE ARE TIMES VAMPIRES HAVE TO DO IT TO SURVIVE.
BUT YOU CAN'T JUST MURDER EVERYONE WHO GETS ON YOUR NERVES!
...
YOU'RE THE ONE WHO DROVE THIS GUY NUTS IN THE FIRST PLACE.
IT'S NOT RIGHT TO KILL SOMEBODY FOR HAVING MENTAL PROBLEMS.
IF YOU'D JUST TAKE THE TIME TO TALK TO HIM, I'M SURE YOU COULD...
CHAK

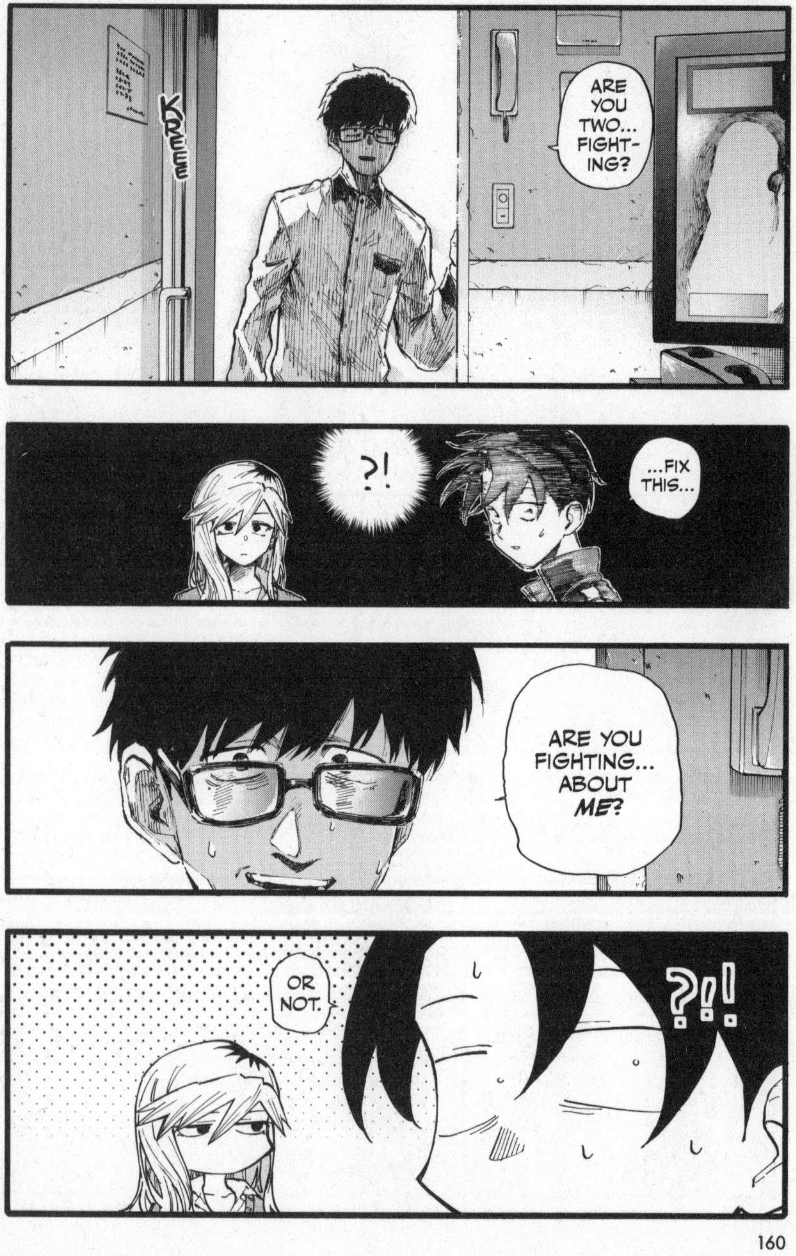
ARE YOU TWO... FIGHT-ING?
KREEE
...FIX THIS...
?!
ARE YOU FIGHTING... ABOUT *ME*?
?!!
OR NOT.

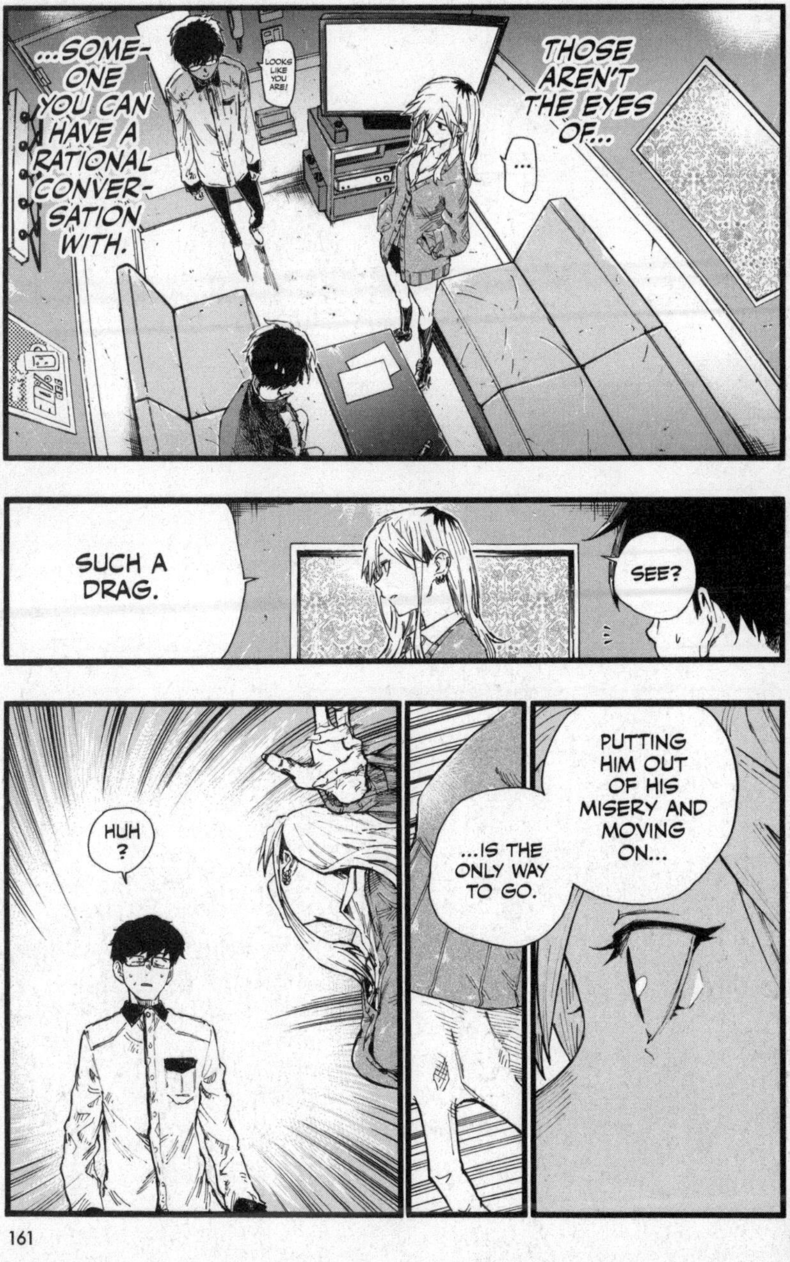
THOSE AREN'T THE EYES OF...
...
LOOKS LIKE YOU ARE!
...SOME-ONE YOU CAN HAVE A RATIONAL CONVER-SATION WITH.
SEE?
SUCH A DRAG.
PUTTING HIM OUT OF HIS MISERY AND MOVING ON...
...IS THE ONLY WAY TO GO.
HUH?

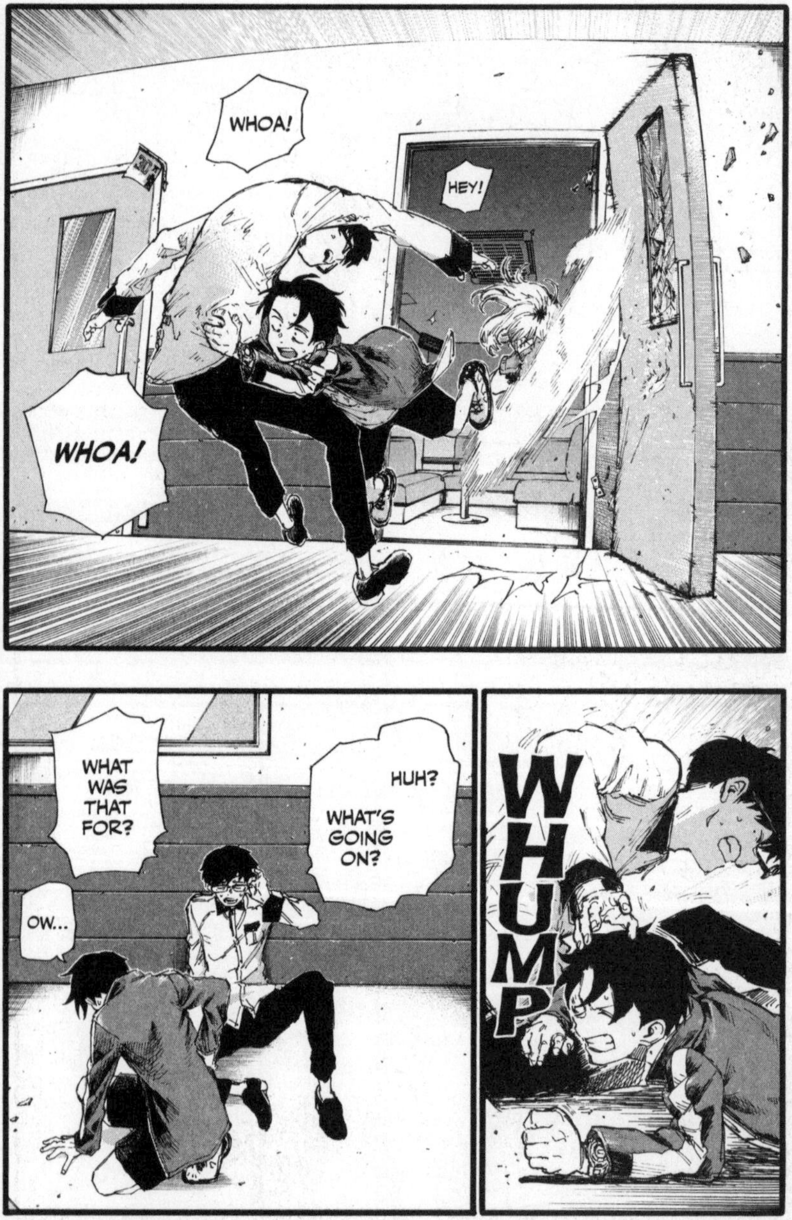
HEY!
WHOA!
WHOA!
WHUMP
HUH?
WHAT'S GOING ON?
WHAT WAS THAT FOR?
OW...

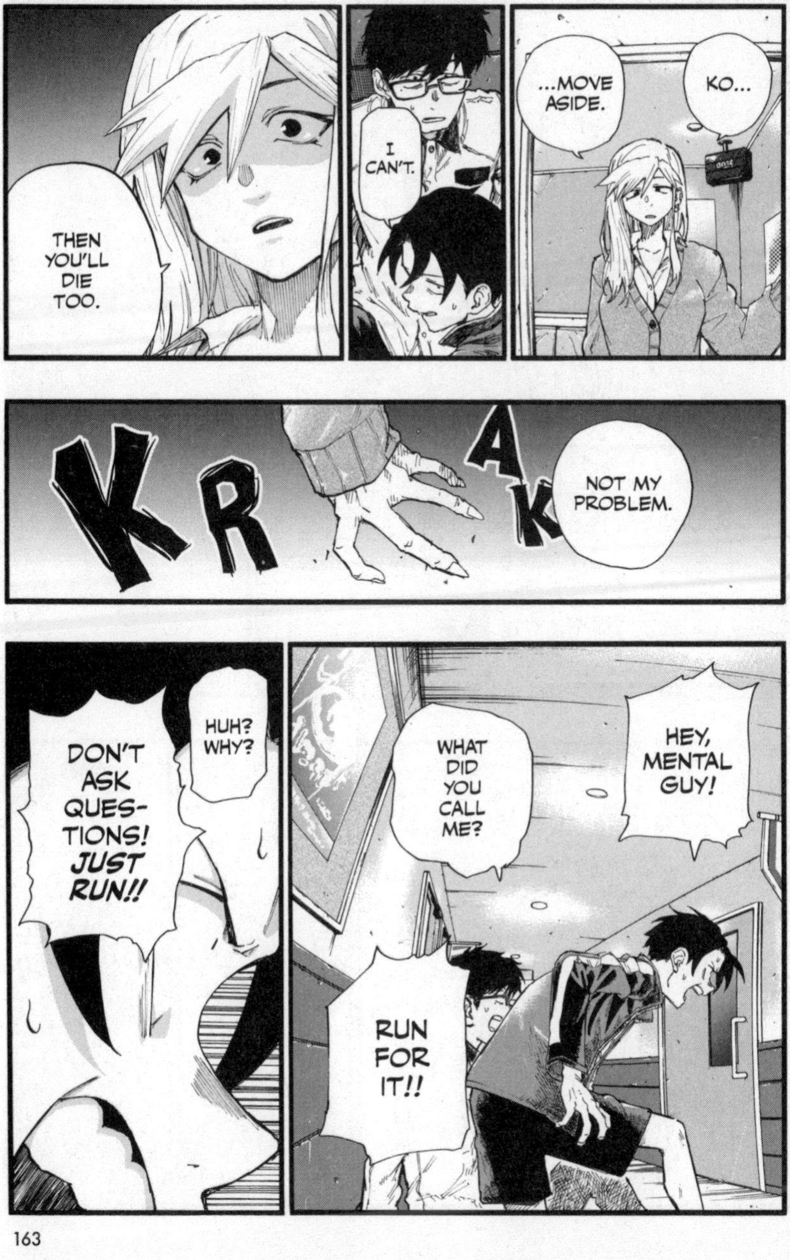
KO...
...MOVE ASIDE.
I CAN'T.
THEN YOU'LL DIE TOO.
NOT MY PROBLEM.
KRAK
HEY, MENTAL GUY!
WHAT DID YOU CALL ME?
RUN FOR IT!!
HUH? WHY?
DON'T ASK QUESTIONS! JUST RUN!!

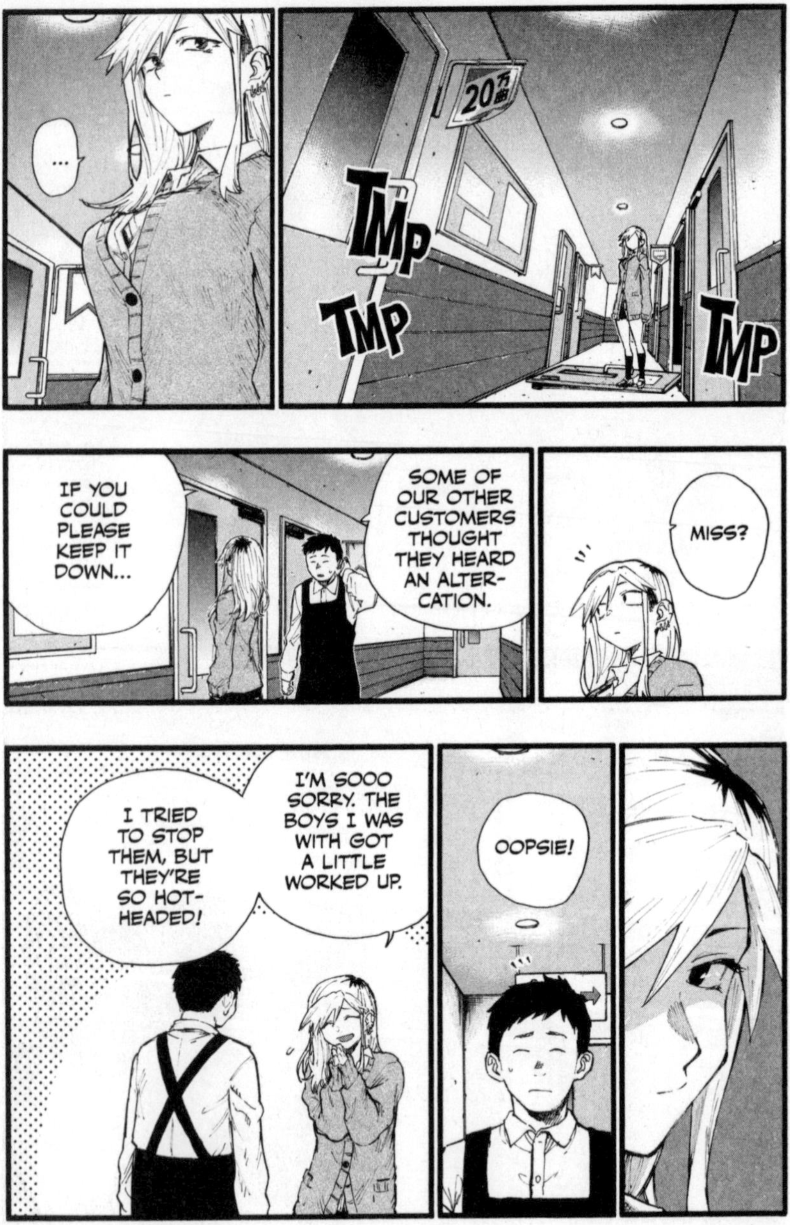
TMP
TMP
TMP
...
MISS?
SOME OF OUR OTHER CUSTOMERS THOUGHT THEY HEARD AN ALTERCATION.
IF YOU COULD PLEASE KEEP IT DOWN...
OOPSIE!
I'M SOOO SORRY. THE BOYS I WAS WITH GOT A LITTLE WORKED UP.
I TRIED TO STOP THEM, BUT THEY'RE SO HOT-HEADED!

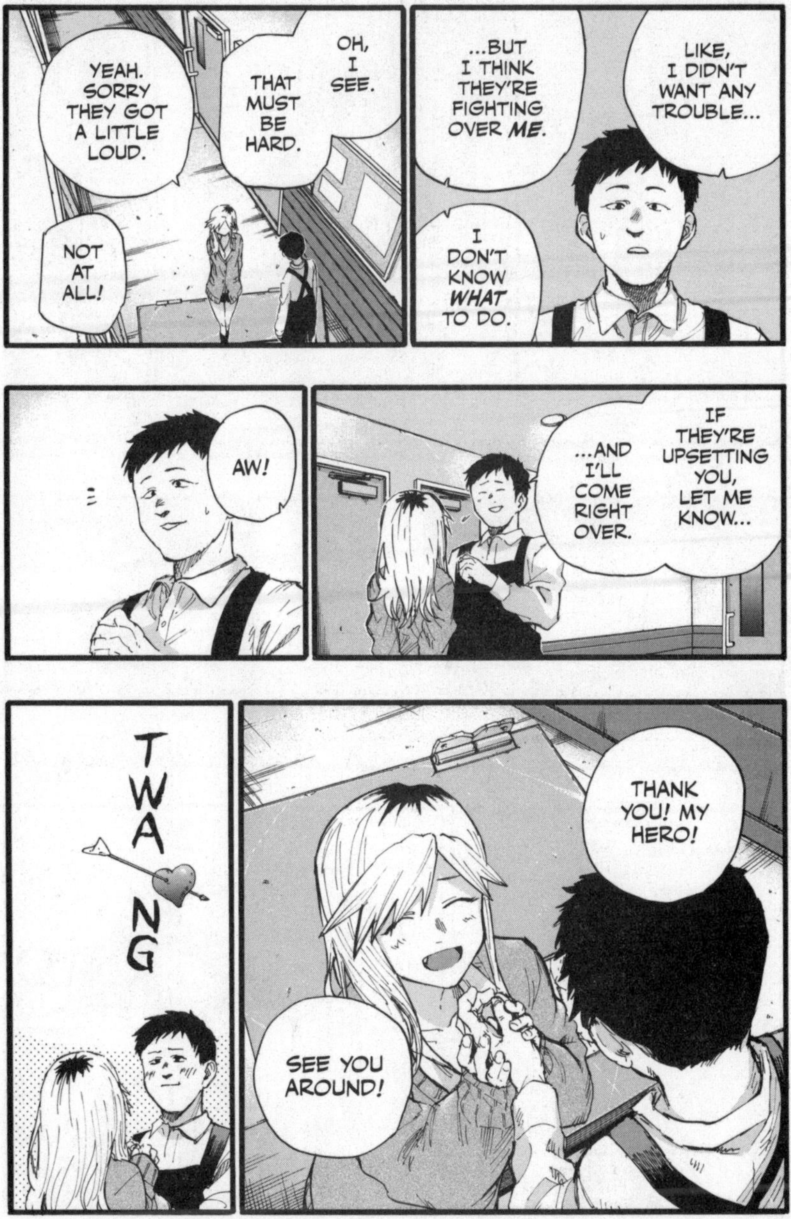
LIKE, I DIDN'T WANT ANY TROUBLE...
...BUT I THINK THEY'RE FIGHTING OVER *ME*.
I DON'T KNOW *WHAT* TO DO.
OH, I SEE.
THAT MUST BE HARD.
YEAH. SORRY THEY GOT A LITTLE LOUD.
NOT AT ALL!
IF THEY'RE UPSETTING YOU, LET ME KNOW...
...AND I'LL COME RIGHT OVER.
AW!
THANK YOU! MY HERO!
SEE YOU AROUND!
TWANG

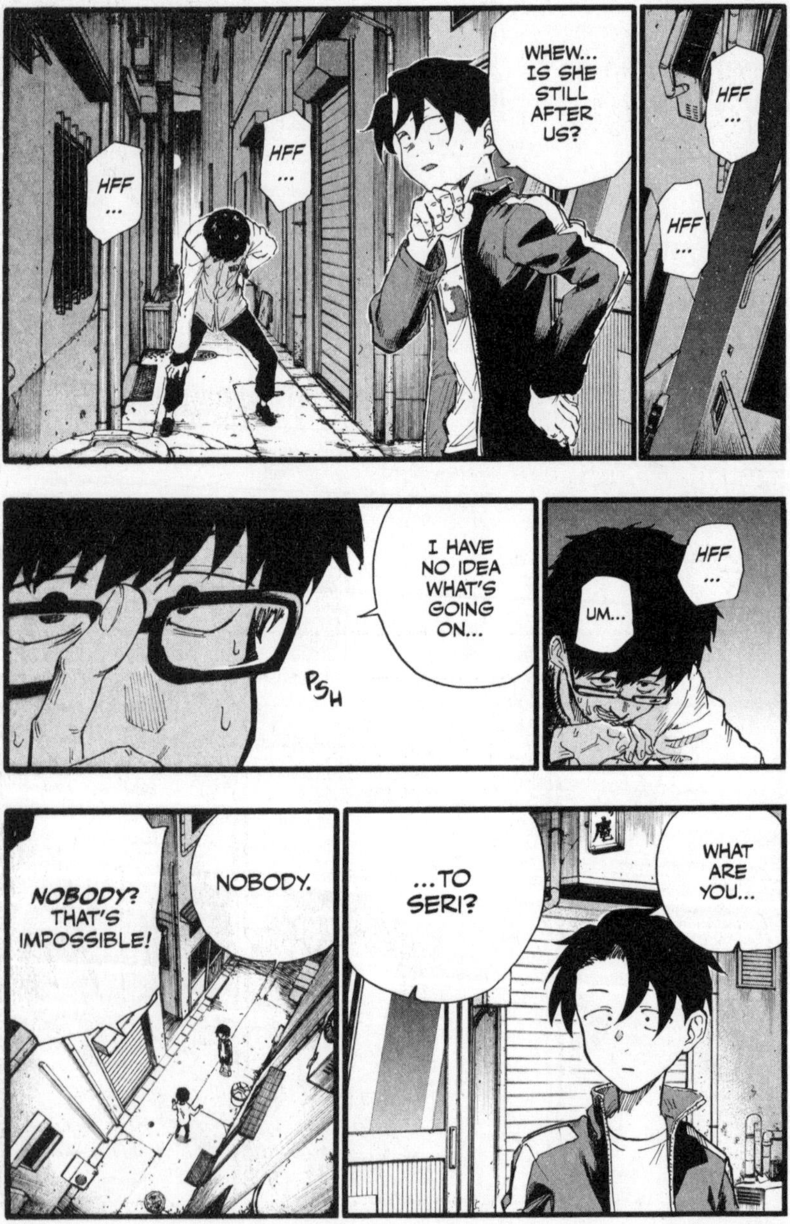
HFF...
HFF...
WHEW... IS SHE STILL AFTER US?
HFF...
HFF...
HFF...
UM...
I HAVE NO IDEA WHAT'S GOING ON...
PSH
WHAT ARE YOU...
...TO SERI?
NOBODY.
NOBODY? THAT'S IMPOSSIBLE!

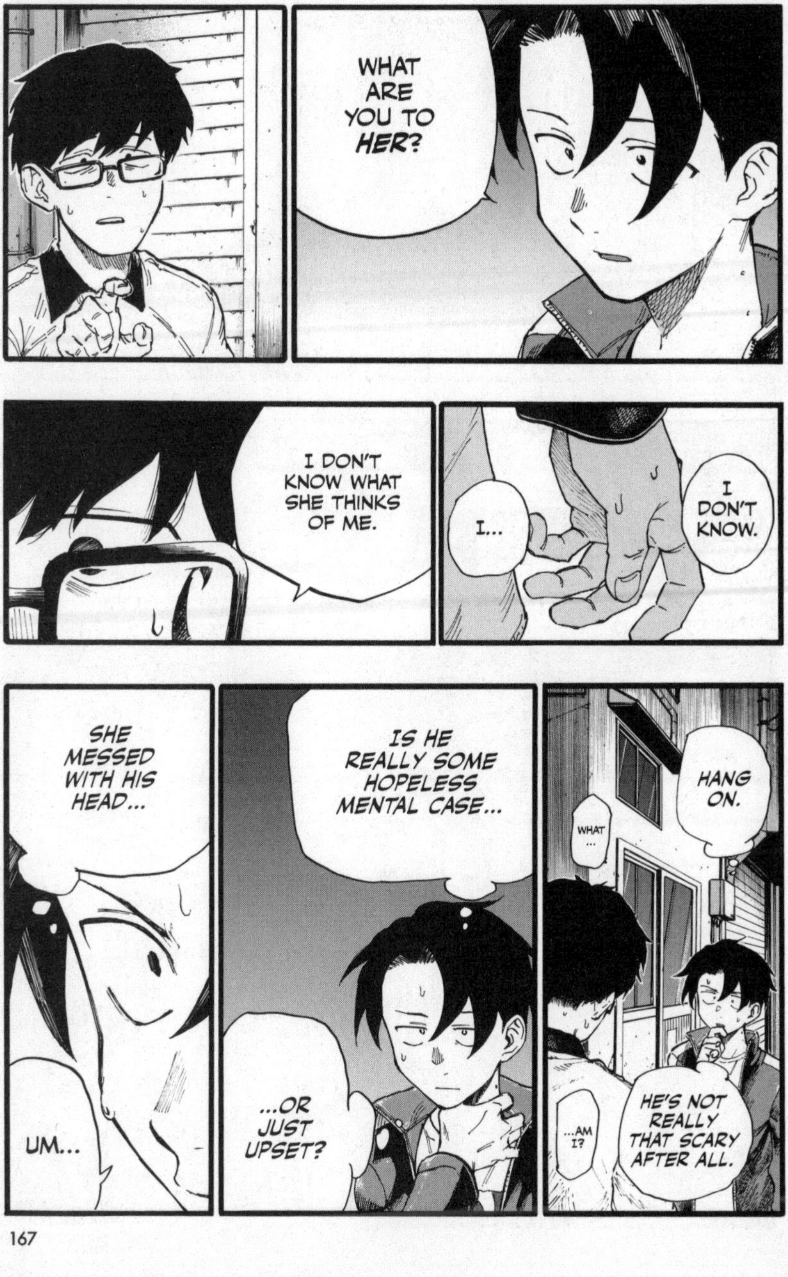
WHAT ARE YOU TO *HER*?
I DON'T KNOW.
I...
I DON'T KNOW WHAT SHE THINKS OF ME.
HANG ON.
WHAT ...
HE'S NOT REALLY THAT SCARY AFTER ALL.
...AM I?
IS HE REALLY SOME HOPELESS MENTAL CASE...
...OR JUST UPSET?
SHE MESSED WITH HIS HEAD...
UM...

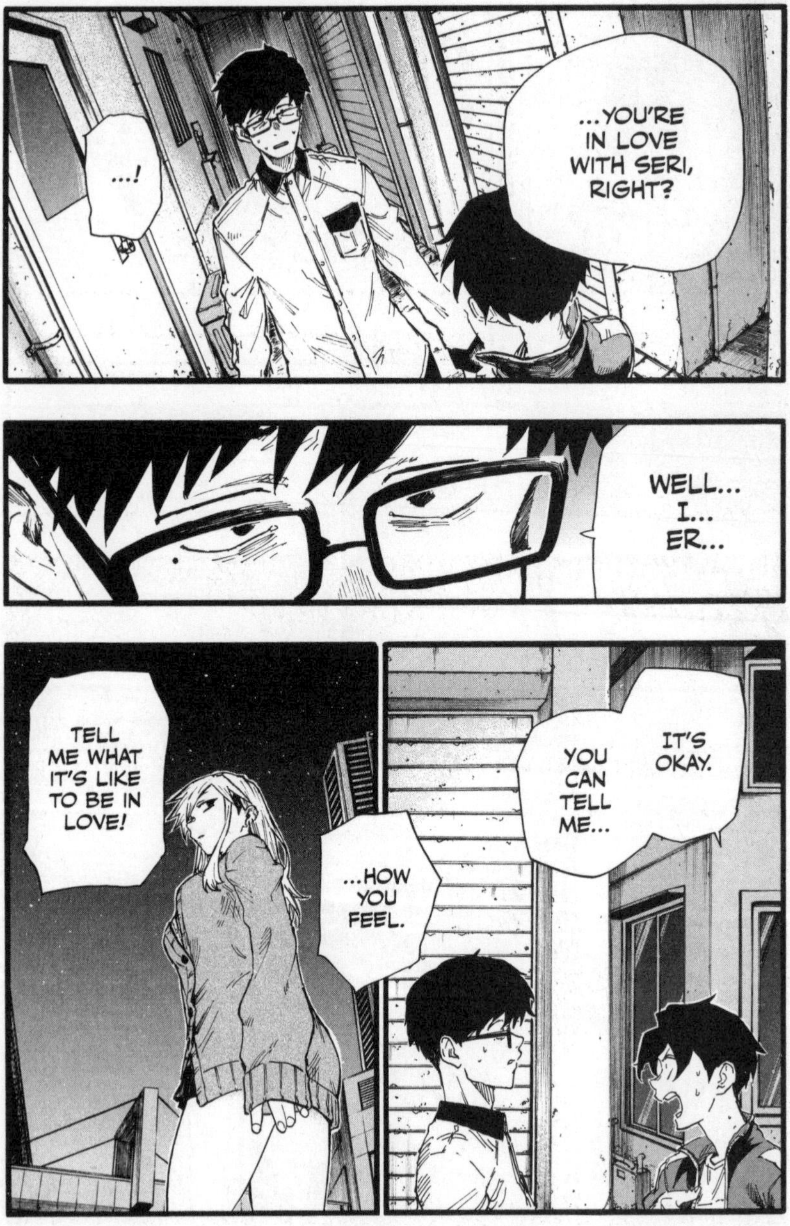
...YOU'RE IN LOVE WITH SERI, RIGHT?
...!
WELL... I... ER...
IT'S OKAY.
YOU CAN TELL ME...
...HOW YOU FEEL.
TELL ME WHAT IT'S LIKE TO BE IN LOVE!

NIGHT 28: LOVE IS BLIND

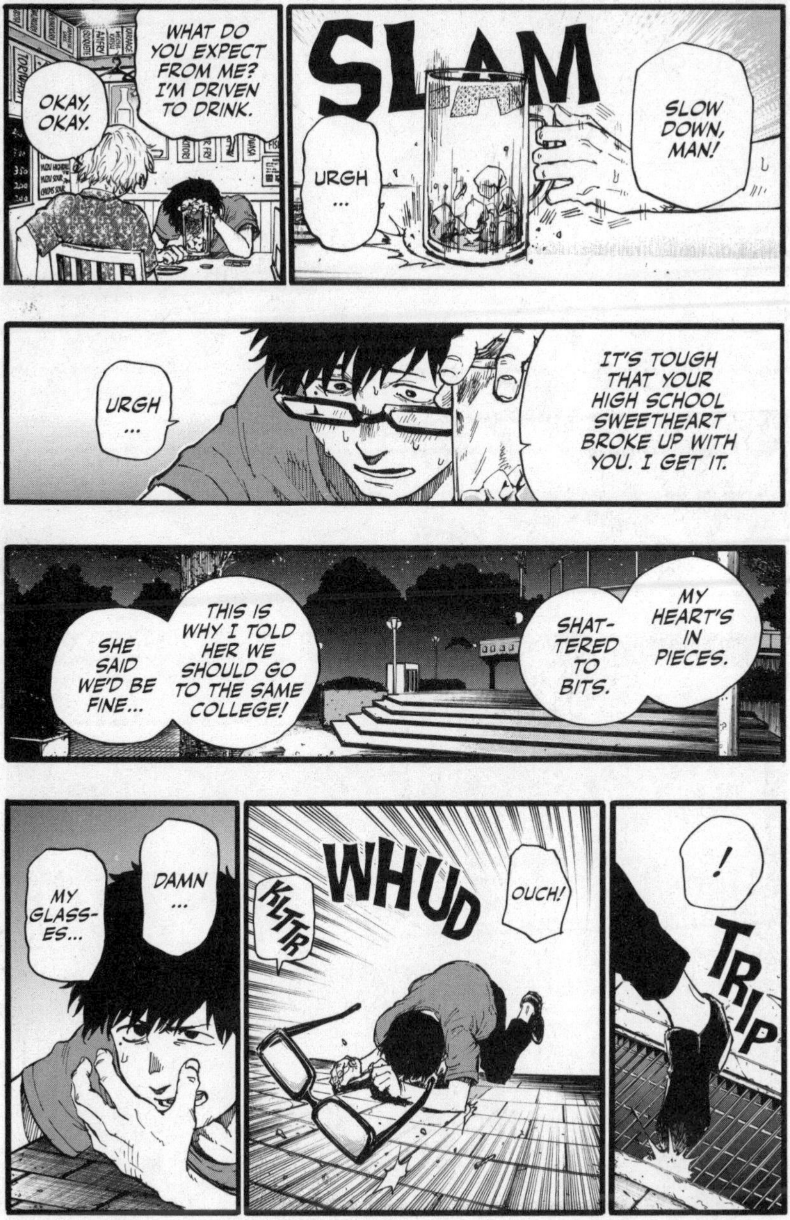
SLAM
SLOW DOWN, MAN!
URGH ...
WHAT DO YOU EXPECT FROM ME? I'M DRIVEN TO DRINK.
OKAY, OKAY.
IT'S TOUGH THAT YOUR HIGH SCHOOL SWEETHEART BROKE UP WITH YOU. I GET IT.
URGH ...
MY HEART'S IN PIECES.
SHAT-TERED TO BITS.
THIS IS WHY I TOLD HER WE SHOULD GO TO THE SAME COLLEGE!
SHE SAID WE'D BE FINE...
!
TRIP
WHUD
OUCH!
KLTTR
DAMN ...
MY GLASS-ES...

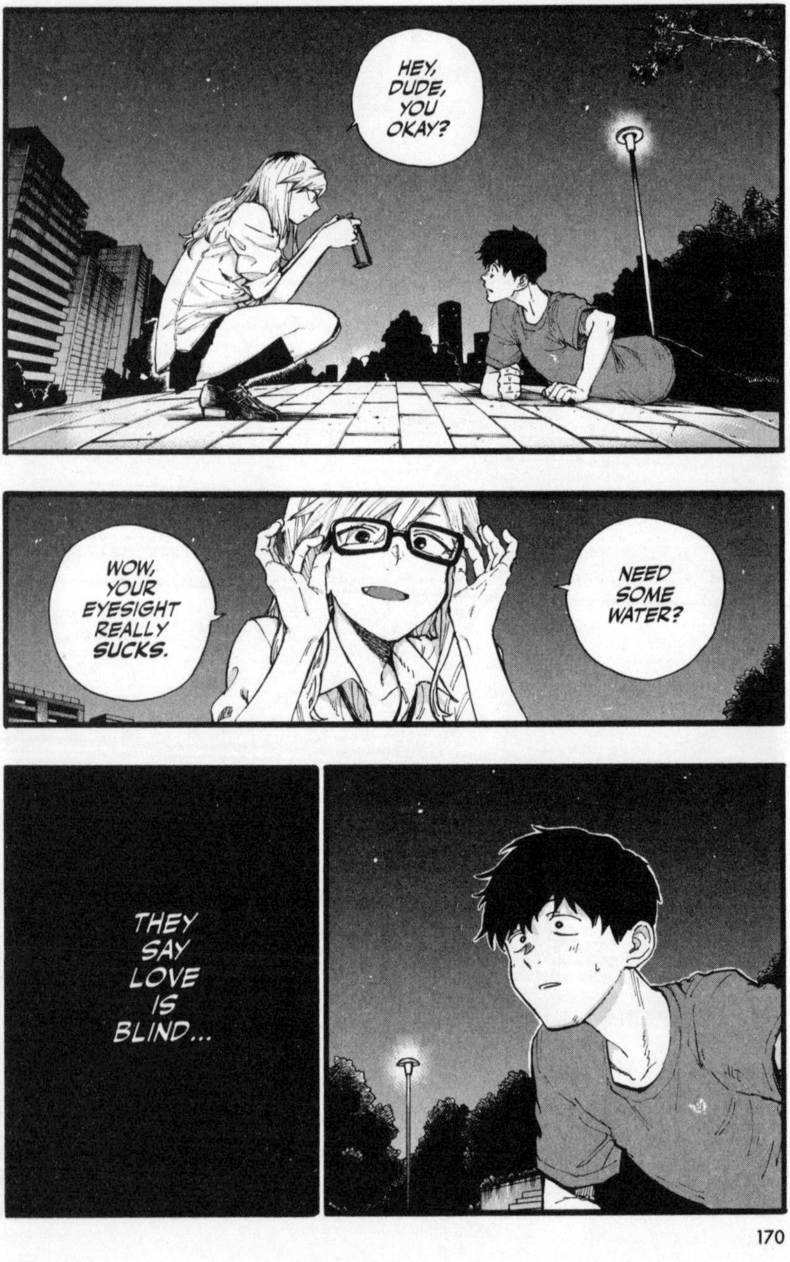
HEY, DUDE, YOU OKAY?
NEED SOME WATER?
WOW, YOUR EYESIGHT REALLY SUCKS.
THEY SAY LOVE IS BLIND...

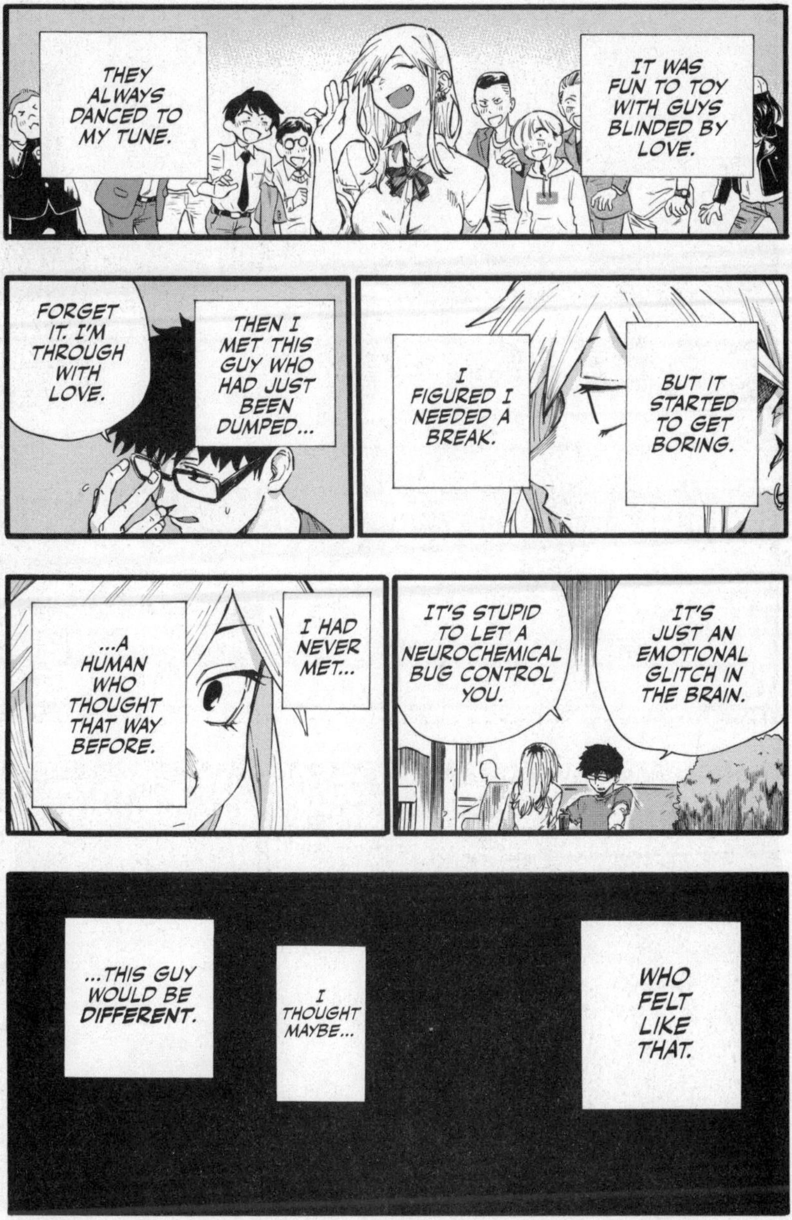
IT WAS FUN TO TOY WITH GUYS BLINDED BY LOVE.
THEY ALWAYS DANCED TO MY TUNE.
BUT IT STARTED TO GET BORING.
I FIGURED I NEEDED A BREAK.
THEN I MET THIS GUY WHO HAD JUST BEEN DUMPED...
FORGET IT. I'M THROUGH WITH LOVE.
IT'S JUST AN EMOTIONAL GLITCH IN THE BRAIN.
IT'S STUPID TO LET A NEUROCHEMICAL BUG CONTROL YOU.
I HAD NEVER MET...
...A HUMAN WHO THOUGHT THAT WAY BEFORE.
WHO FELT LIKE THAT.
I THOUGHT MAYBE...
...THIS GUY WOULD BE DIFFERENT.

THEY SAY LOVE IS BLIND.
TO SOME EXTENT, THAT'S TRUE.
...
OH YEAH? HOW SO?
WELL...
?
...WHEN YOU'RE IN LOVE, YOU PRODUCE A LOT OF DOPAMINE.
A NEUROTRANS-MITTER THAT'S SECRETED WHEN YOU FEEL PLEASURE.

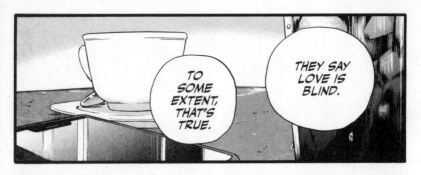

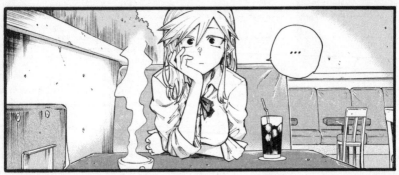

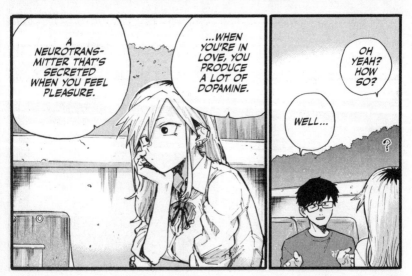

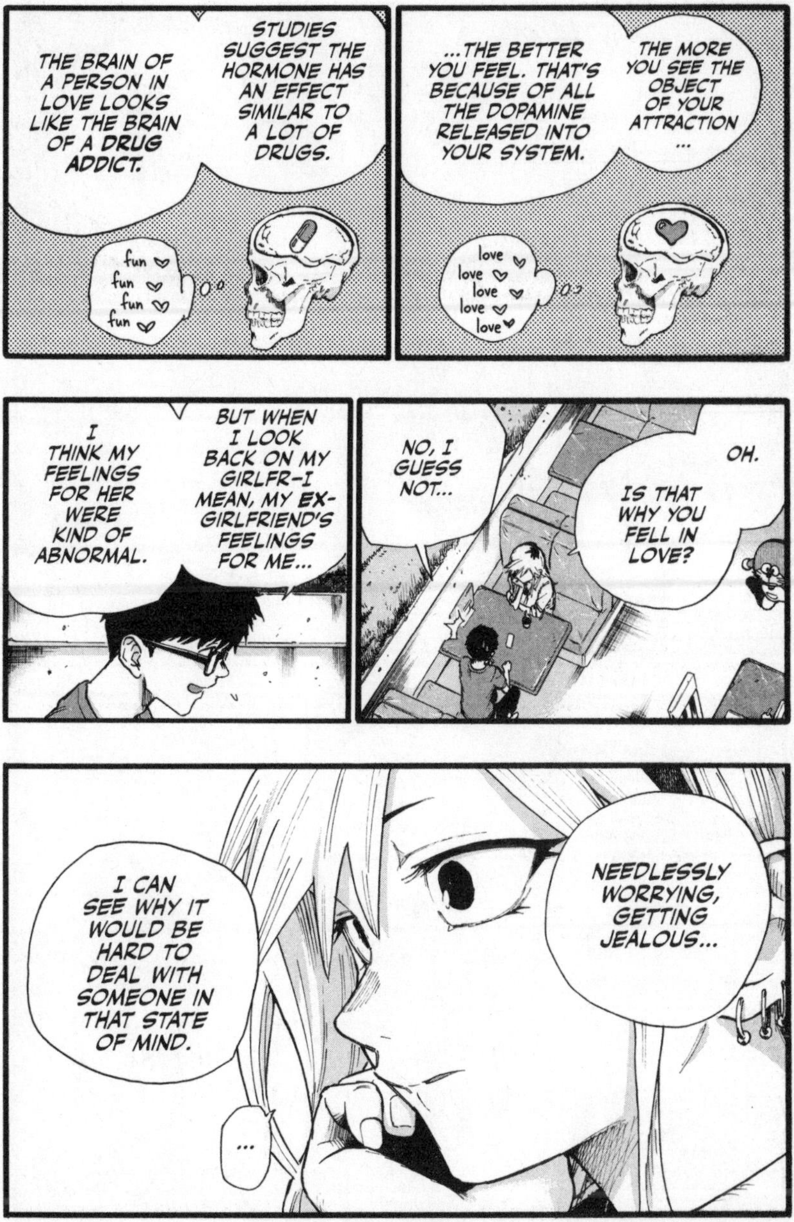
THE MORE YOU SEE THE OBJECT OF YOUR ATTRACTION ...
...THE BETTER YOU FEEL. THAT'S BECAUSE OF ALL THE DOPAMINE RELEASED INTO YOUR SYSTEM.
love love love love love
STUDIES SUGGEST THE HORMONE HAS AN EFFECT SIMILAR TO A LOT OF DRUGS.
THE BRAIN OF A PERSON IN LOVE LOOKS LIKE THE BRAIN OF A DRUG ADDICT.
fun fun fun fun
OH.
IS THAT WHY YOU FELL IN LOVE?
NO, I GUESS NOT...
BUT WHEN I LOOK BACK ON MY GIRLFR–I MEAN, MY EX-GIRLFRIEND'S FEELINGS FOR ME...
I THINK MY FEELINGS FOR HER WERE KIND OF ABNORMAL.
NEEDLESSLY WORRYING, GETTING JEALOUS...
I CAN SEE WHY IT WOULD BE HARD TO DEAL WITH SOMEONE IN THAT STATE OF MIND.
...

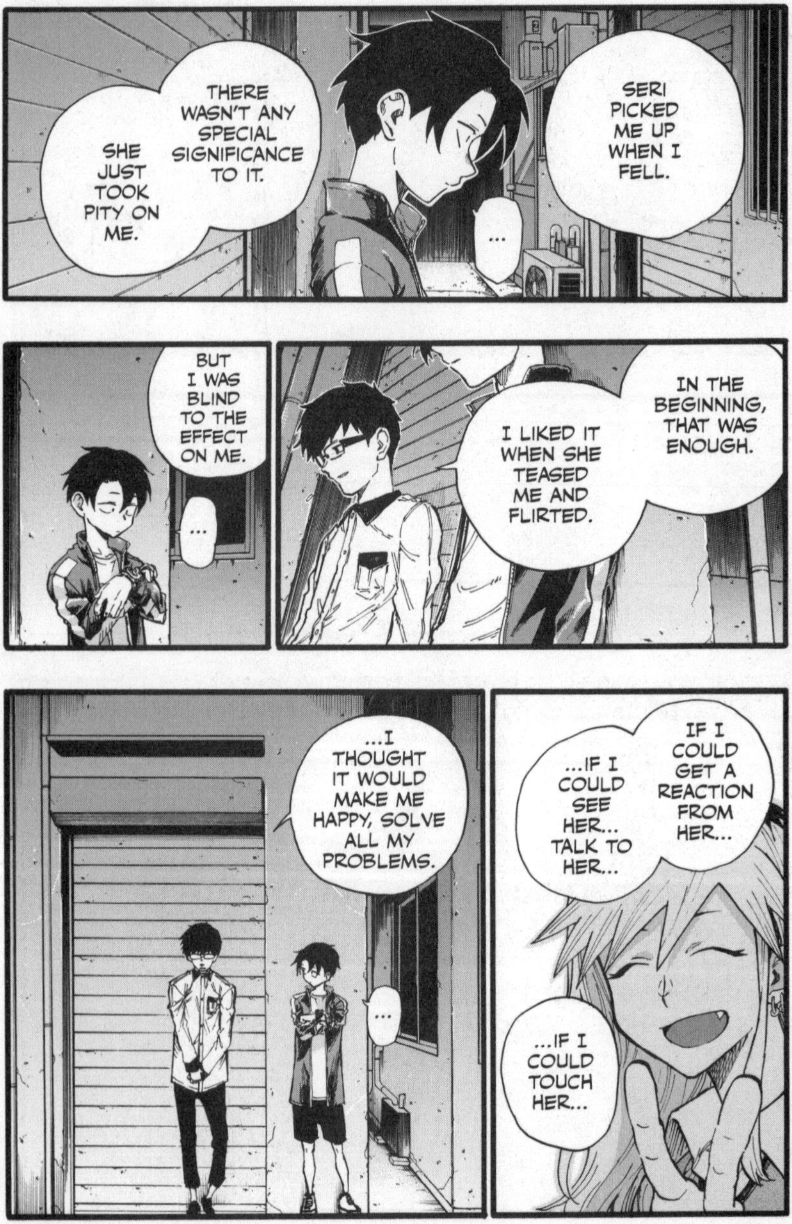
SERI PICKED ME UP WHEN I FELL.
...
THERE WASN'T ANY SPECIAL SIGNIFICANCE TO IT.
SHE JUST TOOK PITY ON ME.
IN THE BEGINNING, THAT WAS ENOUGH.
I LIKED IT WHEN SHE TEASED ME AND FLIRTED.
BUT I WAS BLIND TO THE EFFECT ON ME.
...
IF I COULD GET A REACTION FROM HER...
...IF I COULD SEE HER... TALK TO HER...
...IF I COULD TOUCH HER...
...I THOUGHT IT WOULD MAKE ME HAPPY, SOLVE ALL MY PROBLEMS.
...

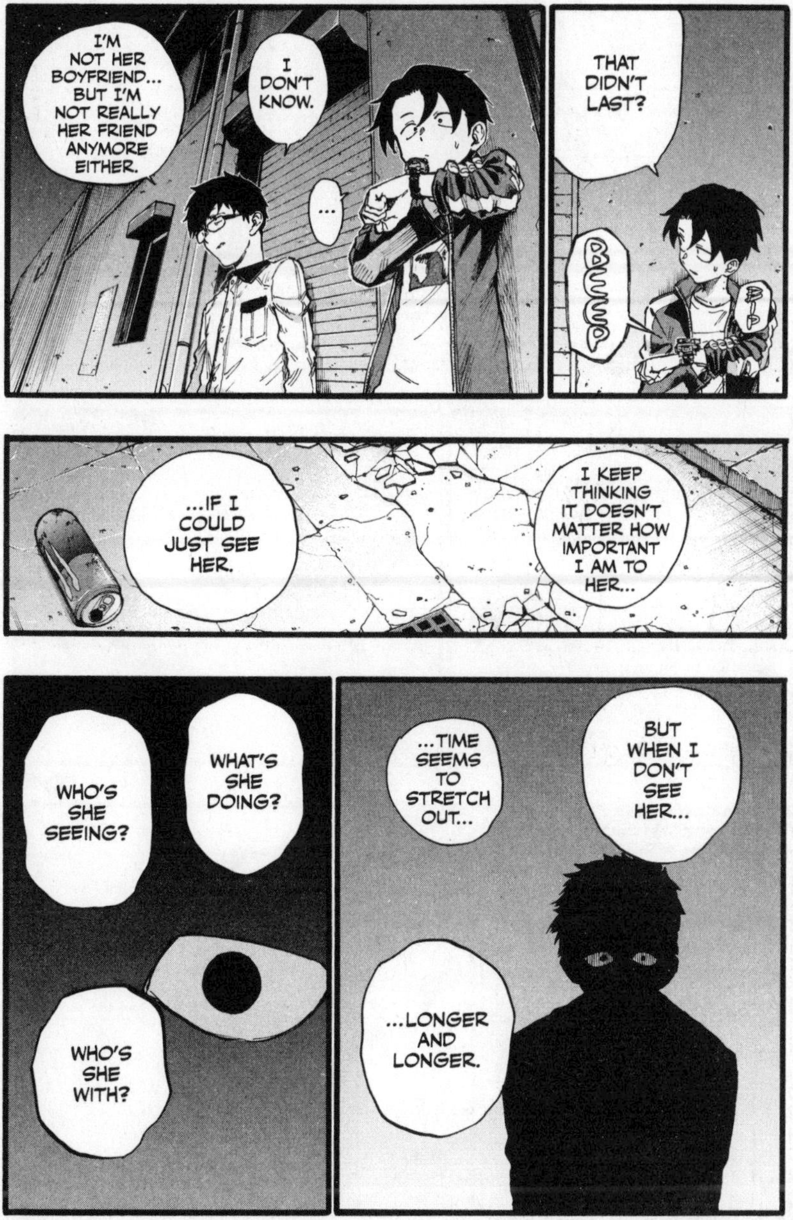
THAT DIDN'T LAST?
BIP
BEEEP
I DON'T KNOW.
I'M NOT HER BOYFRIEND... BUT I'M NOT REALLY HER FRIEND ANYMORE EITHER.
...
I KEEP THINKING IT DOESN'T MATTER HOW IMPORTANT I AM TO HER...
...IF I COULD JUST SEE HER.
BUT WHEN I DON'T SEE HER...
...TIME SEEMS TO STRETCH OUT...
...LONGER AND LONGER.
WHAT'S SHE DOING?
WHO'S SHE SEEING?
WHO'S SHE WITH?

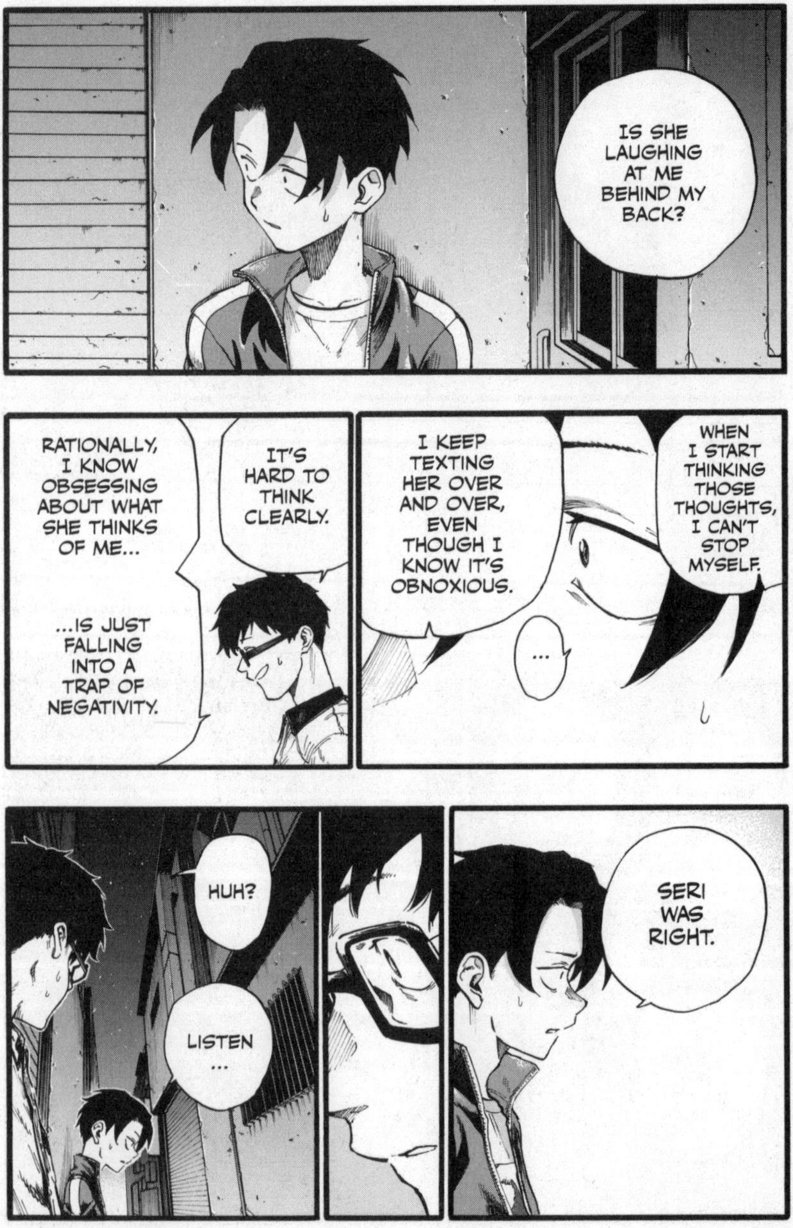
IS SHE LAUGHING AT ME BEHIND MY BACK?
WHEN I START THINKING THOSE THOUGHTS, I CAN'T STOP MYSELF.
I KEEP TEXTING HER OVER AND OVER, EVEN THOUGH I KNOW IT'S OBNOXIOUS.
...
IT'S HARD TO THINK CLEARLY.
RATIONALLY, I KNOW OBSESSING ABOUT WHAT SHE THINKS OF ME...
...IS JUST FALLING INTO A TRAP OF NEGATIVITY.
SERI WAS RIGHT.
HUH?
LISTEN...

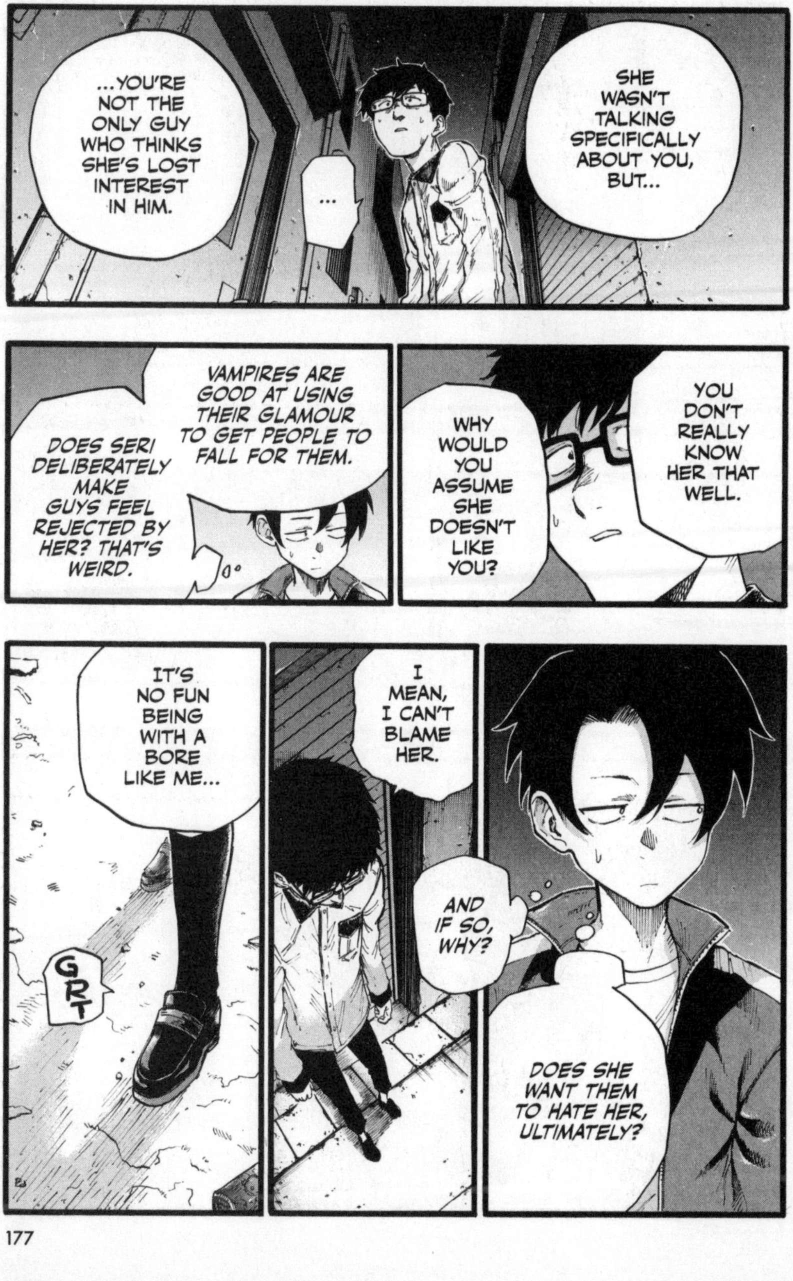
SHE WASN'T TALKING SPECIFICALLY ABOUT YOU, BUT...
...
...YOU'RE NOT THE ONLY GUY WHO THINKS SHE'S LOST INTEREST IN HIM.
YOU DON'T REALLY KNOW HER THAT WELL.
WHY WOULD YOU ASSUME SHE DOESN'T LIKE YOU?
VAMPIRES ARE GOOD AT USING THEIR GLAMOUR TO GET PEOPLE TO FALL FOR THEM.
DOES SERI DELIBERATELY MAKE GUYS FEEL REJECTED BY HER? THAT'S WEIRD.
AND IF SO, WHY?
DOES SHE WANT THEM TO HATE HER, ULTIMATELY?
I MEAN, I CAN'T BLAME HER.
IT'S NO FUN BEING WITH A BORE LIKE ME...
GRT

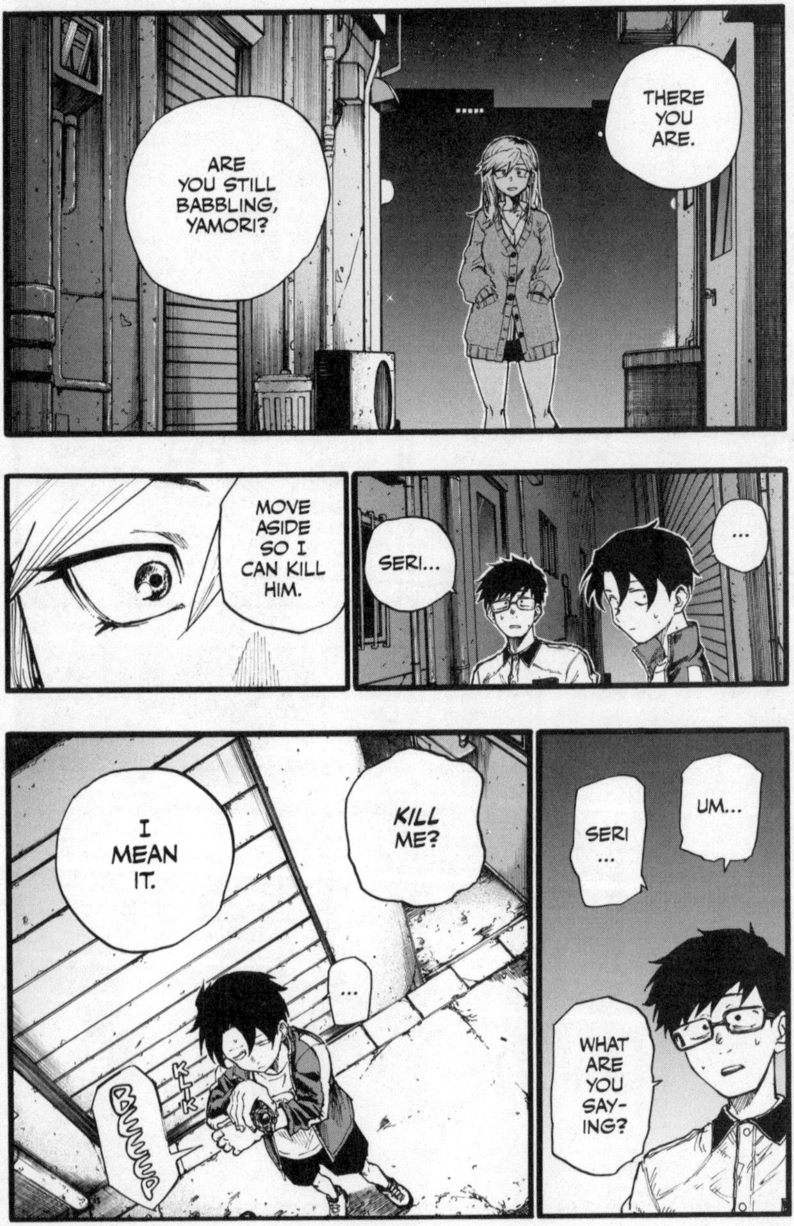
THERE YOU ARE.
ARE YOU STILL BABBLING, YAMORI?
...
SERI...
MOVE ASIDE SO I CAN KILL HIM.
UM...
SERI...
WHAT ARE YOU SAYING?
KILL ME?
I MEAN IT.
...
KLIK

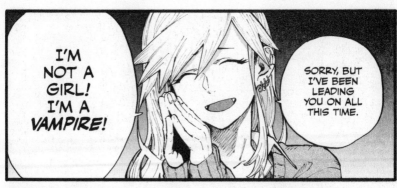

SORRY, BUT I'VE BEEN LEADING YOU ON ALL THIS TIME.
I'M NOT A GIRL! I'M A *VAMPIRE!*
I LOOK FOR HUMANS TO FALL IN LOVE WITH ME...
...AND CHAT THEM UP TO SEE IF THEY'VE GOT THE RIGHT STUFF TO BE TURNED INTO A VAMPIRE.
IT HAS TO BE SOME-BODY WHO'S ATTRACTED TO ME, SEE? OTHERWISE IT DOESN'T WORK.
...?
W-WHAT ARE YOU TALKING ABOUT?
DON'T STRAIN YOUR BRAIN.
BEEEP
!
...
YOU'LL BE DEAD IN A SEC.
NO.
HUH?
I WON'T LET YOU KILL HIM!
NO WAY!
I SEE.

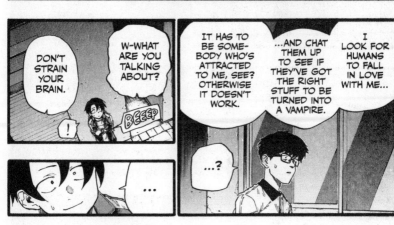

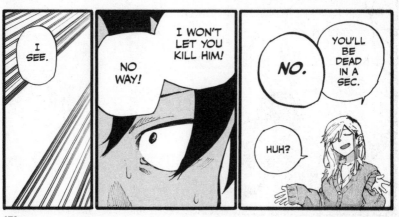

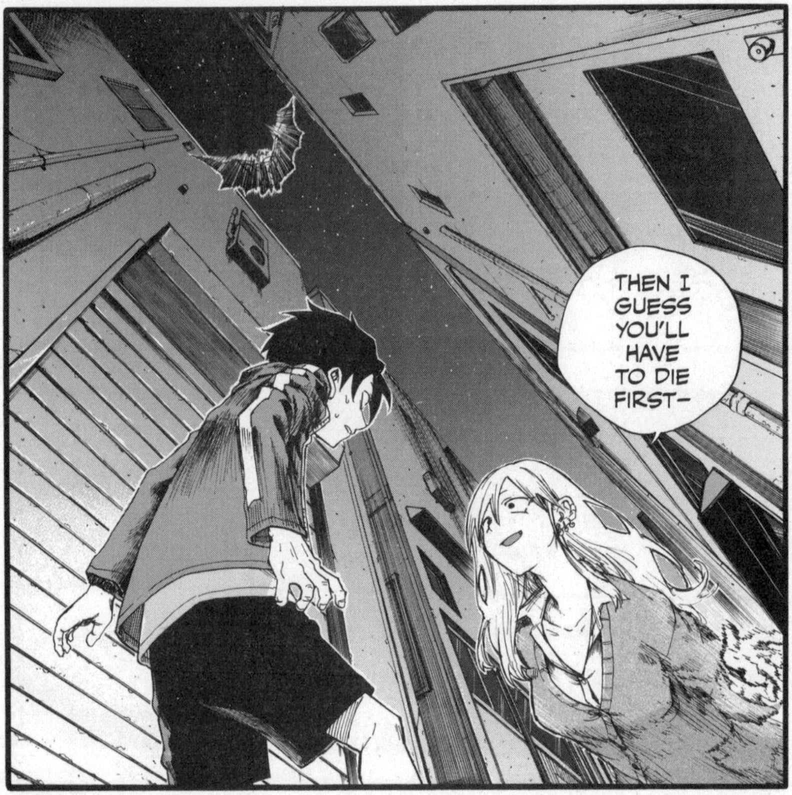
THEN I GUESS YOU'LL HAVE TO DIE FIRST–
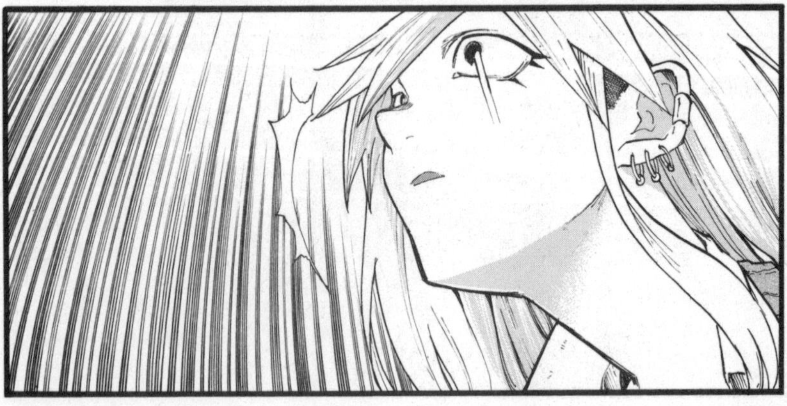

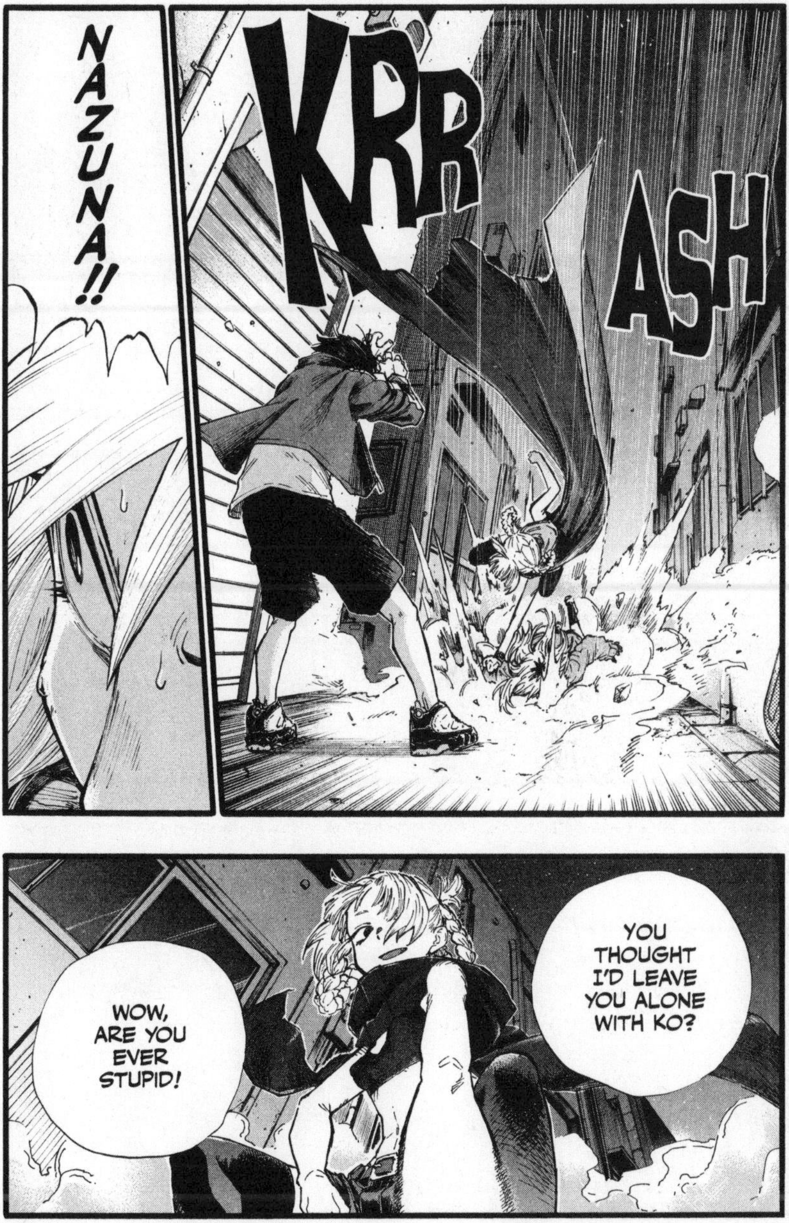
KRR ASH
NAZUNA!!
YOU THOUGHT I'D LEAVE YOU ALONE WITH KO?
WOW, ARE YOU EVER STUPID!

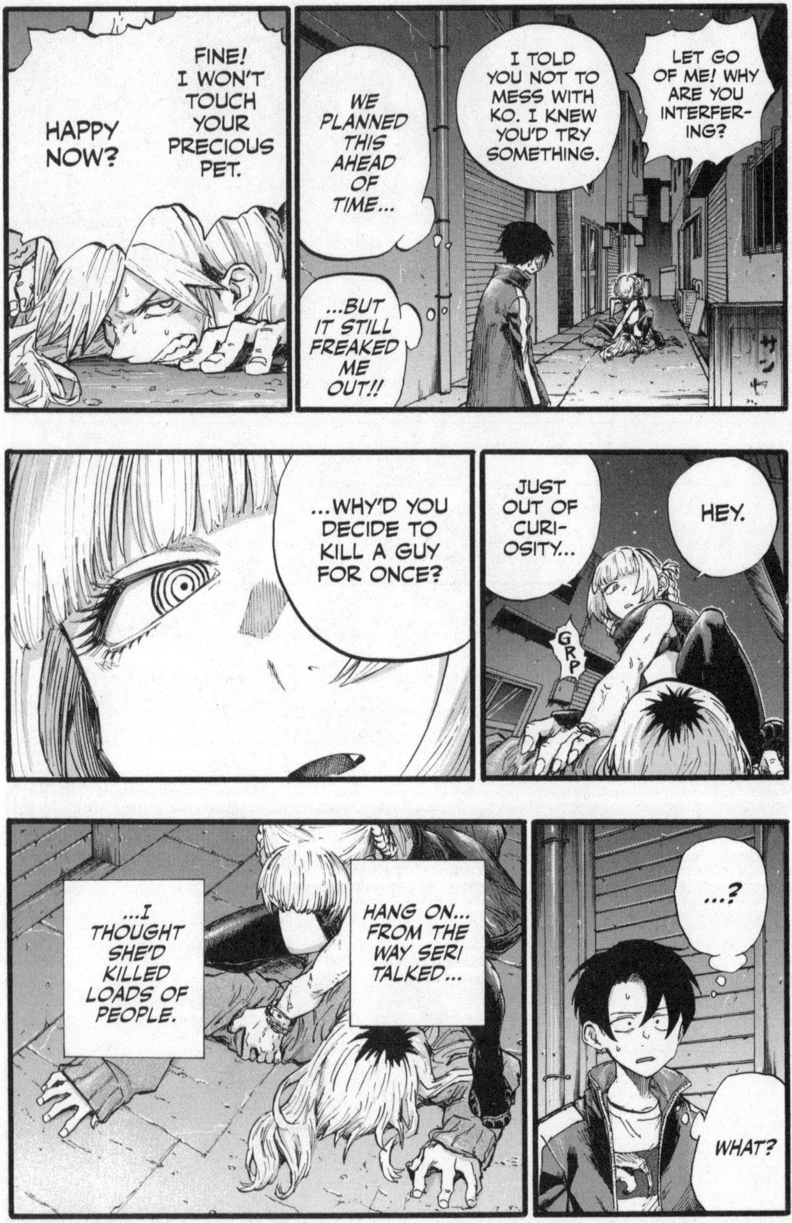

LET GO OF ME! WHY ARE YOU INTERFER-ING?
I TOLD YOU NOT TO MESS WITH KO. I KNEW YOU'D TRY SOMETHING.
WE PLANNED THIS AHEAD OF TIME...
...BUT IT STILL FREAKED ME OUT!!
FINE! I WON'T TOUCH YOUR PRECIOUS PET.
HAPPY NOW?
HEY.
JUST OUT OF CURI-OSITY...
GRP
...WHY'D YOU DECIDE TO KILL A GUY FOR ONCE?
...?
WHAT?
HANG ON... FROM THE WAY SERI TALKED...
...I THOUGHT SHE'D KILLED LOADS OF PEOPLE.

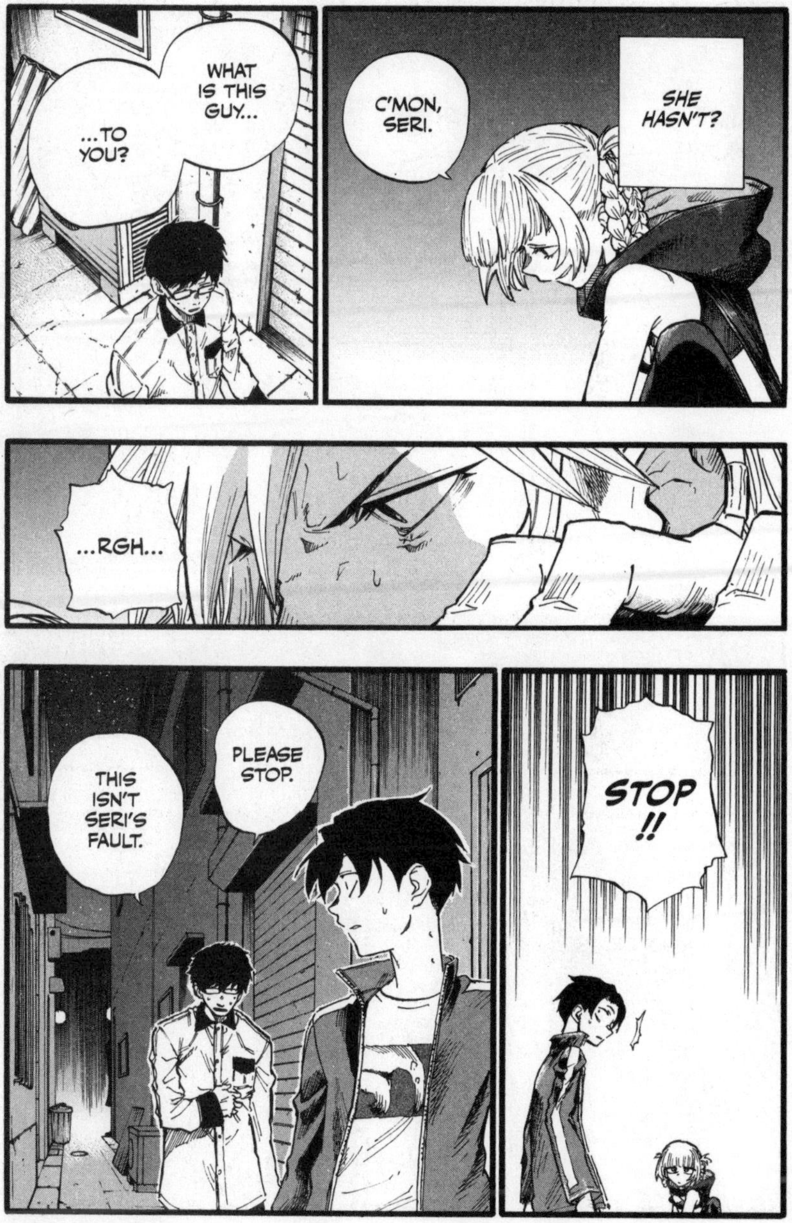
SHE HASN'T?
C'MON, SERI.
WHAT IS THIS GUY...
...TO YOU?
...RGH...
STOP !!
PLEASE STOP.
THIS ISN'T SERI'S FAULT.

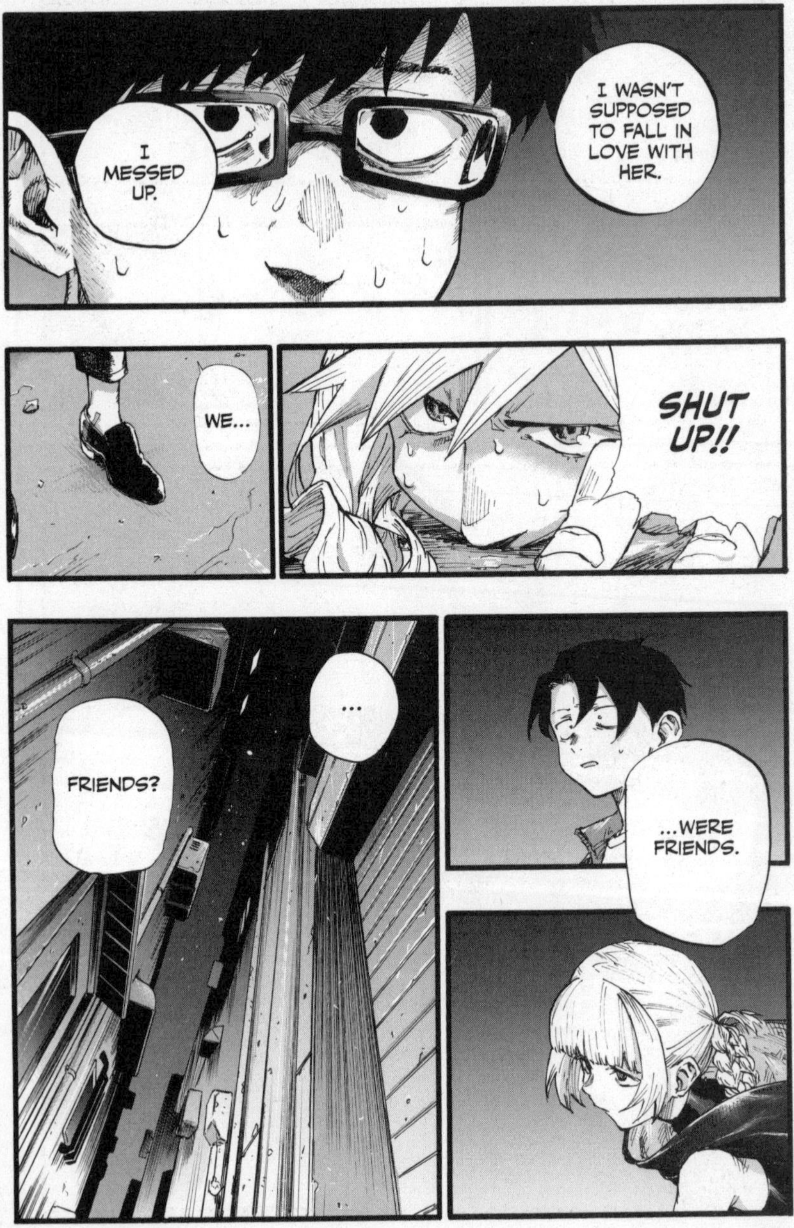
I WASN'T SUPPOSED TO FALL IN LOVE WITH HER.
I MESSED UP.
SHUT UP!!
WE...
...WERE FRIENDS.
...
FRIENDS?

NIGHT 29: NO FAIR

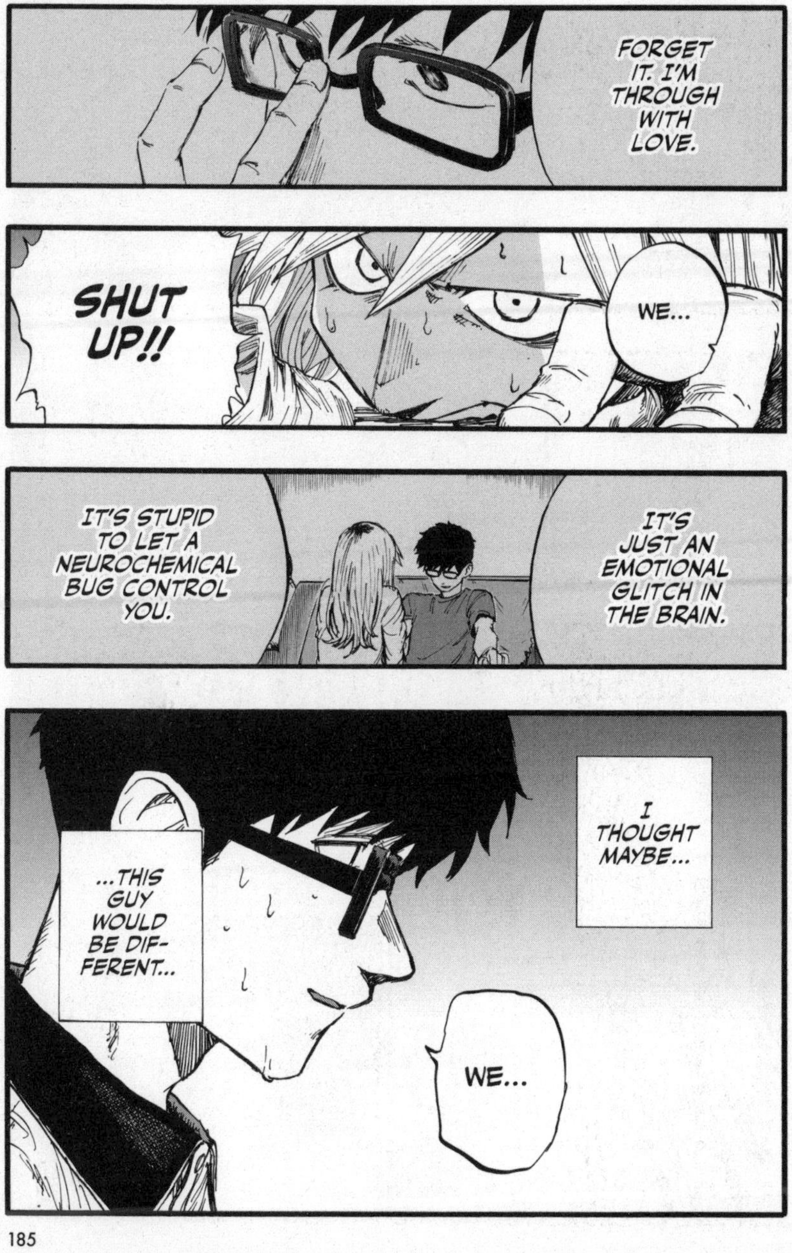

FORGET IT. I'M THROUGH WITH LOVE.
WE...
SHUT UP!!
IT'S JUST AN EMOTIONAL GLITCH IN THE BRAIN.
IT'S STUPID TO LET A NEUROCHEMICAL BUG CONTROL YOU.
I THOUGHT MAYBE...
...THIS GUY WOULD BE DIF- FERENT...
WE...

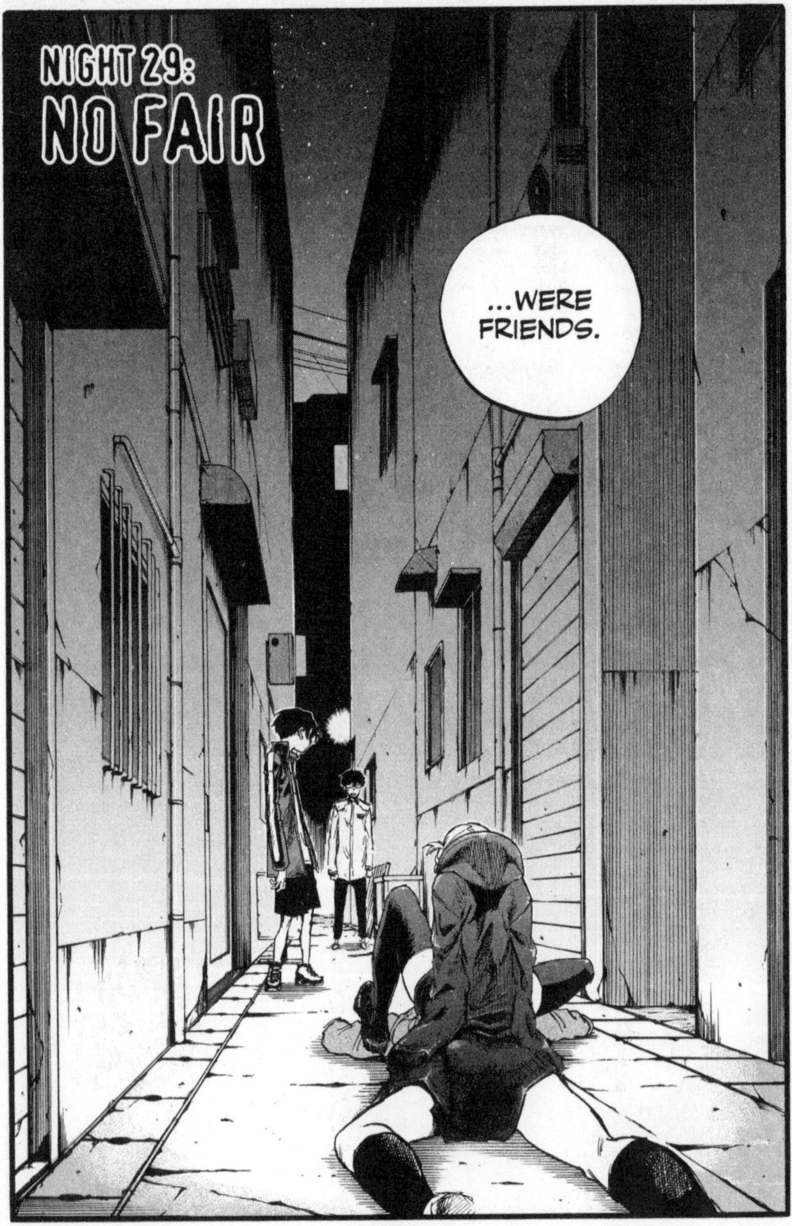
NIGHT 29:
NO FAIR
...WERE FRIENDS.

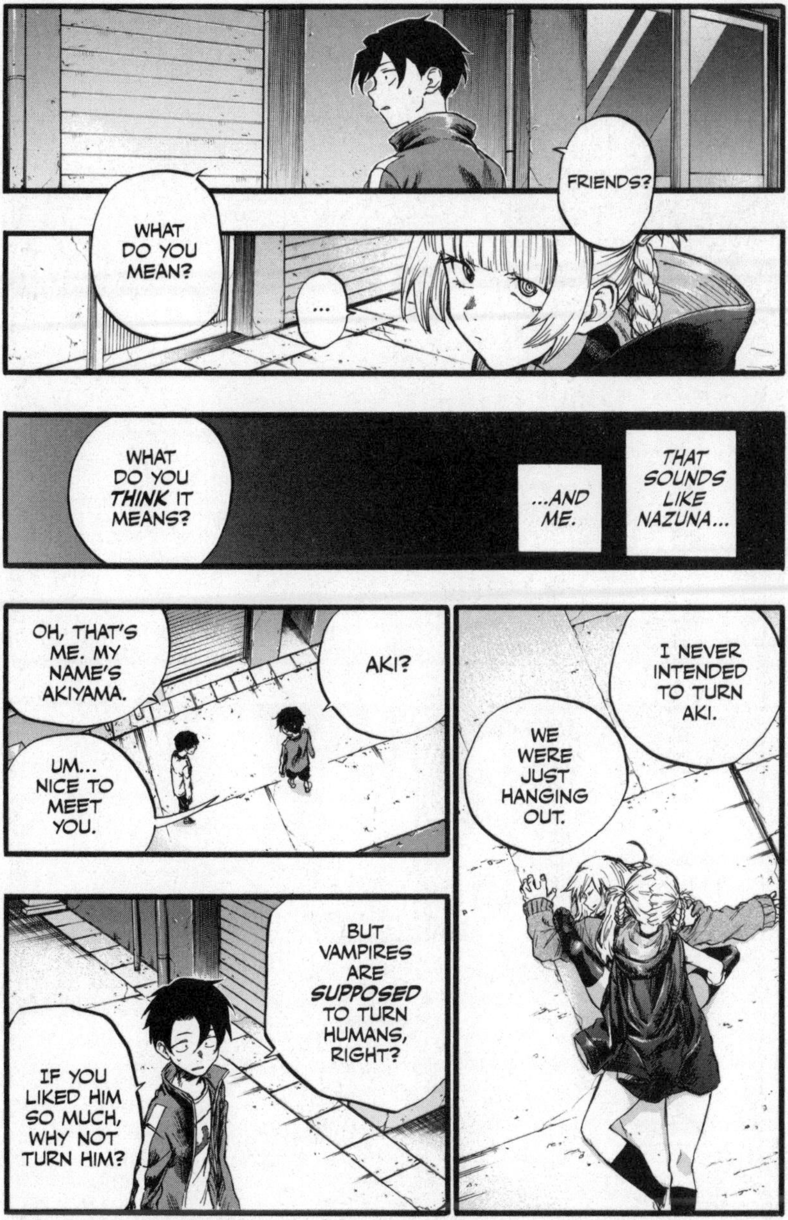
FRIENDS?
WHAT DO YOU MEAN?
...
THAT SOUNDS LIKE NAZUNA...
...AND ME.
WHAT DO YOU *THINK* IT MEANS?
I NEVER INTENDED TO TURN AKI.
WE WERE JUST HANGING OUT.
AKI?
OH, THAT'S ME. MY NAME'S AKIYAMA.
UM... NICE TO MEET YOU.
BUT VAMPIRES ARE *SUPPOSED* TO TURN HUMANS, RIGHT?
IF YOU LIKED HIM SO MUCH, WHY NOT TURN HIM?

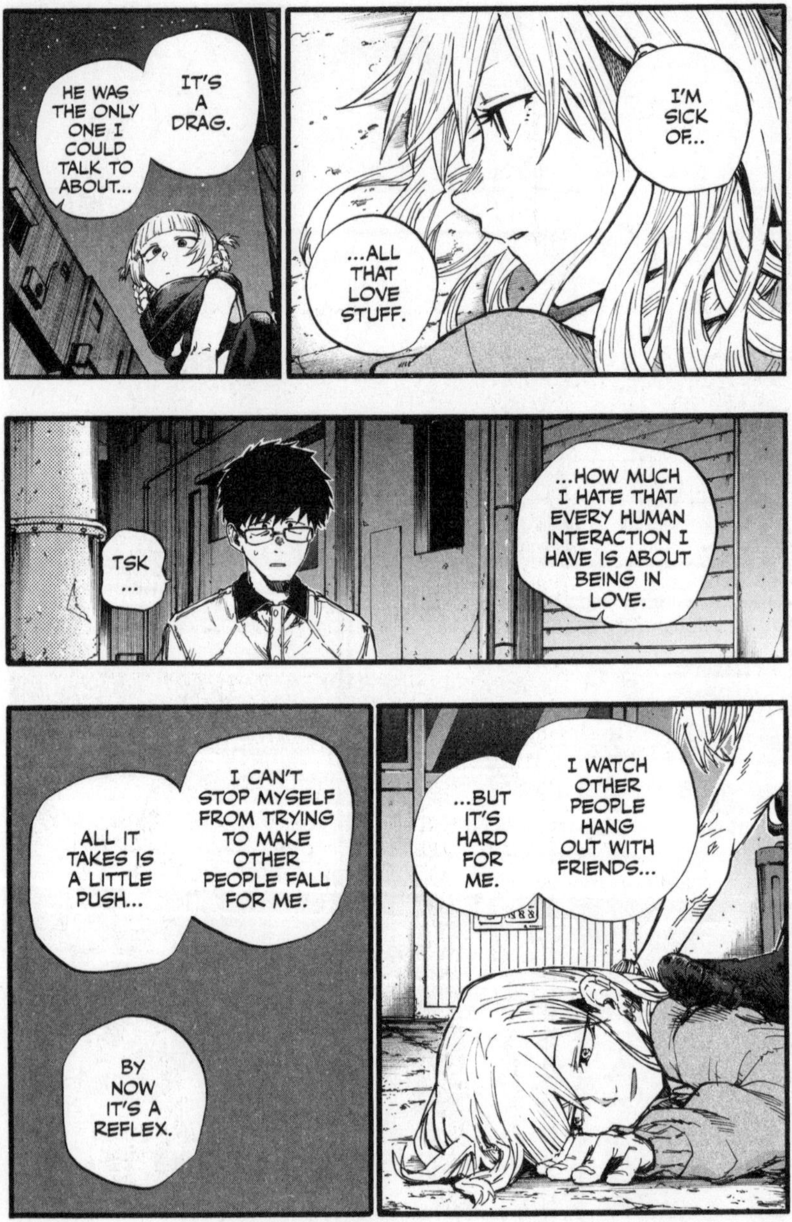
I'M SICK OF...
...ALL THAT LOVE STUFF.
IT'S A DRAG.
HE WAS THE ONLY ONE I COULD TALK TO ABOUT...
...HOW MUCH I HATE THAT EVERY HUMAN INTERACTION I HAVE IS ABOUT BEING IN LOVE.
TSK ...
I WATCH OTHER PEOPLE HANG OUT WITH FRIENDS...
...BUT IT'S HARD FOR ME.
I CAN'T STOP MYSELF FROM TRYING TO MAKE OTHER PEOPLE FALL FOR ME.
ALL IT TAKES IS A LITTLE PUSH...
BY NOW IT'S A REFLEX.

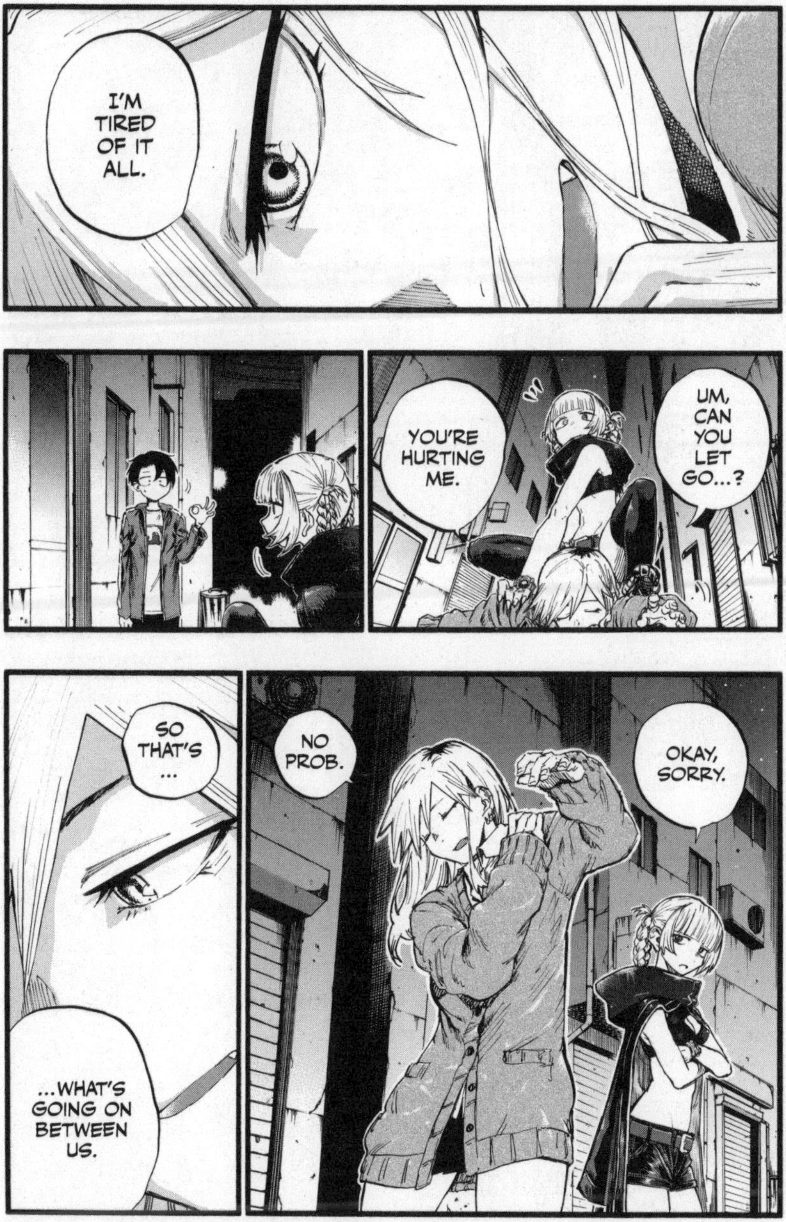
I'M TIRED OF IT ALL.
UM, CAN YOU LET GO...?
YOU'RE HURTING ME.
OKAY, SORRY.
NO PROB.
SO THAT'S ...
...WHAT'S GOING ON BETWEEN US.

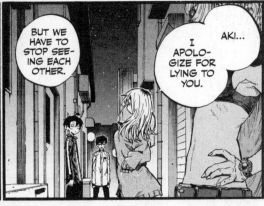

AKI... I APOLOGIZE FOR LYING TO YOU.
BUT WE HAVE TO STOP SEEING EACH OTHER.
IT'LL BE BETTER FOR BOTH OF US.
I CAN'T GIVE YOU THE KIND OF RELATIONSHIP YOU WANT.
AND WE CAN'T GO BACK TO THE WAY THINGS WERE.
WE'RE STUCK IN A VICIOUS CIRCLE.
LET'S JUST PRETEND ALL THIS NEVER HAPPENED.
OKAY?
...
...

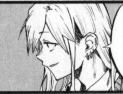

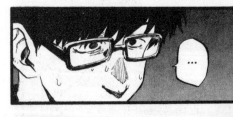

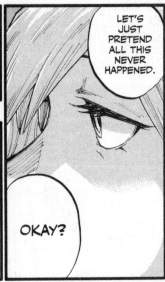

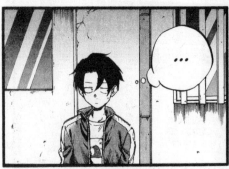

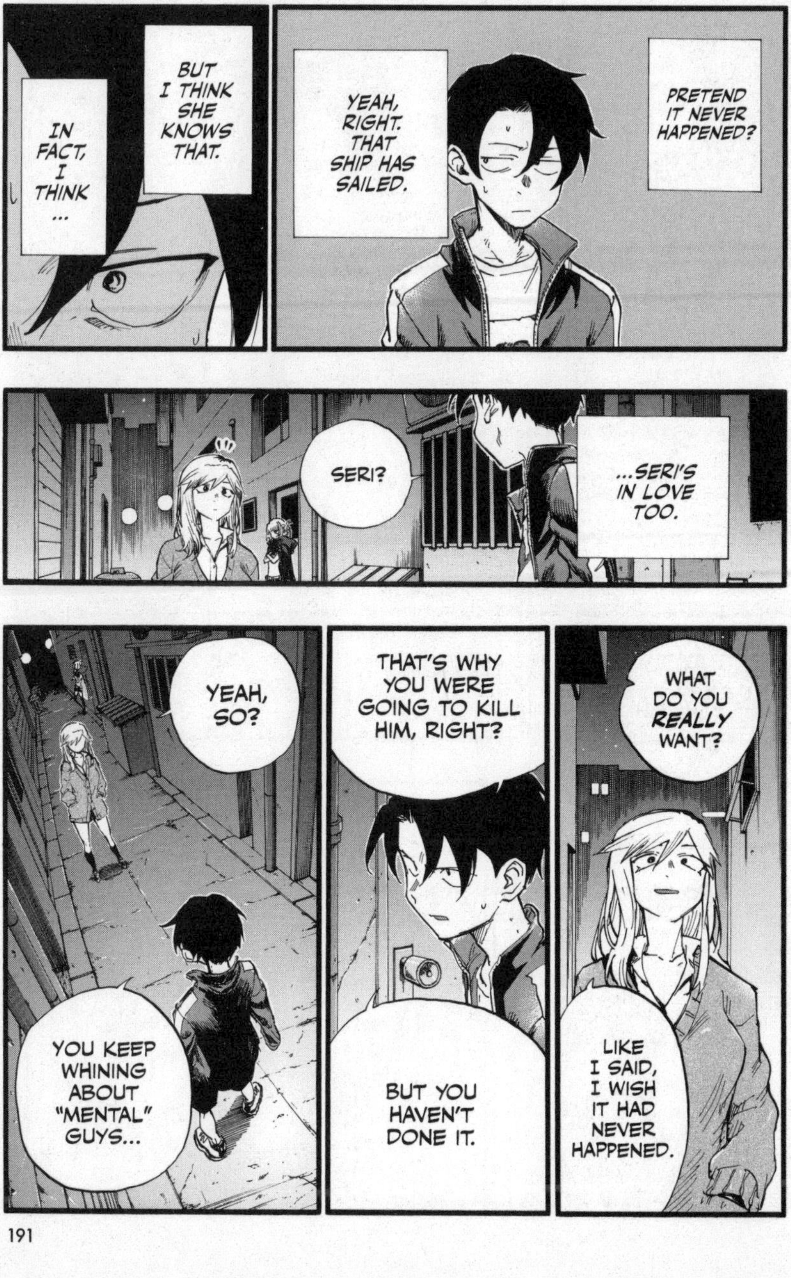
PRETEND IT NEVER HAPPENED?
YEAH, RIGHT. THAT SHIP HAS SAILED.
BUT I THINK SHE KNOWS THAT.
IN FACT, I THINK ...
...SERI'S IN LOVE TOO.
SERI?
WHAT DO YOU REALLY WANT?
LIKE I SAID, I WISH IT HAD NEVER HAPPENED.
THAT'S WHY YOU WERE GOING TO KILL HIM, RIGHT?
BUT YOU HAVEN'T DONE IT.
YEAH, SO?
YOU KEEP WHINING ABOUT "MENTAL" GUYS...

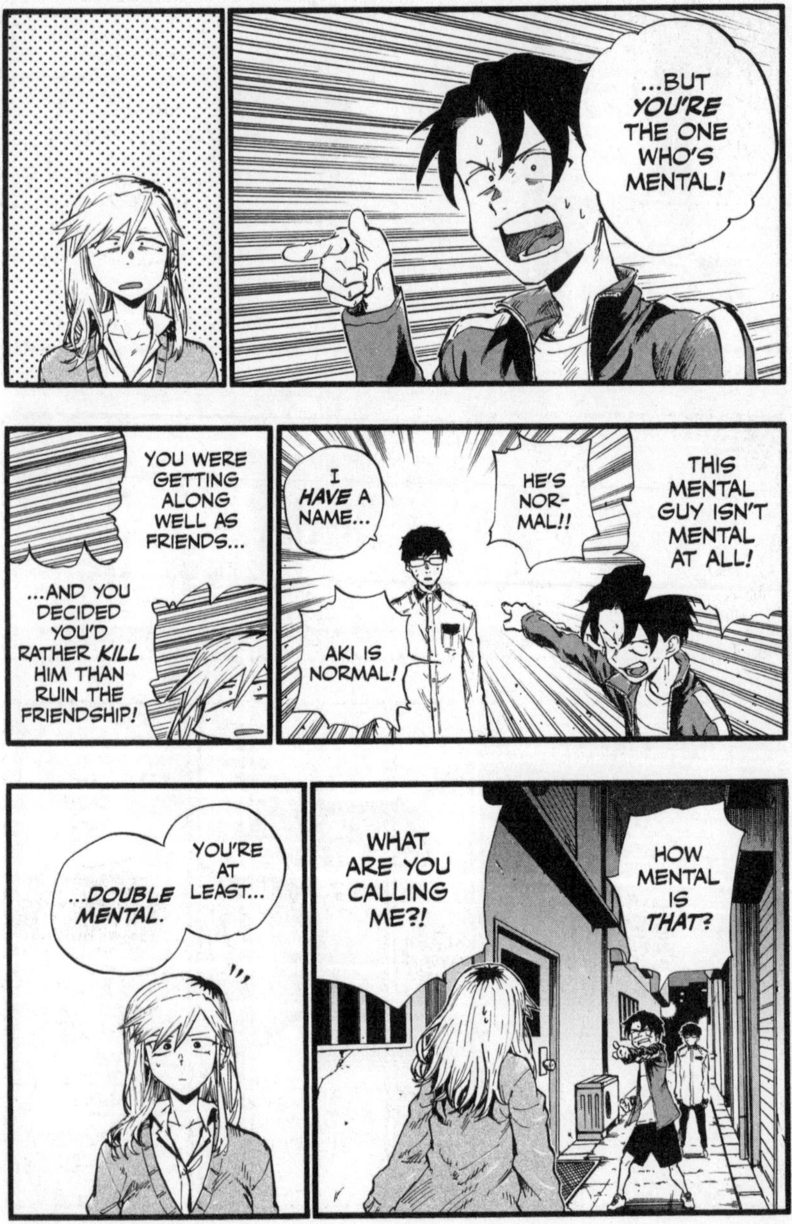
...BUT *YOU'RE* THE ONE WHO'S MENTAL!
THIS MENTAL GUY ISN'T MENTAL AT ALL!
HE'S NOR-MAL!!
I *HAVE* A NAME...
AKI IS NORMAL!
YOU WERE GETTING ALONG WELL AS FRIENDS...
...AND YOU DECIDED YOU'D RATHER *KILL* HIM THAN RUIN THE FRIENDSHIP!
HOW MENTAL IS *THAT*?
WHAT ARE YOU CALLING ME?!
YOU'RE AT LEAST...
...*DOUBLE MENTAL*.

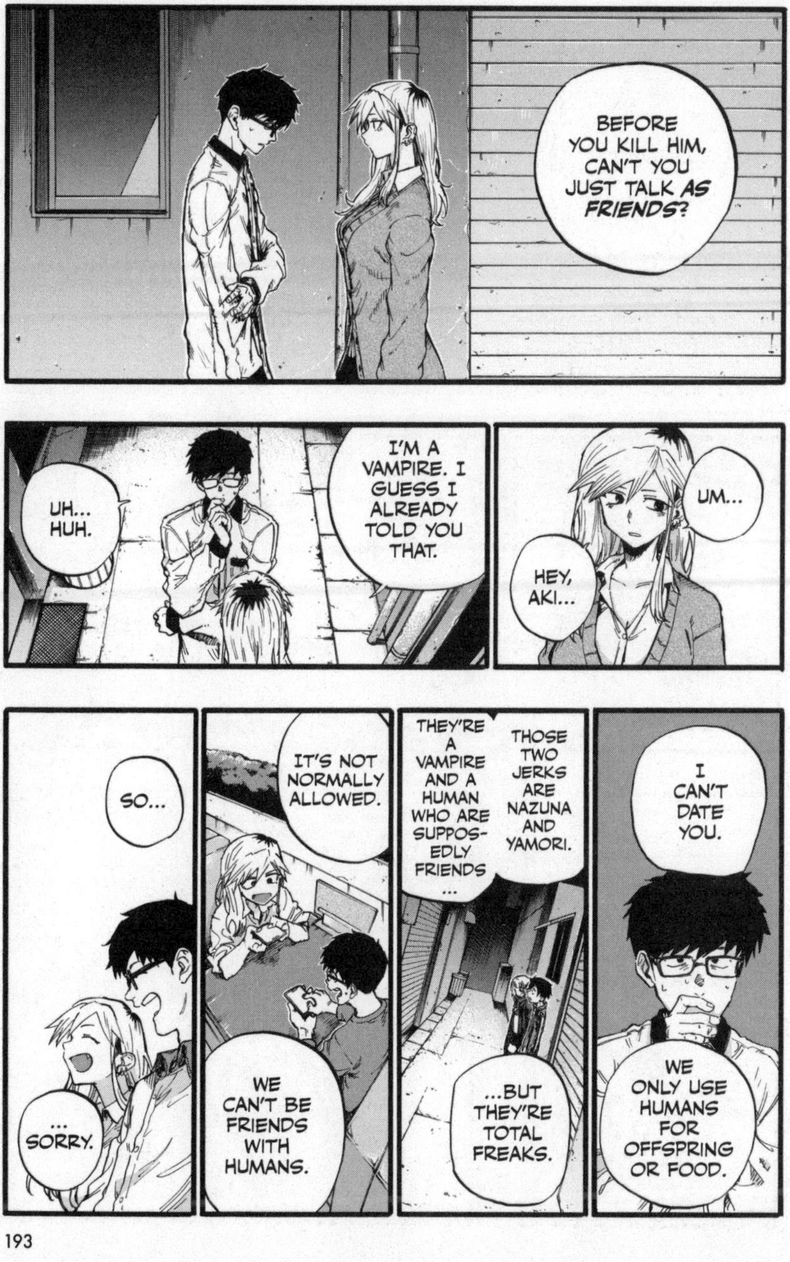
BEFORE YOU KILL HIM, CAN'T YOU JUST TALK *AS FRIENDS*?
UM...
HEY, AKI...
I'M A VAMPIRE. I GUESS I ALREADY TOLD YOU THAT.
UH... HUH.
I CAN'T DATE YOU.
WE ONLY USE HUMANS FOR OFFSPRING OR FOOD.
THOSE TWO JERKS ARE NAZUNA AND YAMORI.
THEY'RE A VAMPIRE AND A HUMAN WHO ARE SUPPOS-EDLY FRIENDS ...
...BUT THEY'RE TOTAL FREAKS.
IT'S NOT NORMALLY ALLOWED.
WE CAN'T BE FRIENDS WITH HUMANS.
SO...
... SORRY.

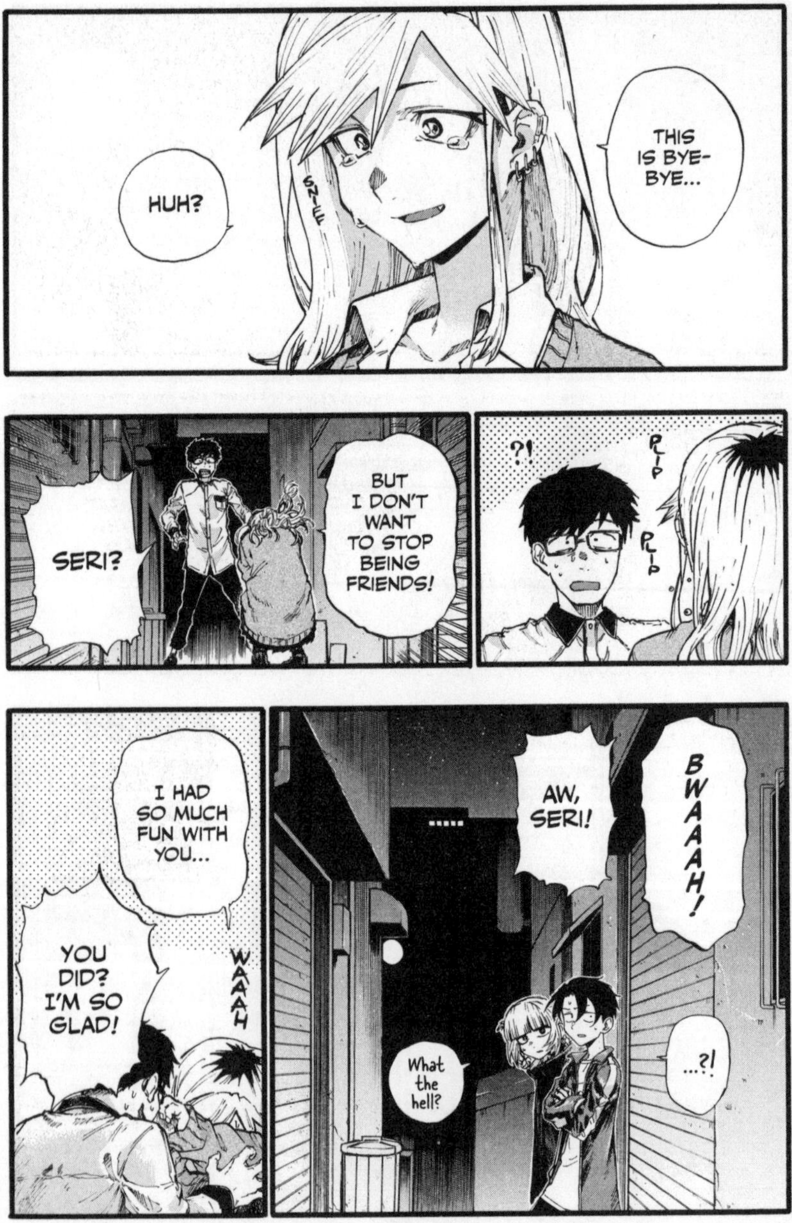
THIS IS BYE-BYE...
SNIFF
HUH?
?!
PLIP
PLIP
BUT I DON'T WANT TO STOP BEING FRIENDS!
SERI?
BWAAAAH!
AW, SERI!
...?!
What the hell?
I HAD SO MUCH FUN WITH YOU...
WAAAH
YOU DID? I'M SO GLAD!

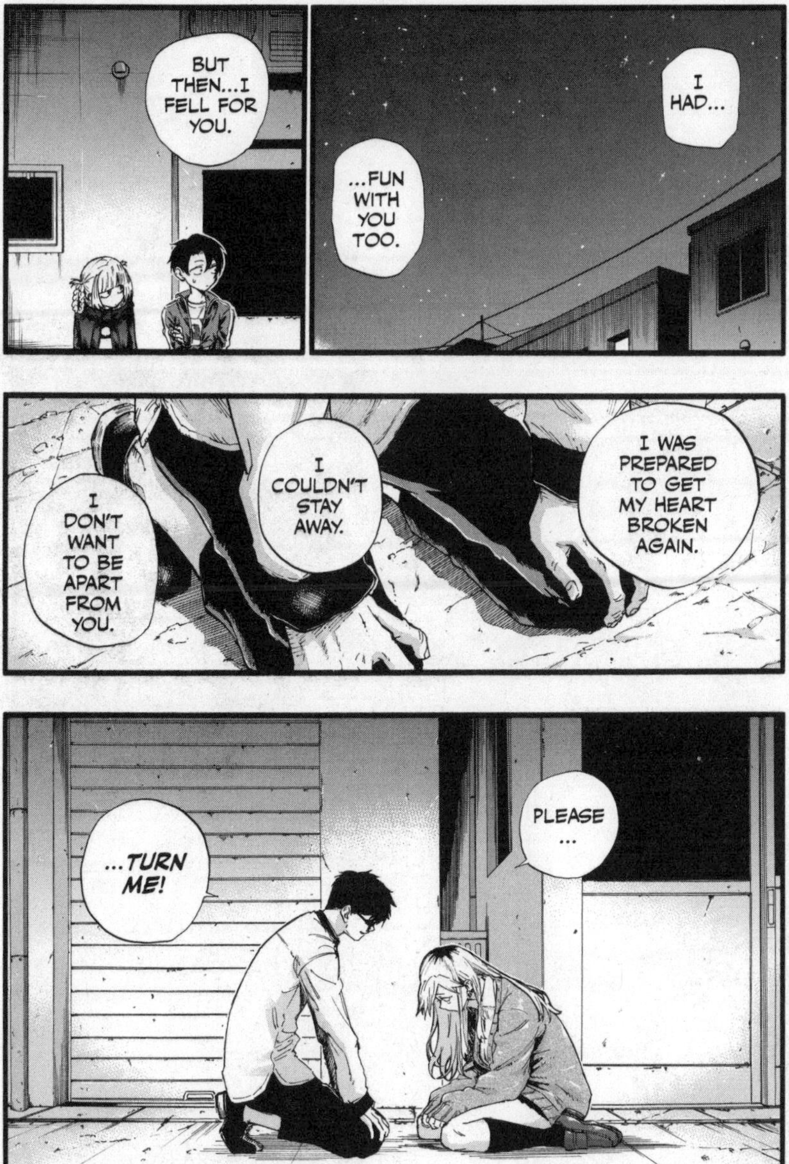
I HAD...
...FUN WITH YOU TOO.
BUT THEN...I FELL FOR YOU.
I WAS PREPARED TO GET MY HEART BROKEN AGAIN.
I COULDN'T STAY AWAY.
I DON'T WANT TO BE APART FROM YOU.
PLEASE...
...TURN ME!

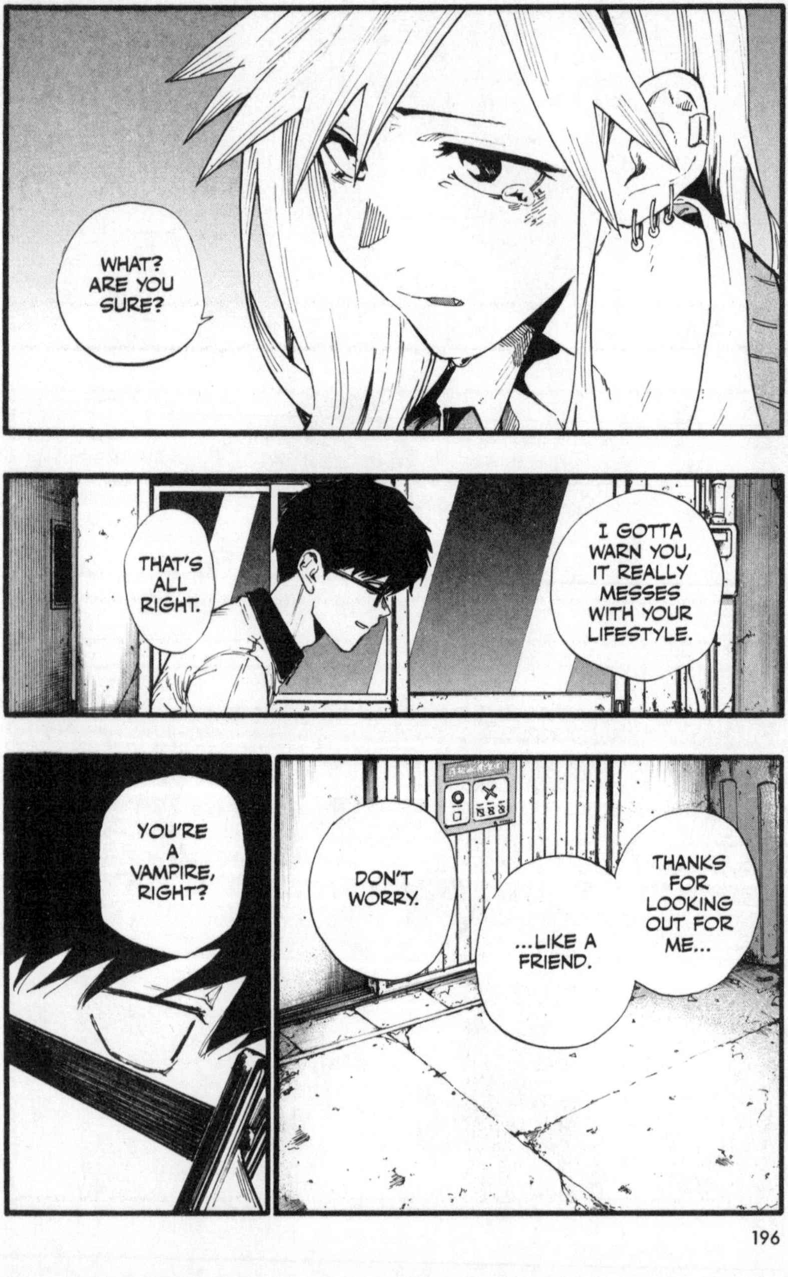
WHAT? ARE YOU SURE?
I GOTTA WARN YOU, IT REALLY MESSES WITH YOUR LIFESTYLE.
THAT'S ALL RIGHT.
THANKS FOR LOOKING OUT FOR ME...
...LIKE A FRIEND.
DON'T WORRY.
YOU'RE A VAMPIRE, RIGHT?

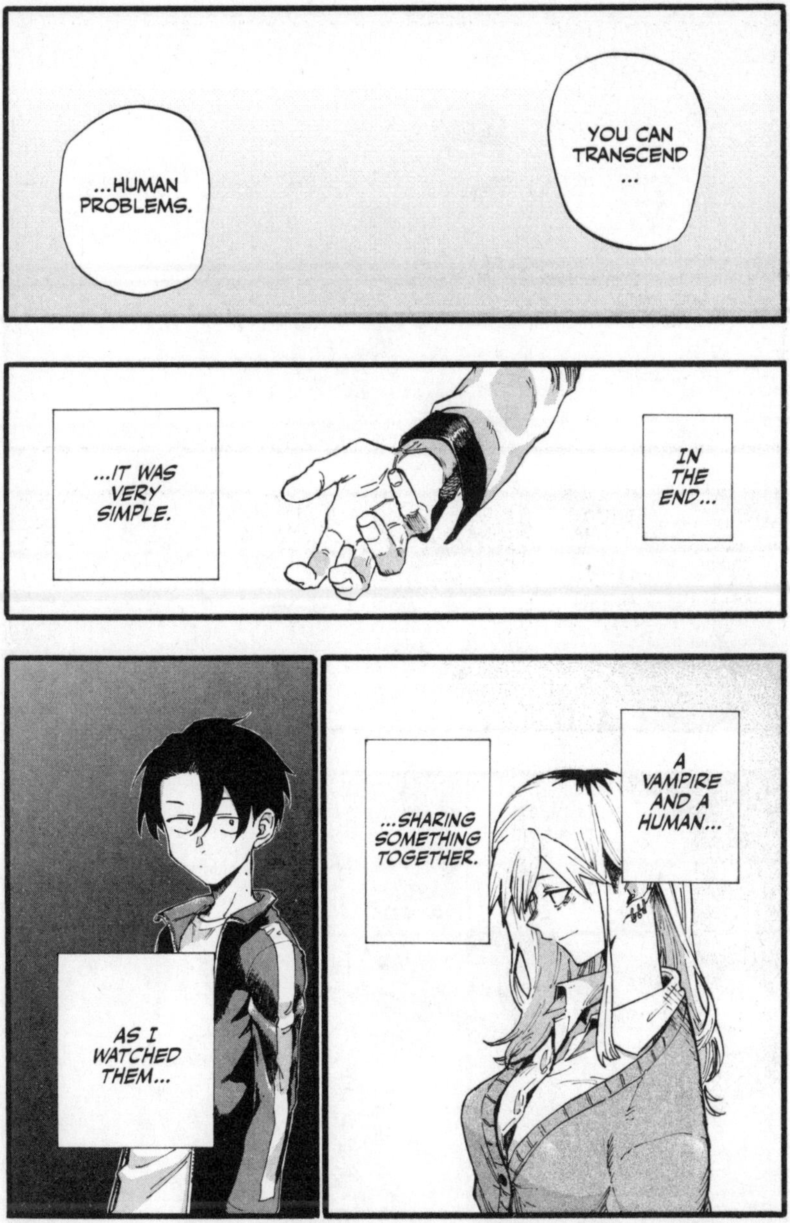
YOU CAN TRANSCEND ...
...HUMAN PROBLEMS.
IN THE END...
...IT WAS VERY SIMPLE.
A VAMPIRE AND A HUMAN...
...SHARING SOMETHING TOGETHER.
AS I WATCHED THEM...

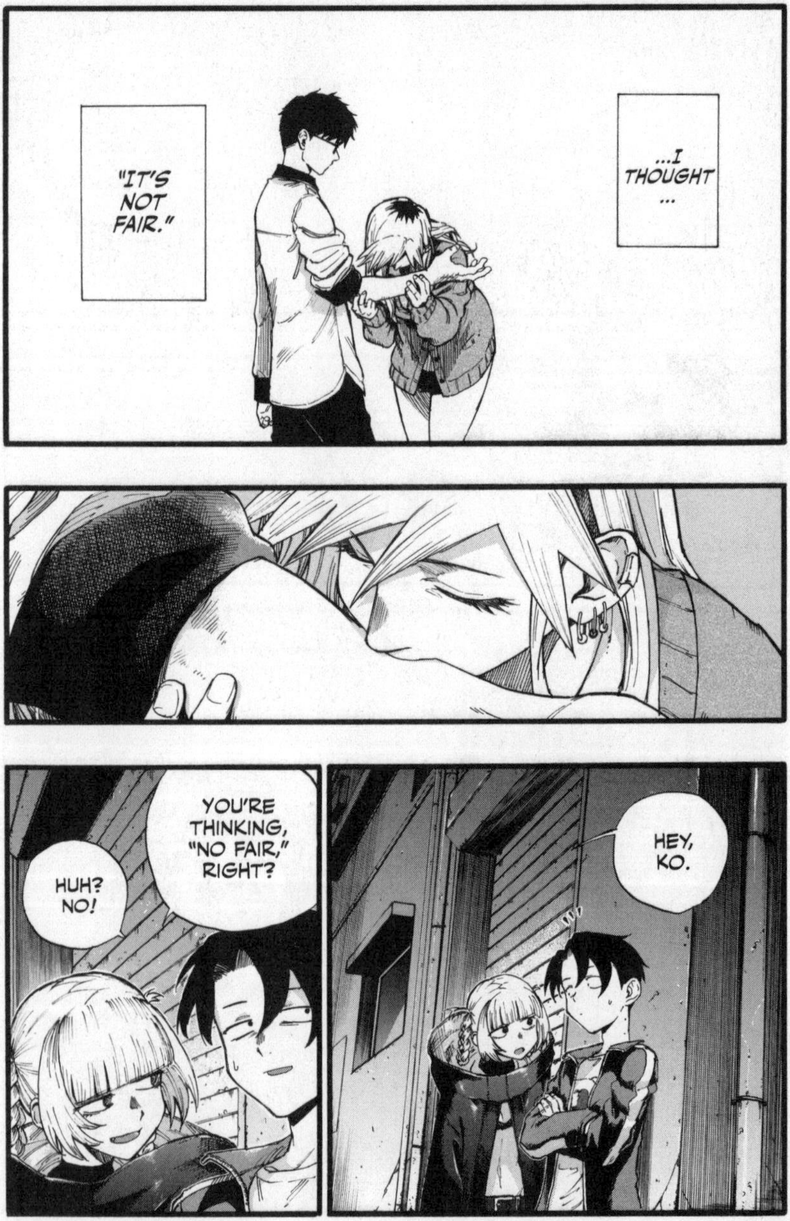
...I THOUGHT ...
"IT'S NOT FAIR."
HEY, KO.
YOU'RE THINKING, "NO FAIR," RIGHT?
HUH? NO!

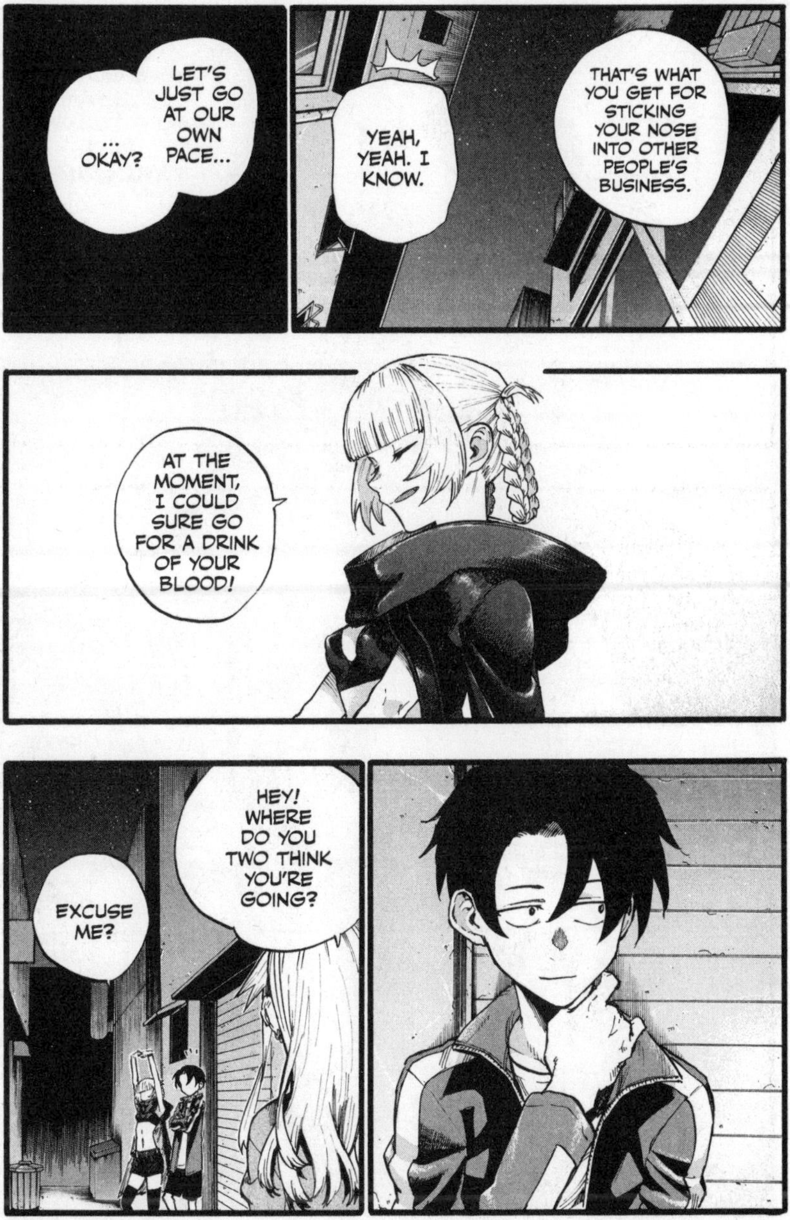
THAT'S WHAT YOU GET FOR STICKING YOUR NOSE INTO OTHER PEOPLE'S BUSINESS.
YEAH, YEAH. I KNOW.
LET'S JUST GO AT OUR OWN PACE...
... OKAY?
AT THE MOMENT, I COULD SURE GO FOR A DRINK OF YOUR BLOOD!
HEY! WHERE DO YOU TWO THINK YOU'RE GOING?
EXCUSE ME?

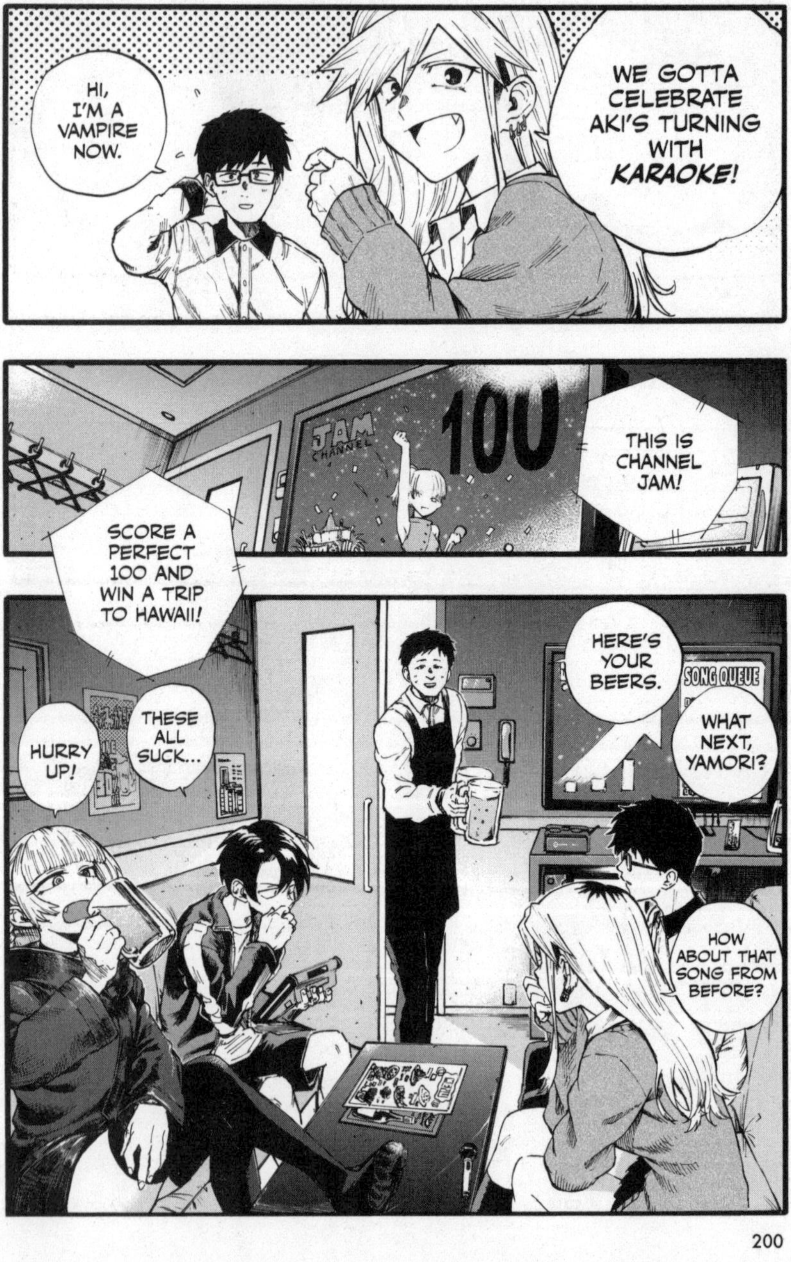
WE GOTTA CELEBRATE AKI'S TURNING WITH ***KARAOKE!***
HI, I'M A VAMPIRE NOW.
100
JAM CHANNEL
THIS IS CHANNEL JAM!
SCORE A PERFECT 100 AND WIN A TRIP TO HAWAII!
SONG QUEUE
HERE'S YOUR BEERS.
WHAT NEXT, YAMORI?
HOW ABOUT THAT SONG FROM BEFORE?
THESE ALL SUCK...
HURRY UP!

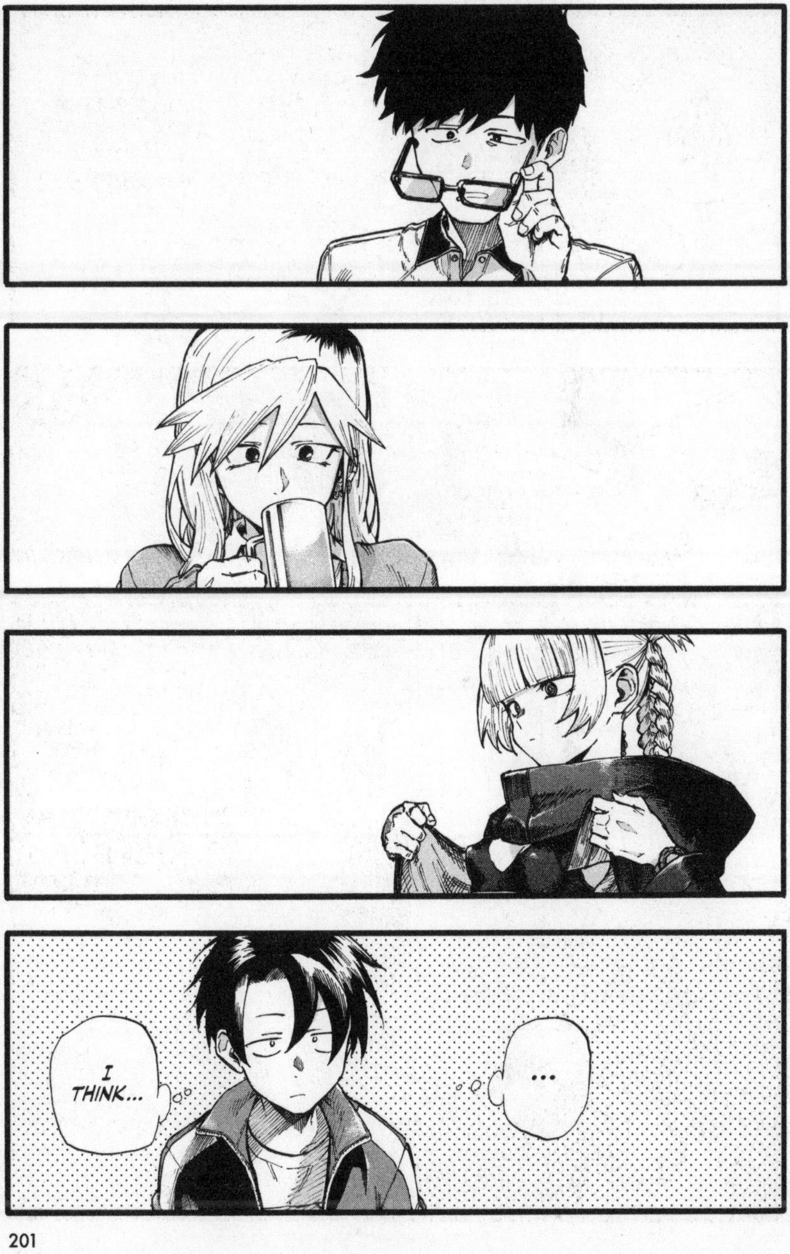
...
I THINK...

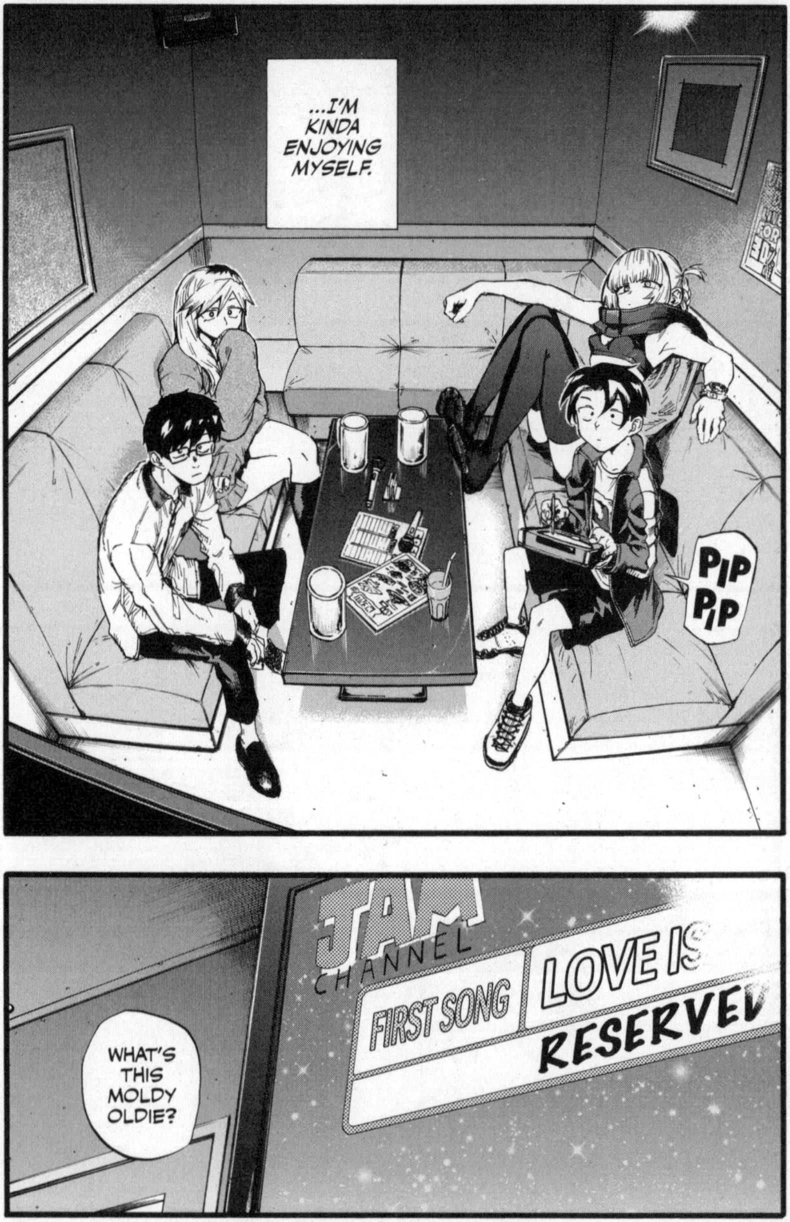
...I'M KINDA ENJOYING MYSELF.
PIP PIP
JAM CHANNEL
FIRST SONG
LOVE IS
RESERVED
WHAT'S THIS MOLDY OLDIE?

CALL OF THE NIGHT 3 • THE END

Call of the Night

Seri

all of the Night

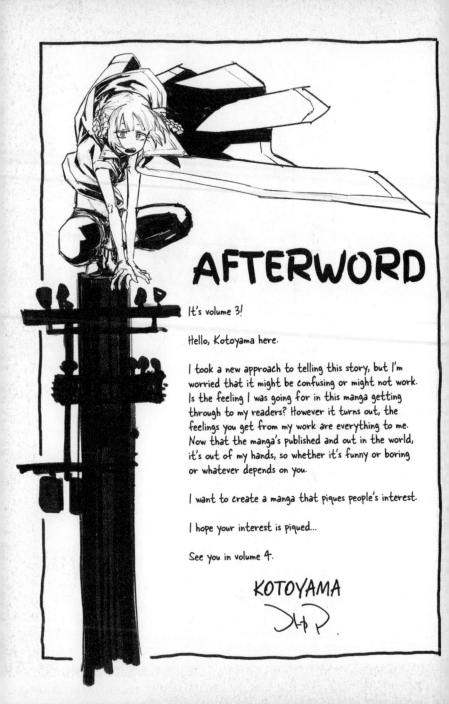

AFTERWORD

It's volume 3!

Hello, Kotoyama here.

I took a new approach to telling this story, but I'm worried that it might be confusing or might not work. Is the feeling I was going for in this manga getting through to my readers? However it turns out, the feelings you get from my work are everything to me. Now that the manga's published and out in the world, it's out of my hands, so whether it's funny or boring or whatever depends on you.

I want to create a manga that piques people's interest.

I hope your interest is piqued...

See you in volume 4.

KOTOYAMA

I have bad posture.
I try to improve it, but before I know it,
I'm sitting in an awkward position again.

—KOTOYAMA

KOTOYAMA

In 2013, Kotoyama won the Shonen Sunday Manga
College Award for *Azuma*. From 2014 to 2018,
Kotoyama's title *Dagashi Kashi* ran in *Shonen Sunday*
magazine. *Call of the Night* has been published
in *Shonen Sunday* since 2019.

Call of the Night

⟨ 3 ⟩

SHONEN SUNDAY EDITION

Story and Art by

KOTOYAMA

Translation – **JUNKO GODA**
English Adaptation – **SHAENON K. GARRITY**
Touch-Up Art & Lettering – **ANNALIESE "ACE" CHRISTMAN**
Cover & Interior Design – **ALICE LEWIS**
Editor – **ANNETTE ROMAN**

YOFUKASHI NO UTA Vol. 3
by KOTOYAMA
© 2019 KOTOYAMA
All rights reserved.
Original Japanese edition published by SHOGAKUKAN.
English translation rights in the United States of America, Canada, the United Kingdom,
Ireland, Australia and New Zealand arranged with SHOGAKUKAN.

Original Cover Design – Yasuhisa KAWATANI

Printed in Canada

Published by VIZ Media, LLC
P.O. Box 77010
San Francisco, CA 94107

10 9 8 7 6 5 4 3 2 1
First printing, August 2021

viz.com

shonensunday.com

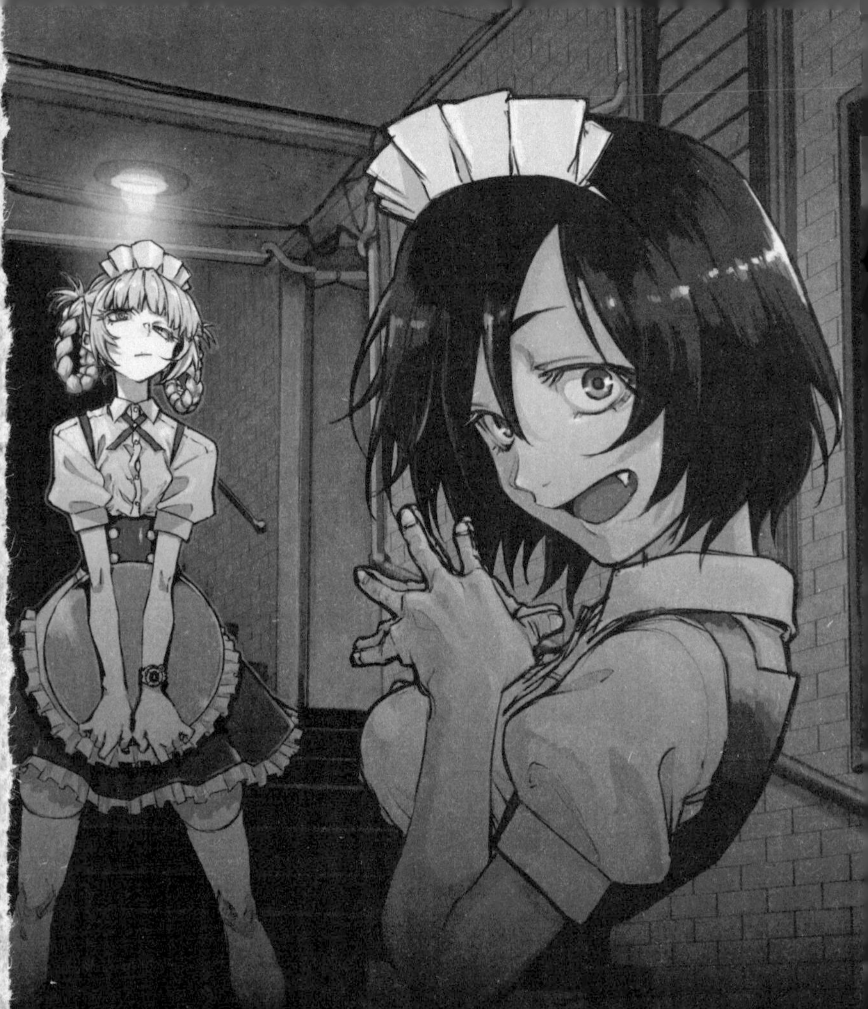

VOLUME 4

Nazuna can't let her guard down for a second now that a flock of hot vampire women is interested in Ko's hot blood! Then, when she takes a shift at a maid café where the customer is always right, the vampire is always wrong! Akira meets the girl Ko rejected before he met Nazuna, and Ko meets a private detective searching for someone he knows. Plus, a late-night visit to Ko's school to ghostbust spooky legends provides a glimpse into the drawbacks of giving up your humanity.